THE NEW LIFE OF GRACE

PETER FRANSEN, S. J.

THE NEW LIFE
OF GRACE

Foreword by John MACQUARRIE

HERDER AND HERDER

1972
HERDER AND HERDER NEW YORK
232 Madison Avenue, New York 10016

Translated by Georges Dupont, S.J.

Imprimatur: Hector Cunial, Vicar General
Rome, February 14, 1969

© 1969 by Desclee Co., Inc.

ISBN: 665-00017-0

Library of Congress Catalog Card Number: 69-20373

Printed in the United States

TABLE OF CONTENTS

PART TWO: WHAT MAY WE EXPECT FROM GRACE?

FOREWORD

There will never be too many books on grace, for grace is at the very heart of the Christian experience and, indeed, sums it up in a single word. But because the word "grace" points to this central experience, with all its depth and mystery and even its elusiveness, good theological books on the subject are by no means common. It is easier to become rhapsodic over the theme than to subject it to the believing yet critical and analytical reflection which is proper to the theologian. The present book combines in a remarkable way the *experience* of grace in its many dimensions—"outflowing and inflowing life," "interior strength," "presence of God," and so on—with the *theology* of grace, the attempt to reach, so far as possible, an understanding of the experience. The author is deeply conscious that in the contemporary world men are no longer content with unanalyzed experience or blind faith, and that the Church owes them a reasoned account of her beliefs so that their experience is supported and deepened by their understanding.

I have said that grace is at the very heart of Christian experience. Fundamentally, it is the awareness of receiving a free and undeserved gift. Through grace we learn that we are not alone in the world, nor must we rely only on our own little resources for life. In spite of all the harshness and bitterness that surround us, there is at work on a still more fundamental level a love which seeks to enter and transform our lives and the lives of all men. But when we try to conceptualize this experience, we find it hard to do so, and there may be times when we wonder whether, after all, the skeptic may not be right when he tells us plainly that grace is an illusion.

Unfortunately, the skeptic's arguments are strengthened when he points to some of the popular and traditional ways in which Christians have thought of grace, and in which they have misconceived it as something almost physical, something to be quantifiably measured and mechanically transmitted. The mystery of grace is certainly not one that can be fully grasped, but we advance far in our understanding of it when we turn from impersonal to personal models. The little parable of inter-

personal relations from which this book sets out determines
the tone of the whole subsequent discussion on the nature of
grace.

In the past, we have made the mistake also of thinking of
grace in too narrowly ecclesiastical terms. Is it possible that
the quite secular man has some experience of grace? For instance,
when he feels the joy of being alive, when a nameless thank-
fulness comes over him—is this not a stirring of grace? Our
very existences are a free gift from God, so that there is a kind
of grace in existence itself and even those who do not profess
belief in God may know the stirrings of grace within themselves.
It is a further merit of this book that it breaks down the
barriers that we have sometimes tried to build around grace in
tying it too narrowly to the explicit Christian community of the
Church. Such restrictions contradict the very nature of grace.
If God has blessed his Church with a singular outpouring of his
grace, this must be so that Christians will be able to recognize
and strengthen all manifestations of grace throughout the
creation.

John Macquarrie,
Union Theological Seminary,
New York.

INTRODUCTION

This book on grace has been written not without serious apprehension. It is a formidable assignment to provide within the limits of a book all that is necessary for an adequate, clear insight into one of the most central and most debated tracts of our Christian belief. Students of theology attend lectures on it for a whole year, four times a week; and usually they do not succeed in touching on all the aspects of this rich and intricate subject. Writing a book on grace is not made easier for an author when he realizes that many of the prospective readers are unfamiliar with theological methods.

Viewed from God's side, grace signifies first and foremost the wealth and majesty of God's love which enfolds *us all* in one gesture and, at the same time, speaks *to each one of us* in accordance with our most intimate dispositions and, so to say, from within the individual situation in life peculiarly our own.

Grace, seen from God's side, signifies the sheer reality of the Blessed Trinity: Father, Son and Holy Spirit. It means our eternal election by the Father, the cardinal fact of the redemption by the Son dying on the cross and rising on Easter Sunday, the Lord's enduring presence in our history till the last day, through the power of the Holy Spirit—a presence which comes to us as an actual reality in the Church, by the medium of the sacraments and of the word of Christian preaching.

Viewed from man's side, grace signifies rebirth in Christ. It denotes a mysterious but nonetheless eminently real stream of life which wells up from the deepest stratum of our being where it rests securely in the creative hand of God, up through all the slowly developing stages of our personality, irrigating and permeating the innumerable areas of our complex psychology, yet never ceasing to be a divine life, a purely gratuitous gift, God's constantly renewed and freely bestowed love. In the language of the Greek Fathers and the Byzantine theologians, grace is a new light which, on the day of our baptism, rises like dawn on the dim, remote horizon of our personal self, and in the soft morning glow of life dispels by slow degrees the darkness of sin and weakness—all this in preparation for and as a pledge of the midday splendor of a radiant eternity.

Every portion of our being has to be regenerated by grace: spirit and person, intellect and will, all our spiritual powers, from the psychic ego with its own peculiar temperament and character down to the lower psychosomatic regions of our animal bodily life with its obscure drives, its countless determinisms, its unconscious or semiconscious reactions. *All these* have to be reborn through grace.

Grace unites God and man. More exactly, grace is *God's way of meeting* man whom He came in search of and found lost in the solitude of an earthly sinful nature. In this meeting, God's love takes to itself man as he is, the whole of him, and makes of him a child of the Father, with and in the only begotten Son, through the power of the Holy Spirit.

Grace is the marvelous point of contact between two worlds: the world of the triune infinitude, and that of the utter nothingness which is man.

The writing of this book wants to witness to a cheering mandate. Today it is the believing laity itself that begs for a fuller, richer insight into the faith. As a Lutheran lay-movement in North Germany expresses it so finely in its motto, "The laity challenges the Church," our educated lay people look for answers to the grave religious questions of our time. At this very moment and throughout the world, there is manifest in many towns, great or small, a movement seeking for "religious understanding." Shall we at long last see the end of that irritating, smug, inert and conventional Catholic life that sedulously dodges all religious problems, shirks all subtler queries of conscience, and rests satisfied with a determined set of religious practices (euphemistically called "blind faith") or with a half-convinced Christian life, or, if need be, with the vain excitement of mass demonstrations? This movement and search for a more enlightened knowledge of the faith could be compared a few years ago with the hushed timidity of an awakening spring. Since then the Council has aroused the Church. Theology, religious and moral problems are today news items in the daily papers. Our age has discovered anew the significance of the Spirit Who guides the Church.

The time has come to put a stop to a critical situation threatening the faith. The educated classes take it for granted that general culture and professional knowledge and skill keep pace with man's growth in responsibility toward the state and human society. Should a Christian not realize that he must outgrow the immature religious knowledge and practice of his high school and college days? The men and the women of our time should be possessed of the same courage, the same eagerness for study, work and responsibility as was shown by those of past centuries.

A lack of balance between secular culture and religious knowledge might be condoned, perhaps, in periods of quiet and peace, when traditional customs rule uncontested. In times of stress and strain, however, when many old ways of life are breaking down and new ones are still unformed, the interior tension between an underdeveloped religious consciousness and a fully developed professional competence can only raise doubts and dismay in the hearts of good Christians and bitterness and defection among the lukewarm.

*
* *

It is by no means easy for an adult to approach matters of faith with an unprejudiced mind. Mathematicians, doctors, scientists psychologists, lawyers and politicians unconsciously tend to bring to their study of religion the trusted canons of their respective specialities. They reflect on religion—and " do theology "—in the light of scientific methods, or from a political angle, or in conformity with the formal precision of a jurist.

Theology is a science like other sciences. Like them, it has its own proper object and is governed by its own special laws and methods. To these theology must hold fast if it is to be true to itself.

These introductory remarks will justify the divisions of our book:

I. What is grace?—or the application of theological methods to our subject matter.

II. What should man expect from grace?—or glimpses into some important points of contact between the theology of grace and the secular human sciences.

PART ONE

What is Grace?

In order to set the problem in its proper light from the start, we shall avail ourselves of a parable. The rich symbolism of parables, tales or examples has the advantage of enlightening the mind to a surprising degree on one or another of God's secret dealings with man. Christ Himself had recourse to parables to teach the ineffable, to communicate to His hearers what had to remain hidden. Parables respect mysteries and speak to the whole man.

A parable

Once upon a time there was a young girl, an orphan, who grew up in coarse surroundings. Her foster parents were hard and rough, and had never wanted her. Never as a baby or as a growing child had she known the subtle intimacy of a true home. She had never been loved.

And then she grew into a young woman. Daily encounter with disparagement, egotism and brutality hardened her heart. All she knew was self-defense, daily surly bickering to make sure of a minimum of security and right. To the best of her knowledge, it had always been so in the past, and it would remain so in the future: biting in order not to be bitten—the law of the jungle. She had no faith in man; she had not even faith in herself.

Her whole appearance betrayed the solitude in which the soul of her youth was living. She toiled and moiled, dressed in cheap, graceless attire. Her one means of escape from hopeless emptiness was rough and rowdy amusement. Selfish, suspicious and uncouth, with bitterness distorting her mouth, she was aware that she had no beauty and that what men wanted was her body for a few lustful moments.

There lived in the same city a young man, hale and strong. His sunny youth, spent in the midst of loving parents, brothers and sisters, shone in his gaze and sang in his voice. His step and speech were assured and firm, as is the case with those who have found peace. He was a good man.

One bright morning in spring, the miracle happened. The young man met the girl by chance. Moved in his innermost self, his heart went out to her. With the eyes of love, he saw right through and beyond her shabby vulgarity. He looked out for her; he spoke to her with the simplicity of a conquered heart. But she laughed in his face at first, addressed him in crude, unmannered language. She thought he was ridiculous.

But tact, patience and respect found their way at last to a remnant of yearning which lay still unwithered in the depth of the girl's being. For the first time in her life, she was appreciated for her own sake—the greatest need of human nature. Yet the beauty he discovered in her came not from her but from his love.

Love has been a creative power since the beginning of the world. The young man's deference and appreciation stirred up in her a nascent self-reliance, a foretaste of peace and quiet, of inner self-assurance. And timidly, gropingly, the young woman awakened to first love. She shyly began taking care of her appearance, though gaudily still and without elegance. His tenderness and his example refined her taste. Beauty came to her with the first smile.

Soon they became absorbed in each other. They steadily drew together in a selfless exchange of pure mutual love. What had happened really?   Or better: what had come into being? That girl had been granted a great favor, a matchless present, a gift she did not deserve: the favor of love.

After the long, barren winter of her youth, a seed had been sown in her innermost self; it was ready to spring into life. Though still very much herself, she was already another person. She experienced a soothing security, welling up from unsuspected regions within her; she grew steadily in strength and depth, in proportion as her formerly cherished convictions were pulled up by the roots. It was like a painful dying. All the distrust, hatred and vindictiveness she had so far nursed in herself, whatever she had clung to with the despair of a drowning person, she had now to let go; she had to resign herself to the sensation of being stripped bare, bereaved of all. A harrowing agony, indeed, but one of which life is born.

Like a ship tossed on the waves and driven from her course, the girl tried another tack. She steered to the unknown: she made *the leap of faith in another*. The aggressive self-assertiveness, the armor in which she had shielded herself so far, was torn off her. She attempted *the leap of hope in another* who would in the future stand surety for her. Meanwhile, an unsuspected marvel happened: she felt enriched by her new state of bereavement, secure and anchored in her surrender. Faith and hope ripened into *real love*, the final leap, indispensable to anyone who wants both to lose himself and to find himself in another. The girl had lost everything she had, but what she lost she recovered superabundantly. She ceased putting her trust in appearances and now saw more deeply into things. She discovered the beauty of her surrounding world—the setting sun, the violet in the shade, the light in the eyes of a child, the laughter in a voice. She saw everything through the eyes of her beloved. She became another being altogether; for the first time, she was her true self. Her injured youth lived on in her, but it now began to develop along the lines of generosity and disinterested care of others—in a wealth of gratitude.

A beautiful tale, indeed. The one thing in it which leaves us somewhat skeptical is whether there ever was a young man powerful enough to work such a miracle. We read of the custom in honor among the conquistadores that when they were caught in a storm at sea, they vowed marriage with the first penniless girl God would put on their path after a safe return home, with the proviso, naturally, that the girl be sound of limb and morals. Whatever view one takes of the parable or of the conquistadores' custom, it is sure that only a very pure and powerful love can change bitterness and hatred into a return of love. No mere man, however, can achieve even that much, for wickedness is rooted more deeply in our nature than we dare suspect. That is why there had to appear a Man without sin, a Man possessing God's own heart. And when He came, the tale became reality.

God's own parable

Holy Writ tells of that Man. Already in the Old Testament, Yahweh speaking to the Jews said: "Can a mother forget her infant, be without pity on the child of her womb? Even should she forget, I will never forget you. See upon the palms of my hands, I have written your name; your walls are never before me" (Is 49:15). "I have led them with bonds full of humaneness, with ropes of love; I was with them as one who raises a nursling to his cheek, I bent over him to feed him" (Os 11:4).

The parable of a moment ago we did not invent. It is told in more gripping language by Ezechiel. The prophet speaks, in chapter 16, of the unique, undying love of God for the faithless city, Jerusalem, which prefigures the whole of mankind and the Church.

"So saith the Lord God to Jerusalem! The land of thy origin and birth is Chanaan; thy father was an Amorrhite, and thy mother a Cethite [pagan lands turned away from God]. In this manner wast thou born, in the day of thy nativity, thy navel was not cut, neither wast thou washed clean with water, nor rubbed with salt, nor wrapped in swaddling clothes. No eye had pity on thee to do any of these things, out of compassion to thee; but thou wast cast out upon the open field, because no one thought thy life worth while.

"I, then, passed by thee and saw thee sprawling in thy blood; and I said to thee when thou wast in thy blood: Live. I bathed thee in water and washed the blood off thee, and anointed thee with oil; I made thee look as fresh as the flower of the field. And thou didst increase and grow great, and advancedst, and camest to woman's ornament: thy breasts were fashioned and thy hair grew; and yet thou wast naked and full of confusion.

"And again I passed by thee and saw that the time of love had come to thee. I spread my garment over thee and covered thy ignominy. And I swore to thee and I entered into a covenant with thee, saith the Lord God; and thou becamest mine. And I clothed thee with embroidery and shod thee with violet colored shoes; and I girded thee about with fine linen, and clothed thee with garments of silk. And I decked thee also with ornaments and put bracelets on thy hands, and a chain about thy neck.... Thou wast made exceeding beautiful and wast advanced to be a queen. And thy renown went forth among the nations for thy beauty; for it was perfect through the luster I put upon thee, saith the Lord God.

" But trusting in thy beauty, thou playedst the harlot because of thy renown; and thou hast prostituted thyself to every passerby to be his.... [Here the sacred author describes the ' prostitution ' of Jerusalem.] Thou didst also build thee a brothel.... Thou hast made thy beauty to be abominable; and thou hast prostituted thyself to every one that passed by, and hast multiplied thy fornications. [These ' fornications ' will bring Jerusalem to commit the most unnatural deeds.] Adulterous woman, thou hast brought strangers in the place of thy husband. Gifts are given to all harlots; but thou hast given hire to all thy lovers, and thou hast given them gifts to come to thee from every side to commit fornication with thee. " [Ez 16: 3-33]

The significance of this gripping chapter, describing the eternal drama between God and man, will come home to us better when we realize that the term *prostitution,* used by the prophets especially in connection with the covenant, means the sin of idolatry. To commit " fornication " is to betray the Covenant, to renounce and forsake Yahweh as the one true God, to reject His eternal love and to believe in false deities. As most of the cults practiced by Israel's neighboring peoples were mixed with religious prostitution and human sacrifice, the term *fornication* was a telling one to the Jewish mind. In Ezechiel's text, the literal and figurative senses overlap and mix, as in the casting away of children, the offering to the deities, the various allusions to the lewd practices among the people.

Israel's sin is more grievous than those of Sodom and Samaria. God will punish Jerusalem more than any other nation. In the punishment, however, lies also forgiveness, for God remains ever faithful to His first love. It is in this way that we should read and understand the conclusion of the chapter. " Thus saith the Lord God: I will deal with thee, as thou hast despised the oath in breaking the Covenant; and I will remember My Covenant with thee in the days of thy youth, and I will establish with thee an everlasting Covenant. And thou shalt remember thy ways and be ashamed, when thou shalt receive thy sisters, thy elder and thy younger, and I will give them to thee for daughters, but not by thy Covenant. " In this way Jerusalem, capital of God's new people, receives the promise that it will

be given other nations for daughters, namely, the pagans who
live far removed from God and who until now have had no
share in the divine promises. " I will establish My Covenant
with thee; and thou shalt know that I am the Lord, that thou
mayest remember and be confounded, and mayest no more open
thy mouth because of thy confusion, when I shall be pacified
toward thee for all that thou hast done, saith the Lord God " (Ez
16:59-63).

God's graciousness and fidelity

The story became actual truth on the eve of the passion,
when the Man, possessed of God's own heart, told His disciples
in the cenacle: " Drink ye all of this. For this is My blood in the
new Covenant, which shall be shed for many unto the remission
of sins " (Mt 26:27-28).

The Old Testament stresses two of Yahweh's attributes, mercy
and fidelity, or, as the Vulgate calls them less accurately,
" grace and truth. " " All the ways of Yahweh are mercy and
fidely to them that seek after His Covenant and law " (Ps 24:10).
In Psalm 135, the chorus keeps repeating, " Praise ye the Lord,
for He is good. His mercy endureth for ever. " We take it,
then, that divine mercy and fidelity characterize the message
of the Old Testament. And this makes us realize better the
force of St. John's terse, solemn declaration in the opening
chapter of his Gospel: " Of His fullness we have all received,
one grace after another. True, the law was given through Moses,
but mercy and fidelity came through Jesus Christ " (Jn 1:16-17).
Whatever the prophets had sung concerning God's " mercy and
fidelity " became a reality in the New Testament. We have
no longer parables, but actual fact; God came down in person to
us and became man. " The Word was made flesh [that is, a
plain, weak man as we are] and dwelt among us [as did Yahweh
of old, with His people in the desert or in the holy of holies, on
Mount Sion], and we saw His glory [His divine presence, as
on Mount Tabor or after the resurrection], the glory belonging
to the only begotten of the Father, full of grace and truth
[mercy and fidelity] " (Jn 1:14).

The prodigal son

Man finds it hard to believe in love, especially in a love
which forgives and perseveres in the face of betrayal and in-

fidelity. That is why He, who is the incarnate " grace and truth " of the Father, " the radiance of God's glory and the very image of His being" (Heb 1:3), will speak so insistently of God's love for us. Luke has preserved three parables emphasizing the reality we dare not easily accept, the fact that God loves us with unceasing fidelity. Those are the parables of the lost sheep, the lost silver piece and the prodigal son (Lk 15:3-32).

" And He said: ' A certain man had two sons. And the younger of them said to his father: Father, give me the portion of substance that falleth to me. ' " To the Jews, the promised land was their inheritance, which they had received from God Himself. " And he divided unto them his substance. And not many days after, the younger son, gathering all together, went abroad into a far land. " This was not the promised land, but the country of the heathens that lay outside God's Covenant. " And there he wasted his substance, living riotously. " Saying this, Our Lord refers in delicate terms to the sin graphically described by the prophet Ezechiel, the sin of " prostitution, " signifying apostasy and revolt against God.

" And after he had spent all, there came a mighty famine in that country; and he began to be in want. And he went and cleaved to one of the citizens of that country. And he sent him into his farm to feed swine. " Thanks to the latter discreet detail, the apostles (who were Jews) and the simple people of Galilee were sufficiently given to understand into what state of degradation the young man had sunk; to a Jew, swine were unclean animals which he could not tend without defiling himself.

" And he would fain have filled his belly with the husks the swine did eat; and no man gave unto him.

" And returning to himself, he said: ' How many hired servants in my father's house abound with bread, and I here perish with hunger! I will arise and will go to my father and say to him: Father, I have sinned against heaven [that is, against God] and before thee; I am not worthy to be called thy son; make me one of thy hired servants. ' Rising up, he came to his father.

" And when he was yet a great way off, his father saw him, and was moved with compassion, and running to him fell upon his neck, and kissed him. And the son said to him: ' Father, I have sinned against heaven and before thee; I am not now worthy to be called thy son. ' And the father said to his servants: ' Bring forth quickly the first robe and put it on him, and put a ring on his hand [sign of a full reinstatement into his former rank], and shoes on his feet; and bring hither the fatted calf, and kill it, and let us eat and make merry:

because this my son was dead and is come to life again, was lost and is found. ' And they began to be merry. " [Lk 15:11-24]

This Gospel passage is a favorite one with poets and preachers, and justly so. But they usually fail to call attention to what follows in the sacred text, which brings out the difficulty man experiences in acknowledging and accepting God's love. Who among our good Catholics, or for that matter among priests and religious, rejoices when hearing that a public sinner has been reconciled with God on his deathbed? Who in his heart shares the joy which fills the heart of the heavenly Father? Last-minute conversions are commented upon in sarcastic, inconsiderate terms. Such talk seems to betray a hidden regret that, unlike the deceased man, one has not dared to have one's fling on earth for fear of missing a safe arrival in the next world.

The elder brother of the prodigal son showed spite because of the great feast with which the younger brother's homecoming was celebrated.

" And he was angry and would not go in. His father, therefore, coming out, began to entreat him. And he, answering, said to his father: ' Behold, for so many years do I serve thee, and I have never transgressed thy commandment; and yet thou hast never given me a kid to make merry with my friends; but as soon as this thy son is come, who has devoured his substance with harlots, thou hast killed the fatted calf '

" But he said to him: ' Son, thou art always with me, and all I have is thine. But it was fit that we should make merry and be glad, for thy brother was dead, and is come to life again; he was lost, and is found. ' " [Lk 15:28-32]

The word " grace "

We cannot claim to be Christians unless we believe in God's love. " We have seen and do testify that the Father hath sent His Son to be the Savior of the world. Whoever shall confess that Jesus is the Son of God, God abideth in him, and he in God. [For thus] we have known and have believed the charity which God hath to us. God is charity; and he who abideth in charity, abideth in God, and God in him. " Then come the words which, according to St. Augustine, sum up the secret of grace: " Let us therefore love God, because God first hath loved us " (I Jn 4:14-19).

The theology of grace is in the main the theology of God's love for us and of the love which God's first love has caused in us. *Grace* is the English word for the Latin *gratia*. Now, *gratia* has acquired many secondary meanings, both in the technical language of the theologians and in the usage of the Church and the great councils; but its prime Christian meaning comes from Scripture. The Latin Vulgate used *gratia* to translate the Greek word *charis*. All the sacred authors of the New Testament, Paul in particular, have borrowed from the Septuagint the term *charis* to render several Hebrew words conveying meanings reducible to three main ideas: condescending love, conciliatory compassion and fidelity. The basic sense of Christian grace, whatever its later and further technical or non-Scholastic connotations, should always remind us that God first loved us. Let that be its fundamental chord.

"Dearly beloved, let us love one another, for charity is of God. And every one that loveth is born of God and knoweth God. He that loveth not, knoweth not God; for God is charity. By this hath the charity of God appeared toward us, because God hath sent His only begotten Son into the world, that we may live by Him. In this is charity: not as though we had loved God [by our power and means], but because He first loved us, and sent His Son to be a propitiation for our sins" (I Jn 4:7-10).

The covenant of grace

The first part of this book has shown us that any deeper study of the faith must begin with an attitude of attention to what God tells us in the Church, in Holy Scripture and in Tradition. We take for granted that our first parable has caused in us the required attentive attitude and has prepared us to lend an ear to God's own stories concerning Himself.

Here we need do no more than recall to mind the leading ideas of Scripture, to which the preceding pages serve as introduction.

Old Testament themes

The Old Testament is but one long hymn of praise to the love which God showed to His chosen people, Israel. Whenever it describes the divine predilection, the central theme is always the covenant which God freely entered upon with His people. Around this central theme many others group themselves and swell into a powerful polyphony, as for instance God's fidelity and compassion, His patience and forbearance, His love and mercy. God is celebrated in turn as the bridegroom dealing with a fickle and faithless bride, as the shepherd, the vinedresser planting and tending his vineyard, the physician, and the father and king.

Special emphasis falls on the fact that the divine favor bears the characters of being absolutely unearned, gratuitous: God has no need whatever of Israel! "Not because you surpass all nations in numbers, is the Lord joined unto you and has chosen you, for you are the fewest of any people; but because the Lord has loved you and has kept His oath..." (Dt 7:7). "I have loved Israel. I have done this for the sake of My own name" (Is 48:9-11). "For I am God and not a man. I am the saint in your midst" (Os 11:9). "It is not because of you...but for the sake of My holy name" (Ez 36:22). With good reason the

Psalmist exclaims: " Not to us, O Lord, not to us; but to Thy name give glory, for Thy love, for Thy fidelity! Let the gentiles not say: Where is their God? " (Ps 113:1-3).

God Himself—His sanctity—is the motive of His love. The Old Testament never stops underlining the absolute gratuitousness of the divine gift. While Israel keeps forfeiting the Lord's love by its repeated revolts, infidelities and idolatry, God remains true to His Covenant; His word remains forever: He is God and not a man.

God's Covenant with His people

In pre-Christian times, the outstanding fact connected with man's salvation was precisely the Covenant God had concluded with an insignificant nation, the prelude and preparation for the everlasting covenant made in His Son. All the other facts stand grouped around it. Before all else, creation clearly signifies that everything comes from God as a pure gift of love. After it, rank all the memorable events which we learned in the Bible history of our schooldays, the exact bearing of which lay in great part beyond our youthful understanding. Among these events we may mark out the divine promises made to the patriarchs, the calling of Abraham, Israel's deliverance from the bondage of Egypt as an exceptional testimony of God's enduring love, the special providence watching over the Jewish people during the reign of the kings and the period of the prophets. Israel was not only too small and too insignificant a nation to warrant the slightest claim to a special selection, but its increasingly great infidelity and apostasy, its impenitence and obduracy caused it to forfeit all appearance of a claim to it. That is why the main mission of the prophets consisted in proclaiming God's absolute fidelity to His promises, the excellence of His love. They threatened that if Israel kept failing in its allegiance, God would reserve to Himself a " remnant, " and transfer His choice to the poor and the contemptible; He would turn to other nations and make those " poor of Yahweh " henceforth the object of His election. It is not God who abandoned man, but man who abandoned God.

All that God wanted to be to Israel is but a distant fore-shadowing of what He actually is to His " new people, " to the " poor of Yahweh, " to the Church. " For God so loved the world that He hath given His only begotten Son " (Jn 3:16). Herein lies that other element of salvation with which the Christian epoch opened. The unique love of the Father was made manifest to us in Jesus Christ, not so much in spoken words as in deeds: the small, daily marvels narrated in the Gospels, but above all the final consummation of the cross.

The crowning act of the cross has become fully intelligible, as a historical reality, to our faith because of what immediately followed it. Two facts powerfully impressed the nascent Christian community: first, Christ's resurrection and ascension; second, the coming of the Holy Spirit, together with the wonders of spiritual fulfillment and enthusiasm which in the beginning of the primitive Church accompanied this descent and made it visible and tangible.

These facts and realities have at the same time thrown light on the history of the Jewish people as God's chosen race. Whatever had taken place in former times served as a portent, a preparation and a foreshadowing of the central fact of world-history: that God Himself in the person of His Word " was made flesh and dwelt among us " (Jo 1:14) . . . so that we in our turn might (in the bold language of the Greek Fathers) become gods, that is, filled with divine and filial life. St. John pointed this out when he disclosed the higher meaning of Caiphas' prophecy: " Do you not realize that it is good for you that one man should die for the people and not let the whole nation perish? " (Jn 11:50). Caiphas had addressed those words to the Sanhedrin, but John was prompt to reveal the more hidden sense God meant them to convey: " Now, he did not say that of himself, but, being the high priest of that year, he prophesied that Jesus should die for the nation; and not only for the nation, but *to gather together in one the children of God that were dispersed"* (Jn 11:51-52).

The Apostle was more explicit still in his Epistle: " Behold what manner of charity the Father hath bestowed upon us that we should be called and should be sons of God. Therefore, the world knoweth not us, because it knew Him not. Dearly beloved, *we are now the sons of God;* and it hath not yet appeared what we shall be [that is, what it means to be sons of God has not yet been made known]. We know that when He shall appear, we shall be like to Him: because we shall see Him as He is " (I Jn 3:1-2).

Sin and love

It is these *salvific facts* that initiate us still further into the *salvific truths* of our faith, the "dogmas" and articles of faith so frowned upon today in some circles.

We are not here presented with abstract postulates, belonging to some sort of pious geometry, with anxioms fettering creative thought in chains of arid speculation. It is true that faith restrains thought within certain limits, but like all original truth it both restrains and stimulates through the facts.

These facts, voices of God's perennial youth, deliver their enduring message not so much to discursive speculative reason as to the whole man. They lend fertility to thought by leading progressively to fresh, richer and deeper realizations. At the same time, they demand an unambiguous acceptance of their truth, the radiance of divine actuality. Take the Creed, for instance, the summary of Catholic belief: starting with creation, it proceeds like a triumphal march of divine deeds which, from creation till life everlasting, God has done for His people, His Church in general and each one of her members in particular. Thanks to these salvific facts, we are given to understand in what manner it is salvific or in what manner God grants us His grace.

The cross, sign of our perdition

The mystery of grace is the mystery of the way God's love acts with us and for us. Considered as mere creatures, we stand in dire poverty outside the pale of the divine, almighty splendor. We may call that our creaturely isolation from God. Original sin, which our own personal sins actualize still further in life, relegates us not only out of God's glory but under God's wrath. Our creaturely condition is not merely destitute but stained and injured. As we are all born with original sin in our souls, we come on earth in the state of perdition.

Let us understand this well. Original sin in us is no personal, actual sin of ours, but is a state of estrangement from God and of perdition, affecting before God the whole of mankind. God sees us not as isolated individuals but as sharing a responsibility in common. We all fell away from the love of God into perdition with the whole of mankind.

Shakespeare exclaims in *Measure for Measure* (II, ii, 116-121):

> ... But man, proud man,
> Dress'd in a little brief authority,
> Most ignorant of what he's most assured—
> His glassy essence—like an angry ape
> Plays such fantastic tricks before high heaven
> As make the angels weep. ...

These lines are not merely poetic fantasy. The brutalizing experiences of our age have fortunately freed us from the smug, bourgeois conviction that human progress is inevitable. For all that, recent history can give us no more than vague evidence to connect these events with original sin. Taken in themselves, they could be explained on purely natural grounds; they could even be excused and dismissed as commonplace in the context of man's whole history.

If we are committed to the dogma of original sin, that is, to our common state of perdition in the sight of God, we will see that this belief rests mainly on a single fact, the cardinal event of our faith: Christ died for us all.

By the cross we are given to understand that *we all* stand in need of redemption and that, in fact, *we are all* offered and granted the gift of reconciliation. And this shows that also the truth of our inherited state of guilt rests mainly on that cardinal salvific fact of our faith. The Church, later, has done nothing more than *outline and state* in clear terms the basic historical experience of the cross.

The cross, sign of grace

There is more still. The cross reveals to us that God had pity on us, that He came in search of us in our state of perdition and estrangement from Him, that in His fidelity and mercy He never lost sight of us, that He still loves us with a fatherly heart. *And that is grace.*

Grace is not something that hangs high above our heads like the aurora borealis on a frosty night. Grace comes down on us like an abundant dew, permeating us, or like the first breath of spring that stirs nature and awakens it. From grace, that is, from the power and warmth of God's *initial love,* we are made able to look up to Him once again. We know that through faith we are raised, attracted and driven toward Him in sorrow and reciprocation of love. Once again we have obtained the right to live as children of God. Together in and with Christ's filial love, there is born in us a new filial *power* enabling us, in union with Him and through the strength of the Spirit, to cry in very deed and truth, " Abba! Father! " (Rom 8:16-17).

Grace, an outflowing and inflowing life

The conjugate stream, starting from God towards us and returning from us in union with Christ back to God, encompasses the fullness and depth of divine grace. Blessed Jan van Ruysbroeck has patterned the whole of his mystical and theological doctrine on this durable canvas. The mighty ebb and flow of the eternal trinitarian life, from God and Godward, is seen by him as an ocean of love that over and over again floods and fertilizes the world, then carries all things in its sweep back to the original abyss of God's majestic glory.

" Understand now: man shall go out and observe God in His glories with all His saints; and he shall contemplate the riches and the mercy with which God flows, with glories and with Himself and with incomprehensible delights, in all His saints, according to the desire of every spirit. [And man shall see] how the saints themselves, together with all they have received and with all they can do, flow back into that same rich, unique source from which all delight proceeds. This flowing of God demands always a flowing back again; for God is like a sea, ebbing and flowing, ceaselessly flowing into each one of His elect, according to the needs and the worth of each. And in His ebbing He draws back again all men to whom He has given in heaven and on earth, with all they have and all of which they are capable. And from such men He demands more than they can achieve. For He reveals Himself so rich and so merciful and so immeasurably good! And in this manifestation He demands of them love and honor according to His worth. God indeed desires to be loved by us in accordance with His excellence; in this, however, all spirits fail. And so, love is without manner and without fashion. For our spirits do not know how to add yet more to the love that they already bear; for each spirit's capacity for love is finite. And therefore the work of love is constantly begun afresh, so that God may be loved as He demands and as they desire. "[1]

Grace, seen from God's side, signifies that God loves us gratuitously. His love is totally undeserved, first, because as creatures we can lay no claim to any right before God, and second, because our solidarity in evil has caused us to lose without appeal all the privileges God granted to mankind in the beginning. Again, His love is undeserved because in the last analysis all love must find in itself the justifying reason for its existence, and this is supremely the case with God's sovereign love. He loves because He is God and not man, because of His glory and the sanctity of His name.

Grace, an interior strength

God's assurance of His love is never an empty one. "As the rain and the snow come down from heaven and return no more thither, but soak the earth and water it, and make it to be fertile and to give seed to the sower and bread to the eater: so shall My word coming forth from My mouth; it shall not return to Me void, but it shall do whatever I please, and shall prosper in the things for which I sent it " (Is 55:10-11). Consequently, grace, seen from man's side, is a created gift which brings him an inner strength, a lifting urge, a yearning for God. It lays hold of us in the innermost depth of our person, whence it fecundates the multiple layers of our life and blossoms visibly in deeds of holiness, of goodness and joy.

" Now, divine grace, which flows out from God, is an interior compulsion or driving of the Holy Ghost Who, from within us, drives our spirit and incites it in all virtues. This grace flows from within us and not from outside. For God is more truly within us than we ourselves, and His inward driving and urging, natural or supernatural, is closer to us and more interior than our own deeds. And therefore, God works in us from inside outwards, while all creatures work from outside inwards. And because of this, grace and all divine gifts and God's inspirations come from within the unity of our spirit, and not from without, through the senses and its images. "[2]

St. Augustine expressed this double aspect of grace in the terse formula, " *Quia me amasti, fecisti me amabilem,* " " Because

---

[1] Jan van Ruysbroeck, *Die Gheestelike Brulocht,* tr. Eric Colledge as *The Spiritual Espousals* (London: Faber & Faber, 1952), pp. 127-128.
[2] *Ibid.,* p. 21.

You have loved me, You have made me lovable "— and good.
God's love has struck us; its wound burns in our hearts until it is
healed in God.   As St. Augustine said in his celebrated sentence,
" You have made us [in creation and redemption] and turned
us toward You, Lord, and our heart finds no peace until it
rests in You. "

Grace, a presence of God

We are now in a position to enter a little more deeply into the mystery of grace. It is to our advantage that exact thought should be given an entry into the vast sphere of this mystery—though on the condition that we not attempt to debase its secrets by the crude light of our reasoning intelligence, or pretend to measure with the petty yardstick of our reason "what is the breadth and length and height and depth" of God's love (Eph. 3:18). It remains our duty, however, to try to learn our faith better. Respect of God and awe of the divine remoteness do not dispense us from attempting to grasp the momentous meaning of grace in human life. When we make this attempt, we are no longer dealing with Revelation properly speaking but with constructions of the human mind, which are wretched and rickety at best; whatever solidity they have is ultimately borrowed from the certainty of Revelation.

In unraveling the mystery of grace, we find a most appropriate scheme of thought in personalistic philosophy, especially in the description of the *presence* of one person to another. ⌈Grace in general can be described as the secret of God's presence in our life.⌋ And in explaining it this way, we are convinced that we are faithfully following the Master's own teaching. Christ considered no legacy more precious to His Church than His abiding presence with us through the Spirit: "Again I say to you, that if two of you shall consent upon earth concerning anything, whatsoever they shall ask, it shall be done to them by My Father Who is in heaven. For where there are two or three gathered together in My name, *there am I in the midst of them*" (Mt 18:19-20). St. Matthew's Gospel closes with the assurance of an everlasting presence: "Behold, *I am with you ... even to the consummation of the world*" (Mt 28:20). We also have the words Christ spoke in the farewell discourse after the last supper: "If any one loves Me, he will keep My word, and My Father will love him, and We will come to him and *will make Our abode with him*" (Jn 14:23). These words are followed immediately by the parable of the vine and the branches (Jn 15:1-8).

The early Christians did not forget Christ's solemn promise, even in times of persecution. As baptized and believing disciples of our Lord, they knew they were no longer living alone, not even when undergoing abuse and scorn. " You shall greatly rejoice," Peter told them, " if you now must be for a little time made sorrowful in diverse temptations: that the test of your faith (much more precious than gold which is tried by fire) may be found unto praise and glory and honor at the coming of Jesus Christ " (I Pt 1:6-7). The chapter continues, *" Whom having not seen, you love:* in Whom also now, though you see Him not, you believe and, believing, shall rejoice with joy unspeakable and glorified; receiving the end of your faith, even the salvation of your souls " (II Pt 1:8-9).

Faith, then, aims always at securing Christ's presence in our life—an inner, actual presence overflowing with joy through the veil of faith. This is the sense in which we accept Christ's words addressed to Thomas: " Because you have seen Me, Thomas, you have believed [in Christ's resurrection and consequent *omnipresence*]. Blessed are they [both at the time the Gospels were written and ever since] *that have not seen and have believed* " (Jn 20:29).

Grace is the mystery of God's intense, living presence in us. The allegory with which we opened this chapter described this personal reality in terms of psychology and human love. But when we come to consider God and man, we are immediately confronted with a very different matter, simply because God's relations with men do not correspond to men's relations with God or to the relations of men among themselves. The relations between God and men are not the same from both sides and are therefore not interchangeable, though this is the case among men. For instance, we might just as well have told the story of a straying young man who is saved through a girl's pure love.

We should guard against the assumption that man can give or offer anything to God—whether love or joy, pain, homage or holiness—that he has not first received as a gift from God. What is more, when man does freely return the divine gifts to the Father, he does so not by himself alone but together with God, that is, with Christ and the Holy Spirit. These precisions have their importance, for the reason that a Protestant might say that in the domain of grace Catholics assume a presumptive and arrogant attitude before God, considering themselves almost His equals. We Catholics, some might allege, seem to think the divine majesty is indebted to us through our good works and merits. There may indeed be Catholics who in their conduct or teaching lay themselves open to such a charge. But when this happens, we do not hesitate to affirm that their behavior amounts to a perversion of the faith, to a camouflaged sin of Pharisaic pride. To the Corinthians, Paul said very tellingly, " What have you that you have not received? " (I Cor 4:7).

With these precautions in mind, we may now proceed with the theological consideration of grace as the mystery of the *living* presence of one person to another.

On one side stands the Godhead in three persons, Father, Son and Holy Ghost; on the other side we stand, creatures and sinners, but despite this made into the image of God. Veiled in His providence, God speaks to us in every one of the daily events and in the concrete situation of the life He has chosen for us. He speaks to us through the Church and also, without intermediary, in our hearts. He speaks to man with love. He calls each one by his own name, and this name expresses both a commission and a vocation. His word confers upon man the condition, new and peculiarly his own, of being a " you " before God; and here as always, God's word is operative and creative. The Father speaks to me as to a " you, " as to his trusted child reborn and risen already. God's word affects me in the deepest depth of my self; He confers upon this personal core in me a *density* and firmness never suspected before. I am truly *some one* before God because He speaks to me. This is the essential of that creative presence of God in the soul through grace.

Grace, a likeness to Christ

This theological notion, set down just now, is still too incomplete, too bald in its first outline; it should be delved into more deeply by an important addition and correction. Even in grace, it is not we, properly speaking, who stand before God. God's life of love is of itself a unique and intense presence of God to Himself. The Father stands in perfect self-identity, power and intensity before the Son; so does the Son stand before the Father; and so do the Father and the Son before the Spirit. The mystery of grace becomes clearer in outline when we say that through grace, man, while still on earth, is introduced in a hidden though real manner, into the glorious intimacy belonging to the Father, the Son and the Holy Spirit. Our presence to God is a *co*-presence. It is as if through grace, namely, through the loving election and speech of the Father, we are raised to the height of the Son. Grace, then, signifies that by sheer divine love and mercy we are, with and in the Son, permitted to stand before the Father, through the power of the Holy Spirit. It means that we share in the loving conserve of the divine persons. The core of our personality is *spiritually* raised to a re-created density and self-identity (whence the term *supernatural*), enveloped in the unique density and self-identity of the Son. We shall often have occasion to use the term " density " when speaking of what constitutes the core of a person. We shall explain this figure of speech in the chapter on sanctifying grace: *Grace as life's dynamism*. In the meanwhile, it should be enough to say that by this metaphor we want to stress a person's " compactness " wherein the complete subsequent unfolding of personal existence is as yet coiled up by way of dynamic potentiality.

Insofar as the life of grace on earth is already a beginning and an actual foretaste of paradise, what will constitute life eternal is already present in germ—the possibility of living and abiding in the all-surpassing intimacy of the divine Persons. To return to the comparison made earlier, through grace, each one of us is like a drop of water lost in the mighty ebb and

[margin note: Our presence to god]

[margin note: density]

flow of the divine ocean; diffused in the divine life, we are
enabled for the first time to be ourselves in a unique way—ourselves, just because we have become greater than ourselves.

The Son, image of the Father

All this needs to be dwelt upon at some length, especially in
connection with the great scriptural themes which have been
used in great part by Jan van Ruysbroeck.

Holy Scripture presents the Son to us as the visible Revelation
of the Father, as Him in Whom the Father created the world.
"In the beginning was the Word, and the Word was with God,
and the Word was God. He was in the beginning with God.
All things came into being through Him and nothing whatever
came into being without Him.... No one has ever seen God
[the Father]; the only begotten God [the Son] Who is in the
bosom of the Father has made Him known " (Jn 1:1-3, 18).

Soaring to equal heights, the unknown author of the Epistle
to the Hebrews introduced the Son in similar terms: "After
God had spoken of old to our fathers through the prophets,
He has at last spoken to us these days through His Son,
[through] Him Whom He destined to be heir of all things,
and through Whom be made the universe. He, the effulgence
of God's glory and the perfect image of His substance, upholds
the universe by the power of the divine mandate..." (Heb 1:1-3).

A few years earlier, Paul the Apostle had written to the
Colossians:

"He is the image of the invisible God, the firstborn of all
creatures. For in Him all things were created, whether in
the heavens or on the earth, what is visible or invisible,
whether Thrones or Dominations, Principalities or Powers. All
things have been created through Him and for Him. He exists
before all things, and in Him all things subsist. He is also the
head of the body, which is the Church. He is the beginning,
the firstborn among the dead, so that in all things He may
hold the preeminence; for it has pleased [the Father] that in
Him should dwell the fullness [of the Father] and that, through
Him, He should reconcile all things to Himself, whether the
things that are on earth, or things in the heavens, making peace
by the blood of His cross. " [Col. 1:15-20]

In creation and in redemption, the Son stands first. He is
the image of the Father, and in the likeness of this image
the Father has created and redeemed all things. This is the
pivotal fact in the whole history of our salvation.

The countenance of the Son

The ancient Fathers of the Church keenly perceived the unique place held by the Son in both creation and redemption; and they kept it constantly in mind when they drew up the fundamental tenets of their theology. To them nothing was clearer than that man has been created in the image of the Son, and in that same image has been re-created in grace.

For a closer acquaintance with this divine prototype, we shall listen once more to Holy Scripture. Christ spoke of Himself as the Son of Man, the true Servant of Yahweh, and the only begotten Son of the Father.

The name *Son of Man* means nothing more than *man* in the original Hebrew. But this primary meaning, never to be lost sight of, was given an additional connotation by Christ Himself after the glorification on Mount Tabor when He connected it with the two ideas of the suffering servant of Yahweh and the mysterious "son of man" who, according to Daniel's prophecy, "appears on the clouds of heaven" (Dn 7:13).

Perhaps the finest pages in the Old Testament were written by the unknown author, generally called Deutero-Isaias, of the Book of Consolation (Is 40-55). The central figure of that book is the Servant of Yahweh who is to deliver Israel from sin through His sufferings. That is why the unknown author earned for himself the title of " the fifth evangelist. "

Christ Himself acknowledged at some decisive moments of His life that He was the Servant of Yahweh foretold in Isaias. One Sabbath day in the synagogue at Nazareth, He was invited to stand up and read a passage from Scripture. A scroll of the prophet Isaias was handed to Him. He unrolled it and found the place where it read: " The Spirit of the Lord is upon Me, because He has anointed Me. He has sent Me out to bring the glad tidings to the poor, to announce freedom to the prisoners and sight to the blind, to set the oppressed at liberty, to proclaim a year of grace when men may find acceptance with the Lord " (Is 61:1-2, written by Deutero-Isaias, or later by one of his disciples who has been called sometimes Trito-Isaias).

Then He rolled up the scroll, returned it to the attendant and sat down. The eyes of all in the synagogue were fixed upon Him. He then said to them: " This passage of Scripture, which you have just heard, has been fulfilled today " (Lk 4:21).

We find in the New Testament not only a number of passages taken from the Book of Consolation but also many characteristic allusions to a Christology, still in the making at the time the New Testament was being written, and largely based on quotations from Deutero-Isaias. For instance, " Behold, the lamb of

God, who takes away the sin of the world!" (Jn 1:29), and "In Him, God has been well pleased."

We know that St. John built his own theology on Christ's death and resurrection. "'If only I am *lifted up* from the earth, I will attract all men to Myself.' In saying this, He signified the nature of the death He was about to die" (Jn 12:32; see also 3:14; 8:28). It is perhaps less generally known that "being lifted up"—a symbol of the cross, the resurrection and ascension, that is, of all the essential events entering into the work of the redemption—is also a reference to the best-known prophecy of Deutero-Isaias regarding the suffering and triumph of the Servant of Yahweh: "Behold, My servant shall prosper; He shall be *lifted up* and shall be as *greatly exalted* as many were appalled at Him. For His appearance was debased beneath that of man, and His form beneath that of the sons of men. But many nations shall be amazed at Him, and kings shall shut their mouths before Him.... He shall have a posterity, He shall prolong His days; and *what is pleasing to Yahweh will be accomplished in Him*" (Is 52:13-15; 53:10).

Some years before St. John wrote, Paul described the theology of redemption in his Epistle to the Philippians, though in his own personal manner and according to his own cast of mind:

"Keep those sentiments among you which you see in Christ Jesus; He, though subsisting in the form of God, did not cling to the likeness with God as to a prey [as did Adam and Eve]. But he emptied himself, taking to himself the form of servant (Is 53:3, 11-12) and thus becoming like to man [Son of Man]. Appearing as man, He had humbled Himself by *being obedient unto death*, even to the death of the cross. And, therefore, God has lifted Him up and has bestowed upon Him the name above all names.... *Jesus Christ is the Lord.*" [Phil 2:5-11]

The servant is one who obeys, who "does the will of the Father" (Jn 5:30), "whose bread is to accomplish the will of the Father" (Jn 4:34), who will pray: "Not My will, but Yours be done" (Lk 22:42). Thus the trait most characteristic of the Servant is obedience. *It is by His obedience that Christ redeemed us* (Rom 5:19). By sinning, we had become disobedient. Christ has wanted to be in this world of sin, what we, according to the Father's mind, should have been from the beginning, obedient servants of God.

The third characteristic expression Christ used for Himself was "Son of the Father." *Son,* in both Hebrew and Aramaic, can stand for more than one form of relationship—to a person or a people, to God or the devil. Toward the end of His life, Christ gave this rather vague word a clearcut meaning by applying it to Himself in order to mark the intimate connection He has with the Father. Later, both Paul and John determined this sense still further, and spoke of Christ as God's " own Son " and God's " only begotten Son. " Now, what is most characteristic of a son is *love*. God is love, and in Christ that love came down to this earth (I Jn 4:7; 5:4); through His love He saved the world. Sin is essentially self-seeking, a hardening of the heart and pride. Love alone can destroy the power of sin. Christ proved to us the earnestness and intensity of His love by dying on the cross (Jn 15:13; Rom 5:5-8; Gal 2:20).

After the image of the Son　corporate personality

Here we have to take into account a form of thought quite special to the Hebrew mind. Hebrew thinking did not proceed along abstract, metaphysical lines as does Western, which is molded upon the pattern left us by the Greeks. It dealt always in concrete terms, and showed a marked preference for symbols and images. Exegetes have discovered that in the Old Testament, and consequently also in the New, the idea of " sharing " is often expressed by what has come to be called the " corporate personality. " What is said of one person can often be applied to the nation to which that person belongs. This literary genre is often used in the Book of Consolation. In some verses, the Servant of Yahweh is no longer simply the mysterious person described by Isaias, but is also Israel itself as a people; if it is to share in His consolation and triumph, it must share in His sufferings.

That is certainly the way Paul and John understood matters from the start. To them it was perfectly certain that if Christ was the Servant, we had all become servants and slaves of God in Him. And this was so real that in Paul's mind it constituted the special title of honor for all Christians. St. John pointed to the fact that we have become children of God in and through the Son: " To those who received Him and to those who believed in His name, He gave the power of becoming children of God. They are not born of blood, nor from carnal desire, nor from the will of man, but they are *born from God* " (Jn 1:12-13). On another page of his Gospel, the same evangelist reported Caiphas' prophecy concerning Christ's passion, and he was at pains to explain at once the import of those prophetic words. It was an occacion for him to indicate the meaning of both redemption and grace. " He did not say that of himself; but being the high priest of that year, he prophesied that Jesus was to die for the nation; and not for the nation only, but also that He might gather together the scattered children of God " (Jn 11:51-52).

In his first Epistle, John wrote, "Whoever is born of God does not sin, because the seed [of God] remains in him; and he cannot sin, since he is born of God. By this are the children of God and the children of the devil known apart: whoever does not live right is not of God, at least not he who does not love his brethren" (I Jn 3:8-10). In the beginning of that same chapter the Apostle said, "See how God has shown His love toward us: that we should be called children of God, and should *be His children!* Beloved, *we are already* children of God, but as yet it has not been made known what we shall be hereafter. We know, however, that when He will appear [on the ast day] *we shall be like Him,* because we shall see Him as He is" (I Jn 3:1-2).

These words are a striking affirmation of our divine sonship. But St. John was not alone in his affirmation—Paul was equally emphatic: "All those who let themselves be led by the Spirit of God, they are the sons of God. The Spirit which you have received is not one of slavery, leading again to fear. But you have received the Spirit of adoption which makes us cry, 'Abba! Father!' The Spirit bears witness to our spirit that we are children of God; and if children, then also heirs of God and *heirs with Christ, since we share in His sufferings in order to share in His glorification*" (Rom 8:14-17). In his Epistle to the Galatians, Paul connected our participation in the divine sonship yet more explicitly with the redemption and therefore with grace:

"We, too, when we were still minors, were serving in subjection to the elements of this world. But when the appointed time had come, God [the Father] sent out His Son on a mission to us, to be born from a woman and subjected to the Law [of the Jews], in order that He might set free those who were subject to the Law and that we might become sons of adoption. And *because you are sons,* God has sent into our hearts the Spirit of His Son, crying, 'Abba, Father.' You are, therefore, no longer a slave [of the Law]; you are a son; and if a son, then also an heir by God's act." [Gal 4:3-7]

"Abba, Father": these two words are not unlike the opening words of the Aramaic Our Father, the prayer taught us by Christ in person. In this case, we cannot in truth recite the Our Father unless our spirit has a share in the Spirit of God. In the Hebrew idiom, and thus also in biblical Greek, the term *spirit* does not designate the spiritual principle of the human compound, or in other words, the soul; but it signifies, in the Bible, first and foremost the Spirit and the Power of God, the One who later on will reveal Himself as the person of the Holy Spirit. It designates also His gifts, but especially the *whole man,* that is, body and soul living as one person, insofar as it has been filled with the Holy Spirit and, consequently, totally transformed. In this sense, "spirit" stands in opposition to "flesh"; and "flesh," in Paul's writings, means the whole man insofar as he is creature, though especially insofar as he is a sinner standing away from God.

If we can grasp this usage in the sense intended by Paul, John and the other evangelists, we are in possession of the beginnings of a theology of grace. Briefly put, it would amount to this: away from God and as a creature estranged from God, especially if lost through sin, man is nothing more than "flesh." But through the power of God's Spirit—the Spirit of Christ—sinful man becomes "spirit," totally and utterly renewed by God's Spirit. Then and only then does what he has indeed become appear: child of God and heir of God, with and in and through Christ Jesus.

The Apostle Peter summarized this in the well-known text, " Whatever is necessary to life and piety, the divine power has bestowed upon us, together with the knowledge of Him Who called us by His glory and virtue. He has granted us thereby His high and precious promises, so that, leaving behind the corruption of this world with its evil passions, you may *share in the divine nature ...*" (II Pt 1:3-4). Exegetes are probably right in saying that Peter was not thinking at all of the somewhat forced theological meaning which we tend to read in his words today. Nonetheless, Peter's is a bold affirmation. Paul and the author of the Epistle to the Hebrews touched upon the same idea:

" The Lord is the Spirit, and where the Spirit of the Lord is, there is freedom. To all of us it has been given to see with unveiled face the glory of the Lord, and *to be transfigured into an ever-increasing glorious image of Him;* for it is the Spirit of the Lord who works this out " [II Cor 3:17-18].

Put on the new man, the one created *in the image of God,* in justice and holiness [Eph 4:24].

They [our fathers according to the flesh] have corrected us for a short while [in our youth], at their own caprice; but He does so for our advantage, in order that we may *share in His sanctity* [Heb 12:10].

These numerous affirmations in the New Testament are a continuation of a much older tradition which identifies likeness to God with imitation of God in our daily life. Here is what Christ said in the Sermon on the Mount: " But I tell you: love your enemies, pray for those who persecute you; so that you may be children of your Father Who is in heaven, Who causes His sun to rise upon good and evil, and causes rain to fall upon the just and the unjust. For, if you love only those who love you, what claim have you to a reward?...*Be perfect as your heavenly Father is perfect*" (Mt 5:44-48). To Israel of old, Yahweh, in the book of Leviticus, had set the same high standard of conduct: "Be holy because I, Yahweh your God, am holy" (Lv 19:2).

Christ, the prototype of our grace

A good many of our modern theological textbooks enlarge upon the idea of our "assimilation in God" along rather abstract lines, very much as if it were a likeness to the Godhead, to the divine nature as such. But in the light of biblical teaching this notion makes little sense, especially since the word *God* in the New Testament is usually intended to designate God the Father. The theology of God, as found in the Old Testament, has been shifted into that of the Father in the New. As later councils would summarize matters, "the father is the primordial source of all that is divine."

But this rather attenuated tradition has the disadvantage of neglecting what is properly original and unique in the history of our salvation—that we have been re-created in and through the Son, the image of the Father. Likeness to God is thus fundamentally coincident with likeness to the Son. *And this precisely is the essential characteristic which both the divine indwelling and grace develop in us.*

The early Fathers, who as bishops guided and taught the Church, never neglected this truth. It constitutes also one of the most rewarding insights of our mystical tradition. These themes did not escape Ruysbroeck, a man steeped in and nourished on the reading of Scripture. We have been created, and through grace we have been reborn in the image of the Son. In the eyes of our mystic, this is not just an abstract thought; it is something concrete, actual, something intimately bound up with the history of the redemption. In his book *The Perfection of the Sons of God*, he made use of the figurative language of the Bible to designate the various steps of the ladder to Christian perfection. In this respect, he remained of course a man of the Middle Ages, but not for a moment did he forget that Holy Writ uses those various figures of speech to define what forms the essence of all *Christian life*. If we could renounce ourselves and all that is ours in our works, from the moment we come into our naked and imageless spirit [that is, into the depth of our person, where, stripped and freed from images, we are in

nakend imageles spirit

immediate contact with the Spirit of God] we would reach
beyond all things. And in this nakedness, we would be guided,
without any intermediary, by the Spirit of God, and would feel
the assurance that we are truly sons of God [the highest step
we can reach in the Christian life]; for, as says St. Paul,
God's own apostle, " Those who are guided by the Spirit of
God are the sons of God. " You should know, nevertheless,
that *all good believing men are sons of God*. For they were
all born of the Spirit of God, and the Spirit of God lives in them
all; and He moves and urges each individual according to his
habitual disposition to virtue and good works wherein God is
well pleased. But because men do not turn themselves to God
in an equal degree, I shall call some of them faithful servants,
others intimate friends, and still others hidden sons. And yet
all are servants, friends and sons; for they all serve and love
and attend to the one God; and all live and operate by the Spirit
of God. [3]

all men graced

A little while ago, we spoke of the notion of the " corporate
personality " as typical of the spiritual way of thinking. It is
interesting to note how Ruysbroeck very naturally applies to all
Christians the words God the Father spoke on Mount Tabor
(which are taken, incidentally, from Isaias): " All those who
follow Our Lord Jesus Christ hear the voice of the Father, for of
them all He says, ' These are My chosen sons, in whom I am well
pleased. ' Each one of these beloved ones receives grace according to the measure and in the manner that please Him. " [4]

In another page of Ruysbroeck, from *A Mirror of Eternal
Blessedness,* we find a passage still more closely related to
the teaching of Scripture:

" We have also to overcome our senses, to conquer our nature,
to carry our cross and to follow after Christ. In this way we repay
to Him the debt which He paid for us. Through His death and
voluntary penance, we have been *made one with Him* and [have
become] His *faithful servants,* and we belong to His Kingdom.
When we die to our will by accomplishing His will, and when
His will becomes our will, then we are His disciples and His
chosen friends. More still, when we are raised up *through love*
and when our minds stand naked and imageless, just as God
made them, then we are formed by the Holy Spirit and are sons
of God. Mark these words and sentences and live up to them.

stand naked

[3] Jan van Ruysbroeck, *Vanden Blinckenden Steen (The Perfection
of the Sons of God),* in *Werken* 4 Vols.; Tielt: Lannoo, 1946-1948),
[4] *Ibid.,* p. 38.

"When Christ, the Son of God, willed to die for love of us, He surrendered His life into the hands of His enemies till death. And that is how he was *the obedient Servant of His Father* and of all the world. He surrendered also His own will to the will of the Father, and by doing so He practiced the highest justice and taught all truth. He raised His Spirit in most blissful delight and said, "It is all fulfilled"; "Father, into your hands I commend my spirit." Continuing the same verse, the prophet David, in the name of all good men who follow Christ, seems to reply, "Lord, God of truth, You have set me free" (Ps 30:6). For indeed we cannot set ourselves free. But when we follow Christ, as I have shown above, with all the means at our disposal, *our works become one with His works and are ennobled through grace*. That is how He has redeemed us, not indeed through our works but *in His works;* in His merits He has set us free and has redeemed us.

"But if we would feel and possess that freedom, His Spirit must consume our spirit in love and sink it into the bottomless well of His grace and liberal goodness. There our spirit is baptized, set free and made one with His Spirit.... For the will of God has become our will; and that is the root of all true love. When we are born anew of God's Spirit, then our will is free, for it is made to be one with the free will of God. There our spirit, through love, is raised and taken up into one Spirit, one will, one freedom with God.[5]

bottomless grace

Ruysbroeck calls this very sharing in Christ's fullness the "fullness of grace." "He has been given to us out of pure love; in His nature, He is the Son of love. If we are united to Him, we are sons, and in His Spirit we cry 'Abba, Father.'"[6] In a powerful passage, our mystic describes the full flowering of grace, and as a matter of course connects it with the history of salvation: "God's Truth [that is, Christ] speaks within our spirit: 'Look at Me as I look at you, rejoice in possessing Me as I rejoice in possessing you; and as I am you wholly and undivided, so I wish you to be Me wholly and undivided.'"[7] These words describe the relations with and in Christ which grace confers upon us during this life.

These relations are not to be thought of as independent from our personal history or the history of mankind. They all originate in the Son, the ultimate and exemplary cause of all creatures and grace: "'I have seen you from all eternity and before all creation, in Me and one with Me and as Myself,'" which means

[5] Jan van Ruysbroeck, *Spiegel der Eeuwigher Salicheit (A Mirror*
[6] Jan van Ruysbroeck, *Vanden Gheesteliken Tabernakel (The Spiritual*
[7] Jan van Ruysbroeck, *Vanden XII Beghinen (The Twelve Beguines),*

that we were present from the start in the divine, exemplary cause of creation. "'It is there that I have known you, loved you, called and chosen you.'" With this, our history starts on its course. From heaven, the image of the Son is imprinted on man: "'I have created you in My likeness and image.'" And now the incarnation: "'I have taken to Myself your nature and have imprinted on it My image, so that you might be one with Me, without intermediary, in the glory of My Father. I have created My soul with all its powers, and filled it with every gift, so that I could serve and obey your Father and My Father in the human nature we have in common, with all I had, till death. And *out of My fullness of grace and gifts* I have filled your soul and all its powers, in order that you may be like Me, and in My strength and in My gifts serve, thank and praise our God for endless eternity.'"[8]

This lifestream flows through us all as we are gathered into one body; it unites us all in Christ: "See now: *we are all one with God* in our eternal image, because the Wisdom of God [that is, the second person of the Blessed Trinity] is He Who has taken to Himself the nature of us all. But though we are all one in our likeness to God because of the nature which He assumed, we have still to be like Him in grace and virtue if we want to find ourselves one with God in our eternal image, which is God Himself." That oneness and likeness with God the Father in and through the Son, our ultimate exemplar of all grace, is based on the mystery of the incarnation: "After this manner, the humanity of Our Lord Jesus Christ was and is raised and made one with the Wisdom of God (the second person); His soul and all its powers were *filled* and remain filled *with all graces. He* is to us like a living fountain from which we draw whatever we need."[9]

At this point, Ruysbroeck speaks once more of the salvific significance of Christ's earthly life, death and resurrection. Then he passes on to the distribution of grace, dispensed in the Church and through the sacraments: "'Mark well, beloved, what more I have done for you. I have given and bequeathed to you My flesh and living blood, to be food and drink of an all-pervading heavenly savor, and of a nature to suit the desire and taste and experience of every man. I have nourished your passions, your greed and life of the senses with My martyred, glorious body. I have nourished and filled your love and rational life with My Spirit, with My gifts and with the merits whereby I please My Father.'" This passage describes the renewal of our psychosomatic life, of our will and intellect. Ruysbroeck con-

[8] *Ibid.*
[9] *Ibid.*

tinues now with what is deepest and highest in man, namely, what we have called a person's core of density: "'I have nourished and filled your prayer and contemplation with My personality, so that you might live in Me and I in you, God and man, in likeness of virtues and unity of blessedness. My Father and I have filled the world with Our Spirit, with Our gifts and with Our sacraments, according to the desire and needs of everyone. O man, consider Who I am and how I have lived for you and served you, and that I have suffered for you. Be grateful and answer Me according to all your capabilities.'" [10]

Six centuries later, in the Netherlands by the sea, of which Ruysbroeck spoke so willingly, Father Emile Mersch, the well-known theologian of the Mystical Body, renewed the theology of grace and summed it up in the striking title of his article "*Filii in Filio*": grace makes us, each one individually and all in common, "sons of God in the Son." [11]

Servants in the Servant and sons in the Son

It is our intent to build anew the doctrine of grace in accordance with this rich tradition. We, therefore, sum up our foregoing considerations.

Grace springs from God. Since before all time, it lies hidden in the very like of the Blessed Trinity. It is imparted to us insofar as God speaks to us in love, addresses to us His creating and recreating word of love, unites us to Himself in love and, by doing so, establishes in us His presence.

Thanks to this divine presence, in which God unites us to Him and Himself to us, the image of God, prepared by creation, impaired by sin, healed and renewed by redemption, is now at the same time raised and intensified as never before.

All this is brought about not in an abstract and impersonal manner, as if we would be assimilated to the divine nature by a process in which the divine persons have no special role of their own to play. Nor is it brought about apart, so to say, from the history of salvation, in which precisely each one of the divine persons acts and keeps His own peculiar role.

We are redeemed in Christ. It is thus the image of the Son that is imprinted on us; the image of the Son as He made Himself known to us during His earthly life. For our sake, He became the obedient Servant of Yahweh; and we, too, by grace we

---

[10] *Ibid.*, pp. 15-16.
[11] Emile Mersch, S. J., "*Filii in Filio*" *Nouvelle Revue Théologique*, by the Trinity," *The Theology of the Mystical Body*, tr. Cyril Vollert,

— How Grace is imparted —

Insofar as God speaks to us in love,
addresses to us his creating and
recreating word of love, unites us to
Himself in love and by doing so,
establishes in us His presence.

God unites us to Him and Himself to us

creation – sin – redemption

3 theological virtues · the normal expression in
our lives of what in fact we are in our
innermost selves by grace; obedient
servants and loving children

FRANSE '72 p. 38-39

Sin and the New Rit

Each program has been written i
in Western Marylan

* March 7
THE NEW RITE OF PENANCE

Groups are
to meet in
out the par
each progra
interested
group, plea
participati

* March 14
UNDERSTANDING SIN

* Marc

FORMING A

FORGIVE US OUR SINS is a joint p
Maryland, the Western Maryland C
the Archdiocesan Division of Tel
Of Adult Religious Education. M
series and Rev. Francis Sweeney,
resource person.

become obedient servants of God "through and with and in Him", as the final words of the canon of the Mass so solemnly say. He lived on earth as the loving Son of the Father; and we, too, by grace "through and with and in Him" become adopted children of the Father.

The image which the gracious and grace-conferring divine presence imprints on us is thus a concrete one—concrete in its origin, in its formation, in the aim intended. In other words, we are the obedient servants in the Servant, loving children of God together with the Son. It follows quite logically that, as soon as grace calls us, urging us to act in conformity with it, it spurs us on to live in "obedience to the faith" and to yield to the attraction of love. This twofold prompting expresses itself spontaneously in the practice of hope, a hope which we embody in our temporal life through all earthly hardships, dangers and struggles, and which helps us keep our gaze on the final fulfillment awaiting us after death.

In essence, the three theological virtues are simply the normal expression in our lives of what in fact we are in our innermost selves by grace: obedient servants and loving children. The theological virtues are the existential acceptance, the rooting and actualizing of what we are from the moment the Blessed Trinity comes to dwell in us, to unite us to Itself in a vital and creative presence and thus to let us share in Its life. By grace, heaven has begun. "At present, we are looking at a confused reflection in a mirror; but then, we shall see face to face" (I Cor 13:12).

Our unity with the Father and with the Holy Spirit

In explaining the concrete effects which the indwelling of the Blessed Trinity produces, we started from our union in Christ. Our unity with the Father and the Holy Spirit does not fall into second place on that account, as if it were a mere consequence or secondary aspect of the first unity; quite the contrary. It must ever remain the central fact of our faith that the Trinity has come down to us in the visibility of the Son. He is the Word of the Father, the paternal splendor, the Father's perfect image. The Son keeps the role He received in the order of grace as mediator in the redemption. The Son fills not two roles, therefore, but two aspects of one and the same phenomenon: God's dealings with man.

" Of Him it has been witnessed: You are a priest forever according to the order of Melchisedech. And so, a fuller hope has been brought into our lives, *enabling us to draw closer to God....* In consequence, he can, for all time, give eternal salvation to those who approach God through Him, since He is always living to intercede for them. " [Heb 7:17-25]

" This is why He is the mediator of the new Covenant; His death has brought acquittal of all the transgressions under the old Law, so that those who are called may receive the promised eternal inheritance. " [Heb 9:15]

" For God [always meaning God the Father in the New Testament] is one, and one also is the mediator between God and man, the man Jesus Christ, Who gave Himself as a ransom for them all. At the appointed time, He bore His witness; and of that wisdom I am the chosen herald, sent as an apostle—I make no false claims, I am only recalling the truth—to be a true and faithful teacher of the Gentiles. " [I Tim 2:5-7]

Immediate union with Father and Spirit

In and with the Son we return to the Father. Such is the teaching of Scripture. We shall satisfy ourselves in quoting the concluding portion of Paul's important chapter describing Christ's and our resurrection:

" Christ has risen from the dead, the first-fruits of all those who have fallen asleep. For, since by a man death was brought to us, so by a man has come the resurrection of the dead. As all have died in Adam, so also in Christ all shall be made to live. But each one must rise in his own rank: Christ is the first-fruits, and then those that belong to Christ at His coming; after this the completion when he shall hand over the Kingdom to God the Father after He has abolished every other sort of rule, authority and power... And when all things have been completely subjected, then the Son himself will be subject to the One who subjected all things to Him, so that God may be all in all. " [I Cor 15:20-28]

The same truth is brought home to us by the liturgy. With few exceptions, all liturgical prayers are addressed to the Father through and with the Son in unity with the Holy Spirit. Prayer, and above all liturgical prayer, which reflects the faith of the Church in a far purer form than do most private prayers, is the living, personal expression of the order of grace in which we stand and by which we must live.

It would be theologically incorrect to think that the immediate union of the Son with our souls, as described above, unites us with the Father and the Holy Spirit only mediately or derivately. Because of the total mutual immanence of the divine persons within the unity of the divine nature, we come through the Son into immediate contact with the Father and the Holy Spirit. The Father and the Holy Spirit live in us as really and immediately as the Son, notwithstanding the fact that fundamentally grace is granted to us in our quality of servants in the Servant and adopted children in the Son. It would be a serious mistake to look upon a divine person as a means of reaching another divine person by something like a second movement.

Medieval authors are known for their love of apt symbols. Touching on the mystery of the incarnation, they resorted to an illustration that throws some light on how that mystery is worked out and how the person of the Word is united to His sacred humanity. We shall borrow their illustration and use it to explain to some extent the mystery of grace, so closely allied to the mystery of the incarnation.

Imagine, they said, three girls adorning one of themselves for marriage. All three are immediately engaged in the work of adorning, but only one, the bride, is being prepared for the wedding. To apply this to the incarnation, only the second person of the Blessed Trinity, the Word, is " robed " in a humanity; but each one of the three persons has His own immediate active part in working out the incarnation.

The same illustration throws some light on the pattern God follows in communicating His grace; for grace comes to us, along with salvation and redemption, in and through Christ. Fundamentally, the mystery of the incarnation and the mystery of divine grace conferred on man are two different things altogether; but in the language of theology, they have a real analogy. They possess a similarity in structure, because God has connected them closely with each other.

Christ called Himself, and let others call Him, Son of God. Man, too, in a state of grace, is to be called a son of God, but not on the same ground. Christ is the Son of God by nature, and therefore by right, while we are adopted sons, sharing in Christ's sonship. The divine activity which causes us to share in Christ's sonship must be thought of as a *continuation* of the very same divine activity which sent the Son on His earthly mission. From the days of St. Irenaeus, the Greek Fathers expressed this idea in the now classical dictum that God became man in order that man might become " god. " They called the mystery of grace the mystery of our *divinization*. Even today, the Eastern Orthodox use this terminology. We should like to see this grand and rich tradition spread again among the faithful.

Scripture teaches no other doctrine; it speaks frequently and equally of the indwelling of the three Persons and of the indwelling of the Father and of the Holy Spirit. The indwelling of the Holy Spirit is mentioned so often that the theology of the Schoolmen dealt with the dogma of grace as the mystery of the indwelling of the Holy Spirit. Scripture, of course, does not enter into technical precisions; but the writers were aware that the three persons, *each in His own characteristic manner,* work out their indwelling in us. We shall endeavor to examine in some detail what is proper to the action of the Father and to the action of the Holy Spirit.

St. John's teaching

To begin with, we quote two passages from Holy Writ in which John and Paul passed, in the most natural way, from the indwelling of one Person to the presence of the others. In the farewell discourse after the last supper, as reported by John (14:6-26), Christ said, " I am the way, the truth and the life. *No one comes to the Father except through Me.* If you knew Me, you would also know My Father. Already now you know him and see him" (Jn. 14:6-7). Let us observe, in passing, that *to know* and *to see* have a richer meaning in John's language than an English translation lets us suppose. In the Hebrew idiom, *to know* indicates a very personal relationship with another person. He who knows a person loves him, is closely connected with him and lives with him. *To see* has perhaps still greater depth. It indicates a personal experience of God's presence, a contemplation of His " splendor " and " glory "—words which designate the visible signs in which God's majesty manifests itself to us on earth. In nothing has the Father been made more visible here on earth than in His Son, for the Son *is* the " glory " of the Father.

Philip, naïve and outspoken and always ready to drop remarks, did not understand the Master's words. " ' Lord, ' said Philip, ' show us the Father and that will be enough for us. ' ' I have been so long with you, ' Jesus said to him, ' and you do not know Me yet, Philip? *He who sees Me sees the Father.* How do you say: Show us the Father? Do you not believe that I am in the Father and that the Father is in Me? The words I speak to you, I do not speak from Myself; but it is the Father *dwelling in Me* Who does His works. Believe Me: I am in the Father and the Father is in Me. Or else, believe it on account of the works ' " (the signs of His living union with the Father as shown by Christ in His miracles). Hereupon follows the assurance that grace, received in faith and thus reaching each one of us personally, brings with it a share in Christ's intimate union with the Father: " ' Indeed, indeed, I say to you, he who believes in Me shall himself do the works I do; yes, greater than these shall he do, because I am returning to the Father; and whatever you shall ask in My name, I shall do, in order that the Father may be glorified in the Son. ' "

St. John's narrative goes on. Christ now speaks to His apostles about their life after His death: " ' If you love Me, keep My commandments; and I shall ask the Father, and He will give you another Comforter Who is to remain with you forever, the Spirit of truth whom the world is unable to receive because it neither sees Him nor knows Him. But *you know Him, because He abides with you and will be in you.* ' " The presence of the Holy Spirit does not stand in the way of the enduring presence of the risen Lord in our midst: " ' I shall not leave you orphans; *I shall return to you.* Still a little while, and the world shall see Me no more; but you will see Me and *you, too, will live,* ' " will share Christ's life.

St. John now summed up these sentences in pregnant words giving us a comprehensive vision of our fellowship with the Father and the Son in the Holy Spirit: " ' In that day you will

know that I am in My Father, and you in Me, and I in you.
He who has My commandments and keeps them, he it is who
loves Me. He who loves Me [the clearest indication of what
a life in grace means] will be loved by My Father; and I, too,
shall love him, and I shall manifest Myself to him. ' Judas, not
the Iscariot, said to Him: ' Lord, how is it that You will manifest
Yourself to us and not to the world? ' " In the language of
St. John, *world* stands for sinful humanity which refuses to
believe in Christ and therefore does not keep His commandments,
chiefly the commandment of love.

Jesus answered him: " If any one love Me, he will heed what
I say; then My Father will love him, and *We will come to him
and make Our dwelling with him;* but he who does not love Me
will not heed what I say. And the word you hear is not Mine;
it is the word of the Father who sent Me. I have told you all this
while I am still with you. But the Comforter, the Holy Spirit
Whom the Father will send in My name, will teach you everything and will call to mind all that I have told you. " A few lines
further on comes the fundamental parable of the real vine:
" I am the real vine and my Father is the gardener " (Jn 14:6-26;
15:1). We shall return to this in the following chapter.

John used no technical theological terms; he used rather what
is today called freely existential descriptive forms. Yet once
again we notice here what was pointed out before: immanence
in the divine persons and the divine union we possess in both
our salvation and the conferring of grace. Each one of the
persons preserves His own proper traits. It is the Father Who
sends Christ and, at Christ's request, gives us also the Holy
Spirit. It is the Holy Spirit Who will recall all this to our minds
and, by doing so, will finish Christ's work in us. It is in Christ,
the true vine, that we remain united in grace.

St. Paul's teaching

St. Paul's writing unfolds the same rich reality before our eyes,
but from a different perspective. In his Epistle to the Romans,
he tried his best to preserve the Christian message in all its
purity against Jewish converts who wanted to impose a Jewish
spirituality. In the first seven chapters, he entered the lists
against them. He showed the real import of the faith and of
justification, the inefficacy of the Jewish Law in relation to
salvation, and the dangers inherent in a spirituality based on
the Law; and he used the occasion to draw attention to our
deep-seated sinfulness. In chapter 8 (1-17), he called up his own
vision of what a Christian life actually is and should be.

" For those who are in Christ Jesus there exists no condemnation [or sentence passed on sin]. Through Jesus Christ the law of the Spirit of life has set us free from the law of sin and of death. The [Jewish] Law was powerless to do it because of the flesh [that is, our human sinfulness which that Law could never radically cure]; but God [the Father] has achieved this by sending His Son in the likeness of sinful flesh [in the likeness of man] as a reparation for sin: in the flesh itself [that is, as man] He has condemned sin in order that the justice of the law [holiness of life] be accomplished in us who do not live according to the flesh, but according to the dictates of the Spirit. "

Previously we remarked upon the threefold meaning of the word *spirit* in St. Paul. *Spirit* can mean the person of the Holy Spirit, His gifts, or, more often, the whole man insofar as he is " spiritualized " and completely transformed by the indwelling of the Holy Spirit.

" Those who live the life of the flesh [the whole man insofar as he stands under the influence of sin] set their thoughts on sensual things; but those who live the life of the spirit have their minds set on spiritual things. The sensual mind brings only death, but the spiritual mind brings life and peace; for the sensual mind is hostile to God, not submitting itself to God's law; nor can it; they that live according to the flesh cannot please God.

" But you do not live the life of the flesh, but the life of the spirit, *because the Spirit of God* [coming from the Father] *dwells in you*. If anyone does not possess the Spirit of Christ [Paul spoke first of the Spirit of God and speaks now of the Spirit of Christ], he does not belong to Him. *If Christ is in you* [the presence of the Holy Spirit entails the indwelling of Christ], the body, indeed, may be a thing of death because of sin [that is, it will have to die one day], but the spirit is a living thing [that is, you yourself, insofar as you are filled with the Spirit] because of justification. And if the Spirit of Him who raised Christ from the dead dwells, in you, He who raised Christ Jesus from the dead [here Paul reverts to the Father] will give life to your mortal bodies, too, *through the power of the Spirit Who lives in you.* "

A conclusion follows which sums up existentially, and in suggestive language, what Paul envisaged a Christian life to be: " All those who let themselves be led by the Spirit of God are children of God. The Spirit whom you have received is not, as of old, a spirit of fear ruling you by fear; it is the spirit of adoption which makes us cry: ' Abba! Father! ' " The next verses illustrate well the manifold meaning of *spirit* as used in the

New Testament: " *The Spirit Himself* bears witness to *our spirit* that we are children of God; and if children of God, then also heirs of God and co-heirs with Christ, since we share in His sufferings in order to share in His glorification " (Rom 8:1-17).

We may conclude the very fact that in grace and through our living union with the Son we are re-created in His image and likeness gives us an immediate relationship to Him, and this implies an equally immediate presence of the Father and the Holy Spirit. Like the operation at work in the incarnation and redemption, God's action which confers grace upon us is a single divine gesture of love belonging to the three Persons, each exercising His own original and peculiar characteristic.

What is this characteristic, this countenance of the divine persons? And how does it manifest itself in the operation of grace?

The countenance of the Father

As an ancient council puts it, the Father is both first and last, " the font and origin of all that is divine. " He sends the Son, and together with the Son also sends the Holy Spirit, His Spirit. The Son and the Spirit fulfill Their mission by taking us up into Themselves and together bringing us back to the common wellspring of all being, the Father. The election by grace rests with the Father.

The Father lives in us; He unites us immediately to Himself; for He is the origin and therefore the final goal of the living movement which wells up from God and which carries us back to God in faith, hope and charity—" from God to God," as Ruysbroeck would say:

" Mark well with vivid earnestness what it is that we all greatly need. God has, from all eternity, seen and acknowledged us in His Wisdom [the Son]; and He desires that we open our interior eyes and look at Him without reserve. From all eternity He has called us, and He wants us to keep our interior ears steadily open and to listen to the promptings of His grace. From all eternity He has chosen us, and He wants us to choose Him in preference to all creatures. He loves us and has loved us eternally, and He desires us to love Him eternally in return; this is justice: lover united to the beloved, so that the scales be even and equal. "

At this moment the scales stand even and the needle of the balance stands steady. In this comparison of his, Ruysbroeck follows the Western interpretation of justice, which does not fully correspond to the biblical concept.

" Love is eternal. It begins in God and reaches our spirit, demanding a return of love. So starts the exercise of love between God and us, like a golden link that has neither beginning nor end. Our love starts in God and is perfected in Him. He gives Himself to our spirit, and we in return give our spirit to Him [so that the scales may stand steady and even]. Thereby we bear in our spirit the image of God; and *thus we love from God to God, in God and one with God*. We are then wise traders. [Again the simile of the scales: wise traders, who measure the " weight " of their love by the measure of God's love.] For we have given our *all* in return for His *all,* and we have and hold our *all* in His all. Now we are sons, and bear God's image in our spirit, to fulfill the purpose for which we are called [that is, we have been created for the purpose of realizing in ourselves the image of God].... Now we are one with God, without loss or gain [because by living we become what we have been eternally destined to be when God marked us with His seal]. [12]

The mystery of the Father reaches still greater depths. His basic characteristic is to be Father to the Son; it is in this unique and intense relationship with the Son that He expresses His own personal trait. He is Father with all the quiet might, the absoluteness, the self-evident intensity with which He contrasts Himself with the Son in the one divine nature, never ceasing to possess with the Son the identical divine substance. He never ceases to be completely Himself in His fatherhood vis-à-vis the equally intense Self of the Son. The more He is Himself in His fatherhood, the more He and the Son live in each other and share in the wealth of Their common divinity. He keeps His fatherhood while conferring grace upon us. It is He Who, by granting us His presence through grace, makes us His children. In other words, His active presence is no abstract thing. He gives Himself to us *as He is eternally,* that is, as Father and Fatherhood.

" Did God ever say to one of the angels: You are My son, this day I have begotten you? Or again: I shall be a father to him and he will be My son? " (Heb 1:5). In the loving converse between Father and Son, in the birth of the Son from the Father, each possesses His own proper density of person. In the same paternal word of grace and mercy, by which He begets us as sons in the Son, not by nature but by adoption, we

[12] Ruysbroeck, *Vanden XII Beghinen,* pp. 169-171.

receive freely and without merit on our part the new density
of our re-created personality. The paternal gesture is one: it
inclines the Father to the Son, and *stretches out to us* from all
eternity and in accordance with the inner law of life proper to
the divine being. Thus it is that the Father raises and transforms
us into His children in the Son. " Every one who believes that
Jesus is the Christ, is born of God, " wrote St. John, " and every
one who loves the parent who [from all eternity and still now]
begets [him], loves also him who is begotten by him, " that is,
the Son and us all in Him (I Jn 5:1).

With his gaze on that vision, Ruysbroeck elaborated the whole
of his mystical doctrine. No one has shown so vigorously as he
that all reality rests basically on the life of the Trinity. It would
take us too far afield to try to give a glimpse of what Ruysbroeck
has to tell us about the divine image in us, the ultimate foundation of the mystical life of grace. We shall restrict ourselves
to a few brief quotations in which the Father's relations to us in
the Son are sketched in outline: " God's work is God's Son Whom
th Father begets in our spirit. " [13]

" There [in our innermost self] we are, through love, bent back
upon our origin; there we hear the Father's voice which draws
us and reaches us [that is, unites Himself immediately to us];
for in His eternal Word, He says to all His elect: ' This is My
beloved Son, in Whom I am well pleased. ' " [14]
" For the Father has willingly won us [that is, begotten
us], and He has chosen us in His Son. And because of this,
we are gods by grace, though not by nature. " [15]

The countenance of the Spirit

We will now seek to form an idea of how, in the conferring
of grace, the Holy Spirit brings into play and at the same time
infuses His personal characteristic. This property cannot be
easily described. The personal property of the Holy Spirit in its
divine fullness transcends our conceptual powers, just as does
the relationship between the Father and the Son. In my view,
however, theologians embroil their speculative search because
they generally confine their attempt to a purely philosophical
analysis of the operation of love.
The Western theological tradition has recognized the love
of the Father and the Son in the Holy Spirit. Let us accept

[13] Ruysbroeck, *Vanden Blinckenden Steen*, p. 35.
[14] *Ibid.*, pp. 38-39.
[15] Ruysbroeck, *Spieghel der Eeuwigher Salicheit*, p. 212.

this as a first orientation in the inner mystery of the Spirit. Most theologians proceed no farther. They pass on at once to subtle analyses of the dynamism of love, a procedure which perhaps befogs rather than clarifies the mystery.

Holy Writ tells us many other truths about the Holy Spirit. These do not resolve the mystery, of course; nevertheless, they prove to be more illuminating than pure philosophical speculation. We shall have to be brief, contenting ourselves with indicating how we catch a glimpse of the Spirit's own countenance in the light of Scripture. After that, we shall appeal to the mystical experiences of Blessed Jan van Ruysbroeck.

The Holy Spirit revealed Himself in the early years of the Church; He let Himself be known as the gift of both the risen Lord and the Father, and often in a pragmatic, miraculous manner. This unique experience of the primitive Church was set down in Scripture; it forms a first attempt at theology. Luke and John are more precise in this respect than any other sacred writers.

To an attentive reader, it is striking how the *working out* of Christ's task, from the moment of the incarnation till the death on the cross and the resurrection, is attributed to the intervention of the Holy Spirit.

As early as the Book of Consolation, we are told that the Servant of Yahweh will announce justice to the nations and " through His sufferings will bring justice to many " (Is. 53:11), because God " has placed His spirit on Him " (Is. 42:1). " The spirit of Yahweh, the Lord, is upon me, because Yahweh has anointed me. He has sent me to bring the good tidings to the poor " (Is 61:1). When John the Baptist, then a prisoner of Herod, sent his disciples to Jesus to ask whether " he is the one who is to come, " Jesus answered by quoting the words of Isaias referred to just now (Mt 11:2-6; Lk 7:18-23). At Nazareth, on the day that Christ came forward in the synagogue and for the first time spoke publicly of His mission, He cited the Book of Isaias once more before the assembled village: " This passage of Scripture, which you have heard just now, is being fulfilled today " (Lk 4:21).

At the moment of Jesus' baptism in the Jordan, the voice of the Father was heard (Lk 3:22; Mk 1:11; Jn 1:32), and the message of baptism was delivered. The Spirit neither spoke nor acted in any apparent manner; yet He was present under the appearance of a dove, a symbol which probably points to the nature of Christ's mission rather than to Himself. But in that silent presence, so proper to Him, He caused the meeting of Father and Son to be brought to its perfection and completion.

Christ acted, prayed, worked His miracles and preached in

the Spirit: "He, who is sent by God, speaks God's own words; for he gives his Spirit without measure" (Jn 3:34). Christ did not experience the Spirit as a foreign power, as had the prophets of old and as would the apostles later. The Spirit of truth "will glorify Me; for He shall announce to you whatever He has resceived from Me; *for all that the Father has is Mine*" (Jn 16:14-15). The Spirit was to be separated neither from the mission sent by the Father nor from the work of the Son; and yet He remained His original divine Self, giving reality to and *completing* the mission and work. He did this by uniting the *interior* of the Christ-Man more intimately with the Father and by actuating Christ's *external* actions in carrying out His messanic and prophetic function.

What the Spirit did for Christ, He did for the Church as well. The manner of His action was visible and experiential during the years of the Church's infancy. And it is worth noticing that those years were also the period chosen by the Spirit to reveal Himself as a Person.

It was indeed necessary for Christ to "go away" so that the Spirit might reveal Himself (Jn 7:39; 16:7). For the Spirit was the "promise of the Father," the gift left to the Church by the dying (Jn 19:30) and the risen Lord. Everywhere we observe discreetness to be the distinctive mark of the Spirit's operation. The task entrusted to Him does not, in fact, differ from that of Christ; it consists in bringing the work done by the Son in the Father's name to its perfection. "He shall not speak *from Himself* [that is, in His own name]; but whatever He shall hear [from the Son and the Father] He shall speak, and He shall announce to you the events that are to happen" (Jn 16:13). The Master had said the same thing elsewhere in other terms: "I am telling you these things while I am still with you. But the Comforter, the Holy Spirit, whom the Father will send in My name, He will teach you all things, and *will recall to your mind* all I have told you" (Jn 14:25-26).

Christ's prophecy was accomplished primarily on the day the Church was founded on the first Pentecost, in a specific place, the Cenacle, and at a certain date of our history (Acts 2:1-47). In many respects, the miraculous descent of the Holy Spirit resembles the ratification on Mount Sinai of the choice of Israel as God's people. On both days, we observe the "glory" of the Lord manifesting itself in fire and storm; the twelve apostles represented the twelve tribes of the new Israel, and were granted the gift of tongues, that is, an ecstatic speech in which each listener heard his own tongue. In all this, the living unit of the Church in the Spirit is signified, in opposition to the confusion of tongues and the divison of mankind caused by sin and symbolized by the Tower of Babel.

No less significant is the "Pentecost of the Gentiles." In
the presence of Peter, the chief witness, the Holy Spirit came
down upon the pagan Cornelius and his household (Acts 10:11).
Peter would testify on three different occasions "that *these men,
like ourselves, have received the Holy Spirit,* just as He came
upon us *at the beginning*" (Acts 10:47; 11:15-17; 15:8-9). Peter
was fully aware of the far-reaching consequences of this exceptional occurrence: "I do now realize, indeed, that God is no
respecter of persons, but that, on the contrary, anyone of any
nation, who fears Him and acts justly, is acceptable to Him.
He sent the word to the sons of Israel when He proclaimed the
good tiding of peace through Jesus Christ Who is the *Lord of all*"
(Acts 10:34-36).
· While thus manifesting Himself, the Holy Spirit unveiled
His own countenance, His divine Self. We are given a description of it mainly in the Acts of the Apostles, a book that
has been aptly called the Gospel of the Holy Spirit. Exegetes
are agreed in acknowledging that the chief message of Acts
lies in showing how the Spirit confirmed the Church, urging
her to go forth as an apostolic witness and in that capacity to
conquer the world (Acts 1:8, indicating the main theme of the
book).
In Acts, St. Luke did more still: he marked another fruit
of the "gift of the Holy Spirit," namely, the interior consolidation
of the faith in the practice of common prayer, and the reinforcing
of the inner surrender to God. He first indicated each new step
taken by the nascent Church, and then summed up the significance of her growth by portraying the progress of the Christian
community (Acts 2:42-47; 4:32-35; 5:12-16; 9:11; 13:48-52). He
underlined each instance of the union and unanimity of the
brethren, as these were manifested in their practice of pooling
their earthly goods, their joys and their faith. All this, in the
mind of Luke, was the fruit of the Holy Spirit.
Paul and John stressed still more the interior consolidation
of the faith, and marked how the interior surrender of the
brethren, individually and as a society, grew increasingly in
perfection.
The "newness of the Spirit" (Rom 7:6) and the interior
"law of the Spirit of life" (Rom 8:1) stabilize us in our deep,
interior liberty as children of God. *Only in the Spirit* can
we truly pray to the Father: "Abba! Father!" (Rom 8:15-16; Gal
4:6-7); only in Him are we able to believe that Christ is the
redeemer (1 Cor 12:1-3). Only He endows us with true Christian
wisdom and empowers the "spiritual man," the man entirely
filled with the Spirit, to acquire the "mind of Christ" (I Cor 2:10-
16). The noblest outcome of the life of grace, love coming from
God, is reserved to the action of the Spirit: "... because the love

of God has been poured into our hearts through the Holy Spirit who was given to us " (Rom 5:5).

The word _pneuma_ in the New Testament is the nearest equivalent to what today is called _created grace._ Pneuma, or spirit, stands for the whole man when he is totally renewed by the gift of the Spirit. For he then ceases to be " natural man " (I Cor 2:14), that is, " flesh, " and is re-created in a new life, a " renewal of the creature " (II Cor 5:17; Gal 6:15).

The Spirit as gift

Taking a broad view of these elements, we recognize them as various aspects of the operation of grace. They are stamped with the same divine individuality that characterizes the work of the Spirit in Christ: an interior confirmation of the heart in its growing surrender to God, and an exterior radiation of the indwelling divinity in prophetic witnessing. And if that is so, we are entitled to think that the peculiar nature of the Spirit's operation in our life is a distant reflection of the very personal property which He possesses as His own within the Trinity.

He could not but set the seal of His personality on the mission entrusted to Him by the Father and the Son. His mission is to bring the Father's mandate, in the work of the Son, to perfection, to its full existential realization, in each man. And He does this in a twofold movement: first, an _inward movement,_ linking all members of the Mystical Body, in their faith and charity, into one living unit with each other and with God; and second, an _outward movement,_ radiating the Christian message in the apostolate. These two movements are inseparable from each other: the first expresses itself spontaneously in the second, while the second keeps the first actual and genuine.

If we want to describe what is proper to the Spirit and to recognize His divine countenance in the faith, we must attempt to discern His personal characteristic in the operation of grace. Relying on his own mystical experience, Ruysbroeck ventured upon the bold step leading from the visible signs of the Spirit's earthly mission to His hidden mysterious Self within the Trinity.

Ruysbroeck knew, of course, the Augustinian tradition which teaches that the Spirit is the " bond of love " between Father and Son, but he was not fully satisfied with it. He preferred to look upon the Spirit as the principle of unity manifested in the ebb and flow of the trinitarian life: " There we have the Father, together with the Son and with all the beloved, surrounded and embraced in the bond of love: and that is the ' unity ' of the Holy Ghost. It is the same ' unity ' which is at work in the

Holy Spirit principle of unity

outflow [that is, the procession] of the persons and remains so in the return flow of the divine life: it remains a bond of love that can never be undone. " [16]

The following passage gives a deeper insight into the life of the Trinity:

" The nature of the persons is fecund, eternally at work after the manner of the persons. For the Father begets the Son, as another issuing from His nature; and the Son is born of the Father, as God's eternal Wisdom, another in person, but one in nature with the Father. Father and Son pour out from Themselves the Holy Ghost, who is one in nature with Them both. Thus there is oneness in nature and distinction in persons. For in the common relations between the persons, there is reciprocal knowledge and love, flux and reflux between the Father and the Son in the Holy Ghost Who is Their common love. But the unity of the Holy Ghost, wherein the persons live and reign, is active and fruitful [also] in the outward flow making [creating] all things in free liberality [the Spirit], in wisdom [the Son] and in power [the Father]—three properties belonging to the persons. But in the return flow between the persons, the unity of the Holy Ghost is the delight which attracts and envelops the persons, above all distinction, in the bliss of an unfathomable love, which is God Himself in being and nature." [17]

What constitutes the personal property of the Holy Spirit within the trinitarian life should leave its mark on the gifts He bestows on us in our union with the Blessed Trinity: "The Spirit of God is an eternal operation outwards; and He desires that we, too, should work eternally and so resemble Him. But He is also [mystical] repose and [mystical] fruition in the unity of the Father and of the Son and of all His beloved in an eternal rest. "[18]

No wonder Ruysbroeck placed human spiritual perfection in a state of tension, which both carries and bears up the interior life, between action and contemplation, exterior work and interior repose in the delights of God; for in this precisely lies the image of the personality of the Holy Spirit left by Him in our lives.

---

[16] Ruysbroeck, *Boecsken der Verclaringhe (The Little Book of Enlightenment)*, in *Werken*, III, p. 291.

[17] Ruysbroeck, *Vanden XII Beghinen*, p. 71.

[18] Ruysbroeck, *Vanden VII Trappen*, tr. F. Sherwood Taylor as *The Seven Steps of the Ladder of Spiritual Love* (Westminster [England]: Dacre), p. 52.

"The united man [that is, the perfect man] must live for God with the totality of himself, so that he is surrendered to the grace and motion of God, and is docile in all virtues and spiritual practices. In love, he must be raised up and for God die to himself and to all his works, so that he may withdraw [from himself] with all his strength and achieve his transformation into the inconceivable truth which is God Himself. Doing so, he will live by progressing in all virtues, and he will die by entering into God. The perfection of his life lies in these two movements; and these two movements are joined to each other in him as matter and form, as soul and body." [19]

In his concise conclusion, our author associated the riches of such a life with the Holy Spirit: "Because he [the perfect man] maintains and exercises himself in the presence of God, love grows in power in every way." [20]

Ruysbroeck returned to this matter more than once at the end of his book *The Seven Steps of the Ladder of Spiritual Love*, and he proposed it as a faithful summary of his spiritual teaching:

"And so, to go inwards into the quiescent [mystical] fruition and to go outwards to good works, but ever to remain united to the Spirit of God: that is what I mean. For, as we open the eyes of our body, look and close them again so quickly that we are not aware of it, so we die in God and live from God and remain always one with God. Similarly, we shall go outwards into the activity of the life of sense, and go inwards in love, to cleave to God and remain motionless united to God. Mark well: that is the noblest experience we can perceive and understand in our spirit. We must, however, always go up and down the steps of our heavenly ladder in the practice of interior virtues and exterior good works, in conformity with the commandments of God and the precepts of the Church." [21]

The indwelling of the Trinity

We are now in a position to sum up the last two sections. Many a reader brought up on the "classical" theory of grace —a theory mostly confined to theological circles in the Latin Church these last three centuries—has gathered from the preced-

[19] Ruysbroeck, *Boecksen der Verclaringhe*, p. 282.
[20] *Ibid.*, p. 283.
[21] Ruysbroeck, *The Seven Steps...*, pp. 60-61.

ing pages the somewhat uncomfortable impression that we are
wandering far from the subject matter. Let me assure him that
we are right in the heart of the matter; this will become plain
as we go along.

Essentially, grace consists in this: that God, the Blessed Trinity,
loves us. The trinitarian love consists in the union of the
Father, Son and Holy Spirit with us; or better, Their drawing
us into the intimacy of Their own trinitarian life by uniting
us with Themselves.

In conformity with the language of Scripture, this union is
generally called the divine indwelling. We have called it also
the mystery of God's presence. God's active, transforming union
in love imprints the divine image on us; and here the well-
known dictum holds good: "*Amicitia pares invenit aut facit*"
("Friendship is either found among equals or it makes equals
of those it finds"). The notion of *divine image* is just another
approach to the basic conception of grace, which is that we
share in the divine life. "Whatever is necessary to life and
piety, the divine power has bestowed on us, together with the
knowledge of Him who called us by His glory and virtue. He
has granted us therely His high and precious promises, so that,
leaving behind the corruption of this world with all its evil
passions, we may share in the divine nature" (II Pt 1:3-4).

All these various conceptions—divine love, presence, indwelling, image and likeness, sanctification and justification—are
simply different approaches, through different symbolisms, to
one identical reality: that through grace we share in the divine
life.

As long as we abide on earth, our share in the divine life
remains hidden; it is a pledge, a foretaste, a seed, a beginning,
an anticipation of the life of heaven. But what in fact we
already are now will then be made manifest—totally visible,
clearly and explicitly experienced, and fully and existentially
realized. Heaven is the unveiling of what we already are in
and through grace.

A theological inquiry into this participation in the divine
nature should not start from abstract notions concerning the
divine essence and its attributes. For such a participation is
eminently a personal encounter. That is the reason we prefer
to explain grace as a presence of one person to another. And
that was the deeper sense of our first parable.

In grace we first encounter Christ, the one mediator. It is
His image which is imprinted on us; He is the prototype of
creation and of the whole order of grace. We have described
this image in terms borrowed from Scripture. To encounter
Christ signifies that we become servants in the Servant, sons
with the Son. Our status as servants in the Servant means

that our fallen nature is restored to its original dignity, and that therefore the wounds caused by sin are healed. Theologians designate this aspect of grace by the name *gratia sanans,* healing grace. Our position as sons with the Son indicates rather what in theology is called the elevating aspect of grace. It concretely characterizes the *super*natural character of grace. For such an intimacy with the Father and the Son in the power of the Holy Spirit lies outside the range of any merit of ours; it totally transcends mere human possibility.

Such is the image of God imprinted on us when through grace we are united with the Son, encounter Him in the Church and in the sacraments and thus share in His filial life.

The immediate union with the Son brings with it a union with the Father and with the Holy Spirit; both these unions are likewise immediate, and both bear the mark of the characteristic property of the respective divine persons.

The origin of all grace can be traced to the election by the Father. To Him belongs the initiative in granting grace. And as the prime cause He is also the ultimate end; we are called to the Father as the final goal of all grace. He calls us to Himself through grace by adopting us as His children, by uniting us with His Son, by extending the inner trinitarian relationship of fatherhood to us, wherever we are—or better, by assuming us as adopted children into His relations of love with His Son. He speaks to us in His Son. His divine "I," which from all eternity utters to His Son a loving "Thou," is addressed to us as well; He raises us and unites us with His Son, saying, "You are My well-beloved sons." And this precisely is the life of grace.

The Holy Spirit, too, dwells in us. He was at work in Christ, and revealed His action and Himself in the primitive Church. He now extends His operation to us, with the same "discreetness" but also with the same intense motive power. Ruysbroeck often mentions the "drive" or "urge" of the Holy Spirit.

The Holy Spirit reveals His own personality in us. It is through the power of the Holy Spirit that the Father impresses the image of the Son on us. In His role as the Spirit of the Father and the Son, He existentially actualizes this image and carries it to the perfection and fulfillment of a personal acceptance. This He does in a twofold manner. First, inwardly He moves us, joined with the Son, to union with the Father in an upward filial surrender, directing us to the Father and "driving" us on in faith, hope and charity. Second, He simultaneously animates us to display outwardly a complete "obedience to the faith" by our Christian witnessing.

As was the case with Christ and is still the case with the Church, the Holy Spirit is the one in Whom our individual

encounter with the divine persons finds its completion, its
intimate and existential acceptance and realization, its necessary
"commitment." In Him the Father's love reaches its full
and authentic expression, making us into the likeness of the
Son. It is He Who, strictly speaking, is love. For according
to St. John, God, that is, the Father, is love. Nonetheless, the
Spirit is the "bond of love," the divine amen to the primordial
gesture of love which the Father makes in the Son.

It will help here, by way of conclusion, to quote a powerful
passage from the ending of Ruysbroeck's *The Seven Steps of the
Ladder of Spiritual Love:*

"[On the seventh step] the law of love is fulfilled and all
virtues are made perfect. There we are quiescent [in the
mystical experience of God]; and our heavenly Father dwells
in us with the fullness of His graces, and we dwell in Him
beyond all our works and [mystical] delight. Christ Jesus dwells
in us and we in Him. In His life we overcome the world and
all its sins. With Him, we are raised up in love to our heavenly
Father. The Holy Ghost works in us, and we, together with
Him, perform all our good deeds. He cries in us with a loud
voice and yet without words: *Love the Love which loves you
eternally.* His cry is an interior contact with our spirit. His
voice is more terrifying than thunder. The lightnings that
break from it open up heaven to us and show us the Light
and eternal Truth. The heat of His contact and love is so great
that it would burn us up. His contact with our spirit cries
without ceasing: *Repay your debt! Love the Love which loves
you eternally.* With this comes a great impatience, a formless,
unstudied conduct; if we repay more than our love demands,
we incur still greater debts. Love is never silent; without
ceasing, it keeps crying: *Love the Love.* And this is a conflict
quite unknown to uninitiated minds."[22]

This tradition has lived on among our people. It may not
have often soared to the heights reached by Ruysbroeck and
Sister Hadewych, but it has been there, as authentic as life.
Let all we have said be one more warning that we are not very
interested in subtle speculations, but that we want to propose
an undiluted form of Christianity, such as has, in fact, yielded
ripe fruits among our people over the centuries. We want to
deal with matters of life, of true life.

[22] *Ibid.,* pp. 59-60.

Redemption, grace and church

Before we pass on to considering created grace, conferred on us by the divine indwelling, we should free ourselves once and for all from individualistic conceptions. We do not say "personalistic," for that is quite another thing. God's indwelling produces a true solidarity in us, one which achieves its living expression in God's people, the Church, the body of Christ, His Bride in heaven and on earth. First, we shall listen to Scripture in order to familiarize ourselves with its teaching. Second, we shall try to work out these same truths more systematically. Our attempt should produce a unified vision of the Church and grace, two inseparable aspects of the redemption. This chapter is of capital importance. The few practical applications which we shall suggest as we go along will provide proof of the depths which these truths can reach in our lives, if they are considered unflinchingly.

Person and community

Influenced by an atmosphere of dominant individualism, the theology and preaching of recent centuries presented grace all too frequently as no more than an enriching of the individual life of the soul. This, of course, is not accurate. No grace, be it the most intimate, the most exalted mystical gift, is given as a *private* possession. Grace can never be a "thing possessed," simply because it is a life unceasingly flowing out from God and returning to God. Every and all grace is given *in the Church and for the benefit of the Church*, to benefit both the individual receiving it and the community.

If need be, such a view could be vindicated on purely philosophical grounds. Face to face with God, we never stand alone, but together with all other men. God made mankind as one family, and He always sees us as one family. Sin results in division and solitude. It is the role of grace to restore and

consolidate the natural unity of the human race driven apart
by sin.

The same view finds vigorous support today in the study
of the human person. Around the 1920s those who wanted
to be up to date let themselves be carried away by the word
person, not noticing that *person* was frequently mistaken for
personality. In the flush of their enthusiasm, many saw in the
new concept of *person* nothing than an enrichment of the
individual self; they envisaged mainly a free, unhindered self-
development. " To become a person " was more or less synonymous with building up mental acumen, training the will and
achieving freedom to follow one's own conceits, fancies or moods.
That tendency was most noticeable in art. An artist stood apart
from the community. He was a solitary man who, by himself
and at heights inaccessible to common mortals, had to strike
his own path through life.

Many overlooked the paradox that a person discovers himself
as a person in proportion as he renounces himself for the sake
of others. Christ had already pointed in that direction when
He endeavored to unveil the deeper meaning of His death on the
cross, speaking by implication for His disciples as well: " Indeed,
indeed, I say to you: unless the grain of wheat cast into the soil
dies, it remains by itself alone; but if it dies, it bears much fruit.
He who loves his life [in Aramaic, the word *life* is equivalent
to *self*] loses it; but he who hates his life in this world shall
preserve it for life eternal. If anyone wants to serve Me, he must
follow Me; and where I am, there too My servant shall be "
(Jn 12:24-26).

In these words Christ stated a truth that acts as a general
law in the life of all men. I can recall from the days of my
youth a striking experience. There was a young woman who
had chosen a career devoted to art and aesthetics, and was
nevertheless fitful, caustic, thoroughly unengaging. When I met
her again later on, she was a completely changed woman. She
had fully surrendered herself to husband and children, and had
thus found herself. Very likely, many factors had entered into
this change, but the chief reason for her surprising enrichment
was undoubtedly her devotion to her family. Such instances are
not found only among women, as if men could stand by themselves. We are all made for each other; we cannot become
ourselves without selfless devotion, without esteem from others
and for others.

We could appeal to modern psychology, which has discovered
that before a newborn baby is capable of recognizing its parents,
it requires, even for its bodily welfare, love and affection more
than food and hygiene.

But let us go at once to what is highest and noblest in our faith,

to what we know about the Blessed Trinity. The Father possesses
His Self in His fatherhood; the Son is Son because He is totally
turned to the Father. The divine persons are individually so
intensely Themselves just because They are so totally, so radically
in each other and for each other. And that seems to be the
fundamental law of the person. Fashioned in the image of
God, we cannot neglect this law without belittling ourselves.
God is love; man is man in proportion as he loves. Should we
not say that this is so because a man's existence is inextricably
intermeshed with that of others and is spent for others? Man
discovers himself the moment he realizes this fundamental setting
of his life and conforms his conduct to it.

Solidarity in love

Let us return to the subject of love. We have mentioned
previously that the term *grace,* in its primary meaning, signifies
love and fidelity, and therefore solidarity in its highest sense.
It signifies love and fidelity toward God and therefore love and
fidelity toward man. This ought to be self-evident.

In unambiguous language, Scripture says that no one can
follow Christ without love. Scripture confronts us with the
startling paradox that love for God reaches its visible manifestation in love for neighbor?

We like to read about visions and revelations concerning
the hereafter; books on this subject, often quite worthless, seem
to fetch the largest sales. In one passage of the Gospels, Christ
spoke of the last judgment; but as a rule He carefully avoided
whetting human curiosity about such matters. To Peter, who
betrayed curiosity about what was to happen to John, the Master
replied almost curtly, " What is that to you? You just follow
Me " (Jn 21:22). Matthew, however, preserved for us a narrative
which we cannot read often enough:

" When the Son of Man will come in His glory, accompanied
by His angels, He will sit upon the throne of His glory. Before
Him shall be gathered all the nations; and He will divide them
one from another as a shepherd divides the sheep from the
goats. He will place the sheep on His right side and the goats
on His left.

" Then the king will say to those on His right side: ' Come,
you blessed of My Father, inherit the kingdom prepared for
you from the foundation of the world. For I was hungry and
you gave Me to eat. I was thirsty and you gave Me to drink.

I was a stranger and you took Me home; naked and you clothed Me, sick and you cared for Me, in prison and you visited Me.' At this, the just will answer: 'When did we see You hungry and feed You? or thirsty and gave You to drink? When did we see You a stranger and took You home? or naked and clothed You? When did we see You sick or in prison and visited You?' And the king will answer them: 'Indeed, I say to you, as long as you did so to one of the least of My brethren, you did so to me.'

" And then He will say to those on His left side: 'Go far from Me, you the accursed, into the everlasting fire that was prepared for the devil and his angels: for I was hungry and you did not give Me food. I was thirsty and you did not give Me drink. I was a stranger and you did not take Me home; naked and you did not clothe Me, sick and in prison and you did not visit Me.' They, in their turn, will answer: 'Lord, when did we see You hungry, or thirsty, or a stranger, or sick, or in prison and did not minister to You?' Then He will answer them: 'Indeed, I say to you, as long as you did not do so to one of the least of my brethren here, you did not do so to Me' And the latter shall go away into everlasting punishment, and the first ones to eternal life. " [Mt 25:31-46]

Comment seems superfluous. Yet we must admit that it is hard to live up sincerely to Christ's teaching. In case the text of Matthew is not explicit enough, there is also St. John's first Epistle. For John, the supreme characteristic of God the Father is love. This love has come down to us on earth in Christ. And here a surprise awaits us: with all the realism of the mystic, John did not conclude that we have to love God; he concluded that we must love one another. Love for God is apt to conceal many illusions, since we do not see God. The visible, tangible expression of our love for God is brotherly love, the sacrament of our love for God: "Love consists in this: not that we loved God, but that He loved us, and sent His Son to be an atonement for our sins. Beloved, if God so loved us, we too ought to love one another. *No one has ever seen God*; but if we love one another, then God dwells in us, and the love of God has reached its full growth in our lives" (I Jn 4:10-12). Farther on, John said, "If anyone boasts of loving God and yet hates his brother, he is a liar. For he who does not love his own brother *whom he sees*, cannot love God *Whom he does not see*. We have this commandment from Him: he who loves God must love his brother as well" (I Jn 4:20-21). In the eyes of God, every interior disposition should be expressed in humanly visible terms. In this we are given to understand that the Church and grace go together.

The following text in John's first Epistle takes us right to

the heart of the problem: "Everyone who believes that Jesus
is the Christ, is born of God; and everyone who loves the
parent [the Father] loves also the one born of Him. If we
love God and keep His commandments, *we are sure of loving
His children.* For in this consists the love of God, that we keep
His commandments " (I Jn 5:1-3).

How can we love God if we do not love God's children?
It is clear from this alone that grace supposes and confirms
a deep-seated solidarity among men. One might even say that
this solidarity is given the place of honor in Scripture.

Solidarity in the Covenant

As is well known, the promises made to Abraham had been
given in the old Covenant to the nation, not to the individuals.
The Covenant, solemnly sealed on Mount Sinai, bound the
Hebrews together into the chosen people of Yahweh. Prophets
like Isaias and Ezechiel would later stress the personal responsibility of each individual within the chosen people. Still later,
after the exile and a few centuries before Christ, it would be the
Law which bound the people together. And so the rabbis would
look upon the Law as God's outstanding gift to His people.
This legal piety, which found its noblest expression in the strict
observance of the Law, implied that each member of the Jewish
people considered himself personally responsible for the keeping
of the Law. Hence arose the sect of the Pharisees. Their first
aim was good, and we can see in the Gospels that there were
still some pious Pharisees among the contemporaries of our
Lord. It remains always true what St. John repeated so often:
the one, true love of God consists in the observance of His holy
Law.

Unfortunately, the spirituality of some in the sect grew infected
with nationalism and pride. The ideal was to become "a just
man." That is precisely the reason the term keeps recurring
in the New Testament, in order to bring out the true nature
of justice. Among the Pharisees, however, some had persuaded
themselves that, relying *exclusively on their own efforts,* they
could observe the countless ritual and other laws which the
learned rabbis had woven into God's Law. They despised the
nations to whom the Law had not been given. What is worse,
they despised the Jews not of their sect who, for social or
economic reasons or because they were compelled (as in Galilee)
to live in the midst of pagans, were not able to live up to the
strict letter of the Law. It is on that score that these Pharisees,
who should have led their sect to religious excellence, were so

mercilessly condemned by Christ in the Gospels and so vigorously impugned by Paul in the Epistles to the Romans and Galatians.

Christ's attitude brings a serious warning home to us. Christ was God made visible on earth. Now, it is plain from the Gospels that the severe words in which He uttered and therefore revealed God's wrath were not directed against the men whom we priests like to inveigh against, but rather against the pious folk who by their pride denied the true nature of religion. The pride of these Pharisees stood in opposition to God as much as to men. *Their sectarianism denied the true solidarity within Israel.*

Grace as God's Kingdom

But let us return to the theme of solidarity in Christ, the true brotherhood which grace established in us. We have seen how this brotherhood was prepared in the Old Testament, and how certain rabbis and Pharisees deprived it of all meaning. Herein lay the Jewish betrayal in the days of Christ.

Christ came to extend brotherhood through grace. Solidarity was already a grace because it was a noble gift made by the Father. Christ would stress and emphasize our communion in and with Him. But let us ask ourselves: What did Christ preach? Grace? Not grace directly; He preached the *Kingdom.*

The Kingdom is the object of the *Eu-aggelion,* the Good Tidings. The Kingdom of God is said to be present already, but it has still to grow, like a tree in which birds from all over the world may nest. Only at the end of time will it stand fully revealed.

The Kingdom of God primarily gathers together the Jews, the members of the chosen people; but it is also thrown open to all nations It is God's highest gift, His highest grace. After the death and resurrection of Christ, the Kingdom found its first realization and visible materialization in the Church, the new chosen people, symbolized by the twelve apostles who, like the twelve patriarchs of old, form the foundation upon which the Kingdom is built here on earth. Within that Kingdom we all have our home. There and there only *shall we encounter God in humility, faith and love.*

We should like to emphasize here that the notion of the Kingdom of God finds its best elucidation in what we spoke of above: the presence of the Father in the Son by the power of the Holy Spirit. That is the way in which God exercises His kingship. The notion of the Kingdom adds an important trait to our previous considerations: the divine indwelling assembles us all together into one Kingdom. The Kingdom is both invisible, in that God establishes it, and visible, in that it takes shape here on earth. Through grace we are all children of the Kingdom, and thus we all belong to the visible " people of God on earth, " or the Church.

God acquires a people

The apostles linked the image of " God's people on earth, " or the chosen people of the new Covenant, with the central idea of redemption in Christ. We in turn can now purify our idea of redemption and recognize that it is undivided from the doctrine of grace and the Church.

Influenced by ancient Germanic thought and customs about the freeing of serfs and slaves and about the blood money one tribe paid another in the case of manslaughter, the theology of the early Middle Ages built up a theory of redemption which has weighed heavily upon our spirituality to this day. Admittedly, the influence of ancient Germanic times is accidental. We have to look deeper for the real cause. Everyone knows of the law in use among the Jews: an eye for an eye and a tooth for a tooth. Similar customs can be observed among certain tribes in Africa: murder, whether premeditated or not, can be atoned for only by the blood of a member of the tribe that is considered guilty of the murder. Even in fights among children that strange law is observed; a blow can be made up for only by a like blow in return.

This principle of retribution seems to be so widespread that a few theologians have ranked it as a " cosmic law, " a universal law of ethics prescribing that amends must be made for every sin by a proportionate measure of pain and suffering. As such, it would apply also to the divine order, the violations by sin demanding reparation. Only one more step was needed in the application of this law to conclude that Christ, by the infinite value of His passion, atoned for the infinite injury done by sin to the majesty.

Of course, we could not think of denying that Christ offered satisfaction for our sins to the Father, for that is the explicit teaching of both Scripture and the Church. But we may well ask: What does Christ's reparation and satisfaction essentially consist of? Of His love and obedience, shown in His passion and death, or of the weight of His sufferings?

Our question is not a senseless one, for quantitative and juridical conceptions have crept into the theology of penance, confession, indulgences, and even our devotion to the Sacred

Heart. On the religious level, human nature is inclined to seek for what is quantitative and mechanical. Quantitative measures are easy to imagine, and would dispense us from personal commitment and self-surrender. But such are not the ways of speaking in Scripture.

There is no denying that in Scripture we come across words like *redeem, ransom,* and even the commonplace phrase *to buy on the market;* but these expressions are given spiritualized meanings in the theology of Scripture. In essence, Christ's redeeming action lies in this: that the Father has acquired a new people in Christ by the power of the Holy Spirit. Consequently, the redemption is conceived by the evangelists, particularly Paul and John, as a deliverance from sin, but still more as a divine action of taking possession—in the vocabulary of the Old Testament, an action by which God's sovereign power takes possession of a people, makes it His very own and gathers it to Himself. This sense holds good in respect both to immediate deliverance from sin through grace and to ultimate fulfillment in heaven, since it is only in heaven that we shall be fully free from sin, totally belonging to God, definitively accepted into His Kingdom.

[margin note: X's redeeming action]

In this light, the authentic teaching of Scripture assumes great power. Christ's redeeming action is not restricted to the cross alone; the death on the cross is inseparably bound up with the resurrection and the ascension. Like the Jews of the Old Testament, we celebrate the feast of our deliverance on Easter day, not exclusively on Good Friday. Our deliverance is signified in both the death and the resurrection of Christ, and consequently has been accomplished in them both. The resurrection is not just an adjunct, as we have sometimes heard it stated; it is not simply an apologetical proof that the Man Who died on Good Friday was God. This conception, which is still current in some countries, plainly runs counter to the explicit teaching of Scripture, of the tradition contained in the liturgy and of the great Fathers of the Church. This is the error of a theology which has lost consciousness of its dependence on Scripture and wants to base itself on pure speculation. We have actually heard it contended that, compared to systematically built-up speculation, Scripture is but a primitive, raw and naive interpretation of the faith. Had we not better say that it is the other way round?

[margin note: also w/ life]

Redemption through love

Christ, then, did not buy our freedom by the excess of His sufferings, quantitatively measured as an infinite satisfaction,

but *through the love and obedience* which animated His passion
and death.   His love and obedience proved themselves most
tellingly on the cross, but they attained their highest achievement
in the resurrection.

On this point, no doubt is possible in the writings of John
and Paul.   Toward the end of Christ's first farewell discourse,
John put these words on the Master's lips: "... the world must
know that I love the Father and that I do as the Father has
commanded Me.   Rise, let us depart from here" (Jn 14:31).
And Christ got up from the table and went to the Garden of
Olives.   Earlier in the same Gospel, as he was about to begin
the story of the passion, John repeated the same idea in most
solemn language that leaves no doubt about his true thought:
" Jesus, knowing that the hour of His departure from this world
to go to the Father had come, and still loving His own who were
in the world, gave them the utmost proof of His love " (Jn 13:1).
The solemnity of these words is evidence enough that what
was uppermost in St. John's mind was not the episode of the
washing of the feet that follows in his text, but the story of
the passion taken as a whole.   And this is demonstrated still
further in verse 3, the tone of which is equally impressive:
" Knowing that the Father had given all things into His hands,
that He had come from God and was now returning to God,
He laid aside His outer garments, took up a towel and put it
about Him. "   The repetition of the phrases " to depart from the
world to the Father, " " to come from the Father, " and " to
return to the Father " guarantees that John, so fond of playing
on words with complex meanings, had the Hebrew term *pascha*
in the foreground of his thought.   Now, *pascha*, from which we
derive the English word *paschal*, signified for the Jews a crossing
over, a passage, and especially the crossing of the Red Sea into
liberty.   In His second farewell discourse after the last supper,
Christ suggested the same idea when He said, " This is My
commandment, that you love one another as I have loved you.
No one has greater love than this: that He should lay down His
life for his friends " (Jn 15:12-13).

In other, broader contexts, John suggested the same order
of ideas more than once.   For instance, in the narrative of
Christ's conversation with Nicodemus, he wrote:

" The Son of Man must be lifted up [in another section, we
pointed out that " to lift up " refers to the song of the Servant
of Yahweh in the Book of Consolation, Is 53:13-15] as Moses
of old lifted up the serpent in the desert [another image of
deliverance; see Nm 21:8] in order that anyone who believes
in Him may have eternal life.   For God so loved the world that
He gave His only begotten Son, so that anyone who believes in

Him may not perish, but have eternal life. God did not send His Son into the world to condemn the world, but in order that the world might be saved through Him." [Jn 3:14-17]

In His sacerdotal prayer, Jesus prayed for His own and for all the faithful. Death was imminent; a few paces separated Him from the Garden of Olives. And what did Christ expect from the Father? He asked for and expected a union that could be nothing else than a powerful revelation of God's glory:

" I do not pray for them alone [the apostles], but also for those who through their word believe in Me, that all may be one, as you, Father, are in Me and I You, that they too may be one in us, in order that the world may believe that You have sent Me. I have given them the glory which you have given Me, so that they may be one as We are one. I in them and you in Me, that they may be made perfectly one, and the world may know that You have sent Me and love them as you have loved Me.... Your name I have revealed to them and will reveal; so that the love with which you have loved Me may be in them, and I, too, may be in them. " [Jn 17:20-26]

The visible union of which there is question here undeniably witnesses to the glory of the Father, to His grace. " Glory, " in Hebrew usage, refers to the majesty of God insofar as it can be manifested in this world.

John said all this once again in his first Epistle: " He who does not love, does not know God [in Hebrew, not to know God means " not to have true piety "], for God is love. The love of God has been revealed, where we are concerned, by the fact that God has sent His only begotten Son into the world, so that we might have life through Him " (Jn 4:9). This is the way St. John spoke of our redemption—as the visible manifestation of the Father's love in the obedience and love of the Son. Through this love we have received love and have been brought together in a new unity. John went as far as comparing this new unity in grace with the supreme unity existing between the Father and the Son. This is one more illustration of the intimate connection among the three mysteries of grace, redemption and the Church.

Redemption through obedience

St. Paul was still clearer, if this is possible. In Christ's death on the cross, he saw the Revelation and the guarantee of God's love for us:

" While we were still powerless to help ourselves, Christ, at
the fitting time, died for us sinners. It is hard enough to find
anyone who will die on behalf of a just man, though there
may be one who might contemplate dying for a deserving man.
[This is an echo of the Master's words in St John: " No one
has greater love than this: that he should lay down his life
for his friends " (Jn 15:13). In fact, Paul added emphasis to
John's text by saying that Christ died for His enemies.] But
God proves His love for us in this, that, while we were still
sinners, Christ died for us. All the more surely, now that
we have been justified through His blood, shall we be saved,
through Him, from His wrath. Though enemies of God, we were
reconciled to God through the death of His Son; and now,
reconciled to Him, we are surer than ever of having salvation
in His Son's life. " [Rom 5:6-10]

More than once we have referred to the great text from the
Epistle to the Philippians which re-echoes so powerfully the
consciousness the Church has of her faith. This text keeps
recurring in the Mass and the breviary during Holy Week and
Easter Week. It forms the fundamental theme of the powerful
symphony that the paschal celebration ought to be to us; it offers
us the true content of the paschal mystery. " Appearing as man,
He has humbled Himself by being obedient unto death, *even to
the death* of the cross. And therefore, God has lifted Him up
[image of the Servant of Yahweh] and has bestowed upon Him
the name above all names ... Jesus is the Lord " (Phil 2:8-11).
Because of His obedience, Christ was invested with the very
majesty of the Lord, of Adonai. This word was in use among
the rabbis to speak of God's supreme title, Yahweh, " the name
above all names, " which inspired such awe that it was hardly
ever pronounced. The same sacred name also conveys the
idea of what the kingship of Yahweh is. In Christ, God's
Kingdom has been founded and permanently established.

Redemption and community

St. John contemplated our Christian solidarity in its ultimate
source, the Blessed Trinity. Our unity has its origin in the
Father, Who is love, light and life. This love, this light and
this life have been revealed to us in Christ, and are continually
being consolidated by His Spirit. There we discover the root
and ground of our *koinonia,* our communion with each other.
As the Father is one with the Son, so are we one with the Son
and thus with the Father. Our union, consequently, is a share

in the inner divine life, in the grace that comes down from God and returns to God.

St. Paul preferred to see that same unity in its visible form, the Church. Yet he did not shrink from looking upon the unity within the Church as issuing from the Trinity. It is precisely in this that the great " mystery " consists, the " mystery " Paul was commissioned to announce to the Gentiles, who once upon a time had been " so far away " and now were " brought close " to Christ.

" Remember, therefore, that formerly you were called Gentiles ... that in those days [before the Gospel was preached to them] you were apart from Christ, outlaws from the commonwealth of Israel, strangers to the covenant of the promise, without hope and without God in the world. But now [in opposition to " formerly "; the time of salvation has come in Christ] in Christ Jesus you, once so far away, have been brought close in the blood of Christ. For He is our peace, Who made the two nations one, breaking down in His flesh [His human nature] the wall that was a barrier between us, the enmity there was between us. He put an end to the Law with its decrees [the rabbinic Law caused division, not unity]. He has made peace, remaking the two human creatures into one new man in Himself, so that He might reconcile them both in one body to God through His cross, inflicting death upon the enmity. And He came and brought the good tidings of peace [and thus of unity] to you who were far off, as well as to those who were near [the Jews of the Covenant]; for through Him we have both [Jews and Gentiles] access in the same Spirit to God. " [Eph 2:11-18]

Paul followed this up with the lofty conclusion: " So then, you are no longer strangers and aliens [that is, people living in a foreign country]; but you are fellow-citizens with the saints; you are of God's household, built upon the foundation of the apostles and the prophets, the chief cornerstone being Christ Himself. In Him, the whole building, aptly fitted together, grows into one temple dedicated to the Lord; in Him you [the Gentiles], too, are being built in and with the others into one dwelling-place of God, in the Spirit " (Eph 2:19-22).

There we have the " mystery " which Paul preached. Since all eternity, it had lain hidden in the secret of God's designs. It was now revealed in Christ, animated and sealed by the Spirit. Of all this, Paul was the " Apostle, " the one sent to the Gentiles.

Every one of these themes is enunciated in the opening chapter of the same Epistle to the Ephesians, which for this reason has justly been called " an Epistle concerning the nature of the Church ":

" Blessed be God, the Father of Our Lord Jesus Christ, Who has blessed us in the heavens with every spiritual blessing in Christ. In Christ, He [the Father] chose us out before the foundation of the world to be holy and blameless in His sight. In love, He predestined us to become His children through Jesus Christ, in accordance with the good pleasure of His will, to make manifest the splendor of the grace with which He has favored us in the well-beloved, in Whom we have redemption through His blood, remission of sins, by the wealth of His grace that has overflowed in us in an abundance of wisdom and discernment. For He [the Father] made known to us the hidden purpose of His will, the free design which He had determined to carry out in the fullness of time: to bring all things in Christ under one head, those that are in the heavens and on earth [all] in Him.

" In Him, we also [the Jews, in opposition to "you" which follows] have obtained our inheritance, chosen beforehand to suit the purpose of Him who works out all things according to the design of His will, in order that we might serve to praise His glory, we who were the first to hope in Christ. In Him, you too [the Gentiles], after hearing the word of truth, the gospel of your salvation, in Him, you too have believed, and have been marked with the seal of promise of the Holy Spirit, who is the pledge of our inheritance until the [full] redemption of those whom God has acquired to the praise of His glory." [Eph 1:3-14]

The body of Christ

With these truths as a light and a foundation, Paul built up his theology of the Body of Christ. Let us start by observing that the phrase *Body of Christ* has three meanings in St. Paul. It means, first, the human body of Christ which died and rose for us, and on that account was no longer a " psychic " (natural) body but a " spiritual body " (I Cor 15:44), a " body of glory " (Phil 3:22). After that moment, Christ's risen body became the sign of God's presence on earth, and it is now what the temple of Jerusalem was previously for the Jews (Jn 2:19). In St. Paul, it became the cornerstone of the new temple, which is the Church (I Cor 3:10-17; 2 Cor 6:16-20; Eph 2:20:22).

Christ's body remains visible in the mystery of the Eucharist (I Cor 11:24). In the celebration of the Eucharist, Paul experienced the fact that together we form one body—the Church; and this is the third meaning of the word. " The bread which we break [one of the earliest expressions to designate the eucharistic meal: bread must be broken, as was done by Christ, to be distributed], does it not give a participation of the body of Christ? " Then follows a very ancient symbolism which, unfortunately, we have largely forgotten, though it can be detected in the earliest prayers after communion: " The one bread [one because formed from many grains] makes us one body; for the same one bread is shared by many. Look at Israel of this earth: Do not those who eat of their sacrifice associate themselves with the altar of sacrifices? " (I Cor 10:16-18).

In his Epistles to the Corinthians and the Romans, the Apostle almost surely had in mind the image, rather common in the Greek world of those days, in which the term *body* suggested the solidarity among the multitude of citizens belonging to one city. Each has his individual life and occupation, and yet all hang together. In the first Epistle to the Corinthians (12:12-16), Paul did not hesitate to draw inspiration from a Greek tale about the limbs of the body and the stomach, and apply the image to Christian solidarity.

However, in Paul, the Greek symbolism acquires a deeper significance. First of all, as stated above, we form one body by partaking of Christ's body in the Eucharist. In chapter 12 of the first Epistle to the Corinthians, we have these words: " Just as the [human] body is one single thing, though it has many members, all the members of the body, though many, are one body "; and the text continues: " So it is with Christ. " Notice that Paul did not say, " So it is with the Christians. " " In one and the same Spirit, we are all baptized into one body, whether Jews or Greeks, slaves or freemen; and we were all made to drink of one and the same Spirit " (I Cor 12:12-13). The same principle serves to bring these considerations to their conclusion: " So now all together you are the Body of Christ, and individually members of it " (I Cor 12:27). The same conclusion appears in the Epistle to the Romans: " We, though many, form one body with Christ, but as individuals we are members mutually dependent on each other " (Rom 12:4).

Like John, Paul based this unity in diversity on the living unity of the Blessed Trinity. He first established that we cannot possibly be Christians without the immediate influence of the Holy Spirit: " No one can say, ' Jesus is the Lord ' [the earliest Christian profession of faith], unless by the Spirit. " He then continued: " There are different kinds of gifts, but it is the same Spirit. And there are different kinds of service, but it is the same Lord Christ]. And there are different kinds of power [to work wonders], but it is the same God [the Father] Who manifests His power in us all." The text sums up the varieties of spiritual gifts granted by the Holy Spirit, and ends: " But all these are the effects of one and the same Spirit, who distributes them to the individuals according as He wills " (I Cor 12:3-11).

In his later letters, known as the Captivity Epistles, Paul went one step farther. It is only in these writings that he explicitly described Christ as the head of the Body, and called this Body the Church.

Soon after the opening verses of the Epistle to the Colossians, Paul quoted an ancient hymn to Christ, which we have cited in a previous section:

" He is the image of the invisible God, the first-born of all creatures. For in Him all things were created, whether in the heavens or on the earth, what is visible or invisible, whether Thrones or Dominations, Principalities or Powers. All things have been created through Him and for Him. He exists before all things, and in Him all things subsist. He is also the head of the body, which is the Church. He is the beginning, the first-born among the dead, so that in all things He may hold preeminence; for it has pleased God the Father that in Him should dwell the fullness [of the Father], and that, through Him, He should reconcile all things to Himself, whether the things on earth, or the things in the heavens, making peace by the blood of His cross. " [Col 1:15-20]

We are given here a theology of the Church far more profound than is generally suspected. Just as Christ possesses in Himself the indwelling fullness of the Godhead, so also the Church carries within her the fullness of Christ. " And He (the Father) subjected all things under His feet (that is, under His dominion) and has made Him head of the Church, so that the Church is His body, the completion of Him who completes all things everywhere "; or as, perhaps, a better translation of the original Greek has it: " He has given to the Church, which is His body, the fullness of whatever, in every respect, is being fulfilled in all men " (Eph 1:22-23).

The cosmic fullness of the Church, grounded in Christ and therefore in the Father, has as its immediate, visible manifestation the fact that all men, even the Gentiles, are called to the Church. In the verses that follow those just cited, the Apostle dealt at some length with this call, as it affected both Jews and Gentiles, and used it to stress once again our common solidarity in Christ.

Paul was well aware that, with this doctrine, he definitively

broke away from the general rabbinical teaching which he
had learned in his youth, prior to his conversion, at the feet
of Gamaliel in Jerusalem. The rabbis generally taught that
there were three classes of humans whom God excluded from
the blessings of the Law: Greeks (that is, the Gentiles or, as the
Old Testament calls them, the nations), slaves and women
(though these could share through their husbands in the promises made to Abraham). Seen against this background, the
following assertion of Paul in his Epistle to the Galatians stands
out in bold relief: " Through faith, you are all sons of God in
Jesus Christ. For all of you, by your baptism into Christ, have
put on Christ [yet another simile of union with Christ]. Henceforth there is neither Jew nor Gentile, neither slave nor free-
man, neither man nor woman: they are all one in Christ Jesus.
But if you are Christ's, you are the seed of Abraham, heirs in
virtue of the promise " (Gal 3:26-29). In other words, all
without exception would henceforth be members of the new
Israel, God's people on earth, the people of the promise, heirs
of the Kingdom.

Paul saw the image of Christ's intimate union with His Church
realized in a special way in Christian marriage. In the well-
known words of Genesis 2:24, the marriage union is expressed
in typically Hebrew fashion: " and these two will be one flesh, "
that is, one man. The Apostle plainly had this text in mind
when he spoke of the union of Christ with the Church as the
fruit of the redemption:

" For the husband is head of the woman, as Christ is head
of the Church; now he is the Savior of her who is his body.
Well then, as the Church is subjected to Christ, so women are
subjected to their husbands in all things. Husbands, love your
wives as Christ has loved His Church, and has delivered Himself
up for her in order to make her holy and pure through the
bath of water together with the word [that is, through baptism
and faith in the Word], so as to acquire her as a glorious bride,
free from stain or wrinkle or anything like it, but holy and
undefiled. . . . No one has ever hated his own flesh, but each
one has nourished it and cared for it, just as Christ did for the
Church, since we are all members of His body. That is why
man shall leave father and mother in order to attach himself
to his wife; and these two shall be one flesh. This mystery is a
great one; *I am applying it to Christ and His Church* " [Eph 5:23-
32].

Paul did not intend to strain the comparison unduly. Yet
he looked upon the intimacy of the marriage union as a replica
of the standard for all unions on earth: the union of Christ with

His Bride, the union of the head with the Body, the Church.
The example of marriage helps us to realize better how deeply
we are *all* united to Christ. For Paul, the Church was never
an abstraction, but was rather the sum total of her members.
At the same time, this profound truth, the " mystery of salvation "
which gives Christian marriage its ultimate meaning, must
prompt husbands and wives to love each other as Christ loves
the Church and as the Church owes herself to Christ.

Was not Paul justified in proposing union among the faithful
as the highest of Christian duties? In the text we cite below,
he saw this union as rooted in the Trinity; and he had no
difficulty in laying bare the ultimate foundation of our obligation
to foster union, peace and love: " Endeavor to maintain the
unity of the Spirit in the bond of peace. There is but one body
and one Spirit, as you have been called to one hope by your
vocation. There is but one Lord [Christ], one baptism [given us
by the one Lord]. There is but one God and Father of all,
Who is above all, acts through all and dwells in all " (Eph: 4:3-6).

Our unity in its fulfillment

Union is already achieved now; but we must wait until Christ
returns at the end of time for its full revelation. This is what
St. John tells us, especially in the Book of Revelation, the
Apocalypse. In a previous page, we saw how this union
signified for John a share in the union of the Son with the
Father. While St. Paul developed the metaphor of the body,
St. John enlarged upon the image of the vine:

" I am the true vine, and My Father is the vine-dresser. Any
branch on Me that does not bear fruit, He removes; and any
branch that bears fruit, He prunes in order that it may bear
more fruit. You are pruned already because of the word I have
spoken to you. Abide in Me, and I will abide in You. As the
branch cannot bear fruit unless it remains on the vine, so
neither can you, unless you abide in Me. I am the vine, you
are the branches. He who abides in Me, and I in him, he it is
who bears much fruit, for apart from Me you can do nothing.
If someone does not abide in Me, he is cut off like a branch
and withers; and they will gather them up and throw them
into the fire to be burnt up. If you abide in Me, and My words
abide in you, ask whatever you want and it shall be done to you.
In this My Father is glorified that you bear much fruit, and so
you will be My disciples. As the Father has loved Me, so have
I loved you. Stay in My love. " [Jn 15:1-9]

The Church is not mentioned explicitly in the metaphor of the vine. The next to last chapter of the Apocalypse makes up for this omission. Our union with the Father, Son and Holy Spirit is fully achieved only in the Church triumphant, the Bride of the Lamb. In an effort to utter the ineffable and to describe the glory of heaven, St. John searched the Old Testament for appropriate symbols: heaven as the holy city of Jerusalem, God's dwelling among men in the tabernacle of the Covenant; the twelve tribes of Israel and the twelve apostles, the image of God's new people; and finally, an older metaphor of paradise, the stream of living waters described in the prophecy of Ezechiel (47:6-12) and designating the Holy Spirit. St. John concluded the narrative of his heavenly vision by mentioning the Blessed Trinity, which is the beginning and the end of our redemption, our grace and the Church.

"Then I saw a new heaven and a new earth. . . . I saw the holy city, the new Jerusalem, coming down out of heaven from God [as the highest gift and grace], beautiful as a bride adorned for her husband. And then I heard a mighty voice proclaiming from the throne [image of God's majesty], 'Now at last, God has His abode among men! He will dwell among them. They will be His people, and He Himself will be God with them [an ancient expression to denote the Covenant between God and men].' . . .

"Then one of the angels who holds the seven bowls full of the seven last plagues came to Me and said: 'Come and I will show you the Bride of the Lamb.' So, in the spirit he carried me up to a very high mountain, and showed me the holy city of Jerusalem coming out of heaven from God and shining with the glory of God. . . . The city was ringed with a very high wall and twelve gates, at which stood twelve angels; and on the gates were written the names of the twelve tribes of Israel. . . . The city wall had twelve foundation stones on which were inscribed the twelve names of the twelve apostles of the Lamb.

" . . . the city was of pure gold, bright as clear glass. . . . But the temple itself I did not see; for the temple was the sovereign Lord and the Lamb. [Henceforth we live in the immediate presence of the Father and the Son.] And the city had no need of the light of sun or moon; for the glory of God shone upon it; its lamp was the Lamb. . . . .

" [Now comes the Holy Spirit:] Then the angel showed me the river of the water of life [as in paradise], clear as crystal and flowing from the throne of God and of the Lamb, and running down the middle of the city's street. On either side of the river stood a tree of life, yielding twelve crops of fruit [symbol of abundance], one for each month. The leaves of the trees serve to bring health to the nations.

"There will be no longer any profanation in this city. The throne of God and of the Lamb will be there, with His servants to worship Him; they shall see Him face to face, His name written on their foreheads [as a sign of possession]. There will be no more night, nor will they need the light of lamp or sun; for the Lord God will shed His light upon them; and they shall reign for ever and ever [Ap 21:1-22:5].

Scripture's vision

In this section we have wandered leisurely through the luxuriant garden of Scripture. The first impression may well have been rather confusing. Scripture is no formal French garden, like that at Versailles; it is rather like mountain country with pleasant dales, meadows and woods, and here and there a breathtaking vista, all beneath the splendor of lofty ranges and summits. Scripture is not made up of systematic works in which problems are examined singly and worked out methodically. Scripture contains unorganized writings—letters, for instance—and also some historical books, prepared for the purpose of instruction rather than to supply the reader with scientific history, such as he is used to today.

Repeatedly in this section we have come face to face with the central doctrine outlined in the three preceding sections. The Church is not to be conceived of as apart from the living presence of the Father, the Son and the Holy Spirit. One could write at length about the Church and her diverse aspects. To begin with, she was established by the will of the Father. In being and essence, she is and will always remain the Body of the head, who is Christ. Since the day of the first Pentecost, she has been borne up all through her historical development by the power of the Holy Spirit. Recent papal documents call the Holy Spirit the soul of the Body; Scripture calls the Church the temple of the Holy Spirit.

The hidden, vital energy which keeps the Church together and animates her from within is precisely the "living life" of the Blessed Trinity. Now, the Church has no existence apart from her members; she is not a juridical apparatus, or still less an idea hanging in midair. Consequently, whatever applies to the Church applies to the members in which she lives—those who are now her members and those who are destined to enter the Church. We should exclude no one. She is the mother of us all in Christ.

Further, we have seen that the great mysteries of our faith—
redemption, grace and the Church—are not to be thought of as
independent of each other. We have been set free through the
obedience and love of the Son, sent by the Father Who is love.
The Son walked in our midst in the power of the Spirit, the
Spirit of truth and love. The central core of the divine redeeming act lies in this, that the Father took to Himself a
people and made it His very own; He sanctified it in Christ
through His Spirit, freeing it from sin and filling it with grace.
Grace is the fruit of the redemption; but our redemption was
not worked out on a quasi-juridical basis, as if Christ's abundant
sufferings merited a determined quantity of grace—a notion hard
to get hold of, anyhow. Grace must be seen as the natural
flowering of Christ's redeeming action. That being so, grace
cannot be conceived of as separate from the Church, for both
are but aspects of the same reality: salvation.

We shall have occasion to return to this matter. There is
perhaps no more urgent task in theology than to purify our
ideas on this subject. The creative, renovating presence of the
Blessed Trinity has proved itself above all in the redemption.
Sent by the Father and filled with the Spirit, Christ entered
into human history and became God's obedient Servant and
loving Son. In His humanity, He testified to what He, as Son,
ever continues to be within the Trinity: totally surrendered to the
Father in the love of the Holy Ghost.

In this world of ours, estranged from God by sin, Christ
was what we men have been expected to be since the beginning
of the world: God's servants as creatures, God's children by
grace. And that is the way He chose to redeem us, the one
way God thought of and accepted as a fitting expiation and
satisfaction. God is no sadist to be appeased by the sufferings
of a sinner. Does not a true conversion, a true satisfaction and
expiation, consist in a *change of heart,* the *metanoia* Scripture
speaks of?—the conversion from disobedience to obedience, from
pride and self-love and hate of others to love and self-surrender?
To be accurate, we should say that Christ merited for us the
possibility of becoming God's obedient servants and loving children with, in and through Him.

Before God, *to merit* has a different and far deeper meaning
than what it signifies in human relations. This is pretty obvious,
of course, though it is all too often overlooked. Christ's "meriting" for us means that He won for Himself, both as God and as
man, the power to let us share in His obedience and love, and at
the same time obtained God's pardon for us. The life of grace, as
we noted above, is simply this. And because we share in this
change of heart, in this obedience and love; because He has
gathered all of us around Him and unites us to Him through the

power of His Spirit, it ought to be plain that the being and substance of the Church is not be thought of as distinct from grace. In fact, the Church is grace *par excellence,* insofar as she manifests visibly that aspect of grace which binds us all, like brothers and sisters, into a true and everlasting people of God, the new Israel, the people of the promise and of the inheritance.

Until now we have made no mention in this section of those aspects of the Church with which the catechetical instruction and preaching in vogue today have made us familiar. I mean the Church's *authority,* evidenced in a corpus of law and a fairly extended formal organization. Nor have we ventured to say anything about the Church as a society devoted to religious worship, the prominent acts of which are the offering of the Mass and the reception of the sacraments. No harm is done if we shift the emphasis to the Church as a living society, as a *koinonia* which comes alive in a fuller realization of our solidarity and association in destiny, of our true brotherhood in love.

It would be unwarranted to slur over these visible aspects, to push them aside as mere adjuncts or, worse still, to exclude them from the realm of grace. It was fashionable to do so in the nineteenth century, and that fashion has not yet passed. History has known more than one sectarian movement which began with displeasure and embitterment at the blatant abuses displayed in the visible Church, and ended by taking refuge in a purely spiritual conception of what the Church is. Only cowardice flees from reality; and in this instance, cowardice is wrongheadedness to boot. The Church's founder wanted her to be a visible reality for the simple reason that she belongs to a visible world.

And so, if we have dwelt on the fact that we are one society in Christ, we have not for a moment forgotten that the Church, founded by Christ, is a visible Church. Hence our vigorous insistence on this society's need for practical love between its members in order to grow in actually. In the Church, some have been commissioned to exercice authority and others to preach or to sanctify by performing visible ritual actions, that is, by administering the sacraments. Episcopal and sacerdotal authority was instituted by Christ when He sent His apostles on their missions. The sacraments, too, come from Him. For it is the fundamental law of the incarnation and the redemption that God became man so that we might become partakers of the divine life. God leads through the visible to the invisible, that is, to Himself. We cannot proceed better in our discussion than by giving some insight into the meaning of what is visible in the order of grace.

The twofold movement of life within the Church

We may distinguish two movements of life within the Church.
The first is one that comes down from God to us, and the second
goes up from us to God. Otto Semmelroth has named the first
movement the line of initiative and authority proper to the
husband, and the second the line of self-surrender proper to the
bride. Such figures of speech have a suggestive value and
nothing more, though the latter seems to us to be the more
felicitous of the two.

Here again we come across the trinitarian formula so familiar
to the early Church Fathers and to the liturgy: everything comes
to us from the Father through the Son in the Holy Spirit, and
everything must return from us through the Holy Spirit in the
Son to the Father. With Ruysbroeck, we have applied this
hospitable statement to grace. It has the great advantage of
preventing our conceptions about God and grace from stiffening
into static notions. John and Paul applied the same scheme to
the incarnation and redemption; it is thus to be ranked among the
oldest theological axioms. Because it is an elaboration of the
human mind, it needs to be corrected each time we apply it to
God. But it keeps our theological thought " on the move "—
which is the main thing.

We shall then distinguish between the Church as Body of
Christ in the descending movement and the Church as Bride
of Christ in the ascending movement.

The Church as body

Insofar as the Church, *qua* Body of Christ, remains united to her
head, the participates in His messianic and prophetic function.
And to do so all the members of the Church, in and with Christ
and filled with His Spirit, must bear witness to the truth in the
face of the world. We do this principally by living a genuine
Christian life. No one may consider himself dispensed from
this function. Whether or not this deserves to be called the
" apostolate "—an overworked and often misused term—it is the
duty of baptized and confirmed Christians, for it is the Holy
Spirit Who bears witness in them. (He who and exercices
an ecclesiastical office is under the obligation to observe keenly
how the Holy Spirit is operating among the faithful and what
He is stirring up among them.) It is in this sense that the Church
as a whole is infallible in her witnessing, inasmuch as the
members, according to their various statuses (some in free
obedience, others in authority, though all in unity of faith), are

kept within the truth by the Holy Spirit and bear witness to the
truth.   On this basis, we feel called upon to follow the freedom
and boldness which is ours as the voice of the Holy Spirit, in
spite of our conscious weakness and sinfulness. However, as no
guarantee can be had that His voice is to be heard outside the
Church, each one of us is duty bound to test the interior voice
by the faith of the whole Church, though no member of the
Church is exempted, even for a moment, from the obligation of
listening to the voice of the Holy Spirit in his personal life.
If this rule were lived up to, it would banish all danger of
Christian legalism; it would restore to us all the freedom of the
children of God.

The authoritative preaching of the word of God and the
management of the society of the faithful have been entrusted
to a few members within—and therefore not above—that same
society; their ordination is their "sending."   The priestly mandate was instituted by Christ when He sent His apostles on their
mission.   Of that mission the universal episcopate has taken
the lawful and visible succession.

The fact that this mission is realized still further in the
form of definite laws and a concrete organization is inseparably
linked with Christ's express appointment of these men to be
leaders of a visible human society.   Through the centuries,
these laws and this organization will develop and adapt themselves to new conditions of life or to different cultural traditions;
but the substance of Christ's institution must remain intact.
Saying this, we have implied that these visible forms are open
to reform and adjustment, and the Second Vatican Council has
brought this out clearly enough.   But such as they are, they
are no more—or less—than the normally human, historically
determined forms in which the religious authority, willed by
Christ, takes visible shape.   In these manifestations of authority,
we acknowledge the visibility of grace coming to us in the
Church.   We believe this authority to be infallible within certain
limits, which simply means that within these limits we have the
assurance that Christ, head of the Body, speaks to us through
His Spirit.

This is equally clear from the fact that Holy Scripture frequently describes this mission as a form of *diaconia*, a term
meaning *ministerium* or service, which has been preserved
in some European languages.   Priests are indeed the servants
of the Church and of the faithful, but above all they are the
servants of Christ and of the Spirit.   Not for a moment does their
authority harden into a personal possession.   These men are in
the service of grace.

Assuredly, being humans and sinners like ourselves, they
may abuse this authority, using it for their own ends.   But we

firmly believe that Christ's guidance, at work within the Church, will never permit them to debase what belongs to the substance of the message of grace. In other words, the presence of the Blessed Trinity is so sovereignly assured in the ecclesiastical function that the men who are appointed to exercise this function cannot escape from the divine power of grace, whatever their personal sins. We are speaking of the bishops all over the world, in communion with each other and with the See of Peter. History teaches us that priests and bishops, individually or even in numbers, can fall away from God's truth and grace, but that catastrophe overtakes them only when they deliberately take their stand outside the unity of their function. By their sin, they may possibly succeed in shrouding and obscuring the glory of grace, but they are unable to pervert it totally.

Further evidence is had from the duty inherent in the Church's noblest function: her sanctifying mission. In the name of Christ, the Church sanctifies by administering the sacraments, which are all centered upon the Eucharist.

This sacramental duty, more than any other role, highlights in strong relief the Church's inner nature as Body of Christ and her function in the service of grace. The priest or bishop is the ordinary minister of most sacraments (today, some theologians would say that even the sacrament of marriage is no exception). And in the *present order* of salvation established by Christ, only in the sacramental system does it appear that grace comes down to us in a visible manner.

Scholastic theology distinguishes between sacramental grace and extrasacramental grace, the latter meaning grace conferred outside the actual reception of the sacraments. Such a distinction is valid only for the theologian who isolates the sacraments from each other and from the Church, and looks upon them as so many separate " mechanisms " destined singly to " cause " a determined measure of grace. We cannot help thinking that such a view of the sacraments is a rather materialistic one, reflecting the atomism that came to the fore in a later theology. It is not far removed from magic—not, of course, " black magic, " which is practiced against the will of God, but " white magic, " which attempts to dispose of the divine power by means of appropriate formulas. To our way of thinking, the Christians of the Reform and the Oriental Christians are right in protesting against a conception which is influenced by Nominalism, the bane of theology in the fifteenth century, and which unfortunately has infiltrated most theological textbooks and catechisms in the course of the last three centuries.

Sacraments are not vending machines, infusing a certain degree of grace the moment sacramental formulas have been correctly pronounced. Whatever one may say or think, this is a near approach to magic, the negation of all religion. Fortunately, the sacramental practice among fervent Christians is of a better quality than the teaching they have received.

The instant a Christian, animated by faith, allows the desire to receive a sacrament to well up within him, he puts himself under the influence of the grace proper to that sacrament. This is the teaching of classical theology on the subject of spiritual communion and the act of perfect contrition coupled with the intention of going to confession. We do nothing more here than simply generalize this accredited doctrine and apply it to all the sacraments.

The desire to receive a sacrament could very well be concealed in the sincere will to encounter God, even where few or no authentic sacraments are in acknowledged use, as is the case among the Protestants or indeed among pagans. We apply here the doctrine which says that anyone outside the Church can have a genuine, though possibly inexplicit, desire for the Church, a desire that goes by the name of *votum Ecclesiae*. (We are not authorized to separate the sacraments from the Church, for they are the visible and actual sanctifying rites of the Church. But we know that, thanks to the incarnation and the redemption, the whole world has already been sanctified fundamentally.) This is the reason that all human symbols, and thus all religious rites, possess a sanctifying value insofar as they do not stand in opposition to the true religion. What they do not possess is the full guarantee of Christ's living presence. They preserve a real ambiguity outside the Church, and on that score can serve to draw men away from God. In this light, all grace seems to us to be sacramental, because all grace implies to some extent the visibility of the Church.

And thus we reach the true nature of the Christian sacraments, that by which they differ in their inner being from all other religious rites and ceremonies.

The main theme of our last sections has been the living presence of the Blessed Trinity. Grace is unthinkable except as the fruit of the indwelling, a subject we shall return to in our next section. The Church, too, is determined in her inner being by that divine and consequently active presence. For indeed, neither the incarnation nor the redemption, the two fundamental mysteries of our faith, are to be thought of apart from the active election by the Father and the Son's mission in obedience and love, in and through the power of the Holy Spirit. We fail to see on what grounds the sacraments would be exceptions. In the sacraments, the fruits of the redemption are applied to us. In them, we are granted grace within the sphere of the Church. In essence, they are modeled on the incarnation. They are in effect symbolic actions (not separate things or separate causes) which, in their visibility, express the invisible divinity. They thereby make the divine present.

Early theologians did not look at the sacraments differently from us. We remember how, during the war years, our dogma professor who taught us the treatise on the sacraments laboriously set out to prove, against the liberal theology of Adolf von Harnack and others, that the early Fathers of the Church understood the sacraments to be " causes of grace. " We have nothing against the Western classical theology of the sacraments, provided it is not forgotten that no council has defined this doctrine to be of faith, and that even in the West the " causality " of the sacraments is differently explained by different theologians. Each school has its own theoretical technical elaboration which is not part of the dogma itself.

In any event, the painstaking efforts of our professor failed to satisfy us. Deliverance came to us the day we opened a textbook of Greek Orthodox theology entitled *Dogmatic Theology of the Eastern Orthodox Church,* published in Athens at the beginning of the century. In the chapter called " *Mysteria* " (" The Sacraments "), many texts were quoted from the Fathers of the Church attributing the operation of the sacraments to *the action of the Holy Spirit.* With that, light dawned on us. And indeed, not only was this the teaching of the Fathers; it was the common conception embodied in the liturgy, especially in the Eastern liturgy. The latter, in the administration of the sacraments, contained the prayer *Epiclesis,* specially addressed to the Holy Spirit, invoking Him to fill the water, the chrism and the sacred actions with His power and grace. Nothing more was needed to prove that the older theology had never detached the sacraments from their deeper roots, that it had never considered them apart from the creative, effectual presence of the Father in the Son through the power of the Holy Spirit.

This liberating discovery enabled us to combine our doctrine of the sacraments more definitely and more intimately with the doctrine of grace. Until then, the commonly taught sacramental theology had prevented us from seeing these two matters in their true light. But now we were satisfied that the *one source, the one cause and root of grace is the living presence in us of the Blessed Trinity.* If the sacraments, " confer upon us the grace they signify, " as the catechism teaches, then the only source of that grace is none other than the same presence of the Blessed Trinity. And of this the priest is the ordained, visible minister, the representative of the Church or, more in depth, of Christ and His spirit.

God's indwelling is made to bear fruit in us in a visible, experential manner; at the same time it gathers us all together in order to form us into one people of God, both visible and invisible, the Body of Christ, the Church. By this action, the Father prolongs the work of the redemption in Christ and in the power of His Spirit.

All the sacraments bear out this concept, especially the celebration of the holy eucharist. In the Mass the Church is being built up anew, gathered to the Father, and thus sanctified by the Father in the Son through the Holy Spirit.

The Church as bride

The Church is not only the Body of Christ; she is also His Bride. We regard the Church as the God-given sphere within which we can approach God, return to Him in faith, hope and charity and adore Him in spirit Here we find again the second movement started in us by the indwelling of the Blessed Trinity, the movement which leads us back to the Father by the power of the Holy Spirit.

This upward movement is not confined to the purely spiritual level. We have to return to God as we are, as men, with souls and bodies, with hearts and hands. In other words, our adoration in spirit must necessarily proceed from us by way of visible acts of religion and worship, as acts of the liturgy established by the Church.

The Christian cult ought to express itself first and foremost in the liturgy of the sacraments. The sacraments have been regarded so exclusively as " efficacious instruments of grace " that people seem to have forgotten that the sacraments are above all prayers and the Church's public acts of worship. Unless we are blind, this should be the very first thing noticed in the sacraments. The wrong understanding of opus operatum (the efficacy proper to the sacraments), together with the fact that in the Western Church the sacraments have been administered for centuries in a foreign and practically unknown idiom, has had disastrous consequences. How many of the ordinary faithful are still able to recognize a prayer-deed in the Latin formulas all too frequently muttered in an unbecoming rush? Someone might glibly answer that the sacraments are efficacious by themselves, and that the personal holiness and piety of the priest do not affect their fruitfulness. Things have come to such a pass that if any priest or layman dares to insist that those fine sacramental prayers should in all fairness be recited as authentic prayers, that is, with a spirit of adoration, all he does is arouse surprise. "Another of those fanatics! Another of those rabid liturgists! " Remarks of this sort have been heard within the aula of the Second Vatican Council.

as prayers

However unfamiliar and unsuspected it may seem to some, the sacraments are prayers addressed to God and therefore public ecclesiastical acts of worship. In these prayers, so teaches the venerable tradition of scholasticism, the Church " expresses her faith " as the Bride of Christ. All those who participate—he who receives the sacrament, the community around him and not least the officiating priest, the " steward of the mysteries of God "—have their appointed task. Each one takes part in the congregational act of the cult.

We apologize for dwelling at such length on these questions; but to tell the truth, we all need to reform our approach. Matters will improve when the vernacular is reintroduced, for it will then be plain to us all how much our habitual manner of acting is at variance with the words we utter or hear. Is it not a shame that a more becoming celebration of the liturgy is found in countries where Catholics are in the minority compared with the Reform Christians, and, as if that were not enough, have entered into dialogue with the non-Catholics? In so-called Catholic countries or in ghettos, speed and unsuitable muttering are still the rule. The most striking thing we have come across in our reading in this domain is an article in an American review, written before the Council and dealing with the use of the vernacular in the liturgy. Arguing against the use of the vernacular, the author of the article suggests that the faithful might be disedified because they could no longer understand why priests are in such a hurry! Is this not topsyturvy reasoning? Our Lord has said, " When you pray, do not go on gabbling like the heathens who fancy that the more they say, the more likely they are to be heard. You are not to be like them " (Mt 6:7-8). We smile at the prayer drums in use among the lamas of Tibet, and at the hysterical voodoo rites in the West Indies. But are our " Catholic " liturgical performances any better?

In the acts of Catholic worship, we meet again with grace, which Karl Rahner calls " grace received "; grace existentially accepted and lived up to, grace that comes to life in faith and charity. This aspect of grace is as trinitarian as the former ones.

On a previous page, we have seen how, according to St. Paul, we are not able to pray the Our Father except in the Holy Spirit (Rom 8:15-16; Gal 4:3). " I tell you ... no one can say: Jesus is the Lord [the earliest Christian profession of faith] unless it be in the Holy Spirit " (I Cor 12:3). " In the same way the Spirit comes to the aid of our weakness. When we do not know how to pray, the Spirit Himself pleads for us through our inarticulate groans. And he who can read hearts [an Old Testament description of God the Father] knows well what the Spirit means: He intercedes for the saints according to the mind of God " (Rom 8:26-27). No one ever stated more plainly that in prayer, and thus also in grace, God does not exactly come down to our level; instead, He grants us a share in the inner life of the Trinity—a share shrouted on earth in the obscurity of the faith.

Our prayer, then, is carried up by the Holy Spirit; we must add that it does not reach the Father except " through Our Lord Jesus Christ, " as the liturgy says in the final words of its orations. We would look in vain for a better comprehensive view of Christian prayer than the closing words of the canon of the Mass. A moment or two before intoning the Pater, the priest takes in hand both the consecrated bread and the chalice, lifts them in one gesture toward the Father and says, " through Him, and with Him, and in Him, be to You, God and Father, in union with the Holy Spirit, all honor and glory. "

This prayer shows plainly that the celebration of the Eucharist, so central as the sanctifying source of grace and union with God, is no less central as the act of adoration of the Christian cult; it is performed by Christian society as a whole, gathered round the High Priest Jesus Christ.

By now, the reader will agree that the numerous aspects of the faith not only complement each other but basically form one single, simple reality. To convince ourselves of this, we have merely to view them in the pure light of faith rather than consider them as a bewildering maze of laws and impositions, a collection of points of faith and religious opinions that have nothing in common except the fortuitous character of being accepted in the lump by Roman Catholics.

Conclusion

We have come to the end of this important chapter. We began by listening at some length to Holy Scripture, which in varying tones and themes extols our intimate association in Christ. We learned of our condition as God's visible people on earth, the new Israel, which is the external manifestation of what binds us together in depth, like brothers and sisters in Christ. We have shown how this state springs from the Father's election and is brought about by the moving power of the Holy Spirit. We then considered the point more closely and analyzed it in systematic detail—how in the Church we share in the " living life " of the Blessed Trinity that comes to us from the Father in the Son through the Holy Spirit, and how, in virtue of the divine " philanthropy, " we are led back to the Father in Christ through the consummating love of the Spirit.

Created and uncreated grace

Let us first of all define the two rather unfamiliar notions of created and uncreated grace. A bird's-eye view of the historical growth of the first notion will permit us to reduce the reality it signifies to its proper limits. We shall take pains to show that created grace has no existence as a distinct actuality, but that by its inner dynamism it connects us with the Trinity. Each time in the past theologians overlooked this significant aspect, they provoked objections which sometimes had tragic consequences, as for instance in the days of the Reformation when whole sections of Christendom fell away from the Church. I do not maintain that the atrophy of the notion of created grace was the only cause of the Reformation, but it supplied a motive for protest against the then current Catholic theology; it does so still now.

Origin of the notions

In theology, *uncreated grace* stands for God Himself insofar as He communicates Himself to man in love. In contradistinction to this, *created grace* signifies the result God's self-communication produces on man. Evidently that result cannot be God Himself; therefore, it is something other than God, something created, a gift from God.

The notion of created grace has remained practically unknown in the East; in the West, no clearly formulated expression of it was known for eleven centuries. As is the case in Scripture, the term " grace " remained for a long time a rather fluid idea. Without further precision, the word referred above all to the love which is God Himself, or to the presence of that love in us; tacitly and implicitly, it referred to the favor God worked out in man in consequence of His presence.

A time came when something more definite was needed in order to answer several questions raised about basic points of faith. A first question was: If the baptism of children has any real meaning—as defined by several councils in past centuries—what exactly do the children receive, considering that they are still incapable of evincing personal acts of faith and charity? Scripture seemed to indicate clearly enough that no one is sanctified and justified without acts of faith and charity; how then could children be sanctified by baptism? Then came a second question, akin to the first. After we have been sanctified by divine grace, we *remain* children of God; we live in a "state of grace." Yet it is evident that we do not uninterruptedly make acts of faith and charity. What then do we mean when we say that we have received the "virtue" of charity, or that we live in a "state of grace?"

These are simple queries; some might call them naive. But they betray a real need. The same questions are still being asked today. Dealing with the problem became a custom in professional theology even after Peter Lombard, toward the middle of the twelfth century, risked a rather daring reply to the second question. In his celebrated work *Sententiarum libri quattuor,* he quoted Paul's words: "For the love of God has been poured into our hearts by the Holy Spirit who has been given us" (Rom 5:15). From this text he drew the hardy conclusion: our love is precisely the Holy Spirit Who has been given to us. Lombard's work served as a textbook in all the monasteries and universities of Europe till well into the sixteenth century. Every prospective teacher of theology had to start upon his academic career with a series of lectures commenting on the *Sententiae.* Every professor of theology had to face that conclusion of Lombard's and undertake the delicate task of giving it an acceptable meaning. And thus the problem of how the Holy Spirit, as uncreated gift, is related to charity, as created gift in us, came to the fore in terms at once pregnant and insistent. To accept Lombard's bold paradox literally was tantamount to denying all personal activity in the practice of Christian charity. But the respect paid to the *Magister Sententiarum,* as Lombard was called, and the respect due to Scripture made it impossible for theologians simply to bypass the problem raised in those terms.

St. Thomas solved the question in a masterly way, though from too narrow a point of view. This present book is not the place to enter into St. Thomas' technical theological formulas; the reader will be presumed to have some familiarity with the philosophy and theology of Aquinas' time. In the proposed explanation that follows, we shall remain true to St. Thomas' fundamental intuition. It will be more profitable, however, to bring to light the permanent elements which entered into the conflicting opinions of the successive schools and which are still instructive today. History, it is said, teaches us how to live:

it also teaches us how to think. Faulty thinking processes should be carefully avoided, for they never fail to stir up the same reactions. The point we are dealing with is ample proof of this. The question facing us now is: What is the relation between God as gift and His grace conferred on us? Or, how do created and uncreated grace stand in relation to each other?

Luther's doctrine

The young Luther, while still a Catholic monk, wrote against the doctrine of grace current in his day. But he himself had been brought up in this theology; he knew no other, though he was familiar with the German mystics and, of course, with St. Augustine, for he belonged to the order of the Augustinians. And soon, as a youthful professor at Wittenberg, he would be applying himself wholeheartedly to the study of the Bible. The theology of his time would be of no use to him in the pursuit of biblical studies; it could at best irritate him—to some extent, rightly.

What had happened in the theological world meanwhile? Ever since created grace had been cut off from its one and only source, that is, from the interior operation of the indwelling Holy Spirit, it had come to look increasingly like a personal possession, some sort of capital that could be treasured up or put to use at will. From this, an impression could be gained that man acquired some rights before God merely by making good use of that capital. Professional theologians would have been careful not to draw such a conclusion; but the common preacher, who often made short work of prudent nuances in theology, had come to a rather crude notion of what grace is. This, together with the miserable traffic in indulgences at the time and the corruption in ecclesiastical life, was sufficient ground for protest, even for justifiable protest.

We are of the opinion that Luther's initial protest was in fact justified. In his Catholic days, his theology was not always safe: nor was that of many Catholics of the period. It is quite impossible, of course, to form an idea of what Luther's personal conscience was in the later stages of his evolution. Today, no one denies that the Church needed reform. The deep emotion stirred up within him by what he had witnessed in the Church, and perhaps also (as Karl Meissinger, a well-known Protestant historian, surmises) the enormous success he met with in whole regions of Europe, drove him to excess, to a radicalism that ended with expulsion from the Church. We are at one with

Professor W. H. van de Pol in thinking that the poor man, distraught with warring doubts, finally could no longer accept the belief that the visible Church he saw around him was still the Church of Christ. If what we wrote in a previous section has any value, then we can see that it is impossible to reform the Church from outside; reform must come from within. That was Luther's misfortune.

What was Luther's teaching concerning grace? Scripture is explicit enough: we are justified *only* through grace; and we can assert no right whatever to it. Created grace is consequently unable to bind God to us. William of Ockham had already said as much. Luther carried Ockham's reaction to an impassioned rebellion and thus fell to the other extreme: it is meaningless to speak of created grace in any sense, or of any *interior* justifications; we are justified *sola gratia,* that is, *exclusively* through grace. And saying this, he stood by the principal meaning attached to grace in Scripture, namely, God's love for us. Nothing further! He solved the problem of the relationship between created grace and uncreated grace by eliminating one of the terms of the problem.

However, he was too close as yet to Catholic tradition to be satisfied with such a doctrinal simplification. So he kept other elements of the Catholic faith, twisting them into an extreme form of radicalism because of his strong aversion to the ideas commonly received in the schools. As we understand matters, Luther at bottom did nothing else than reject the visible Church he knew in his Catholic days. And therefore, among other things, the one principle of authority he admitted for his religious beliefs was *sola Scriptura,* that is, God speaking to us *exclusively* in Scripture. In this light, the words *sola fide*—by faith alone— which he discovered in the Epistle to the Romans acquired a unique significance. Man is justified neither by his works, nor by any kind of merit, but *exclusively* by faith. Justification is not something granted to him, but "imputed" to him, insofar as God covers his sins with the merits of Christ. And that is why man is justified—only because of Christ. Christ's merits are the sole ground of man's trust in God. Our justification rests on Christ alone and not on ourselves.

Let us add that Luther, and after him more explicitly Calvin, did not at all deny the operation of the Holy Ghost moving us to lead Christian lives. Most Catholic textbooks dealing with the subject take no notice whatever of this point. In Luther's view, we are really sanctified already in this life. This sanctification, however, is of no value *coram Deo* (in the sight of God), that is, here on earth, where only an absolute obedience to the divine sanctity and majesty could be of *any worth*. Here on earth we remain imperfect.

In God's presence, no imperfection of any sort can plead an excuse. And in this perspective, basic in Luther's mind, a half-way obedience is already a formal disobedience. Seen against the background of God's absolute sanctity, there can be no talk of greater or smaller sins.

Therefore, God cannot but condemn us a sinners. At the same time, however, He deigns out of sheer mercy to cover with the merits of Christ this sin of ours, so deep-set in our nature. That is why we are simultaneously sinners and just men. We shall not understand this basic Protestant paradox unless we take into account that Luther, and after him the Reformation as a whole, was the offspring and heir of Nominalism. Nominalism drove a wedge into reality and wrenched it asunder by distinguishing in it two orders of reality: the absolute order of God's freedom and the order of God's providence chosen once and for all.

Similarly, the Reformation, Lutheranism especially, will draw, within our human activity, a distinction between the Kingdom of God and the Kingdom of men, that is the State. And further, in our opinion, the distinction drawn between the sphere of our interior sanctification and the overall extent of our justification suffers largely from the same defect.

Whatever Luther may have preserved of the divine indwelling—which he knew of from mystical tradition—comes undoubtedly to the fore mainly when he speaks of the order of our sanctification, namely, in what he sometimes means to express by the term "*coram hominibus,*" i.e. in our earthly existence. Within this sphere, the sphere of the Church, we may arrive at a certain degree of Christian perfection. However, "*coram Deo,*" in the sight of God, Luther sees the divine indwelling as being nothing more than God's love which, in sheer mercy, acquits us because of Christ's merits, in the sense that, without justifying us interiorly, God considers us already on earth as just men, exclusively for Christ's sake. Luther rediscovered the personal relations between God and man, those relations which the barren scholastic speculations of his time had lost sight of; but he included them into a leaky synthesis that is no longer so sound or orthodox.

Trent's answer

If the Church intended to take into account this "reformed adjustment," she had to show how all human relations with God, without exception, can be reduced to *one living contact,* the contact we have in the indwelling of the Blessed Trinity.

It was the tragedy of the times that such an attempt could not be made then because the theology of those days was powerless to elaborate a truly satisfying answer. Several centuries later, Cardinal Newman would guess the ecumenical significance of an adequate answer when he wrote the Catholic foreword to the new edition of his formerly Anglican *Lectures on Justification;* but by that time it was too late. Christendom lay riven apart for ages.

What was the answer offered by the Church of the sixteenth century. That answer came through the Council of Trent. The popes of the Middle Ages had already given their approval to the development of theological thought concerning "created grace," especially in connection with the baptism of children. The Council of Vienne (France) in 1312 declared that "the teaching which says that in baptism of both children and adults, informing grace and virtues are given, is more probable and in better harmony and agreement with what the saints and the modern doctors of theology have said" (Denz. 483). When we spoke of Ockham, we pointed out that this doctrine was commonly accepted in the Church toward the end of the Middle Ages.

The Council of Trent thus had to answer the objections of the Reformers who rejected this ecclesiastical teaching. That answer, of course, was not easy to give. To begin with, most theologians and bishops present at the Council had been trained along nominalistic lines and were possessed of no better theology than that which Luther had received in his early religious formation. Further, as all the preceding councils had done, Trent intended to hold to the principle of not settling questions freely debated among Catholics. Trent quite intentionally confined itself to condemning Luther's positions insofar as these had drifted away from the Church's general teaching.

The clearest formulation of the doctrine of grace is to be found in the following text taken from Chapter 7 of the *Decree on Justification:* "Finally, the one formal cause [of our justification] is the justice of God, not the one by which He Himself is just, but the one with which He makes us just [this is a quotation from St. Augustine]. And this means that by this gift of His we are renewed in our spirit, and that we are not merely reputed to be so [that is, justice is not merely imputed to us], but that we are really called just and indeed are just, by the fact that each one of us receives his own justice in the measure the Holy Ghost destines to each one (I Cor 12:11) and according to each one's disposition and cooperation" (Denz. 799).

All that Trent could do was reaffirm the general truth in Holy Writ which had been specially and rather precisely formulated in the Western Church in the doctrine of created grace—that through created grace we have become truly just and holy. Trent, however, did not want to use the term *created grace,* and satisfied itself with less technical phrasing which kept closer to Scripture and steered clear of the controversies within the Church. Thus, the Council said that justice " inheres in us, " *nobis inhaeret.*

The significance of the question concerning the relation between created and uncreated grace seems not to have been noticed by Trent. The theology of those days could not tackle the problem. And in that sense it may be said that Trent did not provide a complete answer to the deeper religious objections raised by the Reformation. In fairness, though, it should be admitted that Trent did say something on the subject. Several Lutherans have acknowledged to us that in the last conciliar chapter, dealing with merit, suggestions were made but not fully worked out. That section, which happens to be the most religious one in the *Decree on Justification,* is Chapter 16: " The Fruits of Justification, That Is, the Merit of Good Works and the Nature of That Merit. " It is worth noticing that Trent did not take an easy way out of the problem; it looked at it from all angles in a sort of dialectical movement, starting from God and returning to God. We shall explain this dialectic movement in our chapter on merit. For the moment, let it be enough for us to see how closely the idea of merit is allied with that of the indwelling, or at least with the biblical insight into our living unity with Christ. Here is the text of the Council of Trent:

" Therefore, to men justified in this manner, whether they have preserved uninterruptedly the grace received or have recovered it when lost, the words of the Apostle have to be pointed out: ' Abound in every good work, knowing that your labor is not in vain in the Lord ' (I Cor 15:58); ' for God is not unjust that He should forget your work and the love which you have shown in His name ' (Heb 6:10); and ' do not lose your confidence, which has a great reward ' (Heb 10:35). And so to those who work well to the end (Mt 10:22) and trust in God, *eternal life is to be offered, both as a grace mercifully promised to the sons of God through Christ Jesus* and as a reward promised by God Himself, to be faithfully given to their good works and merits. For this is the ' crown of justice ' which the Apostle declared was laid up for him after his fight and course to be rendered by the just judge, and not only to him but also to all who love His coming (II Tim 4:7-8). *For since Christ Jesus Himself, as the head of His members* (Eph 4:15) *and as the vine of which we are the branches* (Jn 15:5), *continuously infuses strength into those justified, a strength which always precedes, accompanies and follows their good works and without*

*which they could not in any way be pleasing and meritorious
before God,* we must believe that nothing further is wanting to
those justified to prevent them from being considered, by those
very works which have been done in God, to have fully satisfied
the divine law according to the state of this life and to have truly
merited eternal life.   And this eternal life is to be obtained in
[its] due time, provided they die in grace; for Christ our Savior
says, ' If anyone shall drink of the water that I will give him, he
shall not thirst forever; but it shall become in him a fountain
of water springing up into life everlasting ' (Jn 4:14).   Thus,
neither is our justice established as our own from ourselves, nor is
the justice of God ignored or repudiated; for the justice which we
call ours because we are justified by its inhering in us, *that same
justice is from God, because it is infused into us by God through
the merits of Christ.*

" Nor should this be omitted, that Christ promises the person
who even gives a drink of cold water to one of His least ones
that he shall not be without reward (Mt 10:42), and the Apostle
says that our present light affliction, which is for the moment,
prepares for us an eternal weight of glory that is beyond all
measure (II Cor 4:17).   Although in Holy Scripture much high
value is placed on good works, nevertheless, *no Christian should
either trust or glory in himself and not in the Lord* (I Cor 1:31;
II Cor 10:17), Whose goodness toward all men is such that He
want His gifts to be their merits.

" And since we all offend in many things (Jas 3:2), each one
should have before his eyes not only God's mercy and goodness
but also His justice and severity.   Neither should anyone pass
judgment on his own life, even if he is conscious of no wrong;
for the whole of man's life is to be examined and judged not by
the judgment of men but of God, He ' who will bring to light
the hidden things of darkness, and will make manifest the
counsels of hearts; and then every man shall have his praise
from God ' (I Cor 4:5) Who, as it is written, will render to
everyone according to his works (Rom 2:6; Ps 62:13). [Denz.
809-810]

We have printed in italics the conciliar statements which
affirm that our good works can be of value in the eyes of God
only insofar as they have been done in loving union with Christ.
And that is a point which the Post-Tridentine theologians ought
to have worked out.   This view of our living union with Christ
met the Reformers' Christological preoccupations; and, in our
opinion, it brought together in a higher synthesis whatever lay
piece-meal in Luther's teaching.   It is a tragedy that this was
not done.   For, after Trent, Catholic theology continued to shut
itself into an ever more rigid and defensive position.   During
the following three or four centuries, theologians satisfied them-

selves mainly with substantiating the existence of created grace. By and large, they failed to give serious thought to what is in fact the ultimate root of man's interior sanctification: the living indwelling of the Blessed Trinity. And so created grace was understood by the ordinary faithful to be a thing by itself. Only one connection with God was still kept in mind, namely, that it is a gift from God, and is therefore something created. At this juncture, there remained but one more step to be taken, a step, alas, all too often ventured upon in sermons and popular writings: grace, when conferred on man, became his own possession, so to say, a sort of capital that could be stored up and made to yield abundant returns for heaven. Whenever such notions take root in the mind, the doctrine of grace turns into a caricature of what Holy Scripture and the grand tradition of the Church have always taught.

Decadence and reaction

Theologians, steering clear of the Reformers' objections, attached to the sacramental character a meaning it never had. What they took away from grace—likeness and union with Christ—they henceforth attributed to the character. Unfortunately, here as elsewhere, the serious danger arose of conceiving this likeness as a static entity. Spirituality sought for a solution in a more personal love for Christ. But loose from its theological moorings, loose from a solid theology of grace, such a spirituality was threatened with various forms of sentimentalism that really had nothing in common with genuine piety. Sacramental teaching came perilously close to magic—the belief that, by uttering certain formulas, one can automatically procure a determined quantity of divine power. Instead of answering the objections raised by the Reformers, this theology prepared for our " separated brethren " still further grounds for scandal. Happily, the life of faith lived personally by many Catholics was of a better quality than the doctrine served out to them either in religious instructions or from the pulpit.

Many factors ministered to the hardening of this theological position. In the first place, historically, the bitter wars of religion arose in large areas of Europe; one of their results was that human contacts between Protestants and Catholics became practically impossible. In the second place, one form of Catholic theology still paid attention to the Reformation, and that was controversial theology; but controversy has always proved to be a barren variety of theological thinking. In the line of pastoral theology too, the one concern was for self-defense. Further still, when there followed in the wake of the Reformation the *Auf-klärung*, then rationalism, the French Revolution and liberalism, and much later Marxism, the Roman Church seemed to build itself into a religious fortress whose defensive walls rose higher and higher. It is not typical of such a religious attitude that Cardinal Ottaviani gathered together his various addresses and articles about the Church of our days under the significant title *Il Baluardo*, the bulwark, and thus a ghetto, closed up in itself?

The theology of grace had to bear the consequences of all this. The doctrine of grace, as set forth in classroms and textbooks, was reduced to an uninviting short chapter on what had come to be called "sanctifying grace" and long chapters dealing with the endless disputes on the subject of "actual grace." The divine indwelling, no longer the indwelling of the Blessed Trinity, was lost sight of as the living ground and source of created grace. Instead, it was turned into an immediate consequence, a necessary fruit of infused grace—an extremely impoverished understanding, indeed, of what Scripture teaches.

The mind asks itself in amazement how such a theological position came about. Two causes can be singled out. To begin with, one of the principles belonging to the treatise on the Trinity was being wrongly applied. It was held that the Godhead in its unity of nature was alone involved in the creative act, and not the three divine persons in their distinctive properties. It seems to me that this principle deserves to be applied with more nuance than is usually the case in our present-day manuals of theology. St. Thomas was certainly aware of this, though we cannot enter into that question right now. Where grace was concerned, the way of reasoning used to be quite plain: if grace is to be conceived as something exclusively *created*, it comes to us from God in His unity of nature, whence it follows that it unites us to the Godhead and not to the Trinity.

The indwelling can at best be "attributed" to the Holy Spirit, and this in an improper way. It is no more than a symbolical manner of speaking in connection with the idea of Scripture. Here we see an instance of what happens when theological thought fails to listen to God's word in Holy Writ.

A second cause for the decline of the treatise on grace has been a too-wooden interpretation of the first text we quoted from the Tridentine decree. The text says that the infused justice, which is in us and "inheres in us," is also the "one formal cause" of our justification. That being so, theologians thought, it follows that the Catholic doctrine of grace must be based exclusively on "created grace." Such a faulty interpretation is, of course, foreign to the mind of the Fathers of Trent and consequently devoid of all value: it has no authority to bind us in faith.

In short, many theologians were persuaded that the more the Protestants attacked created grace, the more they themselves had to fix their attention on created grace. Let us say in passing, however, that a small minority among the theologians kept protesting through the centuries against the latter assumption. These were never very numerous, but their contribution was of a high quality. They deliberately based themselves on the teaching of Scripture or on the doctrine of the ancient Fathers and the mystical tradition of the Middle Ages. We may point out Leonard Lessius and Cornelius a Lapide. Lessius was deeply influenced by Ruysbroeck, whom he sought to defend against detractors; and A Lapide was an outstanding Scripture scholar. During the seventeenth century, we meet two great patrologists, Denys Petau and Christian Thomasius. During the nineteenth century, we have the theologian M. J. Scheeben and the patrologist Théodore de Régnon. At the turn of this century, G. J. Waffelaert, Bishop of Bruges (Belgium), rediscovered Ruysbroeck, and by his writings initiated a renewal of mystical theology in the Netherlands. These theologians were few and far between, and were as a rule considered unsafe by the professionals of their day. As it happened, their authority and their evidence prevented the doctrine of grace from straying into a blind alley.

Finally, Father Maurice de la Taille and after him Father Karl Rahner contributed a wider view of the technical theological explanation which St. Thomas had provided in his time, adding to its persuasive force. Conditions in theology were such that theologians could still be convinced by scholastic proofs, which explains why De la Taille and Rahner stood a better chance of succeeding than their predecessors had. Within a very short time, De la Taille's key solution made its mark in Europe, and it was soon after still better received in English-speaking countries, especially in America, where a theology thought out in scholastic concepts is still preferred. Many theologians in Europe, while appreciating De la Taille's theory in spite of its limitations, felt that his basic intuition could be improved upon by being expressed in personalistic categories of thought. Two world wars, a completely new start in biblical studies and in the teaching of the Fathers and the mystics, modern philosophy and ecumenism have set theologians free from too cramping an association with scholasticism.

Whatever the method employed, the battle is won. We are at long last fit to face resolutely the problem which every theologian prior to the Council of Trent was confronted with —to answer the extreme paradox set down by Lombard. However, it is no longer Lombard who compels us to reflect on the

problem; it is Scripture itself, together with the teaching of the
early Fathers and theologians, the glorious mystical tradition
of the Middle Ages and, last but not least, direct dialogues with
our "separated brethren" of both the Reform and the Eastern
Churches.

The question before us is: What exactly is the relationship
between uncreated grace, that is, God Himself or the Blessed
Trinity, and our created grace? We can now give an answer.

The lesson of history

In the historical survey we gave above, we purposely stayed
away from technical theological discussions that suppose some
familiarity with the hypotheses of scholastic theology. At the
same time we did not attempt to introduce nuances that could
have delineated more sharply the main outlines of the theological
evolution. That long and often sad history—does it not concern
the glory of the Gospel message?—is more complex than could
be shown in the short space of a few lines. We hope that our
brief survey has not been too obscure for the uninitiated or too
elementary for those conversant with the subject matter.

Priests and laity should know enough of the history of theological thought to appreciate the motives underlying contemporary
reactions. The gratitude many of them expressed after reading
the first edition of this work indicates that the time has come
to write a new treatise on grace for the use of the laity. We
may therefore dispense with all manner and forms of concepts
which view created grace in terms of abstract geometry.

History bears out the contention that the notion of created
grace is not entitled to the central place which it has usurped
in the treatise of grace. Prior to the eleventh century, generations
of orthodox theologians thought and wrote without ever so
much as mentioning created grace. We do not insinuate that
recent developments in the consciousness of the Church have to
be repudiated. The course of history is irreversible. Further-
more, this development has been approved in some of its salient
results by popes and councils, albeit discreetly. Undeniably,
"created grace" has meaning, though it is *not* an independent
entity, *and still less* something that becomes our possession,
that we can dispose of at will or glory in before God as the fruit
of our own strength and endeavor. Created grace, seen in its
inner nature, belongs to a *higher unity*. It is to be thought of
only *within* and *not next to* or *apart from* the mystery of the
trinitarian indwelling in us. This demands some explanation.

The grace of the encounter

Let us begin with an illustration.   When a seal is stamped
on soft sealing wax, this sticky mass receives the impression
of whatever is marked on the metal stamp, like arms or a
motto.   In that operation, activity proceeds from the pressure
exercised by the seal on the wax.   The seal itself, however,
remains unaltered.   The wax is alone formed in the image of the
seal.

Our comparison has one disadvantage.   Sealing wax is totally
passive.   But man is not.   Under the divine influx, man not
only remains completely free but is granted a new and higher
freedom.   And this being so, it would be wise to avoid, as much
as possible, using illustrations from the material order.   Our
inborn tendency to depersonalize grace, and whatever belongs
to the order of grace, is already strong enough.   If grace is love,
it is freedom as well; it is given to free men in order to intensify
their freedom still more.   Our perspective is wrong if we do not
keep this in sight.

But let us hark back to the parable of the young man in
love with a straying girl.   Until the young man met her, the
girl remained lonely, destitute and embittered.   He did not
start by changing her within in order to meet her afterwards.
This supposition would make no sense.   But then, why say so
when speaking of God's dealings with man?   Has He first to
create grace in us and then, as the fruit of grace, to come and
dwell in us?

It was only *while the encounter was in progress* that the
girl really began to be transformed inside.   Of this transformation
their being together was but the sign and the preparation.   Their
bodily presence continued to play an active role later.   Men
cannot draw close to each other in love without a minimum
of visible, tangible contact.   The young man's love expressed
itself spontaneously in his attitude, in his gestures and gifts.
He tried regularly to meet the girl.   In a previous section we
showed that God respects this law of our nature which He has
created.   The Blessed Trinity came in search of us in Christ, the
visibility of the Father in the Holy Spirit.   The divine presence
stays with us in the Church, the Body of Christ.

Togetherness, visible proximity, becomes perspicuous and
meaningful when it occurs in love.   The young man surrendered
himself and all he had.   He began to speak of himself, of his own
life, his home, his joys and worries, his dreams and ideals; he
spoke of what he discovered in her, of what they could achieve
together.   He gave her whatever he bore in himself—his inner
peace, his rich interior life and his happiness.   The small presents
he left her had value only because they came from him and

reminded her of him; they were something of him, or they were something they had admired together, something he prized himself. A woman can be bought with money and costly presents, but her heart is to be won with delicate attentions and with beauty, with what one sets great store by.

Just *because* the young man gave her whatever he had, beginning with what was highest and dearest to him, the girl began to change within. It was the gift of himself, his self-surrendering love, which cured her, raised her to his own level and introduced her into his world.

Are not these the two effects of grace, namely, that grace *heals* us, that it *elevates* us by *raising* us to intimacy with God? And this *because* grace grants us, already on earth, a share in the life of the Son facing the Father in the power of the Holy Spirit.

The one flaw in our parable lies in the fact that no man can boast of being powerful enough to add anything to the personal worth of another. Man is imperfect; he needs another as much as another needs him. But with God the case is different. His love is a creative love. No sooner is His love directed toward us, no sooner does it come down to us, than we are changed by it within. The moment God loves us, we are forthwith attracted to Him from within. We feel urged toward Him. His love wakens in us a hunger for His presense, a thirst for His life. *And that precisely is created grace.* It takes its rise, grows and lives thanks to His presence. As St. Augustine said. " *Quia amasti me, fecisti me amabilem,*" " Because You have loved me, You have made me lovable. "

Grace healing us

We can express this truth in a more abstract manner for the benefit of those who desire to reflect on their faith in a more rationally conscious way. To do so, we shall proceed along the lines of St. Thomas' fundamental intuition, as further elaborated recently by De la Taille and Rahner.

Basically, the mystery of grace rests on the fact that God *gives Himself* to us. He grants us an immediate share in His life. He comes down to us, or to speak more accurately, He takes us up into His inner glory. We remain men, creatures and sinners, but as men we are enabled to share in His life because *He gives Himself to us immediately,* that is, *without anything intervening between Him and us.*

This would be impossible, however, unless man was " adapted " to his new condition. For of ourselves we stand outside this new existence; we have no claim to such a life. We possess neither the strength nor even the aptitude to raise ourselves to such heights, to penetrate unaided into the divine glory.

The interior adaptation of our human nature, called in theological terms *dispositio ultima,* has two aspects: it heals our wounded nature, and it raises us to the level of the divine life.

God's holiness condemns sin; He cannot do otherwise. That is why His indwelling love has to *heal* our sinfulness, not just on the surface, nor merely by diminishing the number of our sinful deeds, nor by " not imputing " our sins, but by attacking sin at its roots, that is, pride and self-glorification. To that end, His indwelling love sows in us the seed of love.

The healing is an actual gift. We are no longer sinners; we have become in fact children of God. Nevertheless, the healing process remains the task of a lifetime. We are indeed just; and we have to become still more just till the day when we shall be fully so in heaven. God respects our nature. Man needs time to become himself, to grow and to ripen slowly. Hence the words of Trent, in the chapter on merit which was quoted earlier: " ... we must believe that nothing further is wanting to those justified to prevent them from being considered, by those very works which have been done in God, to have fully satisfied the divine law according to the state of this life. ... " Luther, in his radical outlook, failed to understand this great mercy of God. At the end of the same chapter, Trent added a last warning:" And since we all offend in many things (Jas 3:2), each one should have before his eyes not only God's mercy and goodness but also His justice and severity. " Sanctifying grace, infused in us by baptism as created grace, is the fundamental orientation of our person, the immersion of our will in the love which we have freely received thanks to the power of the indwelling Spirit, and to which we must give an ever more actualized expression throughout our lives. This is not possible without growth in sanctity. In a former section we characterized the healing aspect of created grace as a share in Christ's obedience. Through grace, we become obedient servants of God in the Servant.

Grace elevating us

The other aspect of grace is that the Father, through His indwelling love, introduces us into the very life of the divine Persons. We are chosen to stand before the Father with the Son in the strength of Their mutual Spirit. Through grace, therefore,

we become children of God in the Son.   In theological language
this is called the *elevating* aspect of grace, because of which
a truly *super*natural life arises in us.   A moment ago we mentioned that we were unable by our own effort to free ourselves
from the anathema of sin; now we have to say that it is absolutely unthinkable that we should raise ourselves by our unaided
effort to the level of the divine life, which is God's sovereign
possession.   Our elevation is an utterly gratuitous gift, the
totally unexpected surprise the message of grace holds in store
for us.

Before we are brought to God's sanctity, our human nature
needs to be " adapted ": it must be purified of all sin.   This
is not juridical fiction; it is rather the divine gift of forgiveness.
When God forgives, His pardon is an actual fact.   His pardon
means a deliverance.   " Adaptation " is still more radically required in order that we be fit to share in the divine life, which
is beyond our powers.   Sanctifying grace prepares us for the
supernatural participation, fits us for such a life.   " For the love
of God has been poured into our hearts through the Holy Spirit
who has been given us " (Rom 5:5).

At this moment we again recall the text and commentary
of Lombard which caused such headaches to so many of his
successors.   In our quality of sons in the Son, we are henceforth
really capable of loving His Father and our Father, His God
and our God, through the invincible power of the Spirit Who
has been given to us and Who dwells in us.   It is indeed *our*
love, our puny, wretched, human love, but love borne aloft from
within and perfected by the love of the Spirit.   For Trent said,
in the chapter we have just cited:

" His goodness towards men is so great that He accounts His
own gifts as their merits, "—yet another of the many texts of
St. Augustine adopted by the Council.   But we should add this:
God's love for men is so great that He recognizes in our love the
love of His Son, because that Love permeates our love through
and through, fulfills and animates it, and brings it back to
Himself.

It should be abundantly clear by now that created grace
may not be conceived of apart from the divine indwelling.
We have endeavored to show this from history.   The nature
of grace itself must bear it out and convince us.   Created grace
is not something standing *in between* God and us; it is no path
to approach God, no ladder to climb up to God, no *means* to
God—at least, not primarily.   But these are negative concepts;
unless we go beyond such representations of grace, we shall
make no progress in knowledge.   The Eastern Christians are
quite justified when they refuse to accept such descriptions of
grace.   They find it self-evident, to put it rather bluntly, that

creaturehood plus created grace cannot possibly bring about a divine life or constitute a share in the divine life.

Created grace does not act as a screen between God and us since it comes into being only because of and within the gesture by which God unites us immediately to Himself. He gives Himself without an intervening medium; He comes to dwell in us and takes us back to Himself. Emile Mersch called this grace *" un être d'union,"* " a unifying being." Created grace is at once the fruit and the bond of the indwelling, originating in the indwelling and sustained by the indwelling; it raises us into an ever-deepening actualization of the indwelling on earth and in heaven. Latin expresses it more tersely: *ex unione, in unione et ad unionem*—arising from our immediate union with God, granted in that union and urging us to that union. We need a dynamic concept, one that lives because it is enveloped in " the living life " which is none other than God Himself.

A personal relationship

To illustrate still better what we have in mind, we had an occasion to be present in the summer of 1961 at a recital in New York by the well-known singer Joan Sutherland. Thousands of people had flocked to the colossal Lewisohn Stadium. The Stadium is so enormous that nothing more could be seen of the singer than a lustrous green spot on an immense podium in the blaze of the high-powered lights. When people go to a recital, they want not only to hear the singing but to watch its interpretation as a whole—the delivery, the expression, the fire animating the singer. Fortunately, we had brought our opera glasses with us. And these enabled us to establish *personal contact* with the singer in spite of the distance. Why otherwise would we take the trouble of going to a concert when machines at our disposal could reproduce the sound better than it was at the actual performance?

To return to our subject matter, did it matter whether our opera glasses were made of gold or of plastic or of steel, in Japan or in Germany? The one thing of interest to us was Joan Sutherland; and that reason was enough to be glad that we had not forgotten the glasses. We wanted to see in her eyes, in her face, in her gestures whatever it was she intended to convey to us. Any piece of art is a message of beauty. That message comes into its own when it is presented by a living person. So we were grateful for the glasses because they gave us a living contact; they linked us with her.

Much of this is applicable to grace. It is of no great consequence to know how many kinds of grace there are, and what they could be called or how they could be defined and described. The main point is that grace enables us to live in *personal contact* with God. Created grace has no other *raison d'être*.

" Because You have loved me, You have made me lovable! " This suggests another thought, which the renowned apostle of reunion, the Abbé Couturier, was fond of introducing when the conversation happened to touch upon true Christian charity. It is often said that charity is a gift of self. But a subtle brand of pride may lie concealed in this definition. We are conscious that *we* have something to give. Does not the greatest love consist in *allowing others* to love us and to give us something of themselves? This thought gives us the key to the mystery of grace. And it is along those lines that we must recast the saying of St Augustine: " Because You have loved us, we are now able to love You. "

Increase and decrease of grace

In the light of the foregoing sections, we grasp clearly how senseless it would be to look upon grace as privately owned capital which we would like to see increase. It is foolish to stand, ruler in hand, on the alert to measure the grace we may have " merited. " The increase or decrease of grace is as much dependent on our surrender to God in grace as on any other factor. We cannot sufficiently emphasize the fact that grace is never automatically granted apart from our free surrender through faith and love. This idea allows us to unmask still another wrongheaded notion about grace.

Grace undoubtedly can increase, and we can, according to Trent, merit this increase. But that has nothing to do with quantity; it merely implies a qualitative intensification of grace. All theologians are in agreement on this point. Despite this, one comes across a trend in classical theology, especially marked during recent centuries, which we think has failed to free itself from the dangerous notion of automatism. As we see it, that notion is a perverted one. It could spread only in circles where the concept of " reified " grace has gained ground.

To speak of an increase or decrease in grace makes sense only when we place ourselves on the personal level of a living encounter between God and man. The Council of Trent defined, in conformity with Scripture, " that each one of us receives his own justice in the measure the Holy Ghost destines to each one

(I Cor 12:11) and according to each one's disposition and cooperation " (Denz. 799).

The "measure" of grace imparted to us is clearly said to be based on a twofold personal decision: on the one hand, God's free election in the Holy Spirit, when He grants grace as He pleases; and on the other hand, our cooperation with and through grace. Where God's decision is concerned, grace is imparted to His good pleasure. In baptism and confirmation, each one of us receives God's formal assurance that such is really His mind in our regard. And we know that God has promised to give us grace in abundance. God's fidelity endures forever. Now, if God has chosen His elect and intends to keep them, it can only be owing to a still greater abundance of grace. For it would be blasphemous to suspect that a special election would in any way turn to our disadvantage. God's love for us is always far in excess of our love in return.

Intensity of grace, however, is also determined by our cooperation. But let us not imagine that this cooperation is patterned even distantly on the model of partnership among humans. To think so would amount to heresy, a form of semi-Pelagianism condemned in the fifth century. It is not at all as if God is committing to our care a large sum of money to which we, on our side, have now contributed a personal share—be it only a token contribution—that comes from us exclusively as our own. If this were the case, we would owe our eternal beatitude to ourselves. For while acknowledging that God has granted us grace in abundance, we would yet hold that it is we who, by our puny contribution, cause the divine loan to yield dividends. Some may take exception to the way we present this view on the ground that it smacks of financial calculations. But we can think of no more apt way to illustrate the quantitative notion of grace.

In point of fact, what is the truth concerning our cooperation in this respect? The truth is that whatever we give to God has been received by us from God. We give because it has been received. The only thing that is and must remain exclusively our own, as compared to what is from God, is sin or the principle of sin: the sloth, the tepidity, the unwillingness to let the divine grace triumph in us.

We take it, then, that grace increases according to God's free election. We know too that this election will, in any eventuality, surpass the measure of our ability to correspond; we cannot keep pace with God's love. Yet grace increases or decreases "according to each one's disposition and cooperation." When we freely consent to God's invitations, when we freely allow ourselves to be borne aloft by His grace, cost what it may in terms of effort and struggle—and that, too, is God's gift—then grace lives in us more intensely. But when we drag our feet, or worse still when we harden our hearts against the divine calling, forthwith the strength of grace is reduced. It lies within our power to block the flow of grace. Where grace wins through, it is certainly because of our cooperation, but still more because of God's love. We can never " glory in ourselves, but in God only " (I Cor 1:29-31; Rom 3:27; 4:2; Eph 2:9; II Tim 1:9).

In the next chapter we shall come back to the mystery of the divine election. Meanwhile, we should like to observe that, starting from another standpoint, we have reached a conclusion identical with the conclusion of our earlier discussion of God's presence: grace is a life of love from, in and through the divine indwelling. That life opens like a flower—*increase* is an unfortunate term—whenever we allow ourselves, in live faith and charity and therefore in personal surrender, to be taken up into intimacy with God. That life slows down, is stunted, whenever we go our own way, rely on self and abandon God. In this connection Trent quoted another of St. Augustine's pithy sayings: " God abandons no one unless He be first abandoned by him " (Denz. 804). Once again, this shows that there can be no question of grace increasing automatically by means of certain practices. He who would hold such a belief exposes himself to the danger of superstition.

Election and freedom

A few moments ago we made mention of one of the most difficult problems in the domain of grace. Not many decades after the Council of Trent, that problem monopolized practically the whole of the treatise on grace. The Dominicans and the Jesuits and later the Augustinians, followed still later by the Redemptorists, elaborated subtle systems of thought and strove with might and main to bring Rome to condemn or at least disapprove of the opposing party. The theological dispute struck the popular mind so deeply at the time that a "victory" — meaning here a disapproving decree from Rome—was an occasion in some cities of the south for military parades, popular rejoicing and fireworks. Television did not exist in those days; if it had, it would have made capital out of the discussions and attracted as many spectators as an international football match does today.

In the end, several popes forbade the contending parties to condemn each other in the future. Among them was Paul V, who on September 5, 1607, said that each religious order within the Church was allowed to keep its traditional system (Denz. 1090). We shall go no farther into these learned speculations except to say that in the course of time the conflicting positions showed signs of drawing a little closer to each other. Since the last war, most European theological faculties and seminaries have consigned all these systems to the museum of theological antiquities. No great loss to the reader. One thing seems clear: the single fact that so many sincere and intelligent thinkers discussed a problem with so much refining skill and subtlety without advancing one step closer to the solution of the problem is ample proof that the method followed during the debate was in all probability not the right one. So much for the reliance we can place on human reason.

For our part, we shall not come forward with a new solution purporting to clear up all difficulties. But we shall endeavor to indicate *why* no completely satisfying answer can be given. There are times when a theologian is in duty bound to be silent.

We can do no better than to imitate the Church, which has been wisely discreet on this topic ever since the days of Augustine. One cannot but regret that this well-advised discretion has not been followed in the post-Tridentine period. Theological thought could have concentrated its energies more profitably on other problems, for instance, the pressing question regarding the relationship between uncreated and created grace. At any rate, the hopeless controversy is the reason the treatise on grace has remained one of the least satisfying parts of the whole of theology.

In the discussion below, we shall try to find out what is of faith in the two concepts, divine predestination and man's freedom under grace; and that will help us assess their religious bearing. In the next chapter, we shall try to confront these two truths with each other; and that will afford us an occasion to get to the bottom of the question, and to sense *why* we neither can nor may attempt to proceed any farther. Human reason left to itself must ever remain incapable of sounding the mystery of God's action.

God remains first

What is of faith on the subject of divine predestination or divine foreordaining? The mere enunciation of these words sends up a red warning flag. It is not safe to try to synthesize the problem in such terms. For in God there is neither a before nor an after; there is only the eternal, unchanging now. Unhappily for us, we are unable to think without the help of our categories of time and space. We have no option but to content ourselves with using deficient words. Scripture could do nothing else, nor can the Church. But let us be warned.

We prefer to use a terminology that is less bound up with the succession proper to time. We prefer to speak of *God's primacy in grace*. But what does it mean?

Paul gave us the true meaning of that expression in the chapters which he devoted to the election of Israel. Paul was a Jew, and as Jew he suffered grievously at the thought that his own people had fallen out of God's favor. He asked himself the question, "Has God rejected His people?" (Rom 11:1). And he replied, "God has not rejected the people which of old he chose for his own.... There remains today a remnant [the 'remnant' of which the prophets spoke] selected by the grace of God. But if it is by grace, then it does not rest on deeds done [in the observance of the Law]; otherwise, grace would cease to be grace" (Rom 11:2-6). The Apostle repeated these thoughts when announcing the main theme of the Epistle to the Romans:

" All alike [Jews and Gentiles] have sinned and have fallen off from the divine glory. And all are justified by God's free grace alone, through His redeeming act in the person of Christ Jesus.... He shows that He Himself is just and that He justifies any man who puts his faith in Jesus. What room then is left for human boasting? It has been shut out. In virtue of what? In virtue of the good works in keeping the Law. By our own strength? No, but in virtue of the law of faith. And our argument is that a man is justified by faith apart from the observance of the Law " [Rom 3:23-28].

At the close of our previous chapter, we referred to a whole series of Pauline texts taken from both the earlier and the later Epistles, in which the same theme is consistently repeated. For example:

" Brethren, think what sort of people you are, you called by God. Not many of you are learned by any human standard; not many are mighty; not many are highly born. To shame the wise, God has chosen what to the world is unwise; to shame what is strong, God has chosen what to the world is weak. God has chosen what is low and contemptible, things of no account, to bring to naught what is now in being, so that there be no room for human boasting in God's presence. It is thanks to Him [the Father] that you are in Christ Jesus; for God made Him to be our wisdom, our justification, our sanctification, our redemption; so that, as Scripture says [Jer 9:22-23]: ' If anyone boasts, let his boast be in the Lord. '

" As to what concerns my own person, brethren, when I brought the divine message to you, I did not come displaying fine words or learning [so highly prized among the Greeks, and not less among the Corinthians]. I had resolved to bring you no other knowledge than that of Jesus Christ, Christ nailed to the cross. I approached you with a distrust of myself, full of fear and trembling. My speech and preaching were not words of persuasive arguments of [Greek] wisdom; they carried conviction by the power of the Spirit; so that your faith might not be based on human wisdom, but upon the power of God " [I Cor 1:26-2:5].

Such had always been the firm preaching of the old prophets; and Paul never deviated from it. To the Ephesians he wrote from his prison, " You owe it to grace that you have been saved through faith; *not to yourselves, but to God's* gift; not to any action of yours, so that no man might boast. For we are His work, created in Christ Jesus to do good works, which God prepared beforehand, so that we might live in Him " (Eph 2:8-9). From these words it ought to be plain that Paul was not condemning good works; he condemned only those on which we *pride* ourselves as if we performed them *by our own strength*. Toward the close of his earthly career, the Apostle wrote a last letter to his beloved disciple Timothy: " Take your share of suffering in the cause of the Gospel, *through the strength that comes from God*. For it is He who has saved us and has called us to a life of holiness, not on the grounds of any work of ours, but because of His own purpose and His own grace " (II Tim 1:9).

On January 25, 531, Pope Boniface II wrote a letter to St. Caesarius, Archbishop of Arles in France, to approve the resolutions passed at the local Synod of Orange as expressions of the true faith; the letter also contains a number of quotations from Scripture: " We rejoice that you, venerable brother, together with some bishops from Gaul, have judged the faith along truly Catholic lines.   According to what you have written to me, you have unanimously defined that the faith, by which we believe in Christ, has been given to us by God's prevenient grace. To that you have added that *nothing can be good in the sight of God* unless man is enabled by God's grace to will this good, to begin this good and to accomplish it.   Our Savior has said, ' Apart from Me you can do nothing ' (Jn 15:16) " (Denz. 200b). This papal pronouncement is a fine expression of what we have called the primacy of God in grace.   God is necessarily the source and goal of the stream of life which grace is for us.

Wrong conceptions

But what exactly do we mean by God's primacy in grace? Our expression is founded on the basic truth of our faith that we are saved through grace and not through our own works, not through works which we can accomplish by our own strength. Not Paul nor any one of the apostles nor the Church has ever denied that we must bend all our strength to doing the will of God, even in the midst of persecution.   But that, too, is a grace, the fruit of God's election.

There is perhaps no truth over which we men of the West, and in fact all men, have been at more variance.   The conflict began in the fifth century.   A pious ascetic, Pelagius by name, a spiritual guide wielding considerable influence among the Roman aristocracy, began spreading a set of ideas which, after a long while, incurred condemnation by the Church.   Augustine led the fight against Pelagius.   It is indicative of the difficulty we have in realizing fully the fundamental Christian truth at stake that for many years the new ideas found support among the churches of both the East and the West.   Even popes wavered long before censuring the new teacher. For one thing, Pelagius' intentions were almost surely excellent. For another, the question raised by Pelagius had not been gone into very deeply, Augustine said; and the Church was then at grips with another, more blatant heresy, Manichaeanism. Manes was not a Christian, but his doctrine greatly influenced the thought of the period. According to Manichaeanism, the body was evil and sinful, and came from the evil one. Only what was spiritual came from God.

As we have mentioned, Pelagius was an ascetic. Against Manes, he defended the soundness of the human will. God is no respecter of persons: He gives an equal chance to all men. We have to decide what our life will be, and we have the power to do so. If we were unable to do so, God could not in fairness reproach us with our failure, because it would be no fault of ours. Pelagius was prepared to admit the existence of some sort of grace. But this grace did not mean much in the main, for it consisted chiefly in the example and teaching of Christ. He may possibly have admitted more; but after so many centuries, and in the absence of documents, we cannot very well ascertain what it may have been.

Human nature, said Pelagius, has not been corrupted by original sin; and original sin is nothing more than the bad example of our first parents. That being so, children are not harmed by it and have no need of baptism. On this point, however, Pelagius later changed his mind, and came to accept that children should be baptized in view of heaven; but he maintained that they had no share in our common guilt. Pelagius intended, above all, to affirm the goodness of creation against Manes' teachings. God alone, and not the devil, created everything; and His work is good. Human will has remained sound. Otherwise God could not take us to account. The Pelagian doctrine, given here somewhat sketchily, died out long ago, though even today we may still hear some of the arguments it used.

The teaching was condemned by the Council of Carthage in 418. That Council stood under the leadership of Augustine, the "doctor of grace," as the Church would call him in later years. But the condemnation did not put an end to its history. It happened that St. Augustine went too far in stating some of his views. With the years, he spoke of God's election in terms all too pessimistic. That was enough to start another reaction, known later by the name of semi-Pelagianism. But what was semi-Pelagianism?

Some pious monks from Sicily and southern France considered the later works of Augustine to be rather hard, and they came up with another doctrine. What they taught concerning grace was richer than what Pelagius had had to say. Grace, they admitted, had truly to heal the consequences of sin within us. But we, too, had to contribute a share, in two ways, mainly. We have to take the first step toward God, very much as the sick man has to call the doctor, as the good thief had to beg to be remembered, and as Zacchaeus had to climb up in a tree before he caught sight of Christ. Second, from the moment we have received grace, we have to persevere in grace. That is *our* responsibility. And so, both the start and the terminus of the spiritual life are determined by our personal cooperation. God sees to the rest, and in the eyes of those pious monks that was a great deal indeed. They made use of the same arguments as Pelagius: God is no respecter of persons; He therefore takes account of what we do on our side, for otherwise He would be unjust.

We are confident that the reader experiences no difficulty in understanding the thinking of the semi-Pelagians. It is plain talk for men of common sense. They will be cheered by the knowledge that Augustine and Thomas Aquinas, the two outstanding theologians of the West, held similar opinions for a short while in their youth. Yet semi-Pelagianism was condemned in 531 by Boniface II when he approved the decrees of the Council of Orange in the letter quoted above; later, it was condemned solemnly by the Council of Trent.

Why is this doctrine indefensible? For this reason: if Pelagianism and semi-Pelagianism are right, then grace is no longer grace. Sanctity would be due to us, to our own personal efforts, to our own good works and not to grace; we would have a right to it. A moment's reflection will show this. If we hold that God has to rely on our cooperation, it follows at once that in the last analysis we owe faith and heaven to ourselves, to our personal cooperation.

The basic error of such a conception is that it looks upon the collaboration between God and man as taking place on *the same level*, as some sort of equal partnership; God *and* man would face each other on a par, and both would jointly have their part to play. The truth is not so simple. We have to affirm absolutely that God's contribution is far, even infinitely, in excess of ours. As long as we attribute *anything*, be it ever so little, exclusively to ourselves, we imply that this minimum of cooperation is the ultimate reason that we are saved. Even while granting that without God we would be incapable of anything, we would nonetheless be claiming that *we* are responsible for the final outcome. And this would empty the Christian message of grace of its innermost meaning.

An illustration might be of some use here. Let us suppose a mighty oil trust, disposing of an army of technicians and immense resources in machinery and capital. Let us suppose also a farmer on a small holding which happens to have oil. The man knows nothing about oil, and of course does not have the money to exploit it. He is asked simply to set his signature at the bottom of a paper placed before him by the lawyer of the oil trust. All that is required of him is a mere scrawl; but that signature will decide whether or not the oil brings any profit to his household.

What is defective in our illustration can be set right by courageously conceiving grace as we did above; grace is a living actuality, so intimately linked with the divine indwelling that it springs from, accompanies and leads to it. With this in mind, we shall think of God and man as standing not next to each other but *within each other*. We are surrounded, enveloped by His love.

We recall a personal experience of ours which happened in August, 1953, at the small Benedictine priory of Chevetogne in the Belgian Ardennes. Several Protestants and Anglicans and some Russian Orthodox of Saint-Serge in Paris had come there to meet with Catholic theologians. The subject for debate that year was precisely the problem of grace. Evening was falling, marking the end of a busy day's discussion. Until that moment, only the Protestants and the Catholics had spoken. The Russians were plainly embarrassed. All our fine distinctions about grace were totally foreign to them. Someone inquired whether they had no contribution to make to the discussion. After a few moments of hesitation, Doctor J. Meyendorff stood up. He is an expert in Byzantine patrology, and is at present a professor at St. Vladimir in New York.

"Well," he managed to say, "our Church, too, had to face this problem sometime in the twelfth century. At that moment Byzantium was having a revival of ancient Greek culture which would eventually spill over into your Renaissance. That pagan influence entailed some danger of Pelagianism. But our Church's reaction to it was very simple. We were in possession of the rich liturgy of the Mass, which brings the living presence of the Blessed Trinity home to us. The Church did nothing more than remind the faithful of that heavenly life, begun by the reception of the sacraments. And that was quite enough."

There is much truth in Dr. Meyendorff's remarks. As long as we hold on to the genuine notion of grace, we shall meet with few problems arising from the Pelagianism still dormant in our culture. No sooner do we detach created grace from the living mystery of the divine indwelling than difficulties will crowd upon us thick and fast. For then we see grace no longer as a life *in* God but somehow as a life *before* God. And thus grace is misconstrued.

Freedom in grace

A serious question remains. It has plagued mankind ever since
the author of the Book of Job composed his meditations on the
sufferings in this world, ever since Paul wrote his Epistle to the
Romans and spoke of the election and infidelity of the Jewish
people. If what we have said so far is indeed the Christian
doctrine, where does our freedom come in?

At this point it is customary in theology to present arguments
purporting to explain the paradox. We shall not follow this
custom. It is not to the advantage of a fruitful theology to strike
a purely defensive attitude; the best apologetics will always
remain the exposition of what is positive in the Christian message of freedom, the freedom of the children of God; yet few
theological textbooks seem to say a word on the subject. He
who looks upon the Church as a bulwark and a ghetto finds this
message embarrassing. But to keep silent about it could be still
more dangerous. Silence leaves the door wide open to a Christian
variety of legalism, and we know Christ's mind on legalism.

Grace calls us to a new freedom, the true freedom. Scripture
leaves us in no doubt about it.

In the New Testament we come across a conception of freedom
which acknowledges the high esteem the Greco-Roman world
had for the freedom proper to its citizens. The free man alone
was reckoned to be fully human; not so the slave or the child
(Gal 4:1-7). It is strikingly noticeable that the idea of freedom
appears seldom in the Old Testament. But some of the New
Testament writers knew well the Greek conception of freedom
and wanted to apply it to what is true freedom: freedom from
sin. We were slaves of sin; now, however, we are all slaves
of God, and are therefore free from sin (Rom 6:6-23). We owe
this gift of freedom to baptism (Rom 6:6).

There is also a higher teaching about freedom in the New
Testament, connecting it with the freedom of the Son and
consequently of all those who share in his filiation. Matthew
reported one of Our Lord's sayings in which it seems to us
that Christ mainly intended to indicate discreetly His divine
sonship; but by the manner in which St. Matthew summed up the
sequence of events, all of us are included in the freedom Christ
spoke of:

" When they [Christ and the Apostles] arrived at Capharnaum,
the collectors of the temple tax came to Peter and asked: ' Does
your master not pay the temple-tax?' Peter answered: ' Yes,
he does.' When he went indoors, Jesus forestalled him with
the question: ' What do you think, Peter: from whom do earthly
monarchs levy tax or toll? From their sons or from aliens?'
' From aliens,' replied Peter. ' Well then,' answered Jesus,

' the sons go free. But in order not to hurt the feelings of those people, go and cast a line in the lake; take out the first fish you hook up, open its mouth and you will find there a silver coin. Take it and make payment to them *both for me and for yourself*" [Mt 17:24-27].

In the Gospel of St. John, we see how Christ gave a completely new connotation to the Jewish conception of freedom. And here, too, our new freedom is presented as linked with the freedom of the Son. Christ had just said, "You shall know the truth, and the truth will set you free." In John, truth is not abstract truth; it is the living word Christ preached, the message which He brought along with and in His Person. Truth is *par excellence* a concrete notion. And it is that doctrine which sets us free.

On hearing Christ's words, the Jews showed anger. "They replied: 'We are descendants of Abraham and have never been slaves to anyone. What do you mean by saying, You will be set free?' 'Indeed, indeed, I tell you,' said Jesus, 'he who commits sin is a slave.'" And now follows the idea of divine filiation: "The slave has no permanent home in the house, but the Son has his home forever in the house [of the Father]. If then the Son sets you free, you will *indeed* be free" (Jn 8:32-36).

To John such a freedom was an evident fact. It is established in us through the preaching of the Word of God, Who is truth and thus strength. It is brought to perfection in us by the Spirit. It confers upon us that Christian "frankness," the untranslatable Greek word *paresis,* meaning literally outspokenness, freedom in speech, self-assurance (see Eph 3:1-2; Heb 3:6, 4:16; I Jn 2:28, 3-21).

Paul, the champion of freedom

Paul is unsurpassed as the champion of Christian freedom. He defended it staunchly against the influence of some converts from Judaism who tried to impose the Pharisaic spirituality on the Christian community. Later as well, his self-assurance caused him many a hardship. It is possible to detect in the old manuscripts how the copyists tried to tone down some of Paul's more energetic expressions, very much as the *Osservatore Romano* censors papal speeches. "Prudent people" of this sort are to be found everywhere. They can speak of their religion only in pious, commonplace expressions, in "consecrated terms." Now, this sort of thing did not suit Paul's book at all.

Christians are not only free from sin (Rom 6:12-23), from the flesh (Rom 8:1-16) and therefore from eternal death (I Cor

15:12-34). They are *completely free from the Law.* " Sin shall no longer be your master, because you are no longer under the Law, but *under the grace of God*" (Rom 6:14). Exegetes have done their best to gloss over the Pauline affirmation. In their view, Paul had in mind only the ritual precepts of the Law abolished with the coming of Christian truth. But Paul meant all law, law understood even as the ethical expression of the natural law.

In chapter 7 of his Epistle to the Romans, where he described the impotence of the Law to save men, he explicitly cited the command, " Thou shalt not covet, " words taken from the ten commandments (Rom 7:7; Ex 20:17; Dt 5:21). According to one of our best Pauline scholars of today, Stanislas Lyonnet, the word *covet* never has a sexual connotation in the Septuagint Greek (that is, the classical translation of the Old Testament which Paul knew and used). Paul had in mind rather the nature of all sin: to want to be like God. Consequently, in citing that one commandment he summed up the whole law, as epitomized in the scene of paradise (Gen 2:17).

Paul, no less than John, was well aware that love for God finds its expression in obedience to God's will, in the observance of the commandments: " Does this mean that we are to sin because we are no longer under the law but under grace? By no means. You know quite well that if you put yourselves in the service of a master, you are slaves of the one you obey; and that is true whether you serve sin, with death as its result; or obedience, with justice as its result. . . . Now, freed from the commands of sin and servants of God, you reap your fruit, an increase of holiness with its final result, eternal life. For the wages of sin are death, while the gift of God is eternal life in Christ Jesus Our Lord " (Rom 6:15-23).

He explained himself more clearly still in another passage: " You yourselves are our letter of introduction, . . . a letter coming from Christ, given to us to deliver, written not with ink, but with the Spirit of the living God "—here another image flitted across his mind, one borrowed from the Old Testament—" one written not on stone tablets, *but in the hearts of living men.* Such is our confidence in God, through Christ. Not that we are, of ourselves, competent and could claim anything as our own. What competence we may have comes from God. It is He who has made us competent ministers of the new Covenant, a Covenant not of the letetr, but of the Spirit. The letter [the written law] brings death, but the Spirit gives life " (II Cor 3:2-6). This text, too indicates that the living, inner operation of the Spirit works out in us a deep trust, not in ourselves but in God. God's law has been written by the Spirit in our hearts, which means that from within it gives us the strength and the resolve to live up to

the will of God in freedom.   In our own language, we would say
to act on our conviction, a conviction which has been given to us
and yet is ours.

St. Thomas Aquinas, too, understood the scriptural text in
that sense.   We shall quote from him because many people
betray some misgiving whenever there is question of freedom
within the Church.   We are not out to defend any " revolution-
ary " views of our own; we stand for a great tradition in the
Church, the tradition of those who wanted to read Scripture and
who dared to think in its light.   The *Summa Theologiae* reads,
" By the word ' letter ' has to be understood any written law
imposed on man from the outside, even the moral precepts
contained in the Gospel " (I, II, q. 106, a. 2; see a. 1).

As we observed on a previous page, it would appear from
the metaphors he used that Paul had before his eyes the prophecies of Ezechiel and Jeremias when composing his Epistle.
Those two prophecies best describe the nature of grace as it was
understood in the Old Testament.

" Behold the days are coming, so says Yahweh, when I will
make a new Covenant with the house of Israel and with the
house of Juda; not the Covenant which I made with their
fathers in the days I took them by the hand to bring them
out of the land of Egypt. . . .   But this shall be the Covenant
which I will make with the house of Israel, says Yahweh: I will
give my law in their bowels, and I will write it in their hearts:
and I will be their God, and they shall be My people.   They
shall no longer need to tell their neighbor, nor brother his
brother: Learn to know Yahweh.   *For, all shall know Me,* from
the least of them to the greatest, says Yahweh: for I will forgive
their iniquity and I will remember their sin no more [Jer 31:31-
34].

Ezechiel, in his turn, mentioned the same divine words and
connected them with the messianic gift of the Spirit.   After
describing the sin of Israel which was punished with dispersal
during the exile, Yahweh promised His forgiveness, not because
of the merits of Israel but because of the sanctity of His name,
because of Himself, out of pure, gratuitous grace.

" Therefore, tell the house of Israel: Thus says the Lord Yahweh:
It is not for your sake that I will do this, house of Israel, but for
My holy name's sake [that is, God's person], which you have
profaned among the nations [the Gentiles] whither you went.
And I will sanctify my great name, which is profaned among the
nations; that the nations may know I am Yahweh, so says the
Lord Yahweh, when I shall be sanctified in you before their eyes.

I shall gather you [as a token of my grace] from among the nations [that is, from your exile] and I will bring you into your own land [the promised land]. And I will pour upon you clean water, and you shall be cleansed from all your filthiness and I will cleanse you from all your idols. *And I will give you a new heart* [for the Jews, the heart is the symbol of the deepest core of a person] and put a new spirit into you; I will take away the stony heart from your flesh and give you a heart of flesh [that is, a living heart]. And I will put My spirit in the midst of you [that is, in your innermost selves], and *cause you to walk in My commandments* and to keep My judgments and do them. And you shall dwell in the land which I gave to your fathers [image of the Church, the new people of God on earth]; and you shall be My people, and I shall be your God [the biblical expression to signify relationship between God and the people after the Covenant]. And so will I deliver you from all your impurities... [Ez 36:22-29; see 11:19-20].

St. John, who owed so much to the prophets, declared unhesitatingly: " You have received from the Holy One an unction [that is, according to present-day exegesis, God's word given by Christ in the Gospel], and *you know all things.* I write to you now not because you are ignorant of the truth, but just because you know it, and because from the truth no lie [no sin] can come. " A few verses further on, he continued: " As for you, the unction which you have received from Him abides in you, and you need no one to teach you; His unction [His teaching concretely presented as visibly revealed in Christ and as the power of His Spirit] teaches you everything; and that is true and no lie " (I Jn 2:20-27). Christ Himself, during His life on earth, testified to the sanctifying strength of the word: " It is written in the prophets: *And all shall be taught by God* [Jer 31:33; Is 54:13]. Everyone who has listened to the Father and has learnt comes to me. Not that anyone has seen the Father; he alone who is from the Father [that is, Christ only] has seen the Father. Indeed, I say to you: *he who believes possesses eternal life* " (Jn 6:45-46).

Christ's living word, His truth, then, is an interior light and an operative force in our hearts. The Father employs it to teach us. That word is constantly revivified in us by the divine Spirit: " He will teach you all things and will recall to your minds whatever I have told you " (Jn 14:25; II Cor 1:21-22; Eph 1:13-14). God's Spirit " will take away the stony heart... and give you a heart of flesh, " so that we can keep God's commandments. Our face is no longer hidden behind the " veil " of the Old Testament, through which we can hear the word of God and yet not understand it: " Until now, when Moses is read, a veil lies upon their minds.   But whenever anyone turns to the Lord, the veil is removed.   For now the Lord is the Spirit, and *wherever the Spirit of the Lord is, there is freedom*" (II Cor 3:15-17).

Freedom and love

Following in the footsteps of the prophets, neither John nor Paul denied that our holiness lies in our obedience to God's will. Obedience, however, is to be new and based on another law, the "law of Christ," which is His living word (Gal 6:2; I Cor 9:21), "the law of liberty" (Jas 2:12; I Pt 2:16; II Pt 2:19), " the law of the Spirit of life " (Rom 8:2).

In this light, we grasp the meaning of the charter of freedom which Paul addressed to his beloved Galatians.   They were simple people, ex-servicemen who, after hard years in the service of the Empire, had been transplanted from Gaul (whence their name) to Asia Minor.   During Paul's absence, they had been dangerously misled by the intrigues of Judaizing Christians who wanted to bring them over to the practice of circumcision and other Jewish observances.

" *Christ has set us free, to remain in freedom.*   Stand firm, therefore, and do not allow yourselves to be put again under the yoke of slavery [of the Law].   I, Paul, tell you: if you let yourselves be circumcised, Christ will be of no profit to you. Once again I declare: every man who lets himself be circumcised is under obligation to keep the entire Law.   If you seek to be justified by way of the Law, *you are severed from Christ, you are fallen away from grace.*   As for us, we hope to obtain justification *through the Spirit and through faith.*   If you are in union with Christ Jesus, neither circumcision nor the lack of it has any meaning.   What matters is faith, operative in love. . . .

" Brethren, *you have been called to freedom.*   Do not turn your freedom into license for your senses; but be servants to one another in love.   For the whole Law is summed up in one commandment: Thou shalt love thy neighbor as thyself. . . .

" This is what I mean: *if you are led by the Spirit,* you will not follow the desires of the senses.   For the desires of the senses go against those of the Spirit, and those of the Spirit go against those of the senses.   They are in conflict with each other, so that you do not do what you will to do.   But if *you are led by the Spirit,* you are not under the Law." [Gal 5:1-6, 13-14, 16-18]

Paul was to see his teaching concerning freedom put to a wrong use, especially by the Corinthians, his problem children. They fondly fancied that they had caught the Apostle's mind perfectly. They took for their motto, " To Christians all things are lawful. " To this Paul replied, " Everything is lawful; yes, but not everything is harmless. Everything is lawful; but not everything is for the good of the others. Let no one seek his own advantage, but rather that of the others " (I Cor 10:23-24).

Thus, the Christians are henceforth allowed to eat of all things, unlike the Jews who were bound by set prescriptions. Paul sees no objection to Christians eating of the meat that had been offered at pagan sacrifices and was now sold on the market by the servants of the temples: " For the earth, with all it contains, belongs to the Lord. " Should it happen, however, that by the eating of such meat they cause scandal to anyone, they have to abstain from doing so out of love for freedom. " Whether you eat or drink, or whatever you are doing [Paul holds fast to his principle to freedom!], do all for the honor of God. Give no offense to Jews, or Greeks, or to the Church of God. For my part, I always try to meet everyone half-way, regarding not my own good but the *good of the many,* so that they may be saved. *Follow my example as I follow Christ's* (I Cor 10:26, 31-33).

The one real danger that could beset such freedom is self-love, self-seeking. That is why freedom can be safe only where love is ruling, as in the case of Paul—or of Christ: " He who loves his neighbor observes all that the Law commands. For, all the commandments: Thou shalt not commit adultery, Thou shalt do no murder, Thou shalt not steal, Thou shalt not covet, and the rest, are summed up in this one saying: Thou shalt love thy neighbor as thyself. Love refrains from doing the neighbor any harm; that is why *the whole law is summed up in love* " (Rom 13:8-10).

With almost hysterical enthusiasm, the Corinthians flaunted the visible and miraculous gifts of the Spirit: the gifts of prophecy, of ecstatic utterances, of tongues or languages. In connection with these, too, the one rule was: the good of the community, the edification of the others (I Cor 14:1-19). And in the preceding chapter, Paul singled out the one gift which acts as a safeguard over all the other gifts of the Spirit, because it is the highest of them all—charity:

" You should aim at the higher gifts. And I shall show you the best way of all. I may speak in tongues of men or of angels; but if I am without charity, I am no better than a sounding gong, or a clashing cymbal I may have the gift of prophecy and know all hidden science: I may have such faith that I can move mountains [and no one has ever sung the glory of faith as Paul did]; but if I am without charity, I am nothing. I may give away all I possess to feed the poor [and according to the rabbis, this was a work by which one could gain extraordinary merit before God] and I may deliver up my body to be burned at the stake [even martyrdom, which should be the highest expression of charity]: but if I have no charity, it all goes for nothing.... Charity will never fail. The time will come when the powers of prophecy will stop, when speaking with tongues will come to an end, when knowledge will be useless. But charity will never fail.... Now three things persist, faith, hope and charity; but of these *charity is the greatest.*" [I Cor 12:31-13:3, 8, 13]

In charity alone does the message of freedom acquire its true significance. They both proceed from the same Spirit, and have been given to us by the Father in the truth, which is Christ, His living Word.

Freedom as conviction

Let us reflect on this for a moment. Though it is no new doctrine, it is rarely spoken of. Most people, perhaps, do not dare reflect on it. We have heard laymen say, " We are Catholics; our bishops and priests do the thinking for us! " And this reminds one of Goethe's whimsical lines: " All wise things have been thought of already; all one can do is try to think them once more. "

One point should be clear: God wants our hearts. No conformism, not even the most pious, can satisfy God's demand. Our hearts have been given to us in order that we may return them.

By the indwelling of the Father, we have become His children in the Son. God does not expect us to behave like strangers; He wants from us the affection of a child of the house. This affection is given us by the Holy Spirit. It is enough that we think along these lines to be constantly brought back to our basic understanding of what grace is: love.

Our status as children is our freedom as well, insofar as we act from conviction, from love. Love alone guarantees fully that this freedom will not lapse once more into the slavery of sin, *which masquerades as freedom.* It is plain from what we have seen on an earlier page, however, that as long as we live on earth, our freedom runs the risk of degenerating. But a risk never abolishes a right, or still less a duty. We are called to the liberty of children of God. This vocation of ours includes a divine demand. And that is the reason we may not keep silent on the subject of freedom. We have no right to do so. If we keep silent, we curtail and belittle the Gospel, Christ's message of salvation.

The law, the guardian leading to Christ

But then. what of the law? Did not God Himself give a law to the Jewish people? The Church, too, imposes on us divine and ecclesiastical laws in the name of Christ; and she reminds us that the laws of the land also oblige in conscience. That being the case, we Catholics land head over heels in a network of laws and precepts which seem to make serious inroads into our liberties, if they do not totally suppress them.

This objection may very well conceal a conception of freedom which has its roots not in the teaching of the Gospel but in the French Revolution and the age of liberalism. For too many people, " to be free " means " to do what we please, " and not " to become what we are. " Freedom is not to be conceived of as directionless energy that can be made to serve life in any conceivable way. We truly exercise freedom only when we do from conviction what we must do, because we are what we are. Freedom in the service of evil, and thus used contrary to our deepest nature, is a thorough degradation of freedom. Evildoing wounds and maims our freedom. We turn into slaves of sin; we become enslaved to self-will. Our freedom can blossom into a higher freedom by the practice of truth, and in no other way. Nonetheless, there is no escaping the impression that there is a multiplicity of laws which we as Catholics must take into account and conform to.

Of the old Law, Paul said that it " served the Jews as a tutor, bringing them to Christ to find their justification in faith " (Gal 3:24):

" This is what I mean: as long as the heir [the child of the house] is a minor, he is no better off than the servant though all the estate is his; he remains under guardians and trustees until the date is fixed by his father. And so it was with us, while we were still minors, like slaves subjected to the elements of this world [especially the stars which, to the Greeks, were the ruling influence over human lives; among the " elements of this world, " Paul ranked the Law of the Old Testament]. When the appointed time had come [as set by the Father], God sent His Son...to ransom those who were subjected to the Law, in order that we might become sons of adoption. To prove that you are sons, God has sent the Spirit of His Son in our hearts, crying: " Abba, Father. " [Gal 4:1-7]

Paul was obviously correct. Freedom, and more particularly Christian freedom, is not just a gift: it is a task. We must conquer freedom; or better, we must freely allow ourselves to be raised to a higher level of freedom. Like everything else belonging to human existence, our freedom has to mature, to become adult and grow in time. And this applies both to the individual man taken by himself and to human society or a nation.

As long as we are minors and remain immature, we need the external support of order and discipline. Moral immaturity may last a long time in some instances, despite progress on the technical, cultural or even intellectual level. And this, too, must be said of both individuals and society.

When all is said and done, the actuality of sin clings to us, preventing us from achieving a true adult age here on earth. Sin, together with its ensuing weaknesses, keeps us in the condition of minors; and in that state, we live with the permanent threat of being unable to put our freedom to unhampered use because of the allurements all around which lead us into temptations. As a result, none of us can really dispense with the external stimulus of a law acting on us as a " tutor " until Christ should come.

This reminds me of a conversation I had one day with a Latin American on the subject of freedom and of the obligation to hear Mass on Sundays. " That is all very well, " the young man remarked after some thoughtful moments, " but if for us there was no danger of committing mortal sin, we would not go to Mass. "

Supposing matters were really so, we are dealing here with an unmistakably immature Christianity, as weak as that of a seven-year-old child who is still unable to grasp the nature of Christian duties that are to be performed on the Lord's day.

It would be nonsense to expect a child to act from conviction, at least in matters more or less above its understanding. Shall we not recall in this connection the words of Paul: " That is why so many among you are feeble and sick " (I Cor 11:30)?

The Church's declaration that we are obliged under pain of sin to hear Mass on Sundays does not make much sense if we see it as no more that a penal law or a traffic regulation, the transgression of which incurs the penalty of a given fine. By her declaration, the Church reminds us of our blindness regarding the vital significance of the eucharistic celebration on Sunday, the Lord's day. To convinced Christians, such a declaration is superfluous—as superfluous as the law of the Easter duties. It is a great pity that the Church should have to enforce on us our highest obligation by means of severe precepts. It all goes to show how far we are estranged from what Christian life ought to be, and how immature we still are.

We cannot do without laws; and this is because of our sinfulness. Paul himself did not hesitate to issue laws and apply them severely. Nor does the Church hesitate; nor have the founders of religious orders hesitated to impose laws on their members. All, though, have been convinced that precepts are no more than aids toward a nobler aim: the freedom that is ours as children of God.

Now, if the law is no more than the "tutor, bringing [us] to Christ," it is plain that its intention is uniquely to train us in the practice of true freedom. Those in charge of educating children both at home and at school ought to keep this in mind. It should also be remembered in the education of the Christian people in the parish, church organizations, religious orders and diocesan societies gathered around the bishop.

Most people in authority dread looking at things in this light. To them it seems far simpler—and more efficient—to set up and maintain a convenient façade by means of impersonal discipline. Grace, the indwelling of God, of the Holy Spirit—those are very fine ideas, but not to be relied upon in actual conduct. Here we have another instance of how latent Pelagianism breaks out into the open. Human administrative efficiency wants to manage things by means of unverifiable "inspirations."

Better perhaps than any other man in our age, Pope John XXIII gave proof of the persuasive power of trust in God and His grace, and of trust in the good will of men. We may safely say that his manner of acting has been a challenge to our times. It would have been quite easy for him to exercise his authority while the first session of the Second Vatican Council was in progress; but he would have achieved much less if he had done so. We heard it said in Rome more than once: "This is nonsense"; "He is a positive danger to the Church." We are merely quoting.

The law is spiritual

But the law is more than a prop to human weakness; "it is holy, just and good" (Rom 7:13). "We know that the law is spiritual" (Rom 7:14). *Spiritual* in St. Paul's vocabulary always means "inspired by the Spirit." The law is always an expression of the divine will. That was God's purpose when He established authority in the world and above all in the Church. "Who hears you hears Me" (Lk 10:16). The apostles never hesitated to follow their mission, though they were conscious that it was a "service" and not the exercise of personal power. Our nature will always find it hard to come to know the will of God; it is the role of the Church to help us with motherly care, to enlighten and guide us in the discovery of the divine intention in our regard. And we believe that, in the exercise of her authority, the Church is led by the Holy Spirit. Authority, then, is truly "spiritual."

The question may be asked, does obedience, though a virtue, remain free? Or better perhaps, how does obedience make us free men? Let us first see what obedience does *not* stand for.

The law does not make free men of us when it is accepted *for its own sake.* We are not thinking now of an external conformity, for that is not true obedience. We are thinking of law considered as duty, and thus already more or less cut *away from its root,* which is the will of the living God. For the law would then contain its own perfection within itself; it would stand for definite human values in the cultural, social, national and even religious domains. To our minds, all these would somehow still appear related to God, but the emphasis would fall predominantly on the human performance, on fidelity to duty, on the sense of discipline, self-respect and solidarity with others.

These values should not be given primacy in our minds; otherwise a very dangerous process is bound to set in. First comes complacency in our own achievements; then we begin to compare what we have done with what others have failed to do. In no time we are esteeming ourselves as superior to the others, and then we look down upon them. From this consciousness are born the well-known categories among men, discernible already among children: we are the "good people," the others are the "wicked ones," the "evil ones."

What Paul described in such tragic terms in Romans 7 repeats itself all too often in the history of each man and of the Christian people. *Sin uses the law,* which may be able to tell us what to do but fails to give us the strength to do it, *in order to rule our lives again*—a very dangerous sin, indeed, in that it is next to impossible to unmask as sin, at least in the eyes of the people whom it affects. It is the sin of the "pious people."

In the end we assume a certain standing before God. We *pride* ourselves on our rights, on our "merits"; we hug our deeds to ourselves and trust that He, *on His side,* will take note of our achievements. "We are proud of ourselves, not proud of the Lord" (I Cor 1:31). Before we realize it, we have wandered into undiluted legalism.

May we not say that this is the reason "virtue" is so often repelling? We have frequently asked ourselves why it is that "exemplary people" in religious communities or parishes fall short of our expectations and in the end do so little, while "unpredictable" types achieve much more. Far be it from us to state this as law of the Medes and Persians; but that instinctive antagonism roused in us sounds an alarm: something is amiss.

The one word suitable here seems to be *smugness*. Matters worsen when legal obedience develops into the kind of fanatical sectarian pride which of old blossomed into Pharisaism. This is a violation of what ought to be an authentic religious attitude. Christ's severe condemnation of such " pious folk " should ring in our ears forever.

We might draw profit from a most practical illustration. We have witnessed in our days the debasement of the noblest word in the Christian vocabulary: in some countries, one may no longer use the word *charity* for fear of evoking bitterness, even contempt and hatred. And this is due to a failure to understand the real import of the Christian message. It is quite easy, alas, to be " charitable " *at the expense* of others as a " practice of virtue "—our virtue, of course. But the very instant it amounts to that, charity is dead.

We have seen, then, how a legalistic attitude toward life can turn us into slaves of presumption and pride, and thus empty us from within of our freedom in grace.

The law, guidance of the Spirit

There is still another aspect of the law which we may not overlook. The law, more especially the written law, can hardly do more than trace a general outline of conduct for us. A law is always abstract; it never covers the living reality. Herein precisely lies its weakness. It may be true that a superior is in a position to judge the personal attitude his subjects ought to adopt in a given situation; but he is not entitled to absolve them from their own responsibility before God.

There is, assuredly, the trite qualifying clause, " where the superior commands no sin "—a clause that never fails to be quoted, and rightly so, but without added commentary. There appears to be a supposition that in barbarian times a rare superior could be found who would thrust a gun into the hand of one of his subjects with the order to shoot an enemy. That may indeed have happened in earlier centuries, as for instance when St. Charles Borromeo, as Archbishop of Milan, visited an abbey somewhere in the Alps and was received with bullets from hot-blooded monks. It is not very likely, however, that superiors these days would be animated with anything reminiscent of Far West adventures. But there are other " sins " of a subtler kind which do not make for commendable obedience. Such are, for instance, dishonesty or forgery of documents, especially in countries where a lax morality has permitted even clerics and religious to hold that any sort of cheating of the government is legitimate as long as one is not caught. Women superiors have to be on their guard in this respect.

We have in mind much more than all this. *Neither the law nor a superior can absolve us from the personal responsibility we have before God.* We have to make God's will our own. The divine will is as actual and real as God Himself; and it includes obligations which no authority can possibly foresee.

We must do our best to preserve that openness, that attentive attitude, that inner *disponibilité,* as the French like to call it. God is a living God, addressing Himself to living men and not to automatons. We must always *look for this personal guidance of God in our lives, within the framework of the precepts of the Church.* That is the obedience which sets us free.

A consequence might be that we will need to contribute our strength to reforming the law or adapting it to modern times, each one according to his state and calling. Each one of us has to remain on the alert for God's voice speaking in his inner soul; each one has to show a genuine *parresia,* an undaunted Christian assurance, even when domineering and clerical-minded authorities do not favor it or indeed are dead set against it. It is a completely wrongheaded notion to say, as did a Roman prelate in the course of a press conference, that the laity and priests have nothing else to do during the Council than await the decisions of the bishops.

Unquestionably, it pertains to the bishops alone, in communion of faith with the pope, to decide authoritatively and in the last resort what reforms are to be made in the Church; and yet, the reforming of the Church is the concern of the Church as a whole.... No authority in the Church can deprive or relieve us of the responsibility we have to God. And this is what confers upon our obedience its high value of freedom and spiritedness.

The main intent of each one of us must be to discover the will of God in his life. This supposes at least an elementary acquaintance with what is called the *discernment of spirits.* The Holy Spirit speaks to us in our lives, in our hearts. And we have to learn to discern His voice. But who teaches such Christian wisdom to the laity or to the priests?

It has become commonplace to say that Ignatius Loyola was the protagonist of iron discipline. Even outside the Church, many have ready at hand the celebrated quotations, " *perinde ac cadaver* "—" as if he were a dead body "—and " like an old man's staff. " Nothing is surprising in this. Ignatius had been a military man; quite naturally, he has been consigned to the appropriate category of professions.

It is unlikely that soldiers were drilled during his lifetime as are our commandos today. And it would be a cheap anachronism to picture Ignatius as a Prussian sergeant-major or a British sergeant of the guard. However, as he wanted the practice of obedience to be the distinctive mark of his Society, it is worthwhile to see his real mind on the subject of this virtue.

In his *Constitutions*, he not only lent his legislation an exceptional suppleness by the added qualification "as far as is possible," but he linked his rules with the immediate guidance of God by frequently repeating the phrase, "according to the measure of the unction of the Holy Spirit." The ultimate rule of conduct he left to religious formed by years of prayer and study is the *discreta caritas,* a wise and prudent love for God. His *Spiritual Exercises* teach the retreatant how to listen to the voice of the Holy Spirit, how to tell inspirations from the moods and whims of the human heart. No one understands the nature of Ignatian spirituality unless he sees in it an alert openness of the mind vis-à-vis the inspirations of the Holy Spirit. It is useless to look in Ignatius' teaching for the "No arguing, please" of Frederick the Great. An obedience descending upon us vertically from on high is a caricature of Christian obedience.

Grace is thus freedom

Grace is love, and therefore freedom; only in this setting can we claim to possess an authentic Christian obedience. And of course, this makes matters much harder. It is far easier to leave to others the task of making decisions and then to seels a safe comfortable refuge in a life of rule-bound acquiescence. God is unsafe, dangerous and uncomfortable. He does not treat us as mental weaklings, but as free men in whom freedom is a reflection of His glory. Christianity stands for responsibility and daring, for courage to live and for freedom. It is no reformatory for straying teenagers.

As a conclusion to this first part: we have seen how grace endows us with freedom and how this freedom reaches its maturity in obedience. In the earlier centuries of the Church, this was so manifest to all that the word *libertas* was chosen to designate the freedom which grace bestows on us. Whenever natural freedom came under consideration, the words *liberum arbitrium* were used.

We end this section with Canon 25 of the Synod of Orange, which put a stop to the semi-Pelagian controversies; the felicitous phrases sum up all we have said about God's primacy in grace and about freedom: "To love God is an absolute gift of God. He Himself gave us the capacity to love Him; He Who is unloved loves us. When we were as yet displeasing to Him, we were loved, so that the possibility of pleasing Him might arise in us. For He poured out into our hearts the Spirit (Rom 5:5) of the Father and the Son, Whom we love with the Father and the Son ' (Denz. 198).

Election and freedom

The following discussion on how to combine the divine election and our personal freedom runs the risk of remaining on a purely academic level as long as these two truths have not been sharply delineated, as we have attempted to do above. Regarding their relationship, someone may ask whether we have an answer to the objection from reason: if it is God Who works out through grace whatever is good in us, how can we be free?

Faith has already provided us with the main answer. If grace is indeed love, then it means freedom. There is nothing so personal, so spontaneous, so free as love. Love is the soul of freedom. But we are able to grasp this only when we do not conceive of grace as a " thing " in us, some sort of directionless energy. Neither may we think of it apart from the divine indwelling. Grace originates from the indwelling, is bred in the indwelling and leads to a more complete indwelling. Grace signifies the personal relations of love.

A number of difficulties spring from the fact that when we think of God's moving power, we present it as an object, and speak of it in images borrowed from the material world.... When I give a push to a carriage, it *has* to budge. When I am given an injection, my fever *must* come down. When I switch on the light, darkness *cannot* remain. In the parable with which we began our study of grace, the girl stayed free because the young man had won her through love, and not through violence and chains.

St. Augustine endeavored one day to bring these truths home to the simple folk of Hippo. He was commenting upon the Johannine text, " No man can come to Me unless the Father, who has sent Me, draws him.... Everyone who has heard of the Father and has learnt, comes to Me " (Jn 6:44-45). It is one of Augustine's finest texts; we hear in it the saint, the theologian and the astute observer of the human heart. All priests read this passage every year in their breviary during the octave of Pentecost.

" Do not think that you are drawn against your will; the mind is drawn by love.... If it was right for the poet to say, Everyone is drawn by his own pleasure ' (Virgil, *Ec.* 2)—not necessity, therefore, but pleasure, not obligation but delight—how much more boldly ought we Christians to say that man is drawn to Christ when he delights in truth, delights in blessedness, delights in justice, delights in life everlasting, all of which is Christ? "

Suddenly, Augustine appealed to the experience of his audience: " Give me one who loves, and he understands what I say; give me one who longs, give me one who hungers, give me one who is traveling in this wilderness and thirsting and panting after the fountain of his eternal home; give me such a one, and he knows what I mean. " Farther on, feeling powerless to express himself adequately, he has recourse to homely illustrations well within the understanding of the people of Hippo: " Hold out a green branch to a sheep and you draw it. Nuts are shown to a boy and he is enticed; he is drawn by what he runs to, drawn by loving it, drawn without hurt to the body, drawn by the bonds of the heart. If then these things, earthly delights and pleasures, have the power to attract when shown to those who love them, since it is truly said, ' Everyone is drawn by his own pleasure, ' does not Christ, as revealed by the Father, attract us? " (*Joan. Evangel.* 26, 4; *PL* 35, 1608).

God reaches our heart

We have now to enter more deeply into this matter. And this will afford us the opportunity to throw light on still another aspect of grace and to correct a widespread misconception.

We are thinking here of the *supernatural* character of grace, about which much has been written these last twenty years and which has been the source of frequent misunderstandings. Augustine's text sets us on the right road. The value proper and peculiar to love is that it moves us to act from within the innermost core of our own person. It is *our* action, though it is at the same time God's gift.

When and how can it be said that violence is done to our freedom? Whenever coercion is brought to bear on us from outside, whenever something is forced upon us by physical might or, more subtly, by psychological pressure or moral constraint. Coercion injures the nobility of freedom because it violently assails the autonomy of the human conscience and person. In other words, the normal exercise of my autonomous human activity, befitting my human dignity, is trespassed upon. Normally, man acts from his own conviction and pursues his own object.

We do not deny the influence of the numerous determinisms

that weigh down our life; in the last resort, however, it is the responsible person who makes the decision. Violence, of any form, breaks into the natural course of my activity and, by applying force to my external behavior, attempts to cut off to some extent and to throw into reverse the source of my activity, my personal conscience.

Love never coerces. *Nor does God.* Man somehow makes exception here, insofar as we are all extraneous or foreign to each other. A man has no real power over the freedom of another man. He cannot reach it; he cannot get a grip on it. To win another man over to his views, he is compelled to employ external means. The discretion he uses according to the occasion may prevent him from interfering with the freedom of the other, and may make him attempt to persuade the other rather than coerce him. But he cannot succeed in persuading the other without a minimum of importunity. Ruysbroeck puts it very neatly: one man works upon another man from outside inwards, but God alone comes to us *from within outwards*.

We have already quoted a text from Ruysbroeck in which these words occur. In the same book, *The Spiritual Espousals,* he harks back to the same idea. As was customary in the Middle Ages, he built this book, considered to be his masterpiece, by way of the threefold commentary on the words of Matthew's Gospel: "Here is the bridegroom! Come out to meet him" (Mt 25:6). These words afford him the special advantage that he is led by the text itself to conceive of his whole theology of the spiritual life as an *encounter*—a basic theme in the theology of grace on which we have dwelt with emphasis. Towards the end of the second part of the book, Ruysbroeck comes back upon the words, "Come out to meet him." And this is to him a welcome occasion to remind the reader that the manner in which we encounter Jesus differs greatly from the way we encounter men. "You know quite well that any encounter is a meeting together of two persons who come from different places, who face each other and are separate from each other. Now, Christ comes from on high as a Lord and generous donor who can do all things. And we come from below as poor folk who of themselves can do nothing, but stand in need of everything. *Christ comes to us from within outwards,* and we come to Him from outside inwards (i.e. through the medium of our external deeds). That is how our encounter is a spiritual one" (Die Gheestlike Brulocht, o.c., p. 202; cf. Colledge's translation *The Spiritual Espousals*).

We have had several occasions to lay bare the root error in our manner of conceiving grace, which is that the imagination induces us to look upon God as upon someone standing on a level with us, like a partner. The experience which ministers to our thinking process has never disclosed to us any other form of "influence." We spontaneously see God's sanctifying action in the light of our human experience; in other words, we think of it in terms of the way one man acts toward another. Nor can we perhaps ever escape completely from this mode of thought. And that is why we should be mindful of this defect whenever we deal with grace. We should imitate the astronomer who knows the structural defects of his telescope and takes them into account in all his calculations.

Let us take another example, one that illustrates strikingly how hard it is for anyone to get out of himself in order to see the behavior of another as it really is. Very few people are able to watch the perplexing and often unpleasant reactions of a mentally weak person and judge them objectively without displaying at once impatience and vexation and without passing moral judgments which are perfectly pointless under the circumstances. A sick man, too, may have "selfish" reactions that have little in common with egotism properly speaking. We behave in a similar way in our dealings with beings of an order lower than ours. We instinctively attribute to the behavior of animals, and today even to electronic machines, a human content they cannot possibly possess. Now, just as we raise this lower world to ours, so quite unwittingly we lower the divine action to our level.

In order not to be misled, we must constantly correct our instinctive way of conceiving God's working in us. God is not standing *outside us,* as one like us; He is *within us.* In the words of St. Augustine, He is *intimior intimo meo,* far more interior to us than we are to ourselves. God is thus interior precisely because He is so totally different from us—because He is the "absolutely other," totally unlike us in being, sanctity and justice —and also because He is equally so totally beyond us. In philosophical language we could say that the absolute measure of His transcendence indicates to us the equally absolute measure of His immanence.

God, then, does not work in us from the outside, violently imposing Himself on us, binding and determining us to do what is good. As Creator, He stands at the wellspring of our existence, at the point where it flows uninterruptedly from His creative hand. He alone can reach our freedom right at its source and yet do it no violence. On the contrary, He renews it and endows it with true freedom. To understand this well, we should keep in mind that freedom is inseparably bound up with truth, or, as the saying goes today, with authenticity. We must freely become what in fact we are. God does that for us by His grace. Any other sort of freedom must necessarily be an enslavement to self.

Nature and supernature

We can elucidate this in yet another way, and it will afford an occasion for clarifying our understanding of the supernatural character of grace. An exact insight into grace is of decisive importance for us to build up an authentic Christian spirituality. We shall attempt to explain what is supernatural in grace by means of a threefold dialectical movement which takes into account all the various aspects of that living reality.

As a first step, we discover grace to be a *pure gift,* a complete surprise. The very revelation of grace acquaints us with this real element: " ... or grace would cease to be grace " (Rom 11:6). Grace is a pure gift because it is given to sinners, to men unworthy of it. And it is still more so because it lets us share in the inner life of the Blessed Trinity, which lies absolutely beyond our reach unless God lifts us up to it. In actual truth, we are already now standing in and with the Son as children before the Father through the power of the Holy Spirit.

No sooner have we said that much than we have to qualify our wording. Our imagination automatically associates the notion that grace is a totally new life with another idea—that if it is new, it is no longer a " human " life, but verges perhaps on the nonhuman. To some people, *super*-nature seems to convey the meaning of *un*natural. And this, too, is false.

However much we emphasize that grace remains the supreme surprise for our nature, we have to affirm with equal force that grace sets our deepest humanity free, precisely because it restores our most authentic humanity to us and by this means *humanizes* us to an eminent degree. This is the second step in our dialectical movement.

As Father Piet Schoonenberg puts it, by grace we *are what we are given to be.* " We could express it differently: what we receive from God, we do not exactly possess, but we are it. " [23] Properly speaking, we do not receive grace; we do not possess it as something foreign to us, or as something entering into us from outside; but *we are our grace.*

Many novels and plays have been written to try to disentangle the ambiguity latent in a gift. Everyone endowed with average discernment sees that of its nature a gift is a " symbol " of esteem, of love. It has a role peculiarly its own in maintaining personal relations between men. For all that, it does not escape the observant mind of some thinkers that a gift also has its shadows. It obtrudes itself on us; it imposes obligations on us; it is a threat to our freedom; it may even be humbling. Alms

[23] Piet Schoonenberg, *Het geloof van ons Doopsel* (" The Faith of our Baptism ") (4 Vols., 's Hertogenbosch: L. C. G. Malmberg, 1955-1962),

and a gift lie only a hair's breadth apart. And so some people might look upon grace as a threat to their autonomy, as a divine importunity.

Such a notion is not correct. What we receive, as a purely gratuitous gift, is at bottom our own self. We do not speak here of God's creative act but specifically of the divine activity of grace. Grace is " a new birth " (Jn 3:7), a " new creation " (II Cor 5:17; Gal 6:15). Ezechiel and Jeremias spoke of a " new heart " (Jer 31:33; Ez 11:19, 36:26). We know today that in Hebrew *heart* is used not so much as a symbol of love but rather as a symbol of the core of our personality. From grace there arises in us a new " I. " In God *we are* what we receive.

To unveil yet more of the rich treasures contained in this view, we can do no better than contemplate, with Father Schoonenberg, the mystery of the incarnation. We discover the highest exemplar of grace in the intimate union of Christ's humanity with the person of the Word. The grace which is ours is but a reflection of the ineffable grace which accrued to the Man Christ in the incarnation of the Son. We share in that grace in a limited and created degree; but further, the meaning of this supreme grace sheds light on the meaning of our own grace. To the Christ Man too, the union with the divine person Who took to Himself that humanity is a sheer, gratuitous grace, though in this concrete instance (that is, if we consider the living Christ Who is unthinkable apart from his union with the Word) we could perhaps risk speaking of a right of Christ's. As we can see here too, at every turn we discover that our notions are limited and unfit to express the ineffable without deforming it.

What was the effect produced in Christ by the singular union between the second person of the Blessed Trinity and the sacred humanity? This: that Christ was the most excellent of men. We often think of Him quite differently; we do not find it easy to think of Christ as a man. We are constantly tempted to surround Him with the phantomlike luster of the superman. The apocryphal writings, dating from the first centuries of the Christian era, succumbed to this temptation. They deal in fables. The high value of the true Gospels lies precisely in the fact that they do not do that.

Father Schoonenberg ventures upon a paradoxical sentence: " In Christ, His divinization was His humanization. " [24] Because of the intimate union between the Christ Man and the Godhead of the Word, the Man grew more intensely man and human. The reason for saying this is, once again, that God does not reach us from outside but from within, from inside the very ground

---

[24] *Ibid.*, p. 139.

of our existence, from inside the intensity care of our person, from inside our " heart "—and *because* He is the " totally other. "

*Super*natural does not at all mean *super*human, and still less *non*human—at least, not in the sense of suggesting that grace either destroys the human values or throws them into the background. On the contrary, they acquire a new significance and worth.

In the spirituality commonly met with in convents and religious writings, a distinction is drawn between the purely natural human values in our life and the " supernatural " ones. The natural values are treated as having little or no consequence unless they are sanctified by a special " good intention, " which has to be *superimposed* on them. The joy of watching a glorious sunset has no supernatural value unless I offer it up to God. A mother loves her children—but that is normal. A man goes to his office—but that is as it should be. If these activities and states are to have any value before God; more especially, if there is to be any " merit " in them in the sight of God, something must be added, namely, a " good intention. " A little more and these people would declare that nothing but the exceptional, the uncommon, counts for anything in God's eyes. Hence they embrace a constrained spirituality that is not met with in the life of Christ or in the lives of most saints.

Of course, this is a wrong notion of the supernatural, the spiritual. The Germans have a name for it: the doctrine of the two stories. On the ground floor are the service quarters, on the top the drawing rooms. God does not deign to appear on the ground floor; He dwells only in drawing rooms! The truth is that our divinization is also our humanization. We have been made children of God in a renovated humanity. God is pleased with our courtesy to others as much as with our prayers, with our enjoyment of nature as much as with our rejoicing in His glory, with our human friendships as much as with our faith, with our justice and loyalty as much as with our charity—so long as we act *with the heart of a child of God*. No special intention is required for the purpose. We shall come back to this aspect of grace in Part II of this book, where we deal with grace as a new and authentic form of humanism.

Undoubtedly—and here we come to the third step of our dialectical movement—sin, our deep-seated pride and selflove remain tragic realities in our lives. Therefore, the humanism given to us by grace has to be protected by grace against the self, the " lower self " which " sees the good I want to do, but fail to do " (Rom 7:19). While on earth, our Christian humanism can never achieve complete harmony or our powers

perfect integration. Our earthly home is the place of our
mortification, of our penance, of self-discipline, of asceticism
and spiritual combat. However, the human in us as such is not
the source of sin; nor is the body, for that matter. Spiritual
pride alone upsets the balance between our bodily and spiritual
endeavors and causes the body to turn into a temptation—as
happens, for instance, in sexual life.

This being granted, we do not object to the practice of
" good intentions "; but we are not in favor of the artificially
added " special intentions " where these do not rise spontaneously. We mentioned earlier that the noblest of Christian
virtues can be made into a caricature by such nonsense: we
" practice charity " at the expense of our neighbor, for God's
sake! The saints have not insisted on the necessity of " special
intentions "; they have stressed the need of *purifying* our intentions. This is a different thing altogether. As long as the
human in us, though reborn through grace, remains beset by
the danger of self-love, our fundamental orientation from within
is threatened with the risk of swerving away from God. That
is why we have to purify our intentions. To redress our sloth,
our *pesanteur humaine,* our human sluggishness, we must renew
our intentions as the occasion requires, and at the same time
refocus them on God. A child does not need to repeat constantly
that it loves its parents. Yet a child acts sensibly when it
renews its affection, so to say, in appropriate circumstances.
And this applies equally well in the spiritual life.

God loves us *as we are.* He calls us to Himself *wherever
we are.* He does not disavow His initial creative act by infusing
grace into us; rather the contrary. His purpose is not to turn
us into something quite different, something that would be neither
angel nor man. As the French put it, with good reason,
" *A vouloir jouer l'ange, plusieurs ont fini par jouer la bête* "—
" Many who have wanted to act like an angel have ended by
acting like a beast. "

A pernicious spirituality of this sort has wrought havoc in
many religious houses and has destroyed several vocations.
Above all, it has thrown discredit on Christianity itself and
has exposed both piety and virtue to odium. We all feel in
our bones that something is amiss in such an attitude, that
dangerous illusions have crept in. Unfortunately also, this
attitude has made it impossible to build up a sound spirituality
for the ordinary layman. It implies that a layman cannot
aspire to holiness unless he somehow renounces his normal
human joys and obligations, that he must borrow something
from the monastic life or else he will stay hopelessly caught
in the toils of mediocrity. But all this is nonsense. A mother
sanctifies herself by fully living up to her motherhood. A father

sanctifies himself by assuming his masculine responsibility both at home and in his work. Friendship, all too often frowned upon in religious houses and educational institutions, is no obstacle to sanctity unless it ceases to be friendship and becomes two-person egotism.

We see from our threefold dialectical investigation that grace is purely and gratuitously grace and at the same time the finest unfolding of ourselves, for the reason that God reaches us in the depth of ourselves. If abnegation and penance are necessary, it is not because we are not allowed to be men but because we are *sinful* men. Let the reader go over the text previously quoted from the Council of Trent on the subject of merit; he will see for himself that the Church has expounded the notion of merit along the lines of the same three aspects we have presented. Grace has nothing foreign about it. Sin alone is inhuman; that is why it is so monotonous.

What election is not

We hope that our considerations have brought home the idea that through grace God raises and refines our freedom and therefore humanizes it. All the difficulties, however, are not yet out of the way. Our faith speaks of grace; but it also speaks of election and predestination. The question now is: What becomes of our freedom in the context of that election and that predestination?

Our first answer will consist in proposing a purer understanding of this mystery, in ridding it of a variety of false notions.

Before the actual shooting of a film, the screenplay is written out in full and set down in a book called the script. Each individual scene is described: lighting, sound, camera angles, décor, costumes, location, interplay of actors, dialogues—in short, whatever has any importance for the shooting of the film. The script girl is entrusted with the specific task of seeing that the script is faithfully followed in all its details. Now, if we think of God as acting along analogous lines, we can imagine that for all eternity He has prepared the script of our human history. The angels would be the script girls, carefully watching that no detail marked in the book is passed over. And then, naturally, we ask ourselves, how can we be free if everything is "written in the book?" The passivity with which many Mohammedans undergo their lives of poverty, giving no thought to seeking any improvement, is to be ascribed to their belief that everything has been "written in the book" beforehand. Similar fatalistic sects have been known to exist in Christendom.

We warned the reader earlier against the defective manner of thinking hidden in such a representation of reality. In God, there neither a " before " nor an "|after "; there is simply an eternal " now. " Of course, we are unable to form an adequate idea of this divine condition. Do what we will, the category of time intrudes itself on our thought.

Sufficient and efficacious grace

Before going deeper into this matter, we should like to present in their correct form a couple of theological notions that came into general use toward the second half of the seventeenth century. During the Jansenist controversy, it became fashionable to distinguish between two kinds of grace; this distinction has eliminated a great deal of work for theologians. Most readers have probably heard of what are called sufficient grace and, still more celebrated, *gratia efficax*. One could translate the latter by " effectual grace, " " infallible grace " or " grace achieving its end. " But each one of these translations touches upon only one aspect of the original idea. Let us call it " efficacious grace, " as is customary. In case the reader has never come across these terms in the past, we advise him to skip what follows and to pass on immediately to the next part of the book. He will miss nothing that was not said before. Experience has shown that many of the laity and priests are vexed by these hapless notions, and this is the only reason we have decided to write something on the subject.

To understand how those notions came about, we should have an idea of what Jansenism taught. On hearing the word *Jansenism,* most people think of an austere moral teaching dissuading the faithful from frequent communion. Jansenism began as a theology of grace and of man. Man, it said, is radically vitiated by original sin, so much so that when he succeeds in avoiding one particular mortal sin, he inevitably falls into another mortal sin, be it only the sin of pride. Moral corruption reaches such depths in human nature that even the just are incapable of keeping some of the commandments, notwithstanding the help of grace. To perform a good action, man needs an " irresistible grace, " called after Augustinian terminology, *delectatio bona victrix,* an " overwhelming attraction to the good, " which necessarily overcomes our inborn inclination toward evil. Those who receive this grace are the elect of God; everyone else is rejected by God. Considering that God has no obligation whatever toward men, He may leave them in their sin if He pleases.

The Church has condemned the Jansenist doctrine, especially the three following propositions. (1) " Some of God's commandments are impossible for the just who wish and strive to keep them [considering the abilities they actually have]; the grace by which these commandments may become possible is also wanting. " (2) " In the state of fallen nature, no one can ever resist interior grace, " which means that grace, when given, is irresistible. (3) " To merit or to demerit [that is, to sin] in the state of fallen nature, it is enough to be free from external coercion but no [internal] necessity " (Denz. 1092-1094). Everyone realizes the fatalistic nature of such a doctrine of grace, which solves the problem of man's election in such gloomy terms.

The Church could not but condemn those propositions. They run counter to the data of faith. They were solemnly defined as heretical by Pope Innocent X, and this was confirmed by Pope Alexander VII (Denz. 1098). Let us observe that the pope concerns himself only with *factual* relations; for the faith is above all about *facts*. To put it differently, it is a *fact* that in the state of fallen nature, that is, the actual state in which we have our existence, God always gives *sufficient* grace to keep His commandments.

Besides this, theology has rightly taken into account the further fact that our freedom becomes true freedom only by growing and developing. Theologians correctly point out that sufficient graces do not deliver us at once from committing this or that sin, but supply at least the help we need to dispose ourselves gradually by prayer and mortification to genuine and complete obedience. All this is fully understood. God deals with us as we are. Freedom has been entrusted to us as a task. We must freely mature into a full freedom. Thus, the notion of *sufficient grace* acquires a more dynamic meaning, in accordance with experience and with the teaching of the saints.

The Church has defined nothing about actual grace, except that in no case may it be looked upon as "irresistible." Man always retains the possibility of rejecting grace; and this Jansenism denied.

The teaching of the Church is plain. Theology, however, " reified " that teaching to such an extent that for a long period it caused more headaches than comfort. What was the reason for this? As we have said repeatedly, grace had been cut away from the indwelling.

Interest in sanctifying grace was on the wane; " actual grace, " or " *gratia adjuvans* " (helping grace) was on the go. It soon became common practice to apply the teaching about sufficient and efficacious grace to actual grace. Inevitably, this led to a blind alley. For if one starts by looking upon sufficient grace as a thing all its own, an isolated entity, one logically concludes that whenever man fails to accept that grace, "sufficient grace" changes into a "purely sufficient grace." By sheer necessity, one lands in the paradox that what was "sufficient grace" proves to be in fact an "insufficient grace," considering that sin has been committed in spite of it. It is easy to understand why the Jansenists made fun of this grace and parodied the invocation in the litanies of all saints, "From all sufficient grace, deliver us, O Lord," an invocation which could not be tolerated. It was condemned by the Holy Office (now the Congregation for the Doctrine of the Faith) on December 7, 1960 (Denz. 1926).

The censure was correct, of course. But it is nevertheless possible to caricature "sufficient grace." What the Church has solemnly defined is that when we sin Almighty God cannot be blamed for it. We alone are at fault, since God's help is sufficient to avoid sin. The substance of this is that we should never speak of an isolated sufficient grace, but rather of grace being sufficient or adequate. We will then steer clear of wrong conceptions. In fact, that is all the faith tells: that God's grace is always sufficient—or better, superabundant.

The same misadventure befell "efficacious grace." No pope, no council has ever defined efficacious grace to be an article of faith. The term, however, contains a real meaning for the faith, and does not suggest the idea of an actual grace isolated and standing by itself, something which achieves its end by itself. Otherwise we adopt a position hardly different from the erroneous notion of the Jansenists, who accepted the existence of "irresistible grace." Dogmatically, in terms of faith, *efficacious grace* can mean only one thing: whenever a man performs a good action, acceptable in the eyes of God, he owes it in the last analysis to God. Here, too, we shall be well advised not to speak of efficacious grace as a thing apart, but rather to speak of *God's primacy in grace* manifesting itself in my good deed. And this brings us face to face once more with the problem we are discussing.

It is clear now that we can safely write a theology of grace without entering into the relatively recent theological speculations about the mechanism of a separate sufficient grace and a separate efficacious grace. We like to stress this point, for experience has shown us how confusing such notions can be.

In her declarations, the Church has never proceeded farther than what she settled in earlier times concerning the difficult problem of our election. We may illustrate this by turning to the controversy in the ninth century over the subject of divine election through grace. A local synod at Quierzy-sur-Oise, France, gave an answer in the year 853 which accurately sums up the fundamental, factual truths of our faith on the question. The answer is valuable mainly because it aptly brings together many former declarations of popes and councils: "We lost our free will in the first man; but Christ our Lord restored it to us. We possess a free will to do good insofar as grace goes before and helps it; and we possess a free will to do evil insofar as grace abandons it. The will we have is free because grace has freed it and has healed it from corruption." The next canon after this considers the same mystery in the wider perspective of God's salvific will, while correcting a few less felicitous expressions occurring in the preceding canon: "Almighty God wants all men without exception to be saved (1 Tm 2:4), though not all are actually saved. The fact that some are lost is to be blamed on them that are lost" (Denz. 317-318). Please notice that the synod deliberately stopped on the threshold of the mystery, and did not propose more than what we, in the course of these pages, have discovered in Holy Scripture.

Election and indwelling

Is it possible to go one step farther? We are probably authorized to consider the mystery from a closer view, but it must be in the light of the divine indwelling as we have expounded it. In the living presence of God, our person is taken up into the intense life of love proper to the Blessed Trinity; as a result, there arises in us an urging of grace to love God ever more and more. In this setting, to speak of "sufficient grace" or "purely sufficient grace" makes little or no sense, unless one chooses to limit himself to the meaning these terms had during the Jansenist controversy. Grace, seen as coming down from God to us, cannot be other than a divine superabundance. All limitations in the stream of God's grace are due to our ill will and sin, as was pointed out before.

When we are careful to take into account the appeal God addresses to us through the indwelling, we might, if needed, speak of "actual grace." But we shall have a more correct view if we speak of God's primacy in grace. God's primacy in grace is unmistakably evident when we place ourselves within the framework of the personal relationships we are able to discern in the divine indwelling. But all becomes obscure from the moment we cut this grace away from the stream of life, which comes from the Father down to us and returns to the Father through the Holy Spirit in the Son.

For that is the personal, living way the Blessed Trinity dwells in us. We beg the reader's forbearance if we keep repeating the same words monotonously at every turn. The doctrine

of grace, and of what is relevant to grace, has been so materialized, so "reified," that whenever a new problem comes to the
fore we must remind the reader of the fact that these personal
relationships of grace remain decisive for the solutions of *all*
problems in the domain of grace.

The divine living presence in us signifies further that God
speaks to us always anew in the concrete situations of our
existence on earth. Our connections with God through grace
never stiffen into abstract relations, much less into mechanical
reactions. The ever-new—we feel tempted to say "alerting"—
presence of God in our daily life is *God's providence.* Any
situation we may have to face in the course of our earthly
career, even sin, even *our own* sin, acquires in this light a
meaning all its own. God speaks to us wherever we may be.
Every situation is marked with its special duty and calling.
God always holds the initiative in my life. As long as I live,
I can never checkmate Him. He remains forever *faithful* to
Himself. He pursues me in spite of my tepidness and my
rebelliousness. And that is the drama (in the original Greek,
drama means action), the dialogue between God and man.
His invitation is ever renewed, always suited to the actual
moment, and thus never an abstract plan that needs patching
up each time something goes wrong with it. Looked at from that
standpoint, the doctrine of God's primacy in grace keeps its
unsurpassed, comforting significance unimpaired. In the second
part of this book, we shall touch a last time upon the reality
of divine providence in our lives.

What holds good in the life of the individual man is equally
applicable to the history of a nation, or of the Church. Of course,
our minds are as yet unfit to follow this polyphonic dialogue
or even to form an idea of it for themselves. Before God,
each one of us has his own name; but at the same time each
remains a living member of one family, of one people, of the
Church, of the immense human society. We have seen previously that God never severs these two real aspects of our existence from each other.

Predestination and history

Our preceding discussion has perhaps given an inkling of
the way God guides man's life; He doesn't suppress it, but
rather renews it and gives it greater depths. This personalistic
mental outlook affords us at least a glimpse of the interior
law, the inner dialectics of providence. Until now, however,
an important aspect has escaped our notice. The Bible reveals

to us that God is the Lord of history. He guides the nations where He pleases. One feels inclined to call it—though not very effectively—the externals of God's providence, the visible aspect of our history, such as the wars and disasters, the rise and fall of nations or civilizations.

But how God leads history we are unable to perceive. It is not even possible to point to an isolated fact as a " sign " of this divine guidance. Christ refused to adopt the Jewish notion that sickness, poverty or disaster overtaking a man in this life is necessarily a punishment for this or that specified sin. Not even the decadence of a nation needs to be seen as a divine punishment of that nation. God's way reach far deeper and wider. Our solidarity in both good and evil breaks across the boundaries of life, whether of an individual man or a family or a nation. · Assuredly, sickness and all manner of evils are consequences of sin and should be thought of as punishment for sin. However, it has not been granted us to perceive the immediate connection between a given disaster and our sins. And so the ultimate sense of history escapes our perception. To unravel and discover its bearing, we should need to be God Himself.

Any recognition on our part of providence and the divine election at work in mankind takes place in the night of faith—a very dark night, indeed, for those who have no faith. We cannot pretend to experience the action of providence to any extent until love makes us realize that grace is life. Sin plunges man into total darkness; and for a man in darkness, the world is utterly senseless. All he can perceive are the troubling exterior appearances of things. That much has been conclusively established by the widely varying experiences different men had in concentration camps during the war. The camps had been transformed, with devilish ingenuity, into veritable hells. Some internees lost all faith, both in man and in themselves. Others, on the contrary, stumbled upon God for the first time in their lives in those surroundings from which, to all appearances, God had been banished. As I see things, it is along such lines that we can best appreciate the value of Father Aimé Duval's religious songs. He has appeared in our midst as troubadour of Christ's living presence in the slums, in the bylanes, in the night, in sickness. We know, of course, that " God writes straight with crooked lines "; but unless we have the faith, we shall notice nothing more than the senseless scribblings of our human history.

At this point, the theologian too must keep silent. He knows, moreover, *why* he keeps silent: not from spiritual cowardice, nor from dull piety, but rather from a sense of awe. We must admit in all honesty that we have no real insight into God's ways. His activity transcends any and all activity within our experience. For God, time does not pass; youth is eternal; the freshness of the first day endures forever. Nor is there in Him any multiplicity of actions, one complementing another. He knows only of one action, reflected somehow in the checkered light and shade of the countless facets of our human history.

Grace means that God has always loved us. Through grace, He returns us to ourselves in liberal love. Such is our belief because He Himself has told us so, in Christ. But how He does it, we can only vaguely surmise.

Grace and history

We may pride ourselves on it: our age has discovered the fourth dimension, namely, time. Whether we always correctly realize what that means, is quite another matter. This was noticeable already in the impatience and early disappointment people displayed in connection with what happened at the Council. A change, of course, as radical as the one started in the Church by Pope John XXIII, will need a full century before it can carry along with it the entire world in its manner of thinking, of behaving and acting.

Impatience is an offspring of pride. It refuses to accept human nature as it is. *Man lives in time.* Surely, not as a fish lives in water; for that is not enough, nor would it be a discovery. *Man is time,* because he belongs to the cosmos which is unthinkable apart from evolution, and because he himself, with the whole of his existence, shares in the evolution. Man is time also because he is the only being within the cosmos to be conscious of this evolution, to measure and investigate its growth, and to influence it actively. His entire life, his feeling, thought and will are soaked in " time. " The past lives in his present and is turned into a preparation for the future. Our human existence is nothing else than to exist growing; and this within the slow majestic unfolding of the universe.

Our pride refuses to accept this. Just another manifestation of the old sin under a new form: the desire to be like God. That is why we grow impatient. Patience is wisdom, divine wisdom. God respects His creation. He made us that way. In spite of our age-old impatience, He patiently allows us to be what we are.

Our impatience affects even our way of conceiving God. To some it seems far more beautiful, and " more divine, " that God should have created in one instant the entire universe with all it contains. Such a conception belongs rather to the domain of the sensational on which the conjurer depends for his living. Does a slowly evolving universe not offer a more grandiose spectacle than the magician's sleight of hand, producing rabbits,

pigeons and flags from his hat? God does not need this sort
of legerdemain to stir us to admiration.

Just because God respects man in his time-bound condition,
we speak today of a *history of salvation*. We have built the
whole of this book on the fundamental vision that the Blessed
Trinity is present in our world in a living manner. And God
materializes this sanctifying presence of His *in time*. Which
is precisely the meaning of the history of salvation. And if this
is so, grace, too, is bound up with history.

Unhistorical conception of grace

Such an outlook is likely to strike many people as something
totally novel. Current theology failed to prepare us for it.
For, scholasticism borrowed its notions from Aristotelian philosophy. Aristotle shaped his notions on the pattern of experiential
" physical " facts. His philosophy turned out to be a *meta-
physics,* a sort of higher physics. More than once we have
pointed out that such a way of thinking betrays a bent towards
more or less quantitative conceptions. It leads us to static
thought. The machine is the only thing in this world which does
not grow to full development. A machine remains forever
what it was. A better machine is its one replacement. From
this there followed a mental bias for abstract, " universal and
necessary " structures.

When theology does not sufficiently take into account the
origin of its notions and figures of speech, which it inherited
along with the Aristotelian method, it will tend to look upon
grace as a datum standing apart from history.

Theologians of this class are willing enough to concede that
created grace in each individual man remains subject to a certain
form of development. Grace, they say, has a beginning; it can
increase or decrease; it can die and normally should reach
perfection in love. But, that growth is conceived to take place
within the confines of each personal life. In other words, the
beginning and growth of grace repeat themselves uniformly in
the life of each man. A process, thus, which, here on earth,
is to be *repeated* over and over again. Further, such a view is
influenced by the current notion that grace is of a purely
spiritual nature and affects the soul only. There is nothing
to tell us that grace permeates the whole of man, even his body.

Such a conception is completely unhistorical. In essence, it
does not differ from the idea of creation which for centuries
was accepted by all as a self-evident truth. According to this

view, it is taken for granted that the various species of either plants or animals reproduce in every instance beings of the same species as themselves: a process that has not ceased to repeat itself century after century, since the first day of creation. Grace, too, is thought of along similar lines, namely, grace would be a ceaseless repetition of the same process of sanctification. Considering that grace, in its purest and most perfect form is to be met with only within the Church and is merited by Christ, those theologians are hard put to it to see how grace, in its abstract, and therefore in its unchanging perfection, can be had as well outside the Church, or even before the coming of Christ. It is very much as if the dollar, standard national currency of the United States, were to be adopted as the standard in another country quite independent of the United States.

A theology of this sort makes it hard for us to answer the queries our age is asking. I cannot forget, for instance, the question an African seminarist asked while I was teaching in the Congo. It should not be overlooked that an African experiences a deep-seated awareness of his relationship with his ancestors; his tribal consciousness and the whole structure of his community life cannot be thought of apart from the lasting presence of his forebears in his life. And in a certain sense, such a way of thinking is more historical than ours. So, the seminarist asked me what had happened to his ancestors, now that he and his whole family had become Christians. His question did not spring from theological curiosity, but rather from an existential urge. Similar questions are bound to crop up more frequently, now that the Church, since the Council, has adopted a more open attitude toward the world—an " openness " which henceforth must be for each one of us a duty of life and not just a sensational novelty.

Our method

On this ground, it is our purpose to prospect a theological region until now hardly opened up. To forestall all misunderstanding, we shall use the term " grace " in the instances only when the same reality is present; whenever it demands it, we shall give preference to a paraphrase. In the present subject-matter, more than anywhere else, the lack of an adequate terminology is a hindrance.

The chapter, which we begin, could easily be expanded into a whole volume. We shall here content ourselves with an outline of a historical vision of history. At the end, we shall ask the momentous question that was brought up before the

Council: how do we recognize in this turn of history the historical saving role proper to the Church in her quality of visible divine grace in this world?

Let us bring a further precision to the question raised. We must keep true to the theological method. Theology offers no answer to scientific queries regarding the evolution of the cosmos, of man or of other like beings. All that theology endeavors to do is to throw light on those data by means of certainties all its own; namely by means of the contents of Revelation.

Theology starts from the knowledge that God's way of acting remains ever true to itself. God's action is one and undivided in its fullness. But within this world of ours, God's one action displays itselfs in millions of facets that might be compared to so many precipices of that one action on history. As a comparison, we may turn to the prism. As is well known by all, the rich white light of the sun is broken up in the prism and spread out in a colorful spectrum. So, in history, too, we may discover many traces of God's presence; but these are *all* due to the one divine activity. The theologian's task consists in recognizing with reverence and awe the divine intention manifested in the many traces we have of God's presence, and in collating them with each other.

An earnest consideration of truths, that are basic in our belief and are—so we saw in a previous section—actual facts, will help us to confront them with each other and to bring us to a better understanding of God's eternal enduring design. This method of proceeding has been called the method of *analogia fidei*; its ground is the comparison we make between the analogical truths and the facts of our faith. We say " analogical," because those facts and truths, though differing from one another, are really related.

We may conclude with an example that will enable the reader to know exactly how we intend to proceed in our work. And it is this: by contemplating the operation of the Holy Spirit in Christ and, later on, in the primitive Church, we can come to a deeper insight into the true significance of the sacrament of Confirmation. How? The descent of the Spirit upon Christ at the moment of His baptism by John, and the revelation of Himself on the first Pentecost day after the Ascension, are two events really distinct from what happens in Confirmation. Nonetheless, the three mysteries are intimately connected with each other insofar as they are manifestations of the unity of God's purpose, namely, " the imparting of the Spirit " to men.

It is along similar lines that we shall now assemble and compare with each other some mysterious facts of faith, and so seek to reach the hidden unity of the divine action which, from within, binds all those mysteries together. Above all, we must hold fast to the capital mystery, the main burden of this book, namely, the different ways in which God lives in this world and actualizes His presence.

God's presence in history

Until now, we have attempted to bring to light the unity of the divine action by starting from the reality of God's presence in the Church and in the Christian. If anyone does not care to think historically, he has no further questions to ask. But he would be wrong in not doing so. The manner in which the divine action revealed itself to us compels us to acknowledge that God has always honored man's historical dimensions. Centuries in advance "from the beginning," salvation was prepared and announced, and in the course of time ever more clearly defined. "In the fullness of time," it reached its perfect stage in Christ. With this, however, the history of salvation was not at an end. On the contrary, salvation has now to be spread throughout the world, preparing mankind for the final revelation of Christ at the "end of time." "From the beginning," "fullness of time," "end of time": by these expressions, Scripture has indeed and unmistakably borne witness to and traced out, for the benefit of our modern philosophy, the reality of the history of salvation.

Nor could it be otherwise; for the God of love is factually present in His creation. We have been told by J. A. T. Robinson how unfortunate it is to speak of a God "there above," or of a God "there beyond." God is the root of our existence, just because He is forever carrying it forward by His creative action. To create does not only mean to bring into being, leaving it to the creature to take care of its destiny. To create means that the whole of a created existence strikes its deepest roots in God and continues to be sustained by Him.

To begin with: in creating, God has revealed Himself as a God of love. Creation is but one aspect (we dare to say: an aspect of secondary importance) of God's action in love and grace. The act of creating is included in a far more glorious reality, namely, salvation. Salvation consists in this: that God has made Himself known to this world as the one and only object of love; or, more profoundly, that from within His own perfection and love, He concerns Himself with the world, that He lets it have a share in the "living life" which is Himself as Trinity; that

He grants us the grace to love Him like and with His Son in the Holy Spirit.

Ruysbroeck found a powerful comparison for this: God is like a sea which sweeps the universe back to Himself. "This flowing of God demands always a flowing back again; for God is like a sea, ebbing and flowing, ceaselessly flowing into each one of His elect, according to the needs and worth of each. And in His ebbing, He draws back again all men to whom He has given in heaven and on earth, with all they have and with all of which they are capable ... God desires to be loved by us in accordance with His excellence. " [25]

With this grandiose vision before us, we shall have to see what theology can say about the history of the world.

The origin of the cosmos

Modern sciences have opened our eyes to the long pre-history of the cosmos. Whether they conceive of the universe as a fixed and closed space, or as a space whose limits are in full expansion, they all say that it has taken millions of years before the world came to its present state. An evolution which is still in progress.

It does not fall within the competence of the theologian to put to the test world conceptions and cosmogonies thought out by mathematicians. But many observed facts seem to indicate that such an evolution did actually take place. The theologian need not ask for more. He leaves to the men of science the care of giving ulterior precision to their world conception by further calculations and observations.

Meanwhile, like any other man, the scientist has his place in the cosmos such as it is at present. Innumerable nebulae are in the process of achieving their evolution at dizzy distances away from us in space. In the sky, the milky way reminds us that our earth is no more than an imperceptibly small planet within the vast system of stars which form the galaxy wherein we live.

The earth, too, has a long pre-history. When it had solidified and cooled, life appeared on its crust, step by step, millions of years ago. Most probably, life evolved on a pattern of increasing complexity and infolding, spreading out into countless branches, some of which have died out, while others proved sources of still further living forms. Some cosmogonies would

[25] Jan van Ruysbroeck, *Die Gheestelike Brulocht*, tr. Eric Colledge as *The Spiritual Espousals* (London: Faber & Faber, 1952), pp. 127-128.

have it that it all began with an explosion. So, too, apparently, life on the crust of the earth.

Such is the picture which the sciences of the cosmos have built up: a vast vision of a dynamic unfolding of matter and life in time and space.

What can we say about it from the point of view of the faith? This much: that it is the world which God carries in His creating hands. All through centuries-old silence prior to the coming of man, God was there, Father, Son and Holy Spirit. God is totally other than the world, and yet, He is its most secret root and deepest source of life. " And the Spirit of God hovered over the waters " (Gen 1:2), as prime origin of its existence and as its ultimate meaning.

In regard to all these millions of centuries, we have no reason to speak as yet of grace in the strict sense of the word. Grace always supposes a responsible person. Nothing prevents us, though, from accepting that there was something like a distant preparation for grace, something diffused throughout the world, a quiet, still force, a more profound meaning, the fruit of God's operative presence in the world. For that world has sprung from the Father; before all time, it was prepared to be a home for the Son, eternal Image of the Father; it was, therefore, breathing with the power of the Spirit. That world was not given over solely to the blind forces of chance combinations between atoms and cells. That world had a meaning and a definite direction, because God dwelt in it, because His love prepared the cosmos for the Son and for the assembly of God's children.

But let us not imagine that God, like an unskilled workman, had constantly and by dint of miraculous interventions to correct the course of history in order to keep it on the right track. He surrendered the world to the forces which He Himself chose to give. And by so doing, God already manifested both His respect for " the work of His hands " and His patience. All the forces, with which He freely endowed nature, were working for Him. He could guide them from within, because He was incessantly maintaining their existence, not from without, but from within.

As we said in a previous part, concerning divine predestination and human freedom: it is because God is so utterly distinct from the world that from within it, He can keep it moving, and has no need to step in even for a moment. We all too humanly fancy that God operates somehow from outside things; for instance, by neutralizing the laws of nature or by bending them to His plan! Now, in the cosmos, such as it was under God's hand, there was present an anticipation of grace, inasmuch as the cosmos had sprung from love, was being sustained by love, and was directed towards a full realization of that same love.

The origin of man

When life on earth had reached an appropriate high level of organic articulation, complexity and interiority, man arose. Theologians who choose to bypass matter, on the plea that it is the exclusive domain of mechanics and chemistry, are compelled at this point to speak of a divine intervention occuring at the moment when God created the human spirit. Their idea is not false, provided one keeps in mind the motive underlying their way of speaking. The Church must be careful to steer clear of any kind of materialism that would look upon the " soul " as nothing more than the highest stage in the complexity of matter. According to the Church, we must hold that man carries in his person " the image and likeness of God "; human life stands qualitatively on a level superior to that of animal life. And the Church wants to safeguard that much.

Modern thought, on its side, is adverse to concede too clean-cut a division between body and soul, because such a distinction fails to give due consideration to the bodily substance of man who is a hundred per cent citizen of our cosmos. Biblical thought meets this modern want halfway; it always thinks of man in the unity of soul and body. The Greek conception of man was entirely unknown to the Semitic mind, and therefore also to Scripture. The Bible knows of the man only as " flesh, " that is, as a finite and eventually as a sinful creature; or, as " spirit, " that is, as the accomplished man in whom the Spirit of God dwells. This biblical distinction is a theological, not a philosophical, one. In any case, Scripture rarely speaks of the " soul " as spiritual principle of the body.

Now that we know God to be actively present in matter and in life, therefore also in pre-human life, we have excluded a primary kind of materialism. God's operative presence in the cosmos is by no means a mechanical, unconscious and neutral force working itself out automatically. It is pre-eminently a personal presence, closely associated with the evolution of life. Its nature is Love. In this light, we have no difficulty in accepting, in the spirit of the Church, an immediate intervention of God in the origin of the spirit; nor do we look upon this intervention as a wholly extrinsic and sudden stepping-in of God. And at the same time, we hold that man remains truly of this earth, and that he does not lose the royal nobility which is his on the ground of being the " image " of God and of having received from his Maker the power to lord it over the animal kingdom (Gen 1:26-27).

On the subject of the origin of man there is much we do not know, much we shall never know with certainty. A moment's reflection suffices to convince us how impossible it is at present to come across archeological remains that would indicate precisely where, when and how man appeared. And for its part, Scripture has nothing to say here either, nothing in the nature of historical experience and evidence.

But Holy Writ does tell us that man, like all living beings, owes his origin to God, and that man, from the first instant of his existence, has been called to the divine intimacy. Ancient figures of speech, taken from oriental literary tradition, impress upon us this truth of faith: the garden wherein God lingers and man may lead a lordly free life, the tree of life, and above all the Covenant God makes with man. Such a man surely belongs to this earth; he was fashioned out of clay.

We are also unable to ascertain to any degree of certainty whether man did actually live in this early state for any length of time. Taking for granted some indications from pre-history, we would say that it is unlikely—though we have no decisive facts to go by. However, it is quite sure and guaranteed by faith that from the start man was offered the fullness of life of grace, with all that this gift implied, first and foremost the call to immortality.

But let us understand this well. When God offers something, something is effected, since, together with His offer, He confers the required ability to accept His gift freely. What we mean to say is that, in fact, God did actually step into our history and that He did strike at man's deepest self, at least under the form of a real invitation which moved man in his inmost being. A modern idea puts it this way: from the first moment man came into existence, God placed him in a situation of grace which conditioned his whole being as person in its deepest ground. We use the word " inviting attraction, " because man had to be spoken to as a free person. He could, at will, either refuse or accept the invitation. If he chose to accept, he had to do so in virtue of the initial attraction and invitation—as we shall see later on in our study on grace. The invitation was a call to a personal love for God which, as such, surpassed human possibilities. It was thus a true offer of grace, and already a grace: really an " offered grace. "

The divine action possesses still a further distinctive mark: it is irrevocable. " Your word, O Lord, forever stands firm in the heavens; Your fidelity lasts from age to age like the earth You created " (Ps 118:89-90). The praise of God's fidelity forms one of the basic themes of the Old Testament, mostly in connection with God's blessings. God has never gone back on His first invitation of man to grace; through it, He maintains the orientation given to human nature in the depth of its being.

The election to grace, God's inviting attraction, has a third property: it is donated to mankind *in Christ;* for it is He who, as perfect man, unites in Himself the whole human race with the cosmos and with God.

This latter characteristic of Christ, however, is not a point of faith strictly speaking. Some theologians do not accept it. They are of opinion that Christ has been given to us as the Saviour only, *because* we sinned. Nevertheless, there have always been some men in the Church to defend the view we propose. It seems probable that Scripture itself suggests this view of world history. Several Fathers have centered the history of salvation on Christ, independently of the consideration of sin. The Franciscan school, especially Duns Scotus, taught so. In our own day, Teilhard de Chardin came close to that conception, although he saw it in a different perspective, the perspective of the sciences. He sees Christ as the " point Omega, " toward which converge all the lines of force of the cosmic evolution. We think that such a view may be safely received in the Church.

The election of the world and of man in Christ is not independent of the consideration of sin. For, in this world-view, Christ is in the first place the Mediator between God and man, and in the second place He is the Saviour of man who refused to accept the first invitation to grace and therefore fell into a state of perdition. Christ's mediation has now to manifest itself as an act of deliverance and reconciliation.

Whether or not man responded to God's invitation, he was and remains, together with the cosmos, ordained toward Christ. Now, Christ is the highest perfection of creation and humanity, the point where God and man meet each other in perfect surrender and love, within the intimacy of a divine Person. All this gains in clarity when set within the fundamental vision of this book: God has created the world to actualize in time His complete and loving Presence in the world. Christ is manifestly the summit, the consummate actualization of the divine presence in our history. And this explains why we detected in the pre-human history of the cosmos a Christward direction which may be looked upon as the earliest prototype of grace. The first man has, from the start, been chosen in Christ.

We can now deal with the typically human question: Why did God not give Christ to the world from the first instant it came into being? Let us first admit that the view we propose makes sense only when we adoringly recognize that *God respects human existence in time.* Unless we accept this, we shall fail to discern much meaning in the divine action; but if we accept it, then we shall see that God did give Christ to the world from its very beginning, and that apart from Christ the world has no ultimate significance. Just as the cosmos took centuries to prepare for the coming of man, so mankind too had to prepare itself for the coming of Christ—we mean, for Christ's first coming and for His final return when He will fulfill " all in all. " We cannot think of a proof more cogent in favor of this historical trend of grace than the evidence that grace converges consistently and factually on Christ. We shall allow ourselves to repeat once more: grace is the actualization in this world of the presence of the Father, the Son and the Holy Ghost. The presence *starts from* the indwelling, is *carried on* by the indwelling and is preparing us *for the total realization* of the indwelling. And of this indwelling, Christ stands out as the highest symbol and, therefore, as its purest actualization, and also its inner driving force.

The Father's one idea of love is realized to perfection in Christ, through the power of the Spirit. The pure presence of the God-with-us, the Emmanuel, produces in the prism of human history a multitude of forms, all of which are borne up by that first and last form of the indwelling, and animated by it from within. In this light, the scriptural expression *" in Christo "* yields its most pregnant meaning and rightly deserves the name of Christological aspect of grace.

We know from faith that man did not accept the first divine invitation. But how the refusal came about, we do not know. In different figures of speech, Scripture tells us no more than " that man wanted to be like God " (Gen 3:5). Those words express what constitutes the core of sin, nothing else. Revelation did not disclose the concrete psychological setting of this original sin. It is probable that in the very primitive form of life led by the first man, the existential option demanded a certain length of time. We should never completely detach that original sin from the sins that followed later, since these continue to echo and to confirm mankind's first refusal. We have tended to separate too sharply these two aspects in sinful mankind; we have thrown all the guilt on the first man. Holy Writ does not speak that way. Scripture always considers together both aspects of sin. It goes further and stresses more emphatically our own personal sins by which we are perpetuating in ourselves the state of perdition.

From the cross we receive complete certitude concerning our common state of perdition. Christ had to die for all men, because all men needed to be redeemed. *All* were " far from God. "

Paul has summed up this condition of man in a few terse lines that form the main theme of his Epistle to the Romans. " For all alike have sinned, and are deprived of the divine glory [God's glory signifies in Scripture the active presence of God's majesty in our history]. And all are justified by God's free grace alone, through His act of liberation in the person of Christ Jesus " (Rom 3:23-24).

But, then, how in the light of faith have we to understand human existence? To begin with: God's word stays forever and His fidelity is without repentance. " God is not a man so that He lies; nor son of Adam so that He goes back on His word. Does He speak and not act? or say and not fulfill " (Num 23:19). Man has never ceased to be called to the life of grace we spoke of earlier. The so-called " pure nature, " that is, a human existence in which divine grace has no part to act, has never existed. The call to grace, so we said a while ago, owes its origin to the divine presence in our actual history. God never left the world although, in the words of Paul, He may condemn our sinfulness by His silence. God's silence during so many centuries down to our own day is God's greatest reproof. It is also our greatest punishment.

Meanwhile, we learn from faith that the call to grace has remained unanswered, since mankind persisted in the first refusal by the personal sins of its members. That call, therefore, never became " grace " in the sense we usually imply, namely, in the sense of mature grace—mature, that is, freely accepted in virtue of God's first love. Grace, thus, has remained unfulfilled.

Karl Rahner names this divine calling in us " a supernatural existential "—in other words, an initial course set to human existence as such, insofar as the latter has been, from its earliest inception, determined in its innermost core by the appeal of God's love. The actual historical existence of man is the existence of one who is *called* to the *love* of God. Classical theology has a name for it: *state,* namely the state of man simultaneously raised to the supernatural (" *elevatus,* " so says scholasticism) and yet refusing to accept it (in scholastic language, " *lapsus,* " fallen state). This paradox signifies within our existence a split, implying a contradiction that reaches right down to the deepest layer of our person, a sort of spiritual schizophrenia, which constitutes the essence of the state of original sin—something we all share in common. Of late, that state has also been described as a sinful " situation. " The term " situation " is a fitting one, provided we understand it well, that is, if we accept it as a philosophical and theological notion defining our existence in its depest roots, and, therefore, if we do not take it as merely representing a psychological experience.

This inner contradiction, hiding in human nature, cannot be done away with by man himself. Christ, Who from all eternity was destined to be the center of our history, fulfills henceforth that function as Redeemer, as " the Lamb who takes away our sins " (Is 53:7; Jo 1:29; 19:36; Acts 8:32-35; I Cor 5:7; I Pet 1:19).

Israel, Christ's herald

About five hundred years before Christ, in the era of the great prophets, the books of the Old Testament received their final elaboration. Older traditions of the Jewish people, narratives of their history handed down from generation to generation, more especially stories concerning the vocation of Abraham, the deliverance from Egypt by Moses, the doings of great kings like David: all these were taken up and preserved in that final reduction.

That is the origin of what H. Renckens, S.J. so aptly styled: *Israel looks back upon its past.*[26] That happened to be the first theology of history. Evidently, numerous historical facts were narrated in the course of this survey by faith. It was not the duty of the authors to set down the exact succession of facts for everything they wanted to narrate, or to indicate accurately places, dates and sources, after the manner of today.

Their task was confined to expounding the religious meaning of Jewish history in the light of the theology of the great prophets. The prophets prefer to speak of Israel's relationship with God, and this in accordance with a threefold scheme which is actually in harmony with history. Let us, for instance, refer the reader to the great text of Ezekiel which we quoted immediately after the parable at the beginning of the second part of our book. What do we read? Before all else, the first election and love of God is solemnly proclaimed. In the light of that love, Israel's infidelity is set forth—Israel which always falls away from God, adores strange gods, and tramples under foot the divine law. But God remains true to His promises. He will make up for disobedience "in the fullness of time," "on Yahweh's great day," the day of the Messiah. Then He will pour out His spirit upon all flesh, and write His commandments no longer on slabs of stone but in the hearts of men.

This tragic dialogue between the slighted, yet eternally faithful love of God, and the bad will of the chosen people takes place within the sphere of the Covenant. Israel's election to be God's chosen people rested on the Covenant which God had made with Abraham and later renewed with Moses on Sinai. Each year on Easterday, that Covenant is recalled to mind; for, from that Covenant, the exodus of Egypt, "in the might of God," stood out as the holiest of symbols, very much what the cross is for us. The latter became the Christian Paschal celebration.

Such was the theological theme which the writers of the Old Testament endeavored to illustrate in their historical books as well. The same dialogue between God and Israel lays bare the

[26] H. Renckens, S.J., *Israels visie op het verleden* (Tielt, Den Haag:

meaning of the history of God's people. It was in this light that they wanted to view and interpret the numerous events of the past preserved by the people in their traditions. That is why it is rather a theological history, a history seen in the light of faith. However much the books of the Old Testament may differ from our present day history books, they contain a sufficient number of historical data to prove, by their very candor, that the authors wanted to write about situations, relationships and ideas which at the moment of their actual occurrence were not quite so evident.

When there is talk today of the " historical " value of biblical narratives, we invariably hear the naive question: Did it all really happen like that? As a rule, such a question is unfair and, alas, receives an unfair answer. The query is made from the point of view of a civilization that has unlearned the sense of what is symbolical or belongs to poetical art, a civilization that has forgotten how other civilizations have at their disposal a great many more discreet and delicate modes of expression to speak about " facts. "

When, for instance, an African, in the course of a palaver, tells fairy-tales about fowls, or crocodiles and monkeys, his real mind is fixed on " true " facts; for he is pleading as he would do in a lawsuit. Lawsuits in Africa are as serious and business-like as they are among us. They think, however, that it is more polite to clothe in poetical language the bare facts of the case, together with the arguments contained in the customary law of the tribe. The chiefs, the judges and the assembly who are listening know exactly what it is all about. An Asian, too, thinks it uncouth to " call a spade a spade "; he prefers symbolical language. Not for a moment has either the African or the Asian the impression that he is amusing himself with fairy-tales. For, that is the language in which business is done, war and peace are made, philosophy and beliefs discussed. Shall we say that the African is not dealing with real facts because he resorts to modes of expression differing from ours? A man who lived in those countries and, on returning home, listens to our so-called learned discussion about Scripture—at least some of the very " learned " speculations—feels ashamed to see so much ado about nothing.

The writers of the Old and New Testament would look in amazement if we were to ask them point-blank: Did you really intend to write about things that happened? We better ask ourselves: What conforms more to " real " happenings, the evidence of a policeman's report giving precise information about age, color of eyes and hair, about weight and height, place and hour—or a narrative which suggests the deeper meaning of the fact, though without attaching too much attention to details which, after all, are very superficial? What would be more "real": a possible photo of the descent from the cross or Michelangelo's "Pieta"? a photo of Erasmus or his portrait by Holbein? a biography of Henry VIII as left to us by one or another chronicler or Shakespeare's tragedy? a possible report made by Pilate for the use of the imperial administration at Rome or J. S. Bach's "Passion According to St. Matthew"? Because Michelangelo, Shakespeare and Bach permit themselves some poetical, dramatic or musical liberties and are less concerned with concrete details about persons and such like things, does it follow that they bequeated to us "myths," meaning pure concoctions or, at least, symbolical expressions of a merely personal emotion?

It is our right to show a preference for accurate detail in historical narratives. But, let us nevertheless summon enough respect for man and many-sided truth to allow another cultural background to express in its own peculiar manner what is historical truth. If it be granted that the Gospel passage telling of the Magi, who came from the east to visit the crib of the Nativity, is intended to remind us that Christ is born also for non-Jews, that would not prevent Matthew from writing about the authentic mission of a real child at the beginning of our era. And if in their account of what happened in history, the evangelists, like the prophets their predecessors, bring out such details as would convey a lesson to their readers, while leaving the rest in the shade, the whole of their narrative is not on that ground necessarily a fairy-tale. Such judgments, argue the critics, are an untutored, shortsighted notion of what is historical truth. The so-styled naiveté of many biblical narratives is perhaps less naive than the scholarly hypotheses that have been published about them.

But now, what do the books of the Old Testament teach about?

The religious and moral insight of the Hebrew people and, later after the exile, of the Jewish people, is clearly the development of very primitive and rather crude notions and customs. It took a long time before the Hebrews possessed an idea of God that stood out prominently above the idea which the surrounding peoples had formed of God. The gods were little more than national or local deities. The grandiose description of the creation, with which Genesis opens, could have come only at the end of a long evolution towards the knowledge of what God is. God is actually God only when He is the creator of the universe, the Lord of history, the God of all nations and ages— and not just a local or national deity.

Conceptions concerning the hereafter were also rather defective among the Jews. And not less so their idea of morality. In the stories of the Old Testament, we see God's patience endlessly at work: He is preparing a people for the coming of Christ. That is, the basic notion of "redemption," such as it is depicted in the Bible, tallies well with the notion we analyzed previously: God recruits a people, He gathers around Him a people wholly His, a people of His election; and all this He does in time: He prepares Himself a people.

At this point, we ask once more the question: Why did it last so long before Christ came? We reply: Had there been no long preparation and education, no deepening of religious faith, no refining of morality, then, the awakening of personal responsibility, at the moment Christ announced His message, would have been incomprehensible. No man can possibly grasp the meaning of a message unless he is to some extent familiar with its contents, unless the queries of like make the answering message acceptable. The whole of our human conduct and endeavor rests on the whole of our past. Where there is no past, or worse still, where the past shuts our eyes and hearts, we remain blind and deaf. It is just this lack of freedom from a previous history which makes it so hard for men to understand each other—as, for instance, when a European meets an African or Asian. The latter have a past that has little in common with our own.

All this applies still more to the domain of religious truths that demand from man a total surrender. God has prepared mankind for the coming of Christ. Under God's guidance, devout and saintly men, the patriarchs, the kings and judges, the prophets and pious ones from among the people have listened to the voice of God. They have testified to the truth and to the light that had sprung up in their hearts. And thereby they have brought their people closer to the light that would one day shine at Bethlehem.

Israel's long history is unintelligible without the enduring presence of God's love in their past. The Jewish people, though, were not loved for their own sake, but for Christ's sake, and at the same time for the sake of us all. Grace had to reach its maturity in man in the manner proper to man: in a spiritual stream whose flow slowly deepened its bed, a stream in which we have all to quench our thirst. The image of grace, as it appears in the description of Paradise, is verified here again. Four streams sprang from the center of Paradise and irrigated the whole earth. Israel was destined to be one of these streams.

A final question: Was the grace, received by the Jews, the same we know of within the Church?

We have seen already that the Jews lived in God's presence, the living source of all graces. Like all men, they lived in a raised state, that is, they were called to the supernatural state

which happened to be combined with a fallen state. We dealt
with this a little while ago. We also described how God was
present in the history of the Jewish people, preparing them for
Christ. All this indicated that God's personal love, finding
expression in this Presence, incited the Jews to listen to the Lord's
voice speaking in the various religious and moral modes of life
which at the time they were capable of grasping and of living
up to. When they listened to God's voice and surrendered
themselves to Him in faith and hope, " grace " came to them
in perfection. It was already Christ's grace, since it was for
Christ's sake that they were loved. Their grace was *historically
ordained:* for the vocation, associated with this grace, moved them
to contribute their share to the preparation for the coming
of Christ. So that their spiritual life took the form of *hope and
expectation.* Grace in the Old Testament was the grace of
advent. Its finest manifestations were the sighs of the Psalms,
the admonitions of the prophets, but chiefly the widely spread
popular expectation of the Redeemer, the Lord's Anointed. That
grace found its final expression in the short prayer of thanks-
giving uttered by the aged Simeon at the moment he held the
Christ child in his arms:

" This day, Lord, Thou givest Thy servant his discharge in
    peace;
now thy promise is fulfilled.
For I have seen with my own eyes
the deliverance which *Thou hast made ready* in the full sight
    of all the nations:
a light that will be a revelation to the heathen,
and glory to Thy people Israel " (Lk 2:29-32).

We can easily imagine the joy of the first Christians who were
all Jews. What their forefathers had so eagerly been waiting
for, was *now* (a little word which keeps recurring in the New
Testament) an actuality. Here is what Peter wrote to his flock:
" This salvation was the theme which the prophets have pondered
and explored, those who prophesied about the grace of God
awaiting you. They searched what time or circumstances the
Spirit of Christ in them was signifying, when He foretold the
sufferings of Christ, and the glories that would follow. And
it was disclosed to them that the matter they treated of was not
for their time, but for yours. And *now* it has been openly
announced to you through preachers who brought you the Gospel
in the power of the Holy Spirit sent from heaven. These are
things that angels long to see into " (I Pet 1:10-12).

Israel's obduracy is to Paul no proof that they are lost
forever. At any rate, the heathen should be grateful to the
Jews for receiving the redemption through the Jews. The

Apostle pushes the paradox further still: "by their disobedience you have been saved," because the apostles, and especially Paul, had been rejected by the Jews and had at once addressed themselves to the heathen. "In the spreading of the Gospel, they are treated as God's enemies for your sake; but God's choice stands, and they are His friends for the sake of the patriarchs. *For the gracious gifts of God and His calling are irrevocable.* Just as formerly you were disobedient to God, but *now* have received mercy in the time of their disobedience, so *now, when you receive mercy,* they have proved disobedient, but only in order that they too may receive mercy. For in making all men prisoners to disobedience, God's purpose was to show mercy to all mankind" (Rom 11:28-32).

That is the spirit of Christ! And it is in this spirit that the Second Vatican Council prepared a special decree on our relations with the Jews. The mercy that has been shown to us, will lead them too back to God's compassion. And we, Christians, we have to permit God to complete, in and through us, His work of mercy and love, until the day fixed by the Lord.

An old query: salvation outside the Church

For millions of years, billions upon billions of men have lived far from Christ, in ignorance of the Covenant, unaware of the Church. That is the great besetting mystery of the history of salvation. Perhaps it does not disquiet us so directly as it does the new Christians in Africa and Asia who remain linked with their ancestors by so many bonds of fidelity, affection and solidarity. Why did God, lover of all men, reveal Himself all these centuries to only a few nations?

The question is as old as the Church. On this subject, H. de Lubac and Y. M. Congar have collected a surprising anthology of a great many texts from the Fathers and the early scholastics. [27] To mediate on those testimonies is a refreshing experience for an unbiased mind. Only then do we realize how far the Church has drifted into a ghetto these last three centuries. Had these texts not been written by an Augustine, an Irenaeus or a Thomas Aquinas, they would have been looked upon in some circles today if not as heresy, at least as erroneous. Great Christians and saints could combine their joy of having been called to the Church with a breadth of outlook on the

[27] Henri de Lubac, S.J., *Catholicism.* A Study of Dogma in Relation to the Corporate Destiny of Mankind (London: Burns, 1950). Y. M. Congar O.P., *The Wide World My Parish.* Salvation and its Problems (London, Darton, 1961).

non-Christians that keeps much closer to the boundless heart of God. We shall quote one or another of those texts, were it only to prove that what we have to say does not stray from the authoritative tradition of the Church.

During the Middle Ages, theological opinions concerning salvation outside the Church were broader than in the nineteenth century. Thomas Aquinas holds quite definite views about it. In his *Summa Theologica,* he poses the rather strange question, typical of the scholastic method of proceeding: " whether venial sin can be had in any one together with original sin, " and without mortal sin. He answers in the negative. The reason which he advances for his reply is based on the theology of the fundamental option, of which we shall speak at length further on in this book. That fundamental option receives from the scholastics a formulation different from ours today. As they see it, the fundamental option consists in orienting oneself and one's activity to the *final end* which includes all other ends *(se ordinare ad finem ultimum)* and, of course, should be the *true* final end *(finis debitus).*

Here is what St. Thomas wrote: " I reply: we must say that it is impossible that venial sin should be found in a man together with original sin and without mortal sin. And this is the reason: before anyone reaches the years of discretion, his youth, during which he has as yet no proper use of his reason, excuses him from mortal sin. *All the more reason* why he is incapable of venial sin [a rather striking remark, of application in the direction of children who are often and too soon plagued with the fear of mortal sin and hell!], at least where there is question of deeds that in themselves are truly venial sins [venial sins of weakness are thus not excluded]. When, however, he begins to have the use of his reason, he is not then fully excused from the guilt of both venial and grievous sins. The first thing a man does at that moment is to deliberate about himself [this St. Thomas explains in the meaning of a fundamental option]. If, that same moment, he orients himself [fundamentally] toward the right final end, he receives *remission of original sin, and this through grace* [for, such an act can be no other than an act of love]. When he does not do so [that is, when he ordains himself to a wrong final end], he commits at the same moment a mortal sin [further on in our book, we, too, shall account for mortal sin in that way], in the measure he has at that age, the possibility of discernment. For, he does not do ' what in him lies ' [a very terse formula to express the requirement for authenticity of life]. And then there will be in him no venial sin without mortal sin—unless it be after he has obtained forgiveness of all through grace " (*Summa Theologica,* I-II, q. 89, art. 6, in c.).

St. Thomas considers, thus, the possibility of salvation purely from the standpoint of the dialectic of grace. Grace is present in man and is stirred up to life at the moment man consciously assumes responsibility for his existence. At that instant, he has to make a fundamental choice with the help of grace within him, and " do what in him lies. ' Otherwise, he turns away from his own truth and, consequently, also away from grace and God.

The men of the Middle Ages were, thus, in possession of the correct principles to uphold an " open " conception of the Church, inherited from the Fathers. Nonetheless, their conception of the Church was no longer as " open " as it had been formerly. And this was due in large measure to the attitude they had adopted towards non-Christian peoples. Their knowledge of the world did not go much beyond the frontiers of Europe and Asia Minor. The only non-Christians they knew of were the Jews, the Muslims and the heretics in their very midst. Beyond that, they had vague notions about Asia and fabulous Ethiopia. Now, the Jews had allegedly crucified Christ and were in bad faith. Crusaders were at war with the Muslims who occupied the Holy Land, ravaged the coasts of the Mediterranean sea and, therefore, were hardly an improvement upon the Jews.

There is one passage, quoted by Paul from the Old Testament and applied by him to the Jews exclusively, a text which the medieval men understood in an absolute sense when they spoke of the faith. " Faith is awakened by the message, and the message that awakens it comes through the word of Christ. But, I ask you: can it be that they have never heard it [meaning the preaching of the Gospel]! Of course they did: their voice has sounded all over the earth, and their words to the bounds of the inhabited world " (Rom 10:17-18; quotation from Ps 19:5). Having nothing better than a few attestations regarding the journeys of the Apostles " all over the world " (what could those words evoke in the mind of a man of the Middle Ages?) and some legends that had sprung up around such traditions, they thought that practically " the whole world " had heard the Gospel.

Consequently, non-Christians who did not profess the faith, were guilty. Quite clearly, such a reasoning is psychologically weak, and historically weaker still. Our reader is sufficiently acquainted with the history of civilization to know that medieval thought was underdeveloped in matters of psychology and history. We ourselves, while teaching in Africa, have noticed that when the human mind is invited and stimulated to reflect seriously upon itself, it ventures its first steps on the level of the abstract and the logical, and only later, after prolonged experience, seeks a deeper insight into the historical aspect of its existence and into the complexity of its psychic articulations. To be capable of grasping the value of a psychological or historical argument, one needs to possess a degree of culture beyond the *prima facie* satisfied abstract and logical reasoning.

Be this as it may (the text from Paul), ignorance of the world outside Europe, imperfect acquaintance with the various psychological and historical forms of religious attitudes toward God as occurring in the then unknown civilizations: all these factors led the men of the Middle Ages to a certain rigorism in their judgment about the practice of religion among the peoples. It is not unfair to them to say that the Fathers of the Church, who lived in the Roman Empire and knew how the diverse peoples within it preserved their different particular historical background, had gained a degree of unified political and cultural maturity which enabled them to frame a conception of the Church more " open " than that of their barbarian heirs a few centuries later.

When in the sixteenth century St. Francis Xavier set out on his missionary labors, he had few problems, at least at the start. The religious rites of the poor Indians where all inspired by the devil: and so, without the slightest misgiving, he destroyed their altars and images wherever he could. But in Japan, his eyes were opened. He recognized among the Japanese religious aspirations which could not all be of Satan's inspiration. It was the same intuition of God's mysterious way with the heathen which would induce the first missionaries to China to attempt new methods. Unfortunately, these latter pioneers were alone in this discovery and experience of theirs. European theologians had not progressed that far. And so, it came about that the more " open " missionary method was condemned. The new outlook would take much time before winning approval throughout the Church.

For centuries, the main motive in missionary undertakings was and remained the freeing of the heathen from the " shadows of death. " Since then we have come to a better knowledge of those peoples. We are acquainted with their religious traditions, with their rites and beliefs. We have discovered that even among the so-called primitive races all is not to be traced back to anxiety of mind or to superstition. For, they too acknowledge a divinity ruling the world. Mystical states are not unknown among such peoples; nor is there absence of touching examples of charity and fidelity, of morality and piety. To speak glibly of idolatry is to misrepresent reality.

The former sharp contrast between light and darkness has faded into numerous nuances of light and obscurity. Progress has not rendered it easier for the Church to realize what her task consists in. Among the younger generation of missionaries it has led to some sort of crisis, or at least to doubts about the

meaning of their labor. But we shall return to this topic in the
following section.

What we shall do here is to examine one or two biblical and
psychological data which may help us to a more careful, more
correct answer. A few eloquent texts from St. Augustine will
allow us to adopt the correct perspective and to justify what we
shall propose. Doing so, we shall rediscover the main theme
of this book: *from* the indwelling, *through* the indwelling, and
toward the complete actualization of the indwelling.

Our faith contains a few fundamental truths on which to base
further reflections. God loves all men without distinction of race
and person. More than others, Paul's admonition to his disciple
Timothy has given substance to this belief. " First of all, then,
I urge that petitions, prayers, intercessions and thanksgivings be
offered for all men: for sovereigns and all in high office, that
we may lead a tranquil and quiet life in full observance of
religion and high standards of morality. Such prayer is right,
and approved by *God our Saviour, whose will it is that all men
should find salvation and come to know the truth.* For there
is one God, and also one Mediator between God and men,
Christ Jesus, Himself man, who sacrificed Himself to win freedom
for all mankind, so providing at the fitting time [that is, the
" fullness of time "] proof of the divine purpose; of this I was
appointed herald and apostle—this is no lie, but the truth—to
instruct the nations in the true faith " (I Tim 2:1-7).

Not without reason, the exegetes point out that when Paul
dictated those words, he did not have before his eyes the question
which confronts us now. He therefore could not very well meet
it to our satisfaction. The heathens Paul knew of were the
" nations " most of which belonged to the Roman Empire; the
other heathens, however, are not excluded. What strikes us most
is Paul's emphasis and insistence in recalling his own mission.
It had been his mandate in a still young Church to testify to
and to fight for the *absolute universality of salvation.*

The Church has availed herself of this Pauline text whenever
a new experience compelled her to view the old problem on a
larger scale and in a wider perspective. At this period of history,
which is ours, most peoples have obtained or conquered their
independence and their first emancipation from their previous
feudal condition. Only now can we fittingly set the problem
in the light of world history. As long as we look upon foreign
people as " barbarians, " for no other reason than that they are
different from ourselves (a phenomenon common to most civilizations), our natural aversion to them makes us reluctant to
accept that they have not been forsaken by God; an unwillingness
growing weaker when we come to respect them as " men. "

From the era of the great prophets onward, Scripture teaches us further that each man will be judged according to his own works. Christ rejected the ancient Hebrew notion, still prevalent in His day, that sin may cause effects pernicious to others. On that point we shall dwell later on in our chapter on sin. Let it be enough to say here that such a notion of sin belongs to the order of magic. Sin, in its full sense, is always personal: it consists in the deliberate rejection of God's love. Yet, we do not insinuate that, through our personal sins, we cannot do damage to our neighbor. Our solidarity enters into play whenever we do good and whenever we do evil. But we cannot commit sin in the place of another. That is impossible.

Better perhaps than formerly, we realize that man, in his religious and moral conceptions, in his customs and behavior, remains greatly dependent on the ideas and morality of his time and cultural surroundings. It is an illusion, an oversimplified fancy, current though among people suffering from a rationalistic idea of the natural law and conscience, to imagine that, in order to free an African instantaneously from all dread, it is enough to explain to him that the spirits have no power over him. After centuries of Christianity, age-old superstitions of that kind have not yet disappeared from our own midst.

As we mentioned previously, it took long centuries before the Jews were in possession of a higher standard of morality and of a more profound conception of what God really is. It took also centuries before Christianity had dispelled from among us all residual pagan ideas. Why, then, expect it to be otherwise with the heathen today? Let us repeat: man lives in time. He is time.

It is precisely on the level of religion, that is, the domain where naturally and owing to awe and dread of the divine the force of tradition is strongest and most enduring, that evolution is at its slowest in time. Such a phenomenon is not only normal, but wholesome. Let us note in passing that an evolution on that level does not always proceed in the right direction. It can spell regress.

In the course of his gradual ascent, an individual who has grown up amid such traditions and is imbued with them from infancy, will have to set his progress in *this* light, if he is to form his conscience. It is commonly said among us that moral conscience is inborn in man. And that is true, but within certain limits only; for, conscience remains to a high degree dependent on the notions and customs of the surroundings in which we have been brought up. More still, our sinfulness may dim the light of conscience, even deform it. The picture of God which man formed for himself has, through the centuries, assumed the most fanciful, and at times the most repulsive, shapes. And the same misfortune befell also the ideas of how God had to be honored and served by man. It should be clear, then, that the maturing process of conscience demands time.

Lastly, the gradual evolution of a religious and moral conscience does not necessarily keep in step with cultural and technical progress. We are aware of this fact in our own milieu. More than one superior civilization welcomed rather crude representations of God, while very primitive modes of life have known very pure manifestations of belief.

Man commits sin only when he acts against his conscience. Considering that conscience remains dependent on prevalent notions about God, religion, civilization and morality, it is possible for a man to make mistakes without necessarily incurring personal guilt.

But, let us come back to the main subject of this chapter: God's presence in our history. As we have seen, theologians generally agree in accepting that all men without exception live in a state in which they remain called to grace. But, textbook theology presents that teaching in a more or less extrinsic, static manner. No question is asked regarding the existential consequences flowing from it for man. In another place, we have explained the nature of that " state " in terms of the living and loving presence of God in the world. The divine presence produces in man a gracious orientation towards truth and good, which God is. Could not this insight help us to learn something more about the " way God deals with man " in pagandom?

We cannot but accept the fact of God's presence in pagans. God loves them as He loves us. He is their God no less than ours. They, too, were created to be redeemed by Christ. In them, too, the Spirit is at work.

Nor was all this entirely unknown in the Old Testament, although the Jews gave it hardly a thought. According to Scripture, God made a Covenant with Noah. Now, Noah was a patriarch, but no Jew. God's Covenant with Israel dates from Abraham. The text we shall presently cite has clearly in view all men. At the end of the deluge, God addressed Noah. The first sentences of that divine speech do no more than restate the doctrine concerning creation; namely that all men and animals depend on God, that they are to multiply on earth, that no man may kill another, and that man is king of creation because he is made in the image of God. The text ends with God's solemn pronouncement of the Covenant He now makes with man—a Covenant of which the rainbow is to be a sign; a sign taken from nature at the close of a rainstorm, and turned into a religious symbol because henceforth it will signify God's merciful love.

" And God spoke: ' Behold the sign of the Covenant which I establish between Me and you and all living things that are

with you, *for all generations to come.* I place My bow in the
clouds, and it will become the sign of the Covenant between
Me and the earth.   When I shall gather the clouds over the
earth and when the bow will appear in the clouds, I shall
remember the Covenant between Me and you and *all living
beings,* that is, all flesh; and the waters shall no more grow into
a deluge to destroy all flesh.   When the bow stands in the
clouds, I shall see it and I shall remember the eternal covenant
between God and all living beings, that is, *all flesh* that is on the
earth.'   And God told Noah: 'this is the sign of the Covenant
which I establish between Me and all flesh that is on the
earth'" (Gen 9:12-17).

Here we have probably one of the most impressive pronounce-
ments of the Old Testament; its solemnity is enhanced by the
almost ritual recurrence of the divine promise.   The deluge
had been the sign of God's anger against the sin of man.
"Yahweh saw that the wickedness of man was very great
on earth and that his heart formed only evil designs all day long.
It repented Yahweh that he had created man on earth, and he was
sad in his heart" (Gen 6:5-6).   "But Noah found grace in the
eyes of Yahweh" (Gen 6:8).   This "just man who walked
with God, heathen and no Jew," was to receive in the name
of all mankind a message of love, a message of mercy and divine
patience: a message delivered for the benefit of all without
exception.

It may well be that the purpose of the story of Job was no
other than to illustrate in the concrete terms of a parable the
meaning of God's providence.   Nothing in that narrative indicates that Job was a Jew.   The Fathers of the Church noticed
this silence; more than once they pointed to Noah and Job
when they spoke of God's dealings with the heathen.   God,
then, has found a "just man" outside the Jewish race.   The
fact is attested by Holy Writ.

The Fathers of the Church were aware of still another perspective by which to approach the mystery.   They frequently speak
of the Church that came into existence since Adam and Abel:
"*Ecclesia ab Adamo, Ecclesia ab Abel,*"   St. Augustine returns
on several occasions to "the one and true religion" which
had always existed unchanged, though it had assumed a variety
of symbols, rites and forms, in accordance with the rhythm of
ages and civilizations.

We shall quote two of St. Augustine's most striking statements.
Before doing so, let us first state briefly the basic conviction of
which the texts are no more than explicitations.   It is our
considered opinion that that conviction must stand even today.
There are other ways in which the Fathers, and St. Augustine,
have tried to state the case—attempts that have been rendered

out of date by the factual history of mankind's religions. But we think that the Augustinian fundamental vision of the problem, as we shall state it, is better than the one prevailing today.

We are wont to say today that the Church is the *normal* way to God, and that outside the Church salvation is normally not to be had. The fact is nevertheless admitted that men do get saved outside the Church; in which case, salvation is due to some exceptional means of God's providence and mercy. Further, we are wont to declare that those " anonymous Christians " have at least implicitly accepted the Church; and while saying so, we fail to notice the shift of accent in our words. St. Augustine will say that those men have always sought *Christ,* even when unaware of it. We cannot, of course, separate the Church from Christ; for she is the Body of the Head. Yet, to our way of thinking, it seems theologically safer to start from Christ rather than from the Church; for this manner of proceeding guarantees that our conception of the Church, as we intend to propose it here, is truly rooted in Christ.

Reacting against a "closed" notion of the Church, Dr. H. Schlette has recently inverted the terms of the thesis.[28] According to him, the non-Christian religions would be the ordinary way towards God, while the Church would be the extraordinary way.

Both these appear to us to suffer from the same defect. Neither of them takes for its starting point the Person of Christ, the one Mediator between God and man; and both undervalue the decisive character of the divine initiative revealed in the grace of the Church. God's gracious gesture is divinely free and, above all, one. *God goes His way with men, and remains eternally true to Himself.* That is the reason why we find it rather unfortunate to distinguish *different* ways by which man may approach God in our actually existing world.

The Fathers have seen this better than we. For them, there is but one Church, "one and true religion," ever since the beginning of mankind. There is only one Christ. And the one essential structure of this one religion is given us in the one *dialectic of grace.* On that ground, we believe that our book will prove very fitting for reflecting on those difficult problems.

The main burden of our book is the loving presence of the Father, the Son and the Holy Spirit in the world; which presence is the prime source and ultimate meaning of grace and, therefore, also of salvation, of redemption and of the "one and true religion," "religion" taken in the sense of man's relations with

---

[28] Dr H. Schlette, *Die Religionen als Thema der Theologie. Questiones disputatae,* Band 22 (Freiburg i. Br.: Herder, 1964).

God. " Since the beginning, " the creation of the world has had no other purpose. Of this movement, from the Father toward us and from us back to the Father, Christ is the revolving pivot: He is the one Mediator. In this light, there can be mention of the Church only insofar as we conceive of her *in Christ,* as His Body, and energized by the one Spirit. When the life of grace is seen for what it is, as arising from, through and toward the indwelling, it is self-consistent always and everywhere, for all peoples and ages. God remains eternally faithful to His word, a word of love. Grace, its offspring, is self-consistent when understood not as an abstract, preter-historical and merely spiritual entity, but as a life which keeps in close step with the history of the life of the human race, encompasses it and animates it in the concrete, whatever the situation in which humanity may find itself. Then, indeed, and in this sense, the Church has always existed; for Christ has always existed for man's sake, and has been consequently forever man's Mediator—whether He was foretold or already come into our midst. And in that sense, too, there has existed, always and everywhere, a " one and true religion, " whether it was being prepared obscurely, or manifestly and fully actualized in the Church. No man has at any time approached God outside Christ's grace.

It should be easier for us now to visualize what Augustine and several other Fathers had before their mind when they pondered over our problem. The first quotation we give now is an extract from one of St. Augustine's letters; for all the world, it looks as if it was written for the sake of the present section of our chapter. A priest, Deogratias by name, had had a conversation with a pagan; the latter prepared a few questions for Augustine's consideration; but too shy to present himself in person before the celebrated bishop, he asked Deogratias to act as go-between. The third question so prepared is exactly the one dealt with in this present section: why did Christ come so late? Did the religious tradition of the Romans not include some ritual and religious practices of true religious content? As we said: this is precisely our present query.

Augustine had the advantage of possessing first-hand knowledge of Roman civilization. We, on the other hand, when we write, for instance, about Hinduism or Buddhism, have generally to rely on second-hand information, often taken from books presenting romantic views on those religions, and not always tallying with the reality. Augustine knew Rome, its civilization, literature and religious modes of expression. Until his dying day, he valued them, loved them. The day on which the barbarian Alaric captured Rome and sacked the imperial city, proved to be one of the most somber of his life. His trust in divine providence was severely shaken; from this interior crisis of his, there sprang up one of his finest works: *On the City of God.*

His reply to Deogratias contains some very valuable remarks. "Therefore, from the beginning of the human race, all those who believed in Him [namely, Christ], and knew Him and have lived a good and devout life according to His commands, whenever and wherever they lived, *undoubtedly were saved through Him.* Just as we [the Christians today] believe in Him, both as remaining with the Father and as coming in the flesh, so the ancients believed in Him, both as remaining with the Father and about to come in the flesh. We should not think that there have been different kinds of faith, or more than one kind of salvation, because what is now spoken of as something accomplished in the course of time, was then foretold as something to come; and because *one and the same thing* [that is, religion] was foretold or is now preached by divine rites and ceremonies, we are not to think that they are different things, or that there are different kinds of salvation. Let us leave to God the choice of anything that is to happen which tends to the salvation of souls of the faithful and the good; and for ourselves, let us hold to obedience. Thus, *one and the same religion* has been outwardly expressed and practiced under one set of names and signs in times past, and another set at present; it was more hidden then and more open now; it had fewer worshippers in olden times, more later on, *yet it is one and the same true religion.* " [29]

A little further on in the same letter, St. Augustine had compared that phenomenon of a "reality" *(res ipsa)*, identically the same under different religious signs, with the phenomenon of languages. The same truths are uttered by means of different sounds and word combinations. He concluded his comparison: "The saving grace of this religion, the only true one, through which alone true salvation is truly promised, has never been refused to any one who was worthy of it; and whoever lacked it was unworthy of it. " [30]

We have still another assertion of Augustine, which is perhaps more striking still, because more concise and set down in writing at a moment of his life when the great doctor examined before God his theological works, correcting when necessary. This reappraisal of his thought appeared in the book entitled *Retractationes.* Be it well understood that the word *Retractationes* does not mean "retractations" in current English, but

---

[29] Augustine, *Epistola 102 ad Deo gratias presbyterum,* 2, n. 12; cf. *St. Augustine's letters,* Vol. 2, translated by Sister Wilfrid Parsons, S.N.D. (New York: The Fathers of the Church, 1953), pp. 155-156.
[30] *Ibid.,* 2, n. 15; cf. Sister Wilfrid Parsons' translation, p. 159.

rather *revisions*. By no means does Augustine mean to imply that in these pages he revokes what he previously taught. Rather, he passes in review his former writings, frequently giving the history of the origin and ulterior development of his thought; here and there, he corrects less fortunate expressions or arguments; or he corroborates his earlier writings.

Touching our present point, no correction is contemplated. On the contrary, fearing that what he had written in the past might be misunderstood, he gives clearer precision to his idea. And it is interesting to note that the sharper definition he gives to his conception in the present instance is, to some extent, opposite to the tendency fairly prevalent today.

In his minor work *On the True Religion,* he has summed up one of his arguments in the conclusion: "This is the Christian religion in our day. To know it and to follow it is the safest and surest way to salvation." [31] Contemporary theology would surely approve of this statement, and would in all probability feel no need of entering into further precision. Not so Augustine. In his *Retractationes* he remarks concerning his affirmation: "This I said thinking of the word [that is, religion] and not having in mind the reality designated by that word. For, *the reality itself (res ipsa),* which we now call the Christian religion, existed already among the ancients, and has never been wanting *from man's earliest beginnings* till the day Christ would appear in the flesh. From Christ's day on, *the true religion,* already existing, received the name of Christian religion. For, when the apostles started out preaching Him [meaning, Christ] after His resurrection and ascension, and when many believed in Him, His followers were called "Christians," for the first time at Antioch—so it is written in the Acts (11:26). That is why I said: 'This is the Christian religion in our day,' not meaning that it did not formerly exist, but that it received this name only then.'" [32] St. Augustine does not at all deny that Christ's Church is the safest and surest way to divine salvation; but, at the end of his life, he is intent on stressing once more the fact that the unique mission of the Church has in no sense undone God's salvific work before Christ. "The reality" existed from the beginning of mankind, and was ordained to Christ. In Christ, then, became manifest what was previously hidden, though it had never ceased to be real.

Here we have what should be called an "open vision" on the Church. Thanks to Pope John XXIII, it has been charismatically revived in the Church. Whenever we still meet with the

---

[31] Augustine, *De vera Religione,* 10, n. 19; *PL* 34, 131.

[32] Augustine, *Retractationes,* 1, 12, n. 3; *PL* 32, 603.

" closed vision, " we have the distinct impression that the Catholic Church has, in her turn, run up a fair score of *sectarian* traits, owing perhaps to the persecutions and divisions suffered during her history. Every sect is inclined to imagine that whoever does not belong to the elect will be consigned to the region of eternal darkness. Now, our age asks whether such narrow views are in agreement with God's view of human history.

Grace among the pagans

It is quite certain that the Fathers of the Church had an understanding far more profound than ours of the history of God's dealings with men. And that is unavoidable for any one who nourishes his religious thought by an assiduous reading of Holy Scripture. From the earliest beginnings, and surely since the day the first man was unjustly put to death, the Church has been in existence, at least as a sign of what was to come. The blood of Abel, a pious man acceptable to God, prefigured the blood of the sinless Christ who was to gather round Him the Church of God. And Abel did not belong to Israel as such. That led the Fathers of the Church into believing that already in prehistory the Church had been born. For, from the start, God predestined a people, assembled it around Him, brought to it new members.

As proof that it was the study of Holy Writ which suggested to Augustine, and some other Fathers, their deeper understanding of the divine salvation as being the work of grace, we have the following declaration of Augustine: " It is by the grace of Him [that is, by the grace of Christ; a more accurate translation has a more forceful ring in it: it is in view of and for the sake of Christ's grace] that the just men of antiquity have found faith and have been borne up by the same grace so that they had the joy of knowing Him in anticipation, and some of them even foretold His coming. Just men like these we can discover among the people of Israel, as for instance, Moses and Jesus Nave, and Samuel and David, and still others. Such just men can also be found either *outside* the [chosen] people of Israel, as for instance, Job, or prior to Israel's election, men like Abraham, Noah, and whoever is spoken of in Scripture or is passed over in silence. " [33]

Now, if it is true that God has never abandoned men, and

---

[33] Augustine, *De perfectione justitiae hominis,* 19, n. 42; *PL* 44, 315.

that His love always dwelt in them—were it only by way of a
nostalgic hankering after His truth and love—it must follow
that His love could bear fruit in them, too.

We might perhaps recognize two levels on which God clearly
and actively " enrolled " new members in the ranks of His people.
The first level is the level of human conscience—what in
biblical language is called the human " heart. " The gentle
appeal of His grace evoked even among pagans a return of love
for God. Divine patience tolerated that this return of love be
expressed in unpolished, at times very imperfect, ways; God has
always accepted men *as they are*. They knew of nothing
better. But, whenever a man has acknowledged in faith and
love that he was made for God, he has then really met God;
in him grace has been at work. And if he has been saved
through that faith of his, he owes it above all to Christ who
alone is man's road to God.

If we look for further evidence, we have the experience
gathered from a better knowledge of peoples and religious
cults. We admit that many among them are oppressed by the
fear of evil spirits, or of the forces of nature, or of one or other
terrifying mental conceptions formed concerning the nature of
God. Others still have their counsel darkened by coarse religious
and moral customs unworthy of man. They do not possess
the full truth, but can only grope after it. There are peoples,
however, who enjoy a higher degree of religious piety, verging
even on mysticism, as is shown in their literature. But more
than these, the simple ones, the anonymous mass, the unknown,
the poor and forgotten ones: whenever with genuine goodness
and truth, they have turned toward their neighbor, they have
found God. None of Christ's words is to be neglected, nor are
we allowed to prefer our academical abstractions to the Lord's
own teaching: " I tell you this: anything you did for one of
My brothers here, however humble, *you did for Me* " (Mt 25:40).
Theologians have given deep thought to what is the minimum
of truth concerning God which man must believe in order to be
saved. They took for their guidance the words of the Epistle
to the Hebrews: " Anyone who comes to God must believe that
He exists and that He rewards those that search for Him "
(Heb 11:6). And so it is, beyond questioning. But in the concrete, such knowledge will come under more than one guise.
It is certain that we must give at least as much authority to
Matthew's text and other like words of Scripture, as to the lines
from the Epistle to the Hebrews; we need them all for the solution of the questions now under consideration.

St. Augustine was aware of this. He was fully convinced
of the decisive power of true love. " It is the Holy Spirit whom
the wicked cannot receive; for, He is the wellspring of which

Scripture says: 'Keep the fountain to yourself, and let no stranger
share it with you'" (Prov 16:17). Augustine follows here a
reading found in an ancient Latin version, but not occurring in our
Bible. "Even though they [the wicked] frequent our churches,
they cannot be numbered among the children of God. They
have no right to the fountain of life. A wicked man can also
be baptized; he can even prophesy.... A wicked man can
receive the sacrament of the Body and Blood of the Lord....
A wicked man can bear the name of Christ, I mean, he can
go by the name of Christian, and yet be a wicked man....
And so, a wicked man can receive all the sacraments. But
to have love and to be wicked at the same time, that is impossible. Love is the proper gift of the Spirit; the Spirit is the
exceptional fount [of life]. The Spirit of God invites us to
drink of it. The Spirit of God urges us to quench our thirst
in Him." [34]

To solve a problem like the one we are considering here,
abstract theories are of no use. God's love is of a more
concrete order, and what He expects from us has to be as
concrete as Himself. In our opinion, some converts from
paganism have left us good evidence of this, those converts
in particular who experienced that their conversion proved to be
the fulfillment of their former life in paganism, rather than a
complete break with it. When we read that a religious-minded
man like John Wu, formerly Chiang Kai Shek's ambassador
to the Vatican, perceives that his Christian faith is the seal and
an enrichment of what he lived in his pagan days, we know
that God's grace was operative in him already then. [35]

We have something similar in the life of communist Michael
Khoriakhov, who from early youth had been schooled in athe-
ism [36] From his own testimony we learn that he encountered
God, in a vague though authentic way, in the complete surrender

---

[34] Augustine, *In epistolam Joannis ad Parthos*, 7, 4, 4; *PL* 35, 2032.
[35] John Ching Hsung Wu, *Beyond East and West* (London: Sheed &
Ward, 1952). See also Wu's *The Interior Carmel*, the threefold way of
love (London, Sheed & Ward, 1954). Also an interesting witness is
Jacques Dournes' *Dieu aime les paiens*, Une mission de l'Eglise sur
les plateaux du Vietnam (Théologie, 54) (Paris: Aubier. 1963).
[36] Michel Khoriakoff, *Je me mets hors la loi* (Paris: Editions du
Monde Nouveau, 1947): « Moscow meant everything to us and, all to
a man, we were prepared to resist till death. In the face of death,
all material values, I mean whatever serves to prop up our religious
indifference, ceased to be values. The one sense (sentiment), necessary
and vital, revealed itself to be "the sense of heaven," the awareness
of a responsibility, immense and incommensurable, not to oneself
nor to the country, but to one whose presence we suddenly realized—to
God," p. 27. Cf. also of the same author: *Moscou ne croit pas aux
larmes* (Paris: Editions du Monde Nouveau, 1951).

of himself to his people during the battle for Leningrad. He grew clearly conscious that only a value, superior to the country, was entitled to exact the complete sacrifice of his life. He asserts further that many among his friends have undergone the same experience. But they failed to keep true to the interior voice speaking in their hearts. It is fidelity to this interior voice that brought him ultimately to Christ. In this instance, too, we note that grace demands total fidelity, that it reaches its perfection in fidelity, and that it normally leads to Christ.

The last step towards the Church is for many people impossible here on earth. Many know neither the Church nor Christ. What they may have read about these had been written by men who knew as little as they. Let us acknowledge, with all due humility, that what we observe among us, Christians, is all too often a caricature of true Christianity. And God respects a powerlessness not of their own making.

This is the place to draw attention to the greatest scandal that keeps many pagans outside the Church: the divisions among Christians. Ecumenism arose precisely in mission countries, though unfortunately not among the Catholics. How can an Indian believe in the God of peace, in the Christ of love and in the Spirit of union when their followers are so divided from each other into so many different Churches?

Beside the level of conscience, there is still another level on which God meets man. Man is not purely interior, not mere conscience. God has always wanted to find man in human actions, in visible human gestures, in the visible worship practiced in human communities.

By His incarnation, Christ sanctified the whole cosmos. The most common things on earth: bread, water, fire, bodily gestures of man, kneeling, folding of hands, congregational prayer: all have been blessed and sanctified in Him. And so, pagan rites also can be channels of grace. They are not necessarily bad in themselves, unless they offend basic principles of human morality. They differ from our sacraments in that their meaning remains ambiguous, and also on account of sin. They can lead to sin; and they can lead to holiness when they are freed from all evil import and are lived up to with a pure heart.

And now we come to a point which we are apt to misunderstand. We say: the sacraments, instituted by Christ, are *sure* means of salvation. And so they are. But the statement is patent of a false interpretation should we imagine that they automatically place eternal happiness into the hands of men.

In the domain of grace, I mean, when it comes to the complete surrender of self to God in faith and love, *nothing differentiates* the pagan from us. St. Thomas Aquinas said as much, though he has his mind on the similarity between the Jews and Christians with regard to the passion of Christ. [37]

Both pagans and Christians alike have finally to come to a true *surrender of the heart* by faith and love. No other way is to be looked for, there is none. Sacraments cannot release us from the greatest of all duties: faith in God, love of God.

The sure guarantee, inherent in the sacraments, stems from Christ. In the sacraments of the Church we have complete assurance—and this time, without a trace of ambiguity—of the loving presence of Christ and of His Spirit testified to in the sacrament; and this guarantee is given to any individual who worthily receives the sacrament. We may add that the sacraments are beyond any possible doubt the adequate means of salvation and are adapted by God to our human nature which must seek to reach Him through the medium of visible gestures and actions. The ritual prayers, used in the administration of the sacraments, teach us the plain truth concerning our salvation in Christ. Herein lies the absolute guarantee of the sacraments; nothing similar is to be had in the rites practiced outside the Church. But let us repeat: not one sacrament *frees us from the fundamental obligation of returning to God love for love.* In respect of this obligation, both pagans and Christians are identically situated. The pagan, though, will find it harder, because he has to reach God through a jungle of degenerate practices, through impure, or at least unsafe, religious notions and ideas.

" *Church, what do you say of yourself?* "

These are the words spoken by Paul VI at the opening of the second session of the Second Vatican Council; they sum up the task before the Council. That is also *the question our age is asking,* as will be clear to the reader who has followed us so far.

The answer, given in former days, was simple and easy to understand. Here it is: all men outside the Church are lost; the Church alone leads men to heaven. In essence, that answer remains always true; but the nuances that ought to qualify it presuppose a deeper insight into the meaning which faith has for each individual man.

At present the Church stands at the crossroads. What is the vocation proper to the Church? and what is its nature? The

---

[37] St. Thomas Aquinas: "By faith in the Passion of Christ, our forefathers [namely, the Jews] have been justified *exactly as we now," Summa Theologica.* III, q. 62, a. 6, in c.

second answer can be given in a satisfactory manner only in the light of the history of salvation.

The facts outrun theological thought. And this is normal in the Church. The Church is no system: she is the living Body of Christ and is energized by the Holy Spirit. She lives on, often enough in spite and at the expense of our theories. For, theology should be built on facts—facts which happen to be God's action in our history.

John XXIII has performed a prophetic task, the significance of which history will judge more accurately than we can do at present. Today, already, we turn dizzy and—the great pity of it!—terrified at the new responsibility thrown upon our shoulders by God in the astounding developments taking place within the Church. Pope John threw the windows of the Church wide open. He established a Secretariate for unity among the Christians and entrusted to it the care of contacting non-Catholic Christians in a dialogue which is to be henceforth an official task of the Church. His successor, Paul VI, has instituted a Secretariate to start relations with non-Christian religions, an assignment far more arduous than the preceding one. In his first encyclical, *Ecclesiam suam,* Paul VI emphasized once again the necessity of " openness " in the dialogue with non-Catholics and non-Christians. Those who have followed the proceedings of the Council are aware that the sudden shift within the Church has frightened and even scandalized a good many people. Some wanted to know whether no treason was being committed against the mission entrusted by Christ to His Church. Others, though relying on the guidance of the Spirit, felt ill at ease and lost on an unfamiliar road.

" Church, what do you say of yourself? " In the fourth century, at the time of Constantine's conversion, and more especially in the tenth century while the fight was on against imperial and princely powers, there sprang up in the Church a conception with which we are well acquainted. It found a well-defined formulation during the Middle Ages. The idea amounts to this: the Church is God's Kingdom on earth. And what that meant to convey carried more conviction formerly than it does now. Under the rule of the pope and the Roman emperor, public and private life had been wholly " christened. " Christian society had gathered to itself many nations and kingdoms within the unity of one faith and one civilization. The Church on earth was a preliminary image of what heaven was to be.

That image, however, or rather that illusion, has been slowly crumbling for centuries. No one denies that Scripture teaches us that the " Kingdom of God " begins on earth; but it teaches us also that it can turn into an actuality only in heaven. God's Kingdom is to be achieved " at the consummation of time, " and not before. Until then, in God's field there grows darnel and corn, that is, good men and bad men. We have learned from experience that political unity and power can neither build up the Kingdom nor preserve it in being. Political power may at times be of use to the Church; but in the past, it has more often fought against the Church and hindered her progress. In any case, the political powers have received from God a mission widely different from that of concerning themselves with matters of conscience and faith, or of interfering with what belongs to the Church. Little by little, the Church herself came to realize that her mission does not consist in meddling with matters of the State, as long as the State does not endanger her religious mission.

We live in a pluralistic world, that means a world in which a variety of religious ideas, of moral codes and ways of life form an odd medley, and yet have to keep up good neighborly relations if our earthly existence is to be at all bearable. The nostalgia for Constantinian times, or for medieval conditions, has not yet died a natural death. Because those better times are part of an irrevocable past, the Church thought she could do no better than, in self-defense, take refuge in a sort of ghetto. Her idea was to endeavor to keep alive the notion of a Church, " Kingdom of God, " as had been held in the Middle Ages, but now within a restricted area and within walls of her own.

Can we recognize in this notion the correct concept of what the Church really is? Whatever the case may be, neither Christ, nor the Apostles, nor the Christians of the early centuries, have acted that way. When Augustine wrote his great work *On the City of God,* he perceived that the frontiers of the City of God and of the City of Satan cut right across the frontiers of the Roman Empire and clean across those of the visible Church. The early Christians were fortunate in knowing that they could place no reliance on the State, nor on social or political organizations. They never thought of trusting in anything except in the power of God as it manifests itself through the interior and exterior guidance of the Spirit. They never fell victim to our modern form of Pelagianism which puts firmer trust in the power of governments, or in the art of modern organization, or in any kind of external influence supposed to favor the birth, the growth and consolidation of the faith. We rejoice to see that such an outlook has been rejected by the Council. Faith is a personal conviction; it grows on conviction.

It is high time we make our choice between those two concepts. Obviously, our choice is not without consequences for practical life, not least for life within the Church. According to the first concept, the ghetto-Church, the bastion-Church, it is enough that all Christians be pious and good, that they faithfully perform their religious duties, that they strictly adhere to the line given by the religious authorities, and leave to their betters the care of searching more deeply into the tenets of faith. When saying so, we have in mind some definite, and not so rare, religious manifestations within Catholicism. Unfortunately, the concept, just now outlined, betrays itself day by day to be less and less viable in our pluralistic world. It has brought in its wake the loss of the workers in many countries; it causes increasing losses among the intellectuals. The walls of our ghetto are badly breached.

In the second concept, the personal conviction of each member of the Church holds a place of pride. Borne up by their conviction, one and all undertake their particular responsibility in whatever fields they may be laboring, whether in private or in public life, in the sciences or in technical pursuits. The religious authorities placed over them by Christ are there to serve and guide them in their respective responsibilities, to stand by them and to cheer them on. Religious authority, so we see in the Gospel, is service of the community. A point not to be overlooked: mature knowledge of the faith, in the measure of each one's capacity and possibility, is indispensable.

As befits a theologian, we started out from the factual evolution taking place in the Church under the guidance of the Spirit.

That evolution was signalized by Pope Paul's pilgrimage to the Holy Land, by his encounter with the Eastern patriarchs, by his addresses to the King of Jordan, a Muslim, and to the President of Israel, a Jew. In the allocution to the Roman nobility, shortly after New Year 1964, Paul VI solemnly declared that the Holy See renounces all merely political and earthly power.

There remains a final question, the most important to us here. Are we to understand that the recent evolution in the Church, which we believe to be God's doing, can help us towards a deeper insight into the nature and vocation of the Church? We think so. For, it enables us to read the Gospels with the clear eyes of the early Christians instead of through the medium of later civilizations.

The Church, in imitation of Christ, is not self-seeking. She belongs to the world, to all who dwell in it, to those who are ignorant of her or, perhaps, ignore her. Like Christ, she is set apart *to serve* men, a duty Pope John was fond of harkening back to. In the conciliar aula, it was often repeated: the Church's primary duty does not consist in seeking to assert her privileges, her rights, or her ascendency. Her one weapon is the power of the Spirit which maintains her in God's truth as Christ preached it. Her most prized privilege is to show love for all men. All very fine, we might think. But the question is: Do we, in the concrete, live up to it in every department of our ecclesial life?

In the last analysis, all our considerations rest on the fact that the Church is the temple of the most Holy Trinity. And this brings us back to the main theme of our book: the living and loving presence of God in our world.

In a previous chapter, we saw how the divine presence has become a reality in the Church, since grace sanctifies us both individually and in communion with all the other faithful. We now want to know whether the same presence is being actualized in history as well. And here we are facing what is grandest in history.

If the Father, the Son and the Holy Ghost dwell in us as living Persons, it follows that their presence in our hearts and in the Church has a bearing on history, at least on history seen from the mysterious "within" where God is leader and mover. It is through the Church—therefore, through her members—that God manifests His love and His truth to all men. The Church has to be on earth the visibility of that love. She must bear witness to that love and announce that truth. Herein lies her service of God and men.

A subject related to what we have said just now is the consideration of a state of mental uneasiness proper to our age. And it is this. In former days, grace was described as the perfection of individual persons. But that is too narrow a view. Even when we take the broadened and more correct view that individual perfection lies in a loving relationship with God, we still run the risk of stopping at that. We shall grant that in this view all earthly hardships are matters of secondary importance when compared with the holiness accruing to us from such a relationship. But then, also, the "human" side of life on earth appears at best to be an occasion for abnegation, for personal merit and the practice of virtue. Now, that is a dangerous view, and all the more perilous if we bolster it up with the theory that, one way or another, the "human" falls outside the range and reach of grace. What have we to think of it?

Is it not as an attribute of God's love, as Christ revealed it to us, that it goes out to the others? It is striking how, in the spirit of the Scripture—not excluding the Old Testament—perfection is spoken of in terms of a commission to go out to men and to bring God to the world. *Grace is inseparable from mission.* And for that matter, so are the sacraments. Each sacrament confers on us a definite *mission* in the Church that has to be fulfilled and bear fruit.

Let us not go to the length of holding in contempt the personal relationship of love with God. Some authors have done that, carried away by the violence of their reaction against too narrow a concept of what personal sanctification truly is. Let us not forget that Christ set us the example of solitary prayer at night in the mountains. And no one has ever loved God the Father and men more than He. Further, the most precious manifestation of love will always be faith, hope and love for God.

It is a fact, nonetheless, that the Gospels, especially the Johannine Gospel, stress the *radiating* power of faith and charity. As to hope: we do not hope for purely personal interests; but all together, as one, we put our trust in God to obtain our common end. St. John never tires of repeating: he who loves God, keeps the commandments, loves the neighbor. According to him, the Father's nature is the love which is revealed to us in the Son, unites us all in and through the Spirit, and turns us toward the neighbor. One feels tempted to say that, in St. John's doctrine, love is a stream moving only in one direction: it comes down on earth from the Father, through the Son in the Spirit, and flows on in brotherly love towards the world. The Apostle appears to take no notice of a love that is just a relationship with God—or, he seems to leave that aspect of love to eternity.

Let us not exaggerate, though. John says very exactly: " Love consists in this: *not that we have loved God,* but that He has loved us and sent His Son as the remedy for the defilement of our sins. Beloved, if God has loved us, *we in turn are bound to love one another.* No one has ever seen God; but God Himself dwells in us *if we love one another;* His love is brought to *perfection* within us " (I Jn 4: 10 ff). In the discourse after the Last Supper, John sums up his profound theology of Christ; he places on the lips of Christ: " It is not for these alone that I pray, but for all those also who through their words put their faith in Me. May they all be one: *as Thou, Father, art in Me, and I in Thee, so also may they be one in Us,* that the world may believe that Thou didst send Me. The glory which thou didst give Me, I have given to them, that they may be one, *as We are.* I in them and Thou in Me, may they be perfectly one. Then the world will learn that Thou didst send Me, that Thou didst love them as Thou didst Me. . . . I made Thy name known to them, and will make it known, so that the love Thou hast for Me may be in them, and I may be in them " (Jn 17:20-26).

A Christianity which would do away with all of profession of faith and love towards the Father—and all prayer implies such faith and love—is no Christianity at all. There does exist today a tendency to hold such a " religion without religion, " and it appeals to J. A. T. Robinson for support. But the Bishop of Woolwich made it clear—alas, mostly in private conversations—that a "religionless" Christianity is to be preferred in cases where religion has degenerated into what he defined as: recourse to a God invoked exlusively when we are at the end of our wits, helpless, recourse to a "*deus ex machina,*" a God who is called in when we can go no further by our own strength. This sort of religion, surely, caricatures God and prayer at the same time. How in the name of common sense can we live "in Christ" unless, with and in Christ, we keep ourselves in the presence of the Father! Attention to the Father entails no estrangement from the world. On the contrary, we can go to the Father, with and in Christ, only when we have both feet solidly planted on this earth.

Grace, we said, is love; it is also love for men in the world. True love cannot live in human nature, as it did in Christ, unless it strikes root in the world as it actually is. Nothing is as real as God; nothing is as real as love. Consequently, grace cannot alienate us from men, or turn us away from the neighbor on the plea of "self-realization." Rather the other way round: love will be a help to us to arrive at the looked-for perfection the moment we forget and forego self for the sake of serving others.

We have here a good proof in support of the truth that "our divinization is our humanization." We sow God's love when we keep ourselves in firm solidarity with all our fellows, when we share in their worries and joys, show great respect for their good will, for their longings and aspirations, when we feel with them in their loneliness and sufferings. That is the moment we serve them in Christ. We shall then also prize whatever ennobles mankind: culture, art, science and technique, civilizations and ways of life, insofar as these do not offend against divine law. We shall sow God's love in this world of ours when we share in the respect which God Himself has for it. Nothing short of this is necessary if we want to experience what a life of grace really is. Sin is the one thing we may not tolerate, either in ourselves or in others; though, with Christ, we may show a predilection for sinners, were it only because we well know how much we ourselves stand in need of forgiveness.

To speak plainly: we shall not expect politics to help to spread or consolidate the faith; but, if we are politicians, we shall behave as witnesses of Christ in the complicated game of earthly politics. We shall scorn neither science nor technical progress; but we shall keep alive the testimony of true faith and carry it with us into the sphere of culture and human knowledge. We shall not place social problems on an equal footing with religion; but we shall imitate Christ in the respect He always had for men, by a spirit of eagerness in the fulfillment

of our social obligations. We shall not pretend that sound
business is incompatible with religious principles; but within
the intricate machinery of national and international economy,
we shall testify that true wealth lies above all in the service
of others. Far be it from us to contend that it is all easily
done. It is a great deal more convenient to divide our life
into two watertight compartments: one set aside for our private
piety and morality, the other reserved for our duties to the
public and to the family; the latter two are, for many, domains
where God does not come in. If that is the idea we have of
"religion," namely, a tiny corner into which we stuff whatever
our human intelligence or our human endeavor cannot deal
with, and therefore is to be left to God, then, indeed, J. A. T. Robinson is right. Our idea of religion is no better than a caricature.

What then is the mission of the Church in the world? A
"closed" conception of the Church will say: she is the people
of the elect; she is the ship God built: at present, she is tossed
on the waters of a fiendish sea—for a time only; she is sure to
arrive in port. If other men in this sinful world care to be
saved, they can do so by hanging on to ropes attached to the
sides of the ship and trailing through the waves. The condition
of such men is critical, desperate. They are buffeted by the
billows of the world, while the elect already enjoy some security;
they are tossed about in the furious sea, but have still the possibility of an "implicit" desire of the Church: unfortunately, the
latter trait does not fit into the picture we have drawn of the
ship in the storm.

Those aboard the ship know that they are saved. Their
duty of love for the neighbor is mainly to try to persuade him to
leave whatever leaky boat he may be in. Beyond this, there is
nothing to be done than to wait till the neighbor comes to his
right senses and gets converted. The conversion of the neighbor
is the object of prayer and sacrifices. Those on board can call
out to the others and entreat them to join the ship, the only
one sailing under God's colors. They consider it their duty to
warn that the world is evil and has turned away from God,
that the sea is full of dangers, that hidden reefs of false teachings
are threatening storms of human passions and deadly pride.
God's ship alone sails in light. Its captain has been given by
Christ a sure compass infallibly pointing in the right direction.
Whoever obeys the captain and his staff is certain of arriving
in the home port.

In this allegory, we have somewhat heightened the characteristic trats of the "closed" notion of the Church. We shall
not deny that other sketches of it are available, more careful
of shades and nuances. For all that, our allegory is not a

caricature. To be convinced of it, one should read some reports sent in during the preparation of the Second Vatican Council, or one or another declaration made in the conciliar aula by some bishops and cardinals. A cursory glance through such papers will prove that the notion we have described is still strong. Did Pope John XXIII not think it necessary, at the opening of the Council, to warn against the " prophets of doom who are always forecasting disaster, as though the end of the world were in sight "? [38]

" They see in the modern age nothing but predication and ruin. They say that, in comparison with the past eras, the present era is steadily growing worse, and they behave as though they had learned nothing from history, which is nonetheless the teacher of life. They behave as though at earlier councils, everything was a triumph for the Christian idea and life and for proper freedom for the Church. " [39]

The " open " conception of the Church is different. It avoids looking upon the Church as the keystone by which everything stands or falls. Christ alone is central. The divine salvific will is the sole motive power in the history of salvation. Father, Son and Holy Ghost are at work in history. Their desire is that all men, without exception, be saved; that is Their aim in actualizing Their gracious presence in history. All through the ages, God's salvific operation keeps unfolding, respectful of the temporal conditions of individuals and nations. Both individuals and nations have nothing to do but to grow toward a slowly maturing love and truth, already present in them.

In this stream of grace, the Church has been assigned the role of *missionary,* servant of truth and love, in imitation of Christ. She is sent directly to all men without exception. As she has not been given the prerogative to settle authoritatively which people have to be lost forever, she is in duty bound to acknowledge in all men the openings by which divine grace can find an entry into them. More still, like Christ, she is principally sent to the sinners, the straying, the loveless; " it is not the healthy that need a doctor, but the sick " (Mt 9:12). And that is what her *service* really is. Should she fail to be true to this calling of hers and push men away, she would renounce her vocation and be untrue to her nature of being the Body of Christ the Head. The real Church may not lock herself up in a fortress, still less in a ghetto.

That is why she ought *to enter into dialogue* with the whole world, not distinguishing between the " good " and the " wicked. "

---

[38] John XXIII, *Inaugural Address to the Council,* Cf. *The Catholic Mind,* December 1962, p. 50.

[39] *Ibid.,* p. 50.

Today we are no longer in doubt that such a dialogue is incumbent on the Church. John XXIII and Paul VI have often enough proclaimed its necessity.

The dialogue should spread in four concentric circles over the entire world. The first dialogue is with the "members of the household of the faith" (Gal 6:10), the members of the Church. In the second place, the dialogue with those who sincerely believe in Christ, but are still standing outside the unity of the Church. Next, the dialogue with those who believe in God, but have as yet no knowledge of Christ. Finally, the dialogue with all men of good will, whatever their persuasion—provided they are sincere and have pity on "man and his woes."

An "open" concept of the Church does not at all spring from credulity or from cheap naive optimism—as John XXIII has been reproached with more than once. Taught by her Lord and by her experience within her fold, the Church knows better than any that sin holds sway over the world. Why should she speak of salvation, deliverance and redemption, unless she is keenly aware of the power of sin in man? Sin frequently finds expression in systems and conceptions of life which run dead counter to the teaching of the love of God. Such systems the Church can never accept. She may never tolerate a compromise at the expense of truth, still less at the expense of love. She cannot but reject such systems.

If we are bent on finding naivete and "simplism" among men, we shall discover them among those who fancy that wickedness in the world is to be had anywhere in an undiluted form. The mystery of man lies precisely in this, that in him good and evil are in perpetual conflict. As we said just now, the Church must of necessity condemn unacceptable systems of thought. But she will not on that account directly include in her condemnation the followers of such systems; she knows full well that some men adhere to such doctrines in good faith and from good motives. Is this not the reason why so many people embrace communism? Do they not do so in the belief that thereby they defend values, authentically Christian, which they imagine the visible Church is scorning? Here, indeed, we stumble upon the great scandal of our age! Some members of the Church, bishops and priests too, support in social questions (as in South America) or in politics (as in Asia and Africa) the established authority which some nations in Christendom employ for the furtherance of their own political power. Such members of the Church are an object of scandal to the humble and the poor; for they mask and disfigure Christ's countenance which the Church ought to show forth. That was the grievous sin of some Catholics in Europe in the course of the nineteenth century.

The Church, then, must enter into dialogue with all men. A dialogue supposes deference paid to the good faith, the sincere intention, even the well-meant illusions of the other party. A dialogue supposes that we want *to encounter* the other party, man to man, in complete esteem and love, that we take him as he is and not as he should be. Paternalism, colonialism and even moral high-mindedness, are all so many blights on the normal relationships necessary for a dialogue. In case we feel obliged in conscience to warn the partner of his mistakes, let us remain humbly aware that we ourselves are " not without sin, " that we in part share in the guilt of the other party, were it only because we have not always given full scope in our own lives to the truth and the love we are bound to serve.

Such an attitude toward man presupposes, therefore, a great trust in man's good will. Christ taught us that no man is pure sin. The faith teaches us that God does not cease to work in the hearts of all men, and that grace is at work everywhere, though there may be no outward sign of such action. That attitude supposes also a great trust in providence, in God's gracious guidance mercifully seeking to bring men back to Himself, often without their knowing it. To the attitude of the " prophets of gloom, " John XXIII opposes Christ's mind: " We feel we must disagree with those prophets of gloom. . . . In the actual course of events, which seem to betoken a new departure in human society, it is preferable to discern the mysterious guidance of divine providence who, in the successive periods of time, attains His purpose by means of man's own labors, and who knows how to use our human differences for the greater good of the Church. " [40]

What in this concept is the true role of the Church? We have seen that, like Christ, she is sent to all men, to be the servant of all men, in and with the One who became man for the purpose of being the servant of all. Shortly before His passion, Jesus declared to His Apostles: " I have set you an example: you are to do as I have done for you. In very truth I tell you: a servant is not greater than his master, nor a messenger than the one who sent him. If you know this, happy are you if you act upon it " (Jn 13:15-17). Christ repeated His lesson on many occasions, because He knew it to be a hard lesson. The history of the Church is proof that His words bear retelling even today; for one still meets with men who somehow arrogate to themselves the word of God entrusted to them and profane God's inalienable power by appropriating some of it to themselves. These ideas need to be hammered into our heads because they are too often overlooked.

[40] *Ibid., The Catholic Mind, a.c.,* p. 50.

And what is the service we expect from the Church? To begin with, it is the service of witnessing to the truth. The Church has been promised infallibility for the sake of preserving the truth confided to her by Christ as a sacred inheritance, and therefore, not for the sake of her own glory: truth must be preserved in the world and bear fruit. The Church unquestionably possesses the whole truth, although some of her members may, on occasion, attempt to diminish or to narrow or even to debase that truth. It is therefore her most sacred duty to ponder the truth entrusted to her and to realize it in all its fullness and purity.

Deep reflection will enable her to propose the truth to men in forms of expression they can understand. She will be on the lookout for fresh and fit wordings of ancient truths. For that is the only way not to betray the truth, since outmoded expressions get stale and meaningless; but their content remains alive and deserves living words. It is also her way of keeping faithful to the mandate of serving men. To refuse to express the truth in terms adapted to the times, and to hang on stubbornly to worn-out formulas, amounts to a refusal of serving the truth to men. For then, the common man would have of learn our language and thus raise himself to our level, while we decline to come down to his. However, in the performance of this duty, there can be no talk of "coming down"; such service is a primary demand of honesty, of fidelity to the living truth, and of love for men.

The Church is commissioned with a further task: the mission of love. The love, which is God Himself, lives in her. She is the temple of the eternal love which animates the Father, the Son and the Spirit in the glowing radiance of Their mutual surrender.

Wherever genuine love for men is in action, the Church will at once encourage and join it; she recognizes the Holy Ghost at work. Christ came, so writes John, "to gather together the scattered children of God" (Jn 11:52). She, too, will acknowledge those same "scattered children of God," enter into a dialogue with them, even though they belong to political parties that do not flaunt her teaching in their flag, even though those children belong to nations and organizations hostile to her. Wherever there is a beginning of love, the Church feels that the Spirit of God beckons her. It is impossible for her to stay away from any movement set up for the furtherance of peace, social justice, aid to underdeveloped nations, support of family life, care of the poor, the destitute, the sick and the deported people. She will do so even though such organizations and associations are not labelled "Catholic."

One could weep when hearing that many Catholic laymen,

not to mention bishops and priests, have nothing but indifference for anything that is established in this domain on an international scale! The Church has all the trouble in the world to enlist competent laymen willing to lend their service to international organizations in the cause of peace and justice; laymen willing to work in association with members of other religious persuasions, or of different opinions. It is really too cheap to rail at the deficiencies of the UN, the UNESCO, the FAO, and similar international efforts. It is greater folly still to allege that in such organizations masonry is striving for its own ends; no better way to blinding oneself to the good that is being done. No simple solutions are to be had in a pluralistic world like ours. No human organization is perfect, not even our own. The results that have been achieved are amply sufficient to move us to liberality, to practice patience in the face of glaring defects. Politics, it is said, is the art of the possible; not so the tyranny of the ideal. It is the mark of an immature mentality to expect nothing but the best. Callow youth alone hankers after unattainable perfection. We should be the first to come forward wherever a human being is in need.

But we shall not come forward unless we are convinced that the mission of the Church is one of service. At the time of the Hungarian insurrection, an airplane, loaded with medical supplies, was held up in a European capital because two Catholic charitable (!) organizations stopped the pilot from taking off until they could agree among themselves which of the rival organizations could set its signature on the gift of supplies. The spirit of service vanishes as soon as we are caught in the toils of " charitable works, " or as soon as we want our gifts to be labelled " Catholic. " Such a mentality strikes a fatal blow at the heart of genuine Catholicism. Yet, to many people this seems the normal thing to do.

The Church is an apostle entrusted with the charge of forwarding God's truth and love. There we have the reason why she has been filled with the presence of the Blessed Trinity. No individual man is ever given a grace which is not at the same time a gift to the community as a whole; and no grace is granted to the Church unless it be for the good of the whole world. Her most precious gift is the privilege of being on earth the Tabernacle of the Risen Lord, not merely in the thousands of tabernacles in her churches, but in the tabernacles of her faithful as well.

It is perfectly true that the Church is the only one to possess authentically the presence of the Lord, as a gift coming from the Father in the power of the Spirit. And it is this living presence which lends meaning and content to our sacramental rites which, unlike any other rites on earth, are destined " to presentiate " (as we should like to say) the gracious presence of Christ. The main purpose of our book is to help the reader realize the truth that the nature of grace consists in that presence.

" Grace " is never given to us apart from a *mission*, or independent of a partaking in the Church's mission to the world. The character which we receive in baptism, in confirmation and in holy orders, the dedication which we get in confession, extreme unction and matrimony: these are all so many aspects of *the one mission proper to the Church*, aspects of her mission to the world. *No doubt is possible: that mission is to all men.* The certainty of grace, salvation and truth received by all in the one true Church is not of a nature to unite us among ourselves in the Church so that it cuts us off from the other men. The divine assurance, source of our confidence and joy, implies an order to go out to the others. This contact with the others is not to be after the manner of an elder brother who off and on stoops to his junior; it has to be a manifestation of the spirit of Christ, a service to mankind.

The presence of the Risen Lord in the Church is more strikingly manifested in the Eucharist, that is, in a sacramental form, since it comes to us as our food for eternal life. Yet, neither this eucharistic presence, the hidden glow that warms our churches, may be regarded as a gift reserved for ourselves alone. Our churches, where the red lamp burns and where the sacrifice of the Mass assembles and unites us into the people of God, our churches are not done justice to unless we come out from them with " our bearing towards one another arising out of our life with Christ Jesus " (Phil 2:5), that is, with our minds eager to go out to men and to help them, in imitation of Christ. The Church can be no other than apostolic. Apostolate is not a function reserved for specialized members of the Church; it constitutes the inner nature of Christianity. True apostolate bears the mark of Jesus " the Apostle and High Priest of the religion which we profess " (Heb 3:1). Apostolate is service to mankind. As such, it ought to model itself on the patience and deference which God is so endlessly displaying in His dealings with men.

The providential role, proper and peculiar to the Church, will come into clear view when we watch it developing in the course of history. What is the meaning of Redemption? As we have seen in a previous page, redemption, in the mind of Scripture, means above all that the Father, in Christ, has prepared and gathered to Himself a people, and that He is engaged in adding new members to His people through the unifying power of the Spirit.

In the present chapter, we have consistently shown that God does not carry the redemption into effect without actually taking into account the nature of man and his involvement in time. Consequently, redemption progressed in time—like a life-giving water that spreads through a desert and lends fertility wherever it reaches, by transforming arid sand into lush oases. The wellspring of this water is Christ who gives His Spirit to quench man's thirst. "Jesus stood and said with a loud voice: 'If any one is thirsty let him come to Me; whoever believes in Me, let him drink.'" As Scripture says: "Streams of living water shall flow out from within him." And John supplies at once the hidden meaning of the biblical text: "He was speaking of the Spirit which believers in Him would receive later; for the Spirit had not yet been given because Jesus had not yet been glorified" (Jn 7:37-39). From "within" the one who believes, from his heart, will flow "streams of living waters" that will bring fruitfulness to the whole world.

For centuries, the Spirit of God has pervaded mankind and will continue to pervade it through all centuries to come. The ideal would be that all "the scattered children of God" be gathered into the fold of one people, in the unity of one faith, one love and one visible Church. Whether that is actually to take place on earth, we do not know. Nor do we know whether so much can be achieved in a world torn apart by misunderstandings and factions rife among well-intentioned men. In this present era, one thing seems plain: many nations and groups of population neither will nor can accept the Church for what she is, namely the household of God. From this, we may not infer that the Church is prepared to leave such men to their lot, as was done occasionally in the past. Where the Church is as yet unable to preach the full truth, she can at least help men to come closer to each other and, thus, closer to God. She can endeavor to bring pagan morality closer to true Christian standards; she can free the people from subhuman living conditions and thus prepare them to look out for objects higher than the bare subsistence level. St. Thomas Aquinas recognized in his day that it is plainly impossible for a man to think of superior moral values and of religious perfection, so long as he is harrowed by the preoccupation of how to secure his daily bread.

Few books offer a more captivating reading than the diary of a simple Negro woman, Carolina Maria de Jesus, who tells of her life in the slums of Sâo Paulo. [41]

The priests, who put in an occasional presence in the "Favela" and preached their sermons on moral or religious points, produced in her the impression of total strangers, as would be the

[41] Carolina Maria de Jesus, *Child of the Dark,* the diary of C.M. de Jesus, translated from the Portuguese by David St. Clair (New York: The New American Library, 1963).

inhabitants of Mars who by chance had landed in the suburbs. They, well fed and well lodged, were of no use to the poor destitutes, because they had no time to visit the slums, or to give aid to the residents. All they did was " to remind them of their duties. "

What holds good for men living in subhuman conditions, as the by now well-known Brazilian archbishop, Helder Pessôa Camara, declared so repeatedly in Rome, applies equally to the cultured nations who see in Catholicism little more than an insignificant Western sect. Missionaries in Japan assert that most Japanese have of Catholicism only foggy notions. Islam, too, seems to be a society almost closed to Christianity. Nevertheless, there is room for the service of the Church. I know, for instance, a Catholic priest, specialized in Islamic culture, who is often consulted by Muslims in questions connected with the theology of the Koran. When we cannot yet openly announce Christ, the Koran affords an excellent opportunity of bringing religious souls in Islam closer to God.

Toward communism, too, there is room for an attitude more evangelical than what is deemed " becoming " in the eyes of " decent-minded " Catholics. Hitler is reported to have said that only hatred is capable of binding a nation together; to be united, a nation should be given something it can hate and persecute. We need only to read some pamphlets, or to listen to some sermons, in order to realize that not a few laymen, some priests too, mistake anticommunism for apostolic zeal. To hate is easy enough. John XXIII achieved more by his goodness than by thundering against communism, and certainly more than by issuing solemn condemnations. This goodness of his is, perhaps, the one thing which " right-thinking " people in the Church are most disinclined to overlook in him. And why, we may ask? Just because we are still plagued with medieval, therefore semi-barbaric, notions about the role of the Church in human society. It is quite possible that our forefathers could think of nothing better for " the defense of the faith " than to draw the sword, to burn men at the stake, to fulminate excommunications. History is there to tell us that always and everywhere the persecuted win sympathy, while the persecutors, though they be justified and in their right, stand to lose the sympathy of all.

In the historic allocution of John XXIII at the opening of the Council, there occurs a passage, unsurpassed perhaps for its radical opposition to " barbaric " notions. " The Church has always opposed those errors. Frequently, she has condemned them with the greatest severity. *Nowadays,* however, the Spouse of Christ prefers to make use of the medicine of mercy rather than that of severity. She considers that there she meets the needs of the present day by demonstrating the validity of her teaching rather than by condemnation. Not, certainly, that there is a lack of fallacious teaching, opinions and dangerous concepts to be guarded against and dissipated. But these are so obviously in contrast with the right norm of honesty, and have produced such lethal fruit that by now it would seem that men of themselves are inclined to condemn them, particularly those ways of life which despise God and His Law, or place excessive confidence in technical progress and a well-being based exclusively on the comforts of life. They are ever more deeply convinced of the paramount dignity of the human person and of his perfecting, as well as of the duties which that implies. Even more important, experience has taught men that violence inflicted on others, the might of arms and political domination, are of no help at all in finding a happy solution to the grave problems which afflict them. " [42]

In those words, we discover Pope John's comforting confidence in human nature, his solicitude to prepare men for the full Christian message when it is as yet impossible to preach it openly; and for the success of this indirect apostolate, he would appeal to man's sense of justice, to his respect for the human person, to a healthy realism based on the lessons of history.

By now it will be clear to the reader that a more biblical concept of the Church admits of many practical consequences for everyday life, as soon as it is disentangled from the by-growths accruing to it since the Constantinian era, the Middle Ages and the "Ancient Régime." Let us hope it does not take more than a century before Pope John's views win upon the Church as a whole.

To conclude this present section, we should like to ask a question: What ought to be the attitude of the Church toward the non-Christian religions?; and more, in particular, what attitude ought those to adopt who engage in missionary labors? Shall we leave the non-Christians to their good faith, or shall we strain every nerve to bring them to "conversion?" The question is a pressing one; it demands an answer.

We vaguely feel that neither of the two suggested answers rings completely true. We may not abandon the non-Christians to their lot. Why not? We have met, at a congress, a professor of missiology who would not rest until he had a juridical answer. The answer we offered failed to carry his conviction. Our answer was: faith in God's love.

And yet, can anyone who has tasted the love of God keep silence about it? Who is the man who locks up within him the happiness of having encountered Christ at least once in his

[42] Cf. *The Catholic Mind*, December 1962, p. 52.

life, and has been favored in Him with joy and consolation?
Such a man cannot keep silent. He will hold high his conviction
in the face of poverty, persecution and spoliation, in the face
even of the bloody feuds through which Africa and Asia are
seeking themselves, in the face too of insecurity and discouragement when schools and churches are burnt down; " for
the love of Christ leaves us no choice, when once we have
reached the conclusion that one man has died for all and,
therefore, all mankind has died " (II Cor 5:14). Paul's spirit
cannot disappear from the Church; his spirit is the Spirit of
Christ. " The sight of the people moved him to pity: they were
all like sheep without a shepherd, harrassed and helpless
(Num 27:17). And he said to his disciples, " The crop is
heavy, but the laborers are scarce; you must therefore beg the
owner to send laborers to harvest his crop " (Mt 9:36-38).

The instant we understand that the special task of the Church
in the world is none other than to be " the salt of the earth "
(Mt 15:13), and the " yeast... mixed with half a measure a flour "
(Mt 13:33), our missionary work will be filled with respect and
patience when confronting the people we go in search of in
their own land, in their own civilization and traditions, in their
own religious mentality. Our zeal for souls will be purified
because it will respect human nature a great deal more than
when it was still tainted, unconsciously perhaps, with remnants
of colonialism, or at least with paternalistic strains which we
carried away with us from the home country.

We know of no better practical solution than the one which
Abbé Couturier suggested for the ecumenical problem: to identify
ourselves more wholly and more generously with Christ's intentions, to pray and to labor in view of a reunion that will come
when Christ wants it and *as* Christ wants it. We, too, shall
persevere with unflagging zeal in our work among the non-
Christians, believers and unbelievers; we shall pray and labor
that they may find Christ *when* He wants it and *as* He wants
it. We need not fear any weakening in our dedication and
effort. Rather the contrary! An eager spirit to oblige those
people will add new zest to our zeal and make our voice more
persuasive than ever. The more our voice is cleared of all
trace of obtrusiveness and self-conceit, the better God's voice
will make itself heard through our human activity, as it did
in Christ.

If we do that, the Church will remain, in the words of Christ,
what she must be: the light of the world, the yeast in the dough,
the temple of God in this earthly city, and the " holy remnant, "
that is the mass of the small and the poor, those for whose sake
God saved the world in the days of Noah. As to the manner
in which all this is to happen, we shall leave it to God's wisdom.

But that is the service we have to render to mankind, of course with the help of grace, the love of Christ that leaves us no choice (II Cor 5:14).

We shall then follow in Paul's footsteps, the man of indomitable zeal for souls, the man who boasted that he had never been a burden to any one " You know for yourselves, brothers, that our visit to you was not fruitless. Far from it; after all the injury and outrage which to your knowledge we had suffered at Philippi, we declared the gospel of God to you frankly and fearlessly, by the help of our God.... We do not curry favor with men; we seek only the favor of God Who is continually testing our hearts. Our words have never been flattering words, as you have cause to know; nor, as God is our witness, have they ever been a cloak for greed. We have never sought honor from men, from you or from any one else, although as Christ's own envoys we might have made our weight felt; but we were as gentle with you as a nurse caring fondly for her children. With such yearning love we close to impart to you not only the gospel of God but our very selves, so dear had you become to us. Remember, brothers, how we toiled and drudged. We worked for a living night and day, rather than be a burden to any one, while we proclaimed before you the good news of God. " Paul is alluding here to the line of conduct he had strictly followed. Though he held that an apostle is entitled to receive his maintenance from the faithful, Paul nevertheless refused all monetary help; he chose to earn his living by weaving tents, the trade he had been engaged in before his conversion. " As you well know, we dealt with you one by one, as a father does with his children, appealing to you by encouragement, as well as by solemn injunctions, to live lives worthy of the God Who calls you into His Kingdom and glory " (I Thes 2:1-12).

The end of time

Scripture has a word declaring that while on earth the Church and the Christians are living " between times ": between the time of Christ's birth and Ascension and the day of His return at the end of time.

This view of our " state of grace " lends to our lives a fresh dynamic tension. Its importance is obvious: it affects our life of faith. Dynamism and hope tell of youth; stagnancy and living in the past denote old age and arrest.

God works out His loving presence in us through grace. But grace is never looked upon by Scripture as a terminus. The beauty of grace is that it always remains a beginning. And with this idea, time reappears in its quality as a constituent element of our state of grace within the Church.

We all know that Christ compared God's Kingdom on earth to a tiny mustardseed: " As a seed, mustard is smaller than any other; but when it has grown, it is bigger than any gardenplant " (Mt 13:31-32). On his side, however, Paul speaks of grace also as a pledge of eternal life: " And if you and we belong to Christ, guaranteed as His and anointed, it is all God's doing. " According to contemporary exegesis, there is no question here of the sacrament of confirmation, but of the Christian doctrine that shapes our lives. " It is God Who has set His seal upon us, and as a pledge of what is to come, has given the Spirit to dwell in our hearts " (II Cor 1:21-22; cf 5:5).

Paul develops his idea further in the eighth chapter of his Epistle to the Romans, the charter of the doctrine of grace. As we remarked on a previous page, the Apostle envelops in what he writes the entire creation. " I reckon that the sufferings we now endure bear no comparison with the splendor, as yet unrevealed, which is in store for us. For the created universe waits with eager expectation for God's sons to be revealed. It was made the victim of frustration, not by its own choice, but because of Him Who made it so; yet always there was hope because the universe itself is to be freed from the shackles of mortality and so enter upon the liberty and splendor of the children of God. Up to the present, we know, the whole created universe groans in all its parts as if in the pangs of childbirth. Not only so, but even we, to whom the Spirit is given as *first-fruits* of the harvest to come, are groaning inwardly while we wait for God to make us His sons and set our whole body free. For we have been saved, *though only on hope* " will be whole, like God's knowledge of me " (I Cor 13:8-12).

The Apostle concludes his chapter on charity with the same hopeful vision of a fulfillment we do not yet possess, except as a pledge of the Spirit. " Love will never come to an end. Are there prophets? their work will be over. Are there tongues of ecstasy? they will cease. Is there knowledge? it will vanish away; for our knowledge and our prophecy alike are partial, and the partial vanishes when wholeness comes. When I was a child, my speech, my outlook and my thoughts were all childish. When I grew up, I had finished with childish things. Now we see only *puzzling reflections in a mirror,* but then we shall see face to face. My knowledge now is partial; then it will be whole, like God's knowledge of me " (I Cor 13:8-12).

With the Church and through the centuries, we are pilgrims of eternity; we form the people of God, wandering through the desert on the march to the Promised Land. The final goal, assigned to us, sets forth clearly the significance of our pilgrimage, the reason and tenor of our journey—and thus the true nature of grace. Our goal is Christ, the full-grown Christ.

"I pray that the God of Our Lord Jesus Christ, the all-glorious Father, may give you the spiritual powers of wisdom and vision, by which there comes the knowledge of Him. I pray that your inward eyes may be illumined, so that you may *know the hope* to which He calls you, what the wealth and glory of the share He offers you among His people in their heritage, and how vast the resources of His power open to us who trust in Him. They are measured by his strength and the might which He exerted in Christ when He raised Him up from the dead, when He enthroned Him at His right hand in the heavenly realm, far above all government and authority, all power and domination, and any title of sovereignty that may be named, not only in this age but in the age to come. He put everything in subjection beneath His feet, and appointed Him as supreme head of the Church, which is His Body and as such holds within it the fullness of him who himself receives the entire fullness of God" (Eph 1:17-23; II Cor 15:20-28). " He will transfigure the body belonging to our humble state, and give it a form like that of His own resplendent body, by the very power which enables Him to make all things subject to Him" (Phil 3:21).

As it was with the Jews of old, our grace is borne up by a new and grandiose expectation: our full union with Christ, through the power of the Spirit. The Church is still living in a period of advent, a new advent, of course, since the Lord has already come. That coming of His will achieve its perfection when history has reached its completion. We may, on no account, allow our hope to shrink to the dimensions of a hundrum bourgeois anticipation of a personal reward in heaven. *All* have received this hope, and *all together* we have on earth to journey to God. Whatever comes from God: the cosmos, life on earth, the admirable human nature God has endowed us with, the nostalgic yearning of countless thousands of men for peace and happiness—all speak to us of the hope living in us. Nothing and no one is excluded unless he himself willed it so. Heaven is not a private concern, a place where we chance to meet together.

It must be admitted that few people, during life, realize this aspect of grace; yet, it belongs to the true nature of grace, even of the grace we receive through the sacraments. Here is what the liturgy says on the Eucharist: " O sacred banquet, in which Christ is received, the memory of His passion is renewed, the mind filled with grace, and *a pledge of future glory*

is given to us. " [43]   We receive baptism and confirmation in
view of eternity; in every severe sickness, we can unite our
sufferings with Christ so that we may rise one day with Him.
Sins are forgiven us in view of eternity.   Even priesthood and
marriage, the two sacraments destined to sanctify and to consecrate to God our life-task on earth, do so in order to prepare
for the blessed return of Christ both ourselves and all those
whom, as priests or married people, we shall have been able to
help.   When Christ returns, God " will be all in all. "

The " divine milieu "

In this chapter we have seen how God's presence is being actualized in and through history.   We have discovered the presence
of the Father, the Son and the Holy Ghost from the first
creative gesture right through the obscure history of a cosmos
in the making.   The same presence is to reveal itself in glory
at the end of time.   For, after all, that is the meaning history
has in the eyes of God: the final consummation is to be the
fulfillment of the beginning, that is, God is to be the Alpha
and Omega, the first and the last word in the history of this
world.

Not a few of those who have read this chapter will have
thought of Teilhard de Chardin's grandiose vision, as set down
more especially in his book *The Divine Milieu.*   Our purpose,
too, was to write about the *Divine Milieu,* within which our
lives bathe and breathe.   But we have followed a different
method.   This latter remark of ours is of importance, to forestall
all misunderstanding, most of all in what concerns Teilhard so
often misconstrued.

Teilhard approaches our problem, so to say, from the outside.
He is out to present the reader with a synthetic view of what
the sciences have so far taught us about the cosmos and man.
As he proceeds in working out his scientific, or at least phenomenological vision, he remains a true believer.   It is in the light
of a firm faith that the man of science in him gropes his way
toward a higher synthesis.   It is permissible not to be in
agreement with his method; one may even feel out of one's
element in it.   His method has to rely on itself for its justification.

We have proceeded along a different path, the path of
theological reflection.   We have taken for granted all the acquired
data of science.   We have tried to solve the same problem from

---

[43] Antiphon at the *Magnificat* on Corpus Christi.

the inside, that is, as God sees the world. In order to know how God sees the world, we have listened to God's voice speaking in the Church, above all God's voice in the Holy Spirit. We have collated divers truths of faith and, in an attitude of awe and adoration, we have sought to decipher, as best we could, God's intentions hidden in the world. The leading thought in all our meditations has been the sure knowledge that God dwells in the world, God one in nature and three in person. God's presence is a presence of love, a presence calling for a return of love.

Both Teilhard and we, each one faithful to his own method, have set forth the same divine mystery: how God invited us to share with Him His inner life; how this actual world is already enveloped in the " Divine Milieu, " from the indwelling, through the indwelling and for the perfect realization of the indwelling.

Grace and merit

The doctrine of merit opens before us still another avenue to the mystery of grace. We shall deal with it in this chapter and take occasion of it to study grace as a whole. One or other subsequent shorter chapter will bear on some partial aspects of grace.

Let us start with a brief phenomenological attempt to grasp the idea of "merit," as men currently understand it. It is surprising how many different meanings shelter under that one word "merit." We shall satisfy ourselves with examining the three aspects of merit that are met with in the teaching of the Church. On the occasion of each one of these aspects, we shall fall back on the fundamental dialectic recognized by Scripture and the Church in the doctrine of merit. We are of the opinion that such a living dialectic is alone capable of clearing the doctrine of merit of many a misunderstanding that does harm to our religious life. Finally, it is good to know that the Christians of the Reformation were opposed most strongly to the Catholic notion of merit. We shall do well to listen to their objections; we shall then realize that we have sometimes given cause to their disagreements with us.

What is merit?

In all languages, the word "to merit" covers many rather different meanings. The first thing to come spontaneously to mind is the wages earned by a workman. Scripture, too, uses the word in that sense. The employer and the employee sign a contract. The contract bestows on the workman a definite right to the pay agreed upon. It is a mutual agreement, sanctioned by that species of justice known by the name of "commutative justice": it implies an exchange and a bilateral force binding on the contracting parties. Such a convention, affecting both sides, possesses its own character. When some-one sells a house, he acquires a right to the sale price; he does not "merit" it. When a man hires out his horse or his cart, he acquires a right to payment; but neither the horse nor the cart can be said to "merit" anything. Merit connotes the performing of an action, and, to speak accurately, an action performed by a human person. A minimum of freedom is strictly required. Rigorously speaking, a slave does not merit, unless the master acknowledges, be it for a moment, the human nature in the slave. At first sight, it would appear that the pay is proportioned to the work done; and time is the more obvious manner of measuring it. Hence our habit of speaking of work-hours. Our age, however, has discovered that the wages do not represent a mathematical proportion; or rather, that legal obligations go beyond the equation: wages $=$ x hours of work. We know now of family wages, of the employer's contribution to various social insurances, child-allowances, paid holidays, and so forth. Of course, we are at liberty to judge of all these different increases of payment as so many manifestations of, and extortions by decadent trade-unionism lusting for power. But Christian philosophy fully endorses these recent conceptions; and it does so against both extreme Marxism and liberalism. Such social supplements form, indeed, part of merit because they involve the work of a person who is rightly entitled to be respected as a member of human society and as one who has his own responsibilities towards family and children—one who has also a right to recreation, to security and safety. All this is proof that wages strike deeper roots in human nature than a merely mutual legal contract agreed upon as between remuneration and number of hours of work. And this is especially the case where a man binds himself to work for another for a stipulated length of time, and thus puts a considerable portion of his life at the disposal of another. We note the same phenomenon on a higher level, where the services asked for and rendered are of such a nature that most languages have recourse to another word. That new word, nevertheless, still expresses what is already conveyed by the simple word "pay." When a doctor, for instance, or a lawyer, makes his services available to a client, he does not speak of wages, but of fees. The work he does cannot be valued in terms of hours spent in it. Not only have doctors and lawyers to devote many years to prepare themselves for their profession, mut they have to keep up their studies. Besides, long experience adds greatly to the value of their interventions. It happens also that the nature of the work asked for requires special personal initiative; and this, of course, cannot be estimated in terms of sheer justice. In sum, the word "fee" gives clearly to understand that "merit" is actually based on the quality of the person who offers his services. And this explains why it becomes increasingly hard to fix the amount of the fee in cases involving greater personal worth, whether along the line of studies, initiative or dedication, or along the line of authority, experience and fame. The fee, consequently, is likely to vary according to the paying capacity of the patient or client. The latter has *to do what he can* to settle the debt he owes to the person who comes to his aid. To offer adequate remuneration for everything, he cannot. Nor is he expected to.

Sometimes we speak also of merit in quite a different connection, with bearing on our present subject. We can "merit" certain honorific distinctions, like the title of *"doctor honoris causa,"* a medal, an international prize, etc. In such instances we have to leave aside all ideas of juridical proportion. In case of necessity, a doctor or a lawyer can have recourse to a sheriff to exact from the client payments in arrears. But in the instances just mentioned, nothing of the sort can be done.

This kind of merit is also spoken of in Holy Writ, by way of illustration only. Paul a city-dweller and therefore well acquainted with the Greek games in the stadium so popular in his day, has this to say: "You know (do you not) that at the sports all the runners run the race, though only one wins the prize. Like them, run to win! But every athlete goes into strict training. They do it to win a fading wreath; we, a wreath that never fades. For my part, I run with a clear goal before me; I am like a boxer who does not beat the air; I bruise my own body and make it know its master, for fear that after preaching to others I should find myself rejected" (I Cor 9:24-27).

We mentioned sport in connection with the Pauline text. Let us not think of commercialized sport; but rather—let us say—of the Olympic games which have kept something of what was traditional in old Greece. Human society offers other examples of what we have in view here.

This "merit" supposes in the one who awards the prize a minimum of interest, perhaps even a degree of spontaneous desire to offer the prize as a *gift*. In former times, the conferring of honors was an important privilege reserved to the crown; it was an opportunity for the sovereign to give public proof of his benevolence. Today, some of the privileges of the crown have fallen to the state; others have been taken over by the nation and are now being exercised by one or another association more or less acting in the name of the people.

There are today associations acknowledged for the high quality of their scientific, cultural or economic activity in society, and authorized to grant distinctions as signs of their benevolence and esteem. Doing so, they act in some measure in the name of the nation.

On his side, he who receives the mark of honor has somehow

"merited" it, so say the customay tedious discourses delivered
on such occasions. In any case, the recipient may not look
upon the honor, conferred on him, as his "due." Notice, though,
that his achievement, scientific or other, "merits" in a manner
peculiarly its own. Think, for instance, of the awarding of the
Nobel Prize. Here we have to take our stand on a higher
level of human relationships, where personal freedom plays
a more important role. On the one hand, there is the free,
almost sovereign initiativeof conferring the gift, and on the
other, we see a life that ought to be highly valued by society
because of the implied personal dedication and of the stake
society has in it. More clearly than in the dialectic of wages
and fees, a third party is here in evidence, human society.
For, though the mark of honor is conferred by the head of a state
or by representatives of one or another association, it is worthless unless the people as a whole are agreeable, were it only by
tacit consent and esteem.

We are still free to speak of "merit," because the person
honored has acquired some sort "right" to it, evidently a
"right" of its own kind. A great writer, whose works are
known for their literary quality the world over, may expect
something like the Nobel Prize. If it happens that he is passed
by, he is entitled to feel that he is unfairly dealt with; but he has
no court of appeal to redress the wrong done. In fact, he would
lower himself if he sought to stand on his "right," just because
his protest would drag the mark of distinction to the level of
legal dimensions of "pay." Besides, he knows that at the bar of
world opinion, his works have already "merited" due recognition.

The organizations or the persons who bestow such prizes can,
evidently, not be compelled by law to choose one candidate
rather than another. Should the choice be manifestly wrong
and marred by unworthy motives, it stands condemned automatically before public opinion. It would convict the association
of betraying the mandate received from society; at the same
time, the actually conferred mark of distinction would turn
out to be devoid of all value.

Plainly, we have to judge here not from the point of view of
legal right but of honor, in respect of both the donor and the
recipient. More than ever, it is an occasion for pointing out that
in "merit" personal worth plays a capital role. In the last
analysis, personal nobility is the determining factor of recognition,
both in the matter of "wages" or "fees," and in the bestowal
of public marks of honor. And it is immaterial whether that
personal nobility shines out in the achievement itself or in the
recognition of the achievement, publicly attested to and "re-
warded."

We are now ready for the highest degree of " merit, " the level where " merit ", properly so-called, vanishes, where the two persons involved are linked together by mutual bonds far stronger and more radical than either right or honor. We mean to speak of the relations born from love. On the level of love, where the nobility of the person finds its purest expression, achievement as such has no place. Here, any human gesture turns out to be a *symbol* of one person surrendering to another. Whether it takes on the shape of a gift or shelters in a life of devotion, anything that betokens self-surrender is neither more nor less than an eloquently rich symbol of the mutual relations of love.

That is why, at this height, the summit of human relations, there can be no talk of " merit " in the strict sense; for, all distance which " merit " necessarily supposes between persons, has vanished. And yet, in love, mutual obligations attain a degree of intensity far beyond what is implied in " merit " as described above. He who bestows his love and knows that it is accepted, acquires an unquestionable " right " to a return of love. But, then, " right " has escaped from the confines of the legal sphere. A man can, of course, compel his wife to stay with him; he cannot force her to love him. But if the woman is unable validly to justify her refusal to love, she lowers herself. Though she does not transgress any established law, she offends against the nobility of love and, *therefore, against herself*.

All our remarks apply more strictly still when we have to do with a love involving a certain degree of inequality between the persons in question, e.g., in the relations of love between father and son. The father gave to the son life, education and name. The son has been since birth the object of the father's love; he is born of it and with it. Should he reject that love, he would lower himself, disown the nobility of his own person and violate the most sacred laws of gratitude. Neither father nor son mention " merit " in their dealings with each other, unless they attach to the word a special sense; their mutual obligations strike deeper roots. And so, love does away with " merit " by the very intensity to which it attains. Achievement, too, disappears; it makes room for the person himself. Man henceforth disposes of nothing better than symbols to express his love; and express it he must; for human nature is such that it has to express its innermost sentiments in external actions, the only medium at his disposal to actualize them. However, love unites persons not through deeds and rewards, but *without intermediaries*. " Merit " in love lies in an encounter with the person himself, and no longer in the giving or receiving of either reward or gift.

Our analysis has not been useless, though it is not yet theology. Starting out from experience, we have used words in the sense they have in daily life. At any rate, it is not superfluous to ascertain the complex many-sided experience latent in the term " merit. "

Textbook scholasticism has often tended to explain merit by comparing it to the mutual juridical relations existing between the employer and the employee—the lowest form of merit. I tried, of course, to correct the comparison by sundry additions and rectifications. *But the starting point was wrong.*

" Theological merit, " as it has been named, should be defined in terms of its own peculiar spiritual content, and not in terms of inferior concrete examples as found in our experience. We could avail ourselves of them, as Scripture does; but, in rigorous theological thought, we have to start from another significant content.

It is quite certain that the textbook notion of merit is not met with in high scholasticism. St. Thomas connects his most telling texts about the trinitarian indwelling with the doctrine of merit; a clear indication that, for him too, the nobility of divine sonship forms the principal basis of merit. Early scholasticism knew already of the principle: " *Par caritas, par meritum,* " which means, " love is the measure of merit. " If that is true, we have to do with an order of things quite different to the order of justice. But then, to speak of " commutative justice, " even analogically, is dangerous.

We should teach a pure doctrine of merit: *religion demands it.* We are in the presence of God's majesty. Beyond all doubt, the late scholasticism of the sixteenth century gave currency to very " matter-of-fact " notions about the fruits of the Mass and the " power " of indulgences, about the merits due to pilgrimages and such like unusual religious practices. Those were notions that stirred up the Reformers' aversion. Nor should we forget that the conflagration of the Reform got started on the occasion of Tetzel's popular sermons about indulgences. The Council of Trent rejected all such conceptions and practices. Unfortunately, the condemnation came forty years late. By then, Christendom lay rent apart.

The dialectic proper to merit

Unquestionably, theological merit differs in kind from the human merits we described in the preceding section. That difference is definitely established by the fact that we cannot possibly consider God and man as " partners "; " partners " taken in the sense of co-workers standing more or less on a same level. This idea we have elaborated in our discussion on semi-Pelgianism. Now, it happens that " commutative justice " necessarily includes the idea of " partnership. "

We see no means to secure an insight into merit if we do not build it on the pattern of a living dialectical structure, such as may be found both in Scripture and in the teaching of the Church or of the saints. " To merit " is *par excellence* what we should like to call an active existential relationship. All notion of laying up merits, whether in heaven or in the so-called treasure of the Church, is to be ruthlessly set aside.

No need here to prove that we have to start from the basic principle: *God's absolute primacy in the dispensation of grace.* We have dwelt often enough on this principle. In the life of grace, God is first in the most radical way.

In my opinion, it is only by consistently basing the entire range of grace on the divine indwelling that we can safely maintain the divine initiative. There exists no grace that is not due to God's initial love; nor is there any merit, beginning with the first step in the faith and ending with the final consummation in eternity. which does not spring from the prevenient initial love of God who lives in us, ever creates and operates in us: *from* the indwelling, *through* the indwelling, *in view of* a fully actualized indwelling.

To avoid the necessity of bringing it in later as a corrective, we have to secure that unexceptionable basic truth. That done, we can pass on to the second moment of the dialectical movement, which is: within the divine initiative, our good deeds are truly ours—as was shown in a previous section—and at the same time, they are truly meritorious, especially when we live in the " state of grace " as children of God.

We fail to see how any one can dare to assert that such a doctrine is not contained in Scripture. As the unsophisticated Christian knows, there are any number of texts in the Gospel where Christ unambiguously speaks of " reward " and " requital. " We deform God's teaching if we slur over this evidence with fine-spun human theories, be they ever so well-intentioned. In those texts, Christ does no more than take over the teaching of the Old Testament, though not the teaching of the Scribes and the Pharisees (Mt 21:28-32; 25:31-46; Mk 10:17-31; Lk 6:17-23; Acts 24:14-16). Those texts say that God rewards each one according to his works (Mt 16-27; Mk 9:41). After Christ, the apostles taught the same (I Pet 1:17; Apoc 2:23; 20:12; 22:12). And so did Paul (Rom 2:6; 14:12; I Cor 5:10; Hebr 9:27).

There is one kind of merit mercilessly rejected by Christ: merit as the Pharisees conceived it (Mt 15:16-20; Mk 7:3-16). In his Epistles to the Romans and to the Galatians, Paul wages

a relentless war against what he calls "works" or "deeds."
Recent studies in late rabbinical teaching and in Jewish sects
in Christ's day leave us in no doubt concerning the mind of Paul
speaking of "deeds." The mere context of his argumentation
ought alone to have been sufficient to enlighten us about his
meaning. Here, it seems to me, some Protestants fall into a
mistake similar to that of decadent scholasticism. They lift
passages out of their literary and historical context, pose them
as hard and fast metaphysical principles that hang high in the
air above time and mankind; and whatever seems, in their
eyes, to be incompatible with those principles, they leave in the
shadow, scriptural teaching not excepting.

But what does Paul mean by "works" or "deeds" which
he will not hear of? They are actions, *performances,* done from
religious motives which a man flaunts and even "glories in"
before God, on the ground that by them he has acquired definite
"rights" in God's sight. Many rabbis had come to the notion
that God's judgment is very much like that of a human judge
who examines and weighs out man's good and evil actions.
That comparison alone betrays the intention of showing that God
is really *bound* by merit. For a judge who disposes of nothing
better than the notion of the tongue of the balance has no
other function than to confirm officially what the scales have
measured. We have seen in the section on semi-Pelagianism
that in such a supposition, man is, *in the last analysis,* the master
of his destiny. Eternal bliss rests finally with *him*; God's
royal *gift* is ruled out; grace is no longer grace.

The Pharisee was the man who took for granted that his
"merits" acquired for him the strict right to appropriate wages,
an instance, therefore, of the lowest degree of "meriting"
according to our preceding analysis. The Pharisee thought of
himself as does a specialized workman; let us remember that he
belonged to the sect of the "pious." A specialized workman
takes pride in his work and craftsmanship and is perhaps justly
conscious of being the only one fit for the job, so much so that
he reckons his employer lucky that he is not working elsewhere.
Among men, such feelings may be manifestations of a legitimate
proper pride in one's particular trade. But, confronted with
God's majesty and the absolute primacy of grace, such an
attitude spells death to any authentic religious sense.

In this connection, and not by way of a metaphysical principle,
we understand why Paul exclaims on the subject of the mystery
of election to grace: "In just the same way at the present
moment a "remnant" has come into being, selected by the
grace of God. But if it is by grace, then *it does not rest on deeds
done, or grace would cease to be grace*" (Rom 11:5-6).

And *in the same light* we have to understand the main burden of the Epistle to the Romans: "All are justified *by God's grace alone*, through His act of liberation in the person of Christ Jesus. For God designed Him to be the means of expiating sin by His sacrificial death, effective through faith. God meant by this to demonstrate His justice, because in His forbearance He had overlooked the sins of the past—to demonstrate His justice now in the present, showing that He is both Himself just and justifies any man who *puts his faith in Jesus*. What room then is left for human pride? [That is precisely our question!]. It is excluded. And on what principle? The keeping of the law would not exclude it [as some Christians seem to have learned from the Jews], but faith does. For our argument is that a man is justified by faith quite apart from success in keeping the law" (Rom 3·24-28). The Epistle to the Ephesians is more emphatic still: "For it is by His grace you are saved, through faith in Him; it is not your own doing. It is *God's gift*, not a reward for work done. There is nothing for anyone to boast of " (Eph 2:8-9).

The reader cannot fail to notice that Paul attaches a second meaning to the word "deeds." The following verse of the Epistle to the Ephesians says: "For we are God's handiwork, created in Christ Jesus to devote ourselves to *the good deeds* for which God has designed us" (Eph 2:10). These "good deeds" show two actual characteristic notes: first, God *designed* us for them, and second, we have *to live* them. It is not remarkable that Paul should state quietly: "He will pay every man for *what he has done*. To *those who pursue glory, honor and immortality by steady persistence in well-doing,* he will give eternal life; but for those who are governed by selfish ambitions, who refuse obedience to the truth and take the wrong for their guide, there will be the fury of retribution. There will be grinding misery for every human being who is an evildoer, for the Jew first and for the Greek also; and for *every welldoer,* there will be glory honor and peace, for the Jew first and for the Greek also. For God has no favorites.... It is not by hearing the law, but *by doing it,* that men will be justified before God " (Rom 2:6-16).

Either Paul does not know what he is talking about and unmistakably contradicts himself within the space of a few minutes, or the word "deeds" has in his writing a twofold meaning; the first taken from the Old Testament, namely from the ancient prophets, and from Christ's teaching, and the second, standing for the misconstrued notion held by the rabbis, more especially by the Pharisees. We have already pointed out in another place that Pharisaism is one of the most natural and spontaneous—as well as one of the most dangerous—deformations of an authentic attitude before God.

Now, it so happens that various Christians of the Reformation came to the definite opinion that the Catholic Church understands the term "merit" in the second meaning rather than in the first. Of course, their misapprehension is largely due to the word itself, "to merit," Etymologically, the word is derived from the Latin "*mereri*" and "*meritum.*" The Greek of the New Testament is happier in its vocabulary; it says: "to be worthy *(axios)* of," or "to receive rewards according to our deeds," or—speaking of God—"to reward," "to repay." To many Protestants, a Latin derivation seems to be "a blot on their escutcheon," too closely allied to Roman law.

This distrust has its roots in history. The Reformation got under way in protest against practices and doctrines that looked dangerously like rabbinism of a very debased sort.

There then befell to the notion of "merit" a fate similar to what happened to the gradual growth of "created grace." In reaction to Protestantism, the theological schools of the time deemed it necessary to stress the idea of "right" in "merit," if only to keep at a safe distance from the Protestant position. That is how a good many theological manuals, as well as catechisms, fell into explaining the Catholic doctrine on merit in an unsatisfactory way. What they had to offer in the end was a doctrine harmful to the faith and purity of religious life.

From this, we see that the objections raised by the Reformation were not always groundless; common practices among sections of the faithful and misrepresentations by sundry textbooks or spiritual books were to blame. But not a few Protestants fell into the same error with which we reproached those theologians, though in the opposite direction. In order to steer clear of anything smacking of Rome, they threw overboard all teaching about merit so "radically" (a word they favored) that they finally deformed the true teaching of Scripture. To preserve only one aspect of scriptural teaching, be it is ever so central, and to discard all the rest, is to fail in fidelity to the word of God. The protest raised by the early Reformation was in the main justifiable. Let us grant that much. But, "it is these you should have practiced, without neglecting the others" (Lk 11:42).

The Church teaches that we can truly speak of merit when we live in a "state of grace." What is meant by a "state of grace" we shall consider in the next chapter. For the moment, it is enough for us to use the words of Scripture: those alone who are children of God and share in the freedom of the Son can merit in the sight of God.

The state of justice itself can in no way be merited, or "grace would cease to be grace" (Rom 11:26). All we can do is prepare ourselves for it, with the help of God's grace. No need to restate what we said on this point when rebutting the denials of the semi-Pelagians. Election to grace, as such, also falls outside merit; but *given the election,* we can merit the glory of heaven. Clear-cut theological distinctions like these, when arranged in orderly sequence, have an air of paragraphs in a lawbook; they seem merely to clothe in words dogmatic sentences that have no organic unity. In reality, that is not so. All those dogmatic statements fall into and form a coherent organic structure. But we shall come to this point later.

Meanwhile, let us not forget that we are endeavoring to interpret merit in terms of a dialectical movement, the only way of proceeding which experience has proved safe. And here let us call to mind our starting point: in the life of grace, God's initial love keeps the exclusive, absolute and radical primacy all along the line, from the first beginnings of faith up to the final glory of heaven. That is the meaning of what we said a minute ago, " within the election. "

However, Scripture does not content itself with stating two affirmations: the first, that everything is grace, the second, that *with grace* we may truly speak of merit. It goes one step further. So does the Church and the teaching of the great saints, who enjoyed a far deeper experience of the sense of faith than we do. And this third dialectical movement suggests a correction required for an adequate notion of merit. We mean a profound realization of our sinfulness.

Of this sinfulness Christ gives us the first warning as reported by Luke: " Suppose one of you has a servant ploughing or minding sheep. When he comes back from the fields, will the master say, ' Come along at once and sit down '? Will he not rather say, ' Prepare my supper, buckle your belt, and then wait on me while I have my meal; you can have yours afterwards '? Is he grateful to the servant for carrying out his orders? *So with you:* when you have carried out all your orders, you should say: ' We are servants *and deserve no credit*; we have done only our duty ' " (Lk 11:7-10). This short parable, suggested by the rural and patriarchal customs of Galilee Christ uses to give us a lesson in humility. We are servants of God. When we do what we have to do, we have done no more than our duty. No room here for boasting. Even the highest degree of holiness is not more than a duty; God is never served and loved enough. In fact, we are always falling short of strict duty.

We have another parable which affords us a still better insight into the mystery of merit. Matthew has preserved it for us. " Many who are first will be last, and the last first. The Kingdom of heaven is like this. There was once a landowner who went out early one morning to hire laborers for his vineyard; and after agreeing to pay them the usual day's wage he sent them

off to work. Going out three hours later, he saw some more
men standing idle in the market-place. 'Go and join the others
in the vineyard,' he said, 'and I will pay you a fair wage';
so off they went. At noon he went out again, and at three
in the afternoon and made the same arrangement as before.
An hour before sunset, he went out and found another group
standing there; so he said to them, 'Why are you standing about
like this all day with nothing to do?' 'Because no one has
hired us,' they replied. So he told them, 'Go and join the
others in the vineyard.' When evening fell, the owner of the
vineyard said to his steward, 'Call the laborers and give them
their pay, beginning with those who came last and ending
with the first.' Those who had started work an hour before
sunset came forward and were paid the full day's wage. When
it was the turn of the men who had come first, they expected
something extra, but were paid the same amount as the others.
As they took it, they grumbled at their employer: 'These late-
comers have done only one hour's work, yet you have put them
on a level with us who have sweated the whole day long in the
blazing sun!' The owner turned to one of them and said,
'My friend, I am not being unfair to you. You agreed on the
usual wage for the day, did you not? Take your pay and go
home. I chose to pay the last man the same as you. *Surely,
I am free to do with my money what I like. Why be jealous
because I am kind?*' Thus will the last be first and the first
last" (Mt 19:30-20:16).

The opening words and the ending of the parable, as we have
quoted them, seem good evidence that what it signifies above all
is the vocation of the Gentiles as compared with that of the
Jews. The Jews were the first called; the heathen came later.
The vineyard is an ageold image used by the prophets for the
Kingdom of God. The Jews were the people of the Covenant.
But the Covenant cannot prevent God from being "kind,"
nor from "doing with His money what He likes," nor, consequently, from calling to Himself the pagans "at the end of
time." Viewed in this perspective, the parable fits better into
our previous chapter.

It keeps, nonetheless, a significance related to what we are
concerned with here. Christ takes the wage-contract for a
symbol of the Covenant. To the "other laborers," the owner
promises a "fair wage." In all probability, this indicates that
God has bound Himself to take into account the labor we do in
His Kingdom. But what is more important is that Christ
immediately changes the image of strict wages understood as
a legal obligation between equals into something quite relative.
In the Kingdom we have no other *rights* than those God *deigns
to give us.* "Surely, I am free to do with my money what I

like. Why be jealous because I am kind?" The two parts of this quotation throw light on each other. God stays absolutely free, not as an arbitrary tyrant might be, but "because He is kind." His preferences never exclude the others.

We are now ready for the third step in our dialectic. In our merit there is never room for "boasting." To begin with, all things come from Christ. "God has chosen things low and contemptible, mere nothings, to overthrow the existing order. And so there is no place for human pride in the presence of God. *You are in Christ* by God's act, for God has made Him our wisdom; He is our righteousness; in Him we are consecrated and set free. And so [in the words of Scripture], 'If a man is proud, let him be proud of the Lord'" (I Cor 1:28-31).

There is still a further reason: even though we are unaware of it, we do not enjoy freedom to act as we like. There dwells in us the reality of sin; and of sin, God alone can judge. To the Corinthians who had accused him, Paul writes: "For my part, if I am called to account by you or by any human court of judgment, it does not matter to me in the least. Why, I do not even pass judgment on myself, for I have nothing on my conscience; but that does not mean that I stand acquitted. My judge is the Lord. So, pass no premature judgment; wait until the Lord comes. For He will bring to light what darkness hides and disclose man's innermost motives. Then will be the time for each to receive from God such praise as he deserves" (I Cor 4:3-5).

"We are no better than pots of earthenware to contain this treasure" (II Cor 4:7). From Jewish history, Paul draws an object-lesson for the Corinthians: "If you feel sure that you are standing firm, beware! You may fall. So far you have faced no trial beyond what you can bear. God keeps faith, and He will not allow you to be tested above your powers" (I Cor 10:12-12).

And to the weak Galatians, he says: "If a man imagines himself to be somebody, when he is nothing, he is deluding himself. Each man should examine his own conduct for himself; then he can measure his achievement by comparing himself with himself and not with anyone else. For everyone has his own burden to bear" (Gal 6:3-5).

In general, Paul and John speak about what in Protestant theology is named "the indicative"—that is, a clear affirmation of what we have become in Christ and the Spirit. Confronting "the indicative" is "the imperative," the equivalent of a command, namely: become what you already are. No one underlines "the indicative" more strongly than John: "He who is reborn child of God does not commit sin, because the divine seed remains in him; *he cannot be a sinner,* because he is God's child" (I Jn 3:9). But that does not prevent the Apostle from writing in the same Epistle: " If we claim to be sinless, we are self-deceived and strangers to the truth. If we confess our sins, He is just, and may be trusted to forgive our sins and cleanse us from every kind of wrong. But if we say we have committed no sin, we make Him out to be a liar, and then His word has no place in us. My children, in writing thus to you, my purpose is that you should not commit sin " (I Jn 1:8-2:1).

Perhaps no writer of the New Testament has set forth " the imperative " as vigorously as James. He said: " My brothers, what use is it for a man to say he has faith when he does nothing to show it? Can that faith save him?...So with faith: if it does not lead to action, it is in itself a lifeless thing " (James 2:14-17). Reading this text out of its context, we would gather the impression that James contradicts Paul by emphasizing ruthlessly the necessity of good works for salvation. And yet, he is also the one who writes firmly: " My brothers, not many of you should become teachers [that is, men exhorting or admonishing others]; for you may be certain that we who teach shall ourselves be judged with greater strictness. *All of us often go wrong* " (James 3:1-2).

But to conclude this third step in the dialectical explanation of merit, unquestionably all grace comes from God; and yet the fact remains that our deeds acquire *value* in God's sight insofar as the nobility of divine sonship shines in them. Nonetheless —and here we have the third step—this merit remains eternally the merit of men who have been freed from sin, of men who are always exposed to the danger of sin, and who daily fall into sin. Where is the man who dares to say that he loves God to perfection, or that he is holy? No saint ever betrayed such audacity.

In conclusion, we advise the reader to take up again and to reread the chapter on justification in the Council of Trent That chapter has been quoted at full length on the occasion of *Uncreated and Created Grace.* [44] It is fashionable today to hold that Trent failed to take into account the religious objections raised by the Reformers. Such a judgment is perhaps an oversimplification that does not tally with historical facts. The decree on justification had been entrusted by the papal legates at the Council to Jeronimo Seripando, Superior General of the Augustinian order to which Luther belonged. Seripando had no love for the scholastic theology of the period; he was familiar with St. Augustine and quite capable of grasping some of the difficulties of his former fellow-religious. It is thus an exaggeration to maintain that the conciliar Fathers were totally blind to the real problem at issue. Seripando, and others with him,

---

[44] Cf. paperback edition, pp. 129-130.

was conscientiously striving for at least some of the justifiable grievances to be attended to.

The same Tridentine chapter proposes what we have in view here. An attentive reader will notice how that chapter in which the Council sums up its doctrine on merit follows the lines of the dialectic structure, which better than any other, takes into account the complexity of reality. The chapter opens with the solemn affirmation that all things come from God. Of all Tridentine decrees, it is the chief document alluding to the indwelling, or at least to our mystical union with Christ. Christ is " the Head of the members " (Eph 4:15), and " the wine carrying the branches " (Jn 15:5). The reality of our merits is described, in finely balanced sentences, in the setting of the primacy of God's grace. And the end of the chapter refers to the idea, so dear to Paul and Augustine, that we may not boast of our merits because we remain always sinners.

By way of synopsis, the council quotes a profound paradox we owe to Augustine's genius: " God's goodness toward men is such that *He wants His gifts to be their merits.*"

Merit as fidelity to the covenant

After a brief analysis of the word " merit," we have paid special attention to the dialectic structures proper to " merit " in God's sight. Unless we take into account the three main moments already dealt with, and unless we apply them *together* in practical life, we shall never succeed in building up a genuine notion of theological merit, nor shall we truly live up to it. We remain forever exposed to the danger of falling into semi-Pelagianism, or, what is worse, into legalistic piety, of whatever brand it be. That would be the curfew, tolling the knell of a dying religion.

We shall now devote three sections to establishing what theological merit is. The first section attempts to discover a more biblical representation of that aspect of grace which several theologians sought to define in terms of legal right. In my early teaching days I followed the latter method. But I abandoned it, because its disadvantages outweigh its advantages. Besides, as a method, it is imposed on us neither by the reading of Scripture nor by the authentic teaching of the Church. The Council of Trent cautiously confines itself to the definition of " true merit," without further specification (Denz. n. 842). And so, we prefer to follow the biblical concept.

In Scripture, it is plain that, in some way, God has bound Himself to reward us. On this ground, several theologians produce biblical allusions to God's promises. God owes all to Himself. He is not bound by our good deeds. That much is abundantly clear.

But God's promises do not stand apart from His salvific action. They are part and parcel of the history of salvation. They acquire within the Covenant their most significant expression. This would go to show that merit, like grace, is not a purely private affair, some sort of spiritual bank for small investors. The Covenant was entered upon with the people as a whole, God's people. All Israel was addressed together. Consequently, in merit we remain jointly and individualy accountable. We injure one another through sin. Through our faith and love, bearing fruit in good deeds, we help each other, since we are al one in the one Church. If the Last Judgment makes any theological sense, it is above all owing to the fact that men will not be judged individually, but the human race *as a whole*. Through creation we all together are made present to God. In grace, we are called together to love. In the eternal reward of heaven, we shall meet together again before God, " that God may be all in all " (I Cor 15:28; Col 3:11; Eph 1:21).

The spirituality of the Old Testament was entirely built upon faith in the Covenant which God has made with Abraham and had renewed with Moses after the deliverance from Egypt. Of that Covenant, the Temple on Mount Zion in Jerusalem was a shining symbol. In the Holy of Holies, above the Ark of the Covenant and the golden tablets of the Covenant, between the golden wings of the cherubim (Heb 9:1-5), there reigned God's " glory, " present in the midst of His people. On the day of the great reconciliation, the " Yom bakkippurim, " the high priest entered the Holy Place; he sprinkled the Ark and the tablets with the blood of the sacrificial offerings, and then came out again to sprinkle the entire assembly of the people as a sign of cleansing and forgiveness (Heb 6:6-7, 13, 21-22).

Yahweh had revealed to Moses the content of the Covenant: " From now on, if you obey Me and respect My Covenant, I shall regard you as My own from among all nations; for the whole earth is my domain. I will consider you a royal priesthood and a dedicated nation, God's people " (Ex 19:5 6). Later, Peter will quote those words in a text containing, most probably, one of the earliest pre-baptismal instructions (I Pet 2:9).

" Moses then came forward and called together all the elders of the people, and exposed before them whatever Yahweh had commanded. Whereupon the entire people, with one mind, replied: ' *Whatever Yahweh has said we shall observe* ' " (Ex 19: 7). If the people obey God's law, they will be blessed by God; but if they reject His word, they will be punished by God (Ex 23:30-33; Deut 28; Lev 26).

In the beginning of this first part of our volume, we have seen that God's fidelity and graciousness are the two marks of the Covenant. The Covenant is a gift of love and mercy. It remains forever, for God's word endures forever.

Parallel and responding to God's fidelity, there stands the people's *fidelity* to the promises made by their fathers. That fidelity has to manifest itself in the observance of the law, in the " search for God, " in " walking before the Lord, " and finally in the " knowing of God "—all of which are figures of speech to express both moral perfection and religious surrender in faith and love. God's fidelity had promised " to bless " the fidelity of the people; and " to bless " is more telling than " to reward. " Fidelity, *hesed* in Hebrew, forms the main tenet of any authentic Jewish spirituality. From this tradition sprang Hassidism, a religious tradition, strongly marked by a mystical vein, which has spread through eastern Europe, and was made known in western Europe and the United States thanks to the works of Martin Buber and Abraham Heschel.

The Church is the people of the New Covenant. Addressing His apostles at the Last Supper, Jesus repeated the solemn words Moses pronounced during the sacrifice that was to seal God's Covenant of old: " This is the cup of the New Covenant sealed by my blood. Whenever you drink it, do this as a memorial of Me " (I Cor 11:25; Ex 24:8; Jer 31:31). Every eucharistic celebration is a ratification of the New Covenant in Christ's blood. In every celebration, God assembles His People as a sign of salvation and redemption.

At his baptism, each of the faithful renews the solemn promises made by the people of Israel. At the beginning of the baptismal ceremonies, the minister speaks in God's name and promises eternal life to all those who will observe the commandments. Immediately after this, the priest reads the commandment which contains all others, the commandment to love. By the express desire of the Second Vatican Council, the same baptismal promises are to be renewed at confirmation and also, these recent years, by the entire community celebrating the Easter vigil.

So, we have promised to God fidelity and love; both are summed up in " obedience to the faith. " God will never be wanting in fidelity toward us, whether in this life or in the next. It is within this sacramental and salvific sphere that theological merit comes into its true meaning (Rom 4:1-5,11).

Merit as growth and maturing process

Trent defines that in " the state of grace " we merit an increase in grace (Denz. n. 842). How must we understand those words?

Certainly not as an automatic process that would be independent of our free response ot grace. For grace is not like capital which at stated periods brings in spiritual interest, to be entered into the book of life, increasing by itself. Such a notion may be resolutely discarded.

Theologians have tried to explain this aspect of grace as a process of spiritual growth. And of this we have in Scripture a few indications. The Gospels describe the Kingdom of God as a field ripening for the harvest (Mk 4:26-29), or as a seed growing to its full size (Mk 4:30-32). Paul distinguishes between the time when the Corinthians were like small children and the adult age he wishes them to arrive at (I Cor 3:1-3; Heb 5:13).

Alluding to himself, Paul confesses that he is not yet perfect. " I count everything sheer loss ... I count it so much garbage, for the sake of gaining Christ and finding myself incorporate in Him, with no righteousness of my own, no legal rectitude, but the righteousness which comes from faith in Christ, given by God in response to faith. All I care for is to know Christ, to experience the power of His resurrection, and to share His sufferings, in growing conformity with His death, if only I may finally arrive at the resurrection from the dead. It is not to be thought that I have already achieved all that. I have not yet reached perfection, but *I press on,* hoping to take hold of that for which Christ once took hold of me. My friends, I do not reckon myself to have got hold of it yet. All I can say is this: forgetting what is behind me, and reaching out for that which lies ahead, I press towards the goal to win the prize which is God's call to the life above, in Christ Jesus. Let us then keep to this way of thinking, those of us who are mature. If there is any point on which you think differently [is Paul ironical here?], this also God will make plain to you. Only let our conduct be consistent with the level we have already reached " (Phil 3:9-16).

In a superb vision of how we all grow in Christ, Paul writes: " And these were his gifts: some to be apostles, some prophets, some evangelists, some pastors and teachers, to equip God's people for work in His service, to the building up of the Body of Christ. So shall we all at last attain to the Unity inherent in our faith and our knowledge of the Son of God—to *mature manhood,* measured by nothing less than the full stature of Christ. We are no longer to be children, tossed by the waves and whirled about by every fresh gust to teaching, dupes of crafty rogues and their deceitful schemes. No, let us speak the truth in love; so shall we fully *grow up into Christ.* He is the Head, and on Him the whole Body depends. Bonded and knit together by every constituent joint, the whole frame grows through the due activity of each part, and *builds itself up in love* " (Eph 4:11-16).

Paul does not speak of the universal Church in a vague and detached manner. We have proof of it in the anguished cry he addressed to the Galatians who had allowed themselves to be led astray by some Judeo-Christians. " It is always a fine thing to deserve an honest envy—always, and not only when I am present with you, dear children. For my children you are, and I am in travail with you over again *until you take the shape of Christ*" (Gal 4:18-19). A little further he writes: " You were running well. Who hindered you from following the truth? " (Gal 5:7).

In the next chapter we shall sketch in more concrete detail what growth in grace is. For the moment, we approach the subject from the angle of merit. How can we merit an increase of grace? How can we merit heaven?

Catholic theology offers many answers to these queries; but not all of them can be acquitted of juridical bias. To ensure correct thinking in this matter, we should always keep in mind the basic principle laid down by the Council of Trent: " Each one receives for himself his own justice [that is, his state of grace] *in the measure* in which the Spirit ' distributes separately to each individual at will ' (I Cor 12:11), and in accordance with each one's dispositions and cooperation " (Denz. n. 799). Those words of Trent are not to be understood in a static sense; they lay down a fundamental dynamic principle. The term *measure*, in the quotation, indicates that grace is ordained to a fulfillment in eternity.

As is the case with everything in grace, growth is thus dependent in the first place on the divine initiative of the Spirit. God grants His grace as He Himself wants to. He distributes His grace unequally among individuals, insofar as He remains absolutely free, bound by no one, never compelled by any one, and He allots to each one an irreplaceable, singular function in the Church. But, at the same time, grace remains in substance identically one and the same, in this sense at least, that the divine superabundant riches lie open to one and all. It is a sign of human pettiness to fear that the election of a few to more outstanding grace can be injurious to others. Since the indwelling God stays with us in our actual personal condition, that is, a condition involved in time, grace persistently urges us to increasingly greater holiness. This is the moment to recall to mind St. Augustine's paradox: " God's goodness towards men is such that He wants His gifts to be their merits. "

But growth in grace depends also on our cooperation, though, naturally *within the limits* of the divine initiative. At the risk of wearying the reader with ceaseless repetitions, we are not to understand this in a diehard, semi-Pelagian sense. God and man do not work conjointly like partners who, notwithstanding a great difference in dignity and power, *meet on a level with each other,* and bring to the task their own separate contribution.

Cooperation, in the last analysis, is measured by God's love. The more we open ourselves to grace by a loving acceptance of God's grace, the more it flowers in us. Or, in other words, grace never comes into full bloom in a life of tepidity and indifference; for then no increase of grace can be merited. No sound theology has ever lost sight of the principle: the greater the love, the greater the grace, and consequently, the greater the merit.

All through this growing process, God respects the human nature which He made and destined to reach its completion in time. In another place we have observed that freedom has been conferred on us as a duty freely to attain to ever greater freedom. Similarly, through love we grow to greater love. In the light of the peculiar and unique nature of grace, we may say: our good deeds " merit " an increase of grace; or, by lovingly accepting grace, we grow in grace and thereby to greater love.

Growth in grace follows the law of the Spirit. The Holy Ghost, so teaches Ruysbroeck, is from within the Trinity the principle that actualizes, perfects and fulfills. Perfection implies a twofold trend: the first one, leading outwards to a heightening awareness of the responsibility we have toward the world of steadily advancing in the authenticity of our witnessing to God; and the second trend, turning inwards to intensify within us simplicity and interiorization. This is the specific grace of the sacrament of confirmation; that is why it has justly been called the sacrament of the adult.

Growth in grace is ordained by the Spirit toward its final fulfillment in Christ. This statement of fact is just another way for us to understand how grace on earth can merit heaven. Heaven is nothing else than the final revelation of what we have become through grace.

Let us return once more to the main theme of this book: God's indwelling presence. The Father, the Son and the Holy Ghost dwell in us. In love They draw us to Themselves and, in time, work out and actualize their indwelling. Step by step our life on earth must be brought into harmony with the rhythm of the divine life itself. After all, growth in grace means that all through life here below we come to a deeper realization of the indwelling of the Father, the Son and the Holy Ghost, and to a knowledge of our sharing in Their life.

Heaven will completely unveil to us what at present we are able to experience obscurely in faith; in heaven we shall see " face to face " (I Cor 13:12). " Because for us there is no veil over the face, we all reflect as in a mirror the splendor of the Lord; then we are transfigured into His likeness, from splendor to splendor; such is the influence of the Lord Who is Spirit "

(II Cor 3:18). " Therefore we never cease to be confident. We know that so long as we are at home in the body we are exiles from the Lord; faith is our guide, we do not see Him. We are confident, I repeat, and would rather leave our home in the body and go to live with the Lord. We therefore make it our ambition, wherever we are, here or there, to be acceptable to Him. For we must all have our lives laid before the tribunal of Christ, where each must receive what is due to him for his conduct in the body, good or bad " (II Cor 5:6-10).

Nothing could be more explicit than John's testimony: " How great is the love that the Father has shown to us! We are called God's children; *and such we are* [therefore, in this life already]. And the reason why the godless world does not recognize us is that it has not known Him. Here and now, dear friends, we are God's children; what we shall be has not yet been disclosed. But we know that when it is disclosed we shall be like Him, because we shall see Him as He is " (I Jn 3:1-2).

We end with one last remark. By now we are alive to the fact that our progress in grace is a growth that can attain to maturity in heaven only. For, there the flower opens to the sun of God's light, that very flower which during the long winter months on earth began by being a seed cast in the soil, and slowly developed into a highly perched bud balancing on a slender stalk. But, does this deserve the name of merit?

It does, undoubtedly. When Scripture compares the development of grace with the growth of a plant, it intends to convey a truth by means of a figure of speech. A free person, a child of God is at stake in this growth of grace. Our dignity as a child of God unfolds in the course of that growth. Life of grace is nothing else than the flowering of the nobility we receive from the indwelling God at the moment divine sonship is conferred on us in baptism.

The Flemish poet, Guido Gezelle, describes beautifully this aspect of grace in a poem of his. A few sober strokes of his pen suffice to mark out our creaturely condition before God: each one is like a flower slowly opening under the quickening power and radiating light of the sun: [45]

> A flower am I
> And bloom before thine eyes,

[45] Guido Gezelle, *Laatste Verzen* (Amsterdam, Veen, 1913), p. 113. Guido Gezelle, Flemish priest and poet, was born at Bruges (Belgium) on May 1, 1830, and died at Bruges in 1899. He was one of the greatest leaders for the revival of Flemish as a literary language. He wrote, in the dialect of his native Flanders, poems inspired by deep religious and philosophical insight. As a lyric poet, he would be great in any world literature.

Oh thou, fierce sun of light!
Eternally thyself
Permitest me, mere nothing
To live before Thee
And when this life is done
Wilt grant me life unending.

Far from Thee am I
Though Thou, mild source
Of all that is alive
Or ever comes to life,
Art nighest me
And send'st into my deepest self
Thine all-pervading glow.

Fetch me, raise me up!
Undo my earthly bonds;
Tear me by the roots! Transplant
Me . . . let me go . . . let
Me hasten to where Summer reigns,
And glorious Sunlight shines.

Then I, before. . .
No, not before thine eyes,
but next to Thee, with Thee,
But in Thee . . . soon . . . shall bloom,
If Thou wilt suffer me,
A worthless thing, to live—
If in Thy changeless light
Thou let me come.

In our phenomenological analysis, we drew attention to the
fact that merit is to be estimated less by performance or achievement than by the dignity of the person who freely expresses
himself in the achievement. We found verification of this
on the level of ordinary wages, but much more so on the plane of
public honors and prizes. This is to be verified further still
in our relations born form grâce. For these are *par excellence*
relations between two persons who have entered into a dialogue
with each other. Much less importance is attached to deeds
than to love expressed in life. And with this we come to the
last section, a complement of the two preceding ones. No sure
insight into merit is possible *unless we take the three aspects
together:* fidelity and obedience to the Covenant, i.e., the Church,
development and growth in grace, and finally the dialectic of
love.

Merit as interior law of love

Love has been mentioned more than once in this chapter. If we admit that Christianity knows of but one commandment that sums up all the others, then there exists but one kind of "good works": love. Scholastic theologians have been unanimous in maintaining the principle, "*par caritas, par meritum,*" love is the measure of merit. All this ought to be plain after what was said in the preceding sections.

What do we offer to God by our "good works," if not ourselves? God has no need whatever of our works. He is waiting for our "hearts." We have to give ourselves to God because God gave Himself to us in Christ. Consequently, our sole merit is not so much eternal happiness in heaven, but rather Christ Himself Who in the Spirit offers us to the Father.

That is what Paul says: "What does it matter? One way or another, in presence or in sincerity, Christ is set forth, and for that I rejoice. Yes, and rejoice I will, knowing well that the issue of it all will be my deliverance, because you are praying for me, and the Spirit of Jesus Christ is given me for support. For, as I passionately hope, I shall have no cause to be ashamed, but shall speak so boldly that now as always the greatness of Christ will shine out clearly in my person, whether through my life or through my death. For *to me life is Christ,* and death gain; but what if my living on in the body may serve some good purpose? Which then have I to choose? I cannot tell. I am torn two ways: what I should like is to depart and *be with Christ;* that is better by far; but for your sake there is greater need for me to stay on in the body" (Phil 1:18-24). "At the word of command, at the sound of the archangel's voice and God's trumpet-call, the Lord Himself will descend from heaven; first the Christian dead will rise, then we who are left alive shall join them, caught up in clouds to *meet the Lord* in the air. Thus *we shall always be with the Lord*" (I Thes 4:16-17).

Paul's firmest affirmation can be read in his Epistle to the Romans: "I am convinced that there is nothing in death or life, in the realm of the spirits or superhuman powers, in the world as it is or in the world as it shall be, in the forces of the universe, in heights and depths—nothing in all creation that can separate us from the love of God in Christ Jesus our Lord" (Rom 8:38). That is the joyous confession with which Paul concludes the precious eighth chapter of his letter from which we quoted so frequently on the subject of grace.

The book of the Apocalypse, in which St. John contemplated the secret of our future in God, ends with a simple invocation that in all probability formed part of the primitive liturgy of the

Church: " He who gives this testimony speaks: ' Yes, I am coming soon.' Amen. Come, Lord Jesus " (Apoc 22:21).

Have these not been the sentiments of the saints? We all know the prayer attributed to St. Francis Xavier:

> *O Deus, ego amo te,*
> *Nec amo te ut salves me*
> *Aut, quia non amantes te*
> *Aeterno punis igne.*
>
> *Tu, tu, mi Jesu, totum me*
> *Amplexus es in cruce:*
> *Tulisti clavos, lanceam,*
> *Multamque ignominiam,*
>
> *Innumeros dolores,*
> *Sudores et angores,*
> *Ac mortem; et haec pro me*
> *Ac pro me peccatore.*
>
> *Cur igitur non amem te,*
> *O Jesu sacratissime?*
> *Non, ut in coelo salves me,*
> *Aut ne aeterne damnes me,*
> Nec praemii ullius spe,
>
> *Sed sicut tu amasti me,*
> *Sic amo et amabo te,*
> *Solum quia rex meus es,*
> *Et solum quia Deus es!*

The Italians are wont to say, " *traduttore, tradittore,*" " to translate is to traduce," which is true enough of most translated poetry. By great good fortune, we possess a rendering of Xavier's prayer done by Gerard Manley Hopkins which ought to satisfy most [46]:

> O God, I love thee, I love thee—
> Not out of hope of heaven for me
> Nor fearing not to love and be
> In everlasting burning.
>
> Thou, thou, my Jesus, after me
> Didst reach thine arms out dying,

[46] *Poems of Gerard Manley Hopkins,* third edition, Geoffrey Cumberlege (Oxford University Press, 1948), p. 188.

> For my sake sufferedst nails and lance,
> Mocked and marred countenance,
>
> Sorrows passing number,
> Sweat and care and cumber,
> Yes and death, and this for me,
> And thou couldst see me sinning:
>
> Then I, why should not I love thee,
> Jesu, so much in love with me?
> Nor for heaven's sake; not to be
> Out of hell by loving thee;
> *Not for any gain I see;*
>
> But just the way that thou didst me
> I do love and I will love thee;
> What must I love thee, Lord, for then?
> For being my king and God.   Amen.

It would not be hard to produce a sizeable anthology of similar prayers taken from the writings of the saints. Such testimony is of value for our faith. In former days theologians used to quote texts not only from the Councils and papal documents, as present-day theologians still do, but they cited also " *testimonia sanctorum* "—testimonies of men whose lives plunged more deeply than ours into the experience of an unalloyed and intense realization of the faith.

In the dialectic of love we have reached what is most exalted in merit, Christ Himself. At this height of love, no trace of calculation is left, which, at first sight, seems bound up with the idea of " merit. " Love is that most excellent bond which secures us to God and—as we may truly say—God to us; for love is a bond far more sacred than any right, far loftier than any nobility, far richer than any honorable prize. In comparison with love, in comparison with Christ Himself, all else vanishes. He remains forever, our one Reward. He has desired to become our Reward because He first loved us. Here more than anywhere else in our meditations so far, the words of St. Augustine find their application: " God's goodness toward men is so great that He wants His gifts to be their merits. " God's gift is God Himself. *He Himself is our eternal reward.*

Theologians have been so convinced that merit is measured by love that they have sought to know what kind of love is required for merit. After all we have said so far, the query verges on vulgar mockery. Yet, it has its use, were it only because it provides an occasion to redress some wrong notions. Many wrong notions have been current among the faithful, and keep recurring in one or other spiritual writing. However, some others have been condemened by the Church.

Two extreme positions must be avoided: laxism and rigorism. Laxism holds that no explicit love is necessary. The presence of the "state of grace" (that is, the state of sanctifying grace) suffices. Rigorism asserts that nothing counts except an explicit act of love, sometimes even an act of pure love of God—that is, an act motivated by nothing below God. This view has been rejected by the Church when she condemned some of the Jansenist propositions (Denz. nn. 1403-1407) and some of Molinos' disciples (Denz. nn. 1227, 1232).

The first position has not been censured, though few theologians would agree with it. It can be given a good interpretation. But if "state of grace" stands for something too static, no more than a created grace, then the position fails to satisfy. The whole question hinges on whether grace may be conceived statically. We shall dwell on this point in the next chapter.

The main defect in the controversy between laxists and rigorists lies in this: when the dispute arose—in the course of the seventeenth century—most theologians tended to restrict love to distinct acts of love. They looked upon love far too much as a separate human action that had to be combined somehow with other human acts like justice or honesty. Those men lived in a period of theological decline. It had become customary in spiritual books and instructions to stress the necessity of a separate good intention for each "good work." The idea has survived till this day; if influences some of the popular practices of devotion to the Sacred Heart. Most ecclesiastical authorities have been wise enough to recognize that one sincere morning oblation suffices for the day. Generally, however, this way of stating the issue smacks too much of a shopkeeper's policy.

It had escaped the notice of the theologians involved in the dispute that love stands for something more than a human act distinct from the countless other human actions in the course of the day. Love consists in an existential adequate expression of the entire human activity as such. We may liken it to an "openness" dynamically ordained, a fully willed surrender of life as a whole, the "soul" of our *entire* activity in the concrete. Needless to add that love, thus understood, will profitably be formulated now and then in distinct acts.

Now, if we conceive of the "state of grace" dynamically, as a fundamental option made by the whole man—as we shall see in the next chapter—there is no problem. In a life, dynamically upheld by love, everything is love, down to man's most commonplace actions. No need, then, to elicit at every turn a special explicit renewal of the "good intention." There remains the *task of purifying* the fundamental intention; for, we are always in danger of slipping back into self-centeredness. The saints demanded no more than this as basis for the spiritual life, on condition that care is taken of progressive purification of that intention. Such purification can be achieved by seeing to it that the fundamental surrender of our life continues to prop up our life in its concrete circumstances, lest it fade away into empty dreams and enthusiastic devotions of an unwholesome kind—" *Schwärmerei* " as the Germans would say.

Indwelling and merit

By way of conclusion, we shall now attempt to present a synthetic survey of the teaching of the Church concerning merit, always from the standpoint of God's indwelling. The Church teaches that we can in no way merit either our election to grace, or the first grace towards conversion, or perseverance. All this we have to hold as a matter of faith; otherwise, " grace would cease to be grace. " In all these aspects of dispensing grace, God's action retains absolute priority. In all things, *a fortiori* in grace, God has the initiative. If we could merit the first grace toward conversion, or the grace of perseverance, the initiative would be ours. We have insisted enough on this point in the section on semi-Pelgianism. [47]

Holy Writ has more to tell us: the state of justice and holiness, which constitutes divine sonship and finds its concrete expression in the possession of sanctifying grace, is an absolutely gratuitous gift. All we can do toward it is prepare ourselves through conversion, with the help of grace. It is God Himself who by consolidating His initial indwelling in us makes our heart ready for the complete actualization of the indwelling in sanctifying grace. Here too, all initiative rests with God. In my opinion, this preparation, due to grace, does not merit the divine sonship in any way, not even in the analogical sense proposed by a few theologians. And our opinion is based above all on the radical urgency of the scriptural affirmations. Consequently, there can be no question of merit here; divine sonship must be guaranteed its quality of pure gift of God. In the light of Scripture, a gradual *preparation* for this highest of gifts cannot be called " merit. "

But, no sooner are we raised to full intimacy *within* the indwelling, no sooner do we become " servants in the Servant " and " sons in the Son, " than our deeds acquire in God's eyes a unique value. And this *only* on the ground of the dignity

---

[47] Cf. paperback, p. 147 ff.

of children of God manifesting itself in our actions—those actions especially which spring from love; for then the Father recognizes in us the countenance of His Son.

The indwelling consolidates God's Covenant in our hearts. Its law is no longer written on tablets of stone, but in the heart, and by the Spirit. We conform our lives to the Covenant through obedience and love; in that very way we make our return to God of fidelity for fidelity. The indwelling is also an interior power fostering our growth to a maturity that must wait till heaven for its full revelation and flowering. Herein consists the operation proper to the Spirit. Finally, the indwelling invites us to love God with our whole heart. In the indwelling, God gives Himself to us and endows us with the means of giving ourselves to Him. He is the sole reward we look to; and *we ourselves* are the sole "work" He expects from us. But this, too, can be fully realized in heaven only. Meanwhile, we remain "unprofitable servants"; for, when doing all we can, we do no more than our duty. In spite of our best effort, we shall always fall short of the mark: God can never be loved enough. We remain short of the mark for the further reason that we continue to sin in so many things, were it only because our life stays infected by self-centeredness. Hence, the impossibility for us to "boast" of our works and to scorn others. We should remember that the grace of the indwelling was bestowed on us who, as sinners, had no claim to it. Worse still, though we be in the state of grace, we continue to commit daily sins which, as we shall see, carry in them the seed of the true sin. Our hearts remain divided.

However, the gnawing consciousness of our sinful condition need neither sadden nor dismay us. On the contrary, it should awaken in us a great joy, because it affords us a deeper understanding of God's great love for us. It ought to spur us on to generosity and forbearance toward others; for we, great sinners, need forgiveness as much as others. It will bring us peace springing from true humility, the humility of one who has been forgiven much.

Let us end this important chapter on merit with a passage from the Gospel of St. Luke, the story of the penitent woman. Contrary to what is generally believed, in all probability she was neither the sister of Martha, nor the sinner of Magdala. Let her be anonymous; she is for us a model of the *penitent love* that should characterize each and every Christian "to whom much has been forgiven."

"One of the Pharisees invited Him to dinner; He went to the Pharisee's house and took His place at table. A woman who was living an immoral life in the town had learned that Jesus was dining in the Pharisee's house and had brought oil of myrrh in a small flask. She took her place behind Him, by His feet, weeping. His feet were wetted with her tears and she wiped them with her hair, kissing them and anointing them with the myrrh. When His host, the Pharisee, saw this, he said to himself, ' If this fellow were a real prophet, he would know who this woman is that touches him, and what sort of woman she is, a sinner.' Jesus took him up and said, ' Simon, I have something to say to you.' ' Speak on, Master,' said he. ' Two men were in debt to a moneylender: one owed him five hundred silver pieces, the other fifty. As neither had anything to pay with, he let them both off. Now, which will love him most?' Simon replied, ' I should think the one that was let off most.' ' You are right,' said Jesus. Then turning to the woman, he said to Simon, ' You see this woman? I came to your house: you provided no water for my feet; but this woman has made my feet wet with her tears and wiped them with her hair. You gave no kiss; but she has been kissing my feet ever since I came in. You did not anoint my head with oil; but she anointed my feet with myrrh. And so, I tell you, *her great love proves that her many sins have been forgiven*; where little has been forgiven, little love is shown.' Then He said to her, ' Your sins are forgiven.' The other guests began to ask themselves, ' Who is this that he can forgive sins?' But He said to the woman, ' Your faith has saved you; go in peace '" (Lk 7:36-50).

Shall we claim the right to think ourselves better than the penitent woman, or despise her on the illusory plea that we have "made it up" to God? Were we the greatest of saints, we would still be sinners whom God has forgiven much, and who might have been, for lack of grace, far worse than the public sinner of the Gospel.

Luther has said that our justice is no better than "soiled linen" (cf Is 64:5). We must disagree with those words if they signify that grace does not really bring us closer to God in new holiness. We may accept them, though, if we see holiness as something dynamic; if we do not forget that without grace we would have turned out worse than the sinners we scorn, and that our depravity remains forever a threat to our acquired holiness.

We may not forget Christ's stern warning: " I tell you this: taxgatherers and prostitutes are entering the Kingdom of God ahead of you " (Mt 21:31). It is true that these words of Christ occur in another context. Christ was addressing the Jews who refused to believe in Him; He drew a parallel between their pious fruitless talk and the sins of the heathen who, in the end, come to repentance and faith: ' What do you think about this? A man had two sons. He went to the first, and said, ' My boy, go and work today in the vineyard.' ' I will, sir,' the boy replied;

but he never went. The father came to the second and said the same. ' I will not,' he replied, but *afterwards he changed his mind and went.* Which of these two did as his father wished?' 'The second,' they said. Then Jesus answered, ' I tell you this: taxgatherers and prostitutes are entering the Kingdom of God ahead of you. For when John came to show you the right way to live, you did not believe him, but the tax-gatherers and the prostitutes did; and even when you had seen that, *you did not change your minds* and believe him " (Mt 21:28-32).

It is in the nature of grace that it is bestowed on sinners. No doctrine on merit may obscure that basic truth of the Gospel, nor can it avoid being qualified by it. Christ said: " It is not the healthy that need a doctor, but the sick. Go and learn what that text means, ' I require mercy, not sacrifice ' (Os 6:6). I did not come to invite virtuous people, but sinners " (Mt 9:12-13).

In heaven we shall realize that our love remains what it was on earth: *love of repentant men.* Nor should our merits, stemming from love, be seen in a different light; we owe everlasting gratitude to God " whose goodness towards men is such that He wants His gifts to be their merits. " If we could persuade ourselves of this truth and apply it to both individuals and the Church as a society, we would see the end of that triumphalism in the Church so brilliantly pilloried on the Council floor by the Bishop of Bruges, Msgr. E. Desmedt. [48]

---

[48] Xavier Rynne, *Letters from Vatican City,* Vatican II, (First Session): Background and Debates (New York: Farrar, Strauss and Co., 1963), pp. 33-34.

Grace, an enduring gift of God

In our previous chapters, we laid the foundations for a comprehensive, living and enriching understanding of the doctrine of grace. In the following chapters we shall deal with such subsidiary questions as throw light on a more limited aspect of that doctrine: we shall confine our inquiry to sanctifying grace. We want to help the reader to integrate into a larger theology of grace what he learned from his catechism. An author who wants to renew a theological doctrine should not neglect bridging the classical conceptions, already known to the reader, and the more modern representation as yet unfamiliar to him. We shall do so and take the occasion to touch upon some practical problems bearing on the spiritual life and on moral theology—though moral applications belong rather to the second part of the book.

In the present short chapter, we shall content ourselves with gathering up what the preceding chapters have taught us. It affords us an opportunity to show how those principles have their significance in our personal piety.

We lay down as a first principle that grace is not to be compared to a sort of spiritual capital that everyone is free to treasure up for future use at will. Nor is grace a "thing" inside us, a kind of supernatural outgrowth of the soul. Nor is it a definite account credited to us in the book of life, a heavenly life-insurance, freeing us from cares and worries regarding both ourselves and God. Such concrete illustrations may, at best and for a short time, call attention to the fact that grace is *really given to us,* truly implanted in us, and not, as Protestants would have it, imputed to us. I am he who is sanctified. I may, and probably shall, still fail to keep true to God, whether by trifling infidelities or by acts of self-will; but it is certain that, by God's power, I am His beloved adopted child. Grace is a new creation (II Cor 5:17).

No need to insist that the divine adoption confers on me no right henceforth to raise myself above other men, or still less to glory before God in the ability to rely, even for an instant, on

myself apart from God or side by side with Him. The quality
in us of child of God, the rights belonging to an adopted son
together, in and through the only-begotten Son—in a word,
grace—*all is a gift uninterruptedly from God.* Not for a moment
do I hold it from myself! Beginning the moment of my baptism
and for a never-ending beatitude, grace remains a living stream
ceaselessly coming to me from God, permeating me through
and through, and drawing me to God. Grace means a receiving
from God continuously, not on the day of my christening only.
Grace is life, is love; there is not an instant when this stream
of love, so to say, stops and solidifies to become my own possession. I am able to believe, to hope and to love only inasmuch
as I am borne on the life-stream flowing from God and returning
back to God—" from God to God, " as Ruysbroeck would say.
The one thing I can pride myself on, the only achievement
which, in the last analysis, I can claim as wholly mine is tepidity
which dams off and silts up the divine inflow, and mortal sin
which shuts it off. But whatever good I do in the sight of God
I owe first and foremost to God, though it is also my good
deed, and thus my merit, insofar as I keep acting *by* God, borne
on and helped by *His grace. In short, evil in me comes from me;
good in me comes from God, yet also comes from me, for it comes
in me from God first.* We know already St. Augustine's felicitous
formula, adopted by the Council of Trent: " God wants His gifts
to be our merits. " Our merits are truly ours, because we
cooperate with God; but whatever we do with God's cooperation,
is in the first place a gift of God and a never-ending grace.

The provincial council held at Quierzy-sur-Oise (France) in
853 found a striking formulation, suitable to our purpose and
consistent with the teaching of former Fathers and Popes. Its
third canon reads: " Almighty God wants all men without
exception to be saved (I Tm 2:4), though in fact all are not
saved. He who is saved owes it to God's saving grace; he who
is lost bears the responsibility of his being lost " (Denz. n. 318).
Notice how the Council deliberately stops short at the threshold
of the mystery of predestination and, therefore, breaks the logical
symmetry of its sentence. No blame attaches to God in respect
of either eternal damnation or sin; but He keeps the initiative
in grace for eternal election to heaven and for every single
good deed.

The reader sees at once the paramount significance of such a
vivid insight into the mystery of grace, that ever-renewed wonder
of love caused by the initial, faithful and unalterable love of God.
That significance does not lie in this only: that the living
dynamic understanding of grace as " permanent flow ' from God
to God ' " affords an answer to the many accusations by Protestants who misapprehend our Catholic notion of grace. The

significance bears mainly on ourselves as we stand before God:
the more intense our endeavor to live up to the actuality of our
unbreakable dependence on God's grace, the deeper and more
thorough our Christian life. One realizes at once that the very
necessity of prayer stands for the obligation to keep in mind and
to act up to the primordial fact of our indebtedness to God at
every moment for all things; and this includes our first longing
for holiness, our free cooperation, our perseverance in the faith.
The love flowing from the Father, the Son and the Holy Ghost
vitally embraces and envelops us; besides permitting us really
to love God and neighbor, it provides us with all the means to do
so. How appropriate here are the words of the father whose
son was possessed by a dumb spirit and who called on Jesus
to cure him: " I do believe, Lord; help my unbelief " (Mk 9:23).
The whole of our Christian life rests on a tension between what
we *by our own selves* want to do in pride and unbelief, and what
we, *by God,* want to do in humility and surrender. The life
of grace comes finally to this: on the one hand, sustained daily
efforts in the practice of mortification, asceticism, and painful
endeavor, and, on the other hand, the acceptance of being borne
aloft on the wings of God's love. We have simultaneously
to steer, to row and to set sail. But rowing and steering are
God's doing in us before we can do it as we should and in
conformity with His will. Grace cannot possibly exist without
profound humility; nor can it be imagined without submission;
these two, humility and submission, are inseparably linked
together and expressed in prayer and faith. The very moment we
attempt to appropriate God's aid or to do it violence from self-
interested motives, grace slips through our sinful fingers; we
become what Christ most abhorred: Pharisees, presumptuous men
who flatter themselves that they can observe the law of justice
by their own strength and for their own glorification. Against
such, the Lord used hard words: " I tell you this: they have their
reward already " (Mt 6:16), a human reward of vain glory and
fame; in God's sight, they stand empty-handed.

Grace, life's dynamism

Keeping within the framework of these considerations, it will
be useful to examine attentively what grace produces and changes
in the dynamism of human life. Man is a strange being: a
spiritual core in material dimensions, a soul and a body, a person
and matter. We should avoid looking upon the two elements
of the human compound as two heterogeneous sorts of things
which chance to be bound together; as if, for instance, the soul

were a lighter substance haplessly locked up in the coarse wrappings of the body. It would be more correct to view the spirit and the body as two poles, whose respective lines of force are directed toward each other and intermingle. In spirit, I am all I am, but as a spiritual center of free activity. In body, too, I am complete self, but after the manner of a spiritualized matter. No definite boundary line can be drawn between the two, sharply marking off where the spirit stops and matter begins; nor is there a moment when we live purely according to the spirit and then, the next moment, slip down to the exclusively animal region of our being. The truth is that my higher powers are present and operative in even the most commonplace, the most lowly activities of the body.

In human activity, several layers of activity are distinguishable. Beneath them all lies the source itself, center of being and action: the personal spiritual core of density, as it issues immediately from the creative hand of God. Ruysbroeck saw this central core "hanging onto" God Himself, as something that would be unthinkable apart from the creative action of God uninterruptedly preserving it. Needless to say that the notion of "depth" is to be taken in a figurative sense. We could as aptly speak of the "highest summit" of the self—a snow-clad mountain peak, lost to sight, beyond the level of gray clouds, from which our spirit, tense and strained, reaches out to the pure vehement light of the divine glory. The latter comparison has the additional advantage of bringing out that we are never given an immediate awareness of what happens at that spiritual altitude. Should someone prefer it, we could borrow the modern terminology of technical psychology (though in a different sense) and speak of a sub-or super-consciousness, of wich we are aware only insofar as it expresses itself in the more tangible concrete actions of the day.

In this book we frequently speak of the deeper *core of density* of our person. The term has not always been well understood in the first edition. In the English language, "density" happens to be sometimes synonymous with "stupidity," which—to say the least—is rather unfortunate. However, in all languages the word has also a technical meaning which we take here in a transferred and figurative use. *Webster's New Collegiate Dictionary* defines "density" as "the ratio of the mass of a homogeneous portion of matter to its volume." In this sense, it is possible to speak of density of water, density of population in a city, in a country or per square mile. The picture we have in mind, when using the word, is one of *cohesion,* close connection between several elements. The term occurs in our pages usually in combination with "core"—"density" serving to define more precisely the image, "core."

While living in America, we have often sought, in conversations with others, another word, another metaphor that would avoid the unfortunate association " density " has in the English language. Nothing satisfactory was forthcoming. There is nothing else for us to do but clarify our meaning.

In a dynamic conception of our personal existence, we should distinguish *the core* of that existence from its many-sided expressions in time and space. The core unfolds into the complex articulations of our human nature in the various forms of being in us: body and soul, will, intellect, and feeling, active powers (known also by the name of faculties), and actual operations. In all those various kinds of being and activity, we remain always a unified person, identical with ourselves. And this is signified by the little word " I. " " I " am the one who sleeps, eats and thinks, loves and suffers. And it is " I, " too, who am the living source of such an ever-varying multiplicity of actions. But this can be thought of only if we acknowledge in the " I " our entire activity as coiled up and compressed, after the manner of a dynamic capability.

We could also have recourse to the image " seed, " as Scripture does, alluding to grace. In a seed, or in an ovum, the complete, full-grown oak, or the adult man, is already present as a positive possibility. But, the metaphor " core, " when applied to a person, says more, especially in the transferred meaning it has in expressions like the " core of the matter, " " the core of a system. " " Core of a person " is often used in a general sense, yet not to our entire satisfaction. That is why we further define it by adding to it the idea, " density. " We do so with the conscious purpose of affirming that present in this personal core is everything belonging to a human existence: the body, together with our situation in the cosmos, the soul, our will and intellect, our nature or form of being, and our concrete ways of acting; but all this is squeezed together and compressed—if the reader will allow me this insistence on the image—into a true existential capability, or better still, into a source of our " existing, " into an autonomous free person.

The notion which we are endeavoring to put across corresponds more or less to what the Semites meant by the word " heart. " Paul Claudel, in his famous allegory, represents " core " as " *anima,* " in opposition to the busy rational " *animus.* " Mystics call it generally " spirit, " in Latin " *mens.* " Faithful to an older tradition, Ruysbroeck speaks of " spark of the soul, " " *scintilla animae,* " or of the " ground " of the soul; and insofar as it rests in God, he calls it our " higher being. " St. Francis de Sales speaks also of " *la fine pointe de l'esprit.* "

In the religious sphere, it is evidently the mystics who have given special attention to this notion. In modern philosophy, the rediscovery of the person and of the existence of an autonomous option of life within a given situation has given to this notion its due importance at the center of interest. The past century fixed its gaze rather on " reason " or " ratio. "

Since our teaching concerning grace leans for support on the tradition of the mystics and on the modern philosophy of the person, we cannot do without that concept. More than anything, we seek to avoid the suggestion that the corporeal in us, and therefore our earthly responsibility, is to be regarded as an accidental or extrinsic aspect of our life of grace. For such a concept surely entails a whole train of woeful attitudes, especially in the domain of spirituality and apostolate. And for our theological interpretations that notion is of special importance, because, so we think, grace is first and foremost a new life, a new freedom in God, a state of kinship, and consequently a new personal " core, " sharing in the personality of the Son standing before the Father in the power of the Spirit: servants in the Servant, sons in the Son.

Within the core of our being reigns royally our person, as wellspring of all our free actions. This person consists in the spiritual possession of self in primary fundamental liberty—thus, in love. It is at this depth of the spirit that love, the pith and marrow of liberty, lies hidden. It is from there that man determines the sense his life will have. For, at that level man faces only one choice: either he chooses God in self-surrender, or he incapsulates himself in pride. St. Augustine wrote that no more than two primary forms of love are possible: " love of God that is ready to trample on self, or the love of self on the verge of scorning God " (Civ. Dei, 14, 28).

The nature of our freedom

Our fundamental will, the very soul of our liberty, utters itself at the level of our spirit, there where dwells our being as a whole, both corporeal and spiritual—condensed, as it were, in a compact core of density. Freedom is not to be characterized, as classical textbooks are wont to do, by what is commonly called " freedom of choice, " " the power consciously to accept or to reject definite and clearly delineated actions, to do them this way or that. " Such a freedom of choice will no longer be possible in heaven—at least not along the same lines—though we shall have reached freedom in its perfection. Besides, such " freedom of choice " we share in common with the animals, albeit in a superior manner; it remains bound up with the peculiar nature of our earthly situation, in which we have to grow into our true self in and through the countless, seemingly trivial actions of our day.

The nature of our freedom lies at a greater depth, hidden in the density-core of our being, where our person utters itself in a spontaneous and creative manner, assumes its full responsibility and, in its own creative manner, accepts itself as a totality in the face of the totality of the actual world which it confronts. Such exercising of our basic will is frequently called " fundamental option ": *fundamental,* because this basic choice lays the foundation for the exercising of our " freedom of choice " as befits human nature; fundamental, because *it gives meaning* to an apparently senseless, or at least trivial variety of actions we have to fill our day with, and because it integrates their capricious discontinuity into a higher, self-consistent and specified direction. It is called *option,* or existential choice, because it is chiefly concerned with the choice I make of my self, from within my total situation, facing all the rest, and therefore facing God. Augustine, as we mentioned a moment ago, speaks of two avenues open to my love: love of the others and, through the medium of the sacrament of brotherly love, love of God. In more technical philosophical terminology we might say: our basic choice falls on one of two objects: either we orientate our whole life towards self in closed-in, self-glorification, or we open ourselves to others in surrender and love, thus encountering God Himself.

The " fundamental option " is not an act apart, one in the series of many actions that serve man in the exercise of his activity. That is why the option may be described as a freely accepted, dynamically tense *orientation* of our whole life, or as a spiritual climate, as a specified direction at greater depth, as the real motivation of our life. It follows that, as such, it does not immediately fall within the scope of consciousness. But we can discern it in the " vocation " that guides and rules a life, in a man's " ideal "—on condition, though, that we empty those two words of their romantic connotation. Since, however, that basic choice manifests itself consistently in the separate actions of the day and is materialized in and through those same actions, the best way for us to identify the real course set by the fundamental option is to watch the actual " inspiration " underlying the many and very disparate actions of the day. No act would be suitable, therefore, that is conscious—in the sense that we do not make the fundamental option as we make up our mind to put on our hat or to go for a walk. But we can detect it in the trend of the multiple acts in which it manifests and actualizes itself. Nor does the fundamental option exist by itself, separate from those concrete actions, for in them it comes to life, to them it lends a content of genuine human value.

From all this follows the idea that our freedom has to flower in freedom to freedom. Human freedom does not come forward like Pallas Athene springing fully armed from the head of Zeus, her father. Undoubtedly, freedom has been bestowed in man as a power, but especially as a *commission, a call to freedom*. We have freely to grow in freedom to an ever-greater, more mature and riper freedom. And this is not achieved in a matter of days or years; it is the task of a lifetime.

As long as we conceive of freedom as a power to do anything in any way, at any moment, or as pure unrestraint and inde-termination limited only by the liberty of other men, we shall experience great difficulty in grasping all this. We inherited this false notion from the French Revolution and from liberalism. Such a formal notion comes in for partial application within the sphere of politics and civil rights, where it is better called tolerance. A modern pluralistic world is unthinkable without a minimum of democratic tolerance which permits the various religious persuasions, conceptions of life and party interests to live peacefully side by side within the unity of a state.

True freedom is not formal; it is meaningful; it is purposeful. It possesses its own truth and its own value; it bears within itself its own specified direction. *It is thanks to the good use of our freedom that we become what we are and must be.* When, in the use of our freedom, we disown what is our essential self before God and men, we injure and debase freedom. Sin is the fully accepted deterioration of freedom. Any mortal sin is like spiritual suicide. True freedom consists in the unimpeded development of our inner being, of what we already are in fact and have further to become in the future. That is why the call to the highest form of freedom belongs to God alone and not, for instance, to the state; the latter is not entitled to sit in judgment on the essential vocation which is ours as men and Christians.

We are now in a position to combine the two ideas just developed, for a more profound understanding of the nature of our freedom: freedom finds its essential expression in our basic choice, and freedom was bestowed on us as a call, a commission freely to become what we are already and have yet to become.

We have reached the adult age of manhood when we are fit to undertake the task of life as it is, with its tangled mass of seemingly trivial occupations, and also when we are fit to face it with an everdeepening conviction, a ripening intent, a firmer grip and a more personal concern. This cannot be achieved in a day or two. It takes a lifetime to reach the adult age of manhood. The " authenticity " of life consists precisely in the fact that our exterior activity harmonizes better and better with our inner conviction and fundamental will. Life then deserves to be called " true, " because what we " do " tallies with what we actually "mean to do"—such is the robustness, the unity, depth and nobility life should have.

Our freedom evolves and attains to maturity proportionally as we insert and connect with our personal, freely accepted orientation of life all the social manners we have been taught or subjected to in our childhood, all the habits we have formed in life, and even our clogging "conformism." That is what Ruysbroeck means when he keeps repeating that human life develops "from outside inwards."[49] The process of our liberation is at the same time a process of interiorization, and also of simplification; we could say: of spiritualization, if that word were not so easily misunderstood. Our basic will never stands isolated; it comes alive only in the actions of the day. A basic will that seeks to evolve into pure interiority degenerates into dreams and false sentiment. On analogous lines, a life built on the sandy multiplicity of trifling actions, ends by being a dry-as-dust activism. Both these misconceptions are all too frequent. Both are errors misjudging our human nature; they fail to see it as it is: a living unity of spirit and matter. No one can with impunity misjudge or neglect those two poles of our being: spirit and matter. Unless we observe punctually and faithfully the numerous obligations we have, as men, toward self and society, our so-called basic will turns out to be just a pious feckless wish. Unless we act in conformity with a convinced, slowly matured and freely accepted orientation of life, our countless daily actions are emptied of their real human nobility and significance.

All this is strikingly brought out in the English marriage ritual, at the moment when the two parties pronounce their mutual consent: "I take thee to my wedded wife, to have and to hold from this day forward, for better for worse, for richer for poorer, in sickness and in health, to have and to cherish, till death us do part, according to God's ordinance; and thereto I plight *my troth.*" Without this fundamental attitude of absolute *fidelity,* married life becomes unbearable, because senseless. Fidelity will be vain as long as it does not express itself in love and conformity with God's law—in spite of life's vicissitudes and, therefore, "for better for worse, for richer for poorer, in sickness and in health."

At first sight, all this might seem to be little more than finespun theory and even cavilling. But he who in his experience of life has gathered some wisdom and some self-knowledge will feel on homeground, even though he might be hard put to it to define what would be the fitting attitudes. Let us imagine four men: a saint, an egotist, a man spiritually underdeveloped

---

[49] Cf. note 2, paperback, p. 52.

and infantile, and someone suffering from an anxiety neurosis. Let us further suppose that the four men lead more or less the same kind of life, have the same social obligations and, by chance, make similar decisions on the same day and engage more or less in the same occupations: they rise in the morning, take breakfast, go to their work, have some relaxation and return home. We take it that, on the level of their "freedom of choice," they come to very much the same decisions. And yet, how different their respective spiritual climate! In the first man, we cannot but admire the loving surrender to God and men, the quiet joy and peace, the calm enthusiasm pervading the whole day. The second man may do a full day's work as efficiently as the first; but in him we sense the hard, proud refusal to think of anyone but himself, and we are repelled. In the remaining two men, the moral worth of life is of a lower quality. The first is insufficiently developed to assume a mature responsibility toward society. True, he does things nicely, as he has been taught to do; he is carried along by the force of his social instincts or acquired habits; but, at the bottom, he remains a child, though his technical and professional training enables him to perform his duties with sufficient precision. The last of the four men lives a life perpetually hovering between freedom and psychic compulsion; an unhealthy anxiety holds him in its grip and determines most of his actions. Any reader, with a modicum of sincerity and self-knowledge, can appreciate the underlying motives which make those lives so very different.

We have dwelt at some length on the nature of the basic choice that lends meaning and value to our lives. We did so because that notion is not widely known, and yet it is most important in the domain of grace. I think that we are justified in building up our doctrine of sanctifying grace on what we learn from the fundamental option. Nevertheless, the exercice of our "freedom of choice" is beset with its own problem—problems arising from the fact that the lives we are bound to accept and to lead are *human lives,* existences proper to beings composed of body and spirit. Borne up on this fundamental option, and closer to the surface, "freedom of choice" can now enter into play. At this level human behavior looks criss-crossed. Not only has free choice to fix itself on one of the numberless possibilities presented by the many-sided interests of man's daily life, but it also has to make its way through a jungle of impulses, tendencies and restraints—luxurious growths of an existence confined to time and matter; or, in psychological terms: free choice has to pass through the bodily and psychic determinisms accruing to human nature from heredity, tempera-ment and actual situation in life. Life in such conditions becomes a daily struggle, a cold war of clever diplomacy in give-and-take with oneself, a series of delaying tactics keeping an eye on the main chance; it becomes a shooting war when we have to overcome ourselves and make dominant what is best in us.

Sanctifying grace as fundamental option

The question arises: Where, in this complexity, does grace come in? Ruysbroeck has neatly indicated that God works " from within outwards. " [50] The Church teaches that, by the grace of His living re-creating presence in the soul, God *heals and elevates* human activity. This healing and elevating dynamism is secretly sown like a seed in the depth of the soul. Thanks to the appeal of the Father's word, we are attracted from within outwards, pulled and driven. Deep down in our being, the rays of God's creative love awaken a gentle hunger, a nostalgic longing, a tender yearning for God. The icy crust of selfishness begins to thaw under the warmth of God's breath. Assenting to the persuasive usage of His presence, our heart unfolds and develops toward Him. Unselfed and closer to God, who is our new basic choice (made by Christians at baptism) and borne along by the driving force of the deep will, our freedom of choice, which we said lies nearer the surface and is exercised in daily actions, now grows in depth, fervor and stability of direction. Such is the normal pattern of growth in the practice of virtue and holiness. The gradual switchover to the multiplicity of human behavior goes on under the gentle pressure of God's inviting presence.

It is not only our basic choice that falls under the influence of God's grace, but from our basic choice we can also pass on effectively to a new life of obedience to God's commandments and to a life of love. We have often heard people speaking of the distinction between sanctifying grace and actual or assisting grace.

We speak of " sanctifying grace " whenever we have in mind God's presence as something that attracts, invites, firmly and permanently holds our basic will directed toward Him; we speak of " actual grace " whenever the same divine indwelling carries and assists our freedom of choice—whether this be done through light given to the intelligence, or through added vigor given to the will, or through a stirring of the heart, or through enrichment and purification of the imagination. One and the same grace heals and renews all those aspects of our human being. Later on we shall return to the unity and multiplicity of grace.

For the moment we shall do no more than connect the classical

[50] Cf. note 2, paperback, p. 52.

notions learned from the catechism with our newly acquired insights into the nature of our freedom; for it is our freedom, which is *from within* re-created, renovated and healed by the Father's election, in the image of the Son, through the unobtrusive action of the Holy Spirit.

We take the liberty here to add an explanation especially for the use of priests who have been taught the traditional scholastic theology; it will help them to bridge the increasingly outmoded notions with a fresh approach to theology. A scholastic theologian may have difficulty in grasping our meaning when we call " sanctifying grace " the basic will as reborn through grace and orientated toward God. These two connotations, though actually completing each other, do not exactly coincide. In classical theology, followed by most catechisms, sanctifying grace is viewed at its first moment, at the stage when it is " infused " grace, permanent " habitual " dynamic orientation of the soul, and insofar as it has been *given* to us in baptism or at the instant when sins are forgiven.

We prefer to adopt a more existential perspective; we view the same sanctifying grace at its second stage, the moment when it is *accepted* by the human person as a dynamic orientation and thereby reaches, as St. Thomas would say, its " full truth. " In other words, we distinguish in one and the same grace a twofold aspect: its aspect of " being given " and its aspect of " being accepted. " Karl Rahner has given currency to that distinction in the theological world, though St. Thomas was not unacquainted with it, at least in his sacramental teaching. An " offered " grace is really given—" infused, " the scholastics would say—and as such, it really modifies our inner being, thanks to the active and re-creating power of the divine indwelling, which imparts *a real capability* to act in grace. " Accepted " grace is the same grace—and this we like to stress—insofar as it is accepted by the human person in and through God's impelling grace. Classical theology views sanctifying grace preferably as an interior gift which permanently directs the soul toward God; the second aspect seems to be neglected. On the other hand, we treat of the same orientation of the person—of the person rather than of the soul—insofar as that orientation, in a further development of grace in reborn man, is accepted by man, assented to and actualized.

As we said above, these two ways of looking at grace do not overlap; yet they actually do complete each other. The one cannot be thought of independently of the other. Both need not be explicitly mentioned in one definition; but to exclude either aspect would amount to misrepresenting dogma. Both definitions of sanctifying grace are admissible in dogma, as long as we keep in mind the respectively chosen standpoints. From the point of view of faith, no objection can be raised against either of the two—except by those who identify scholastic theology with the faith. The Church has never defined the classical interpretation as such, nor imposed it as a matter of faith. On the contrary, the Council of Trent explicitly refused to do so; all it did define is that in justification and sanctification we receive an " inhering " gift. When all is said and done, we should never forget that the divine reality exceeds in richness the systematic outlines any theological construction dares to put forward. Sanctifying grace, as a living reality in us, encompasses more than is contained in the technical notions with which we sketch out and fix one or other of the actual facets of the life of grace.

When we bypass the worn-out and shaky concepts of a decadent theology and return to the vigor of the original scholastic theology, endeavoring for the first time to characterize the state of grace as an habitual orientation toward God, we perceive that both of the definitions referred to are very much alike. An habitual orientation of the soul, known in Scholasticism as " *habitus,* " is preeminently a dynamic notion, quite meaningless if understood apart from an orientation toward action, and therefore toward life. To consider such an orientation mostly as a thing, a sort of capital, a treasure enriching the soul, is surely to impoverish the teaching of Scripture. We go further and say that it is a dangerous misrepresentation of dogma and a disregard for the doctrine of the great masters in scholastic tradition. Sanctifying grace is thus truly another word for a reborn dynamism of life that arises in the depth of our being thanks to the drawing power of the divine indwelling.

We see here once again that created sanctifying grace, as such, is not entitled to a surplus value which by right belongs to the divine indwelling alone, its source and origin. Of its nature, it is totally the fruit of the indwelling and, at the same time, our link with the indwelling Trinity. Prior to all other considerations, there stands the preeminent fact that the Blessed Trinity lives in us, draws us to Itself in grace through the indwelling, and binds us to Itself in faith and love. The divine indwelling operates in us like a stream of life, springing from God and taking us back to God. And this is the reason why the nature of all grace is ultimately nothing but a new dynamism urging us to God in virtue of God's initial attraction and recreating love.

St. John's Gospel mentions explicitly the divine attraction. " No man can come to me, unless the Father, Who sent Me, draw him. . . . Everyone who has listened to the Father and learned from Him comes to Me " (Jn 6:44-45). In a previous chapter, we have quoted a passage from St. Augustine's commentary on this Johannine text; a second contact with it will prove profitable here. [51]

Grace, one and many

Dogmatic textbooks are often discouraging and confusing. The further one reads in them, the greater the variety of graces met with. In the end one fails to see the forest for the trees. And who would dare deny that such has frequently been the case in the history of theology. For all that, the long list of terms in scientific ecclesiastical theology is not altogether superfluous; for most of the definitions of grace owe their origin to the necessity of sharper precision introduced either by the Church or by theologians in their fight against the numerous heresies and errors in the course of centuries. An understanding of those definitions demands in the student, or the reader, a good grasp of the history of dogma.

In this book we emphasized above all the basic truths concerning grace, a few of which have been thrown into the background during the recurrent controversies with the Protestants. Those basic truths are of exceptional importance for a Christian life; they define what exactly our life of grace is. Therefore, in spite of the trees, we shall try not to lose sight of the forest planted by classical theology.

First and foremost: grace is God's love for us, the love of the Father who calls us to be, with the Son, His own children, and who draws us to Himself by the power of the Spirit. Grace is also, though in a derived sense, a created gift, an infused love for God caused in us by God's initial love and working in us as an imminent dynamism of life. It is the latter which people usually mean when they speak of " grace. "

Insofar as this dynamism is seen as a permanent gratuitous gift affecting our nature in depth and keeping it in a " state of grace, " it is designated as " sanctifying grace. " But it is of great importance to keep in mind that the term " sanctifying grace, " in its theologically technical and sharply defined meaning, by no means covers all the treasures grace confers on us.

We have said that this divine dynamism affects us in the depth of our personal density-core, the " heart of man, " the level at which our dual unity of soul and body lies gathered up in its totality and intensity, as yet undifferentiated; the level, too, where our being " hangs " on to God and unceasingly issues from the divine creative hand. At that same level, our real and deepest freedom takes its rise. There freedom is given together

[51] Cf. paperback, pp. 169-170.

with grace and, in a more profound sense, it remains ever in the process of becoming. This freedom in total possession expresses itself in what we have called our basic will: the total surrender of self either to good or to evil, the fundamental commitment to life, the basic choice which determines our attitude toward God and neighbor. On that level, theology will speak of sanctifying grace and, as a further differentiation of the fundamental option, of the "infused theological virtues," faith, hope and charity. The "gifts of the Holy Ghost" describe rather the aspect of active *passivity* in that basic option, with respect to God's sovereign initiative in the guidance of our life. For, the Spirit leads us by means of personal immediate *motions* of the heart.

Our basic will continues to live, though ever hidden, in the varied activities of our daily "choosing will," the "*liberum arbitrium,*" or "free will" of classical philosophy. Insofar as the choice, made by "free will," takes place under the constant influence of the grace which prepares the choice, sustains and perfects it, we may speak of "actual grace," of "assisting grace"; we may bring in also the distinction between "prevenient," "cooperating" and "efficacious" graces. All these different graces can be reduced to light and certainty for the intellect, to strength and perseverance for the will, to consolation and comfort and joy for the mind.

All such technical distinctions, as we find them in catechetical instructions, should not cause us to forget that grace is a living actuality "from God to God," a divine gesture of love. For these distinctions are not to be traced back to different actions and interventions on God's side, but rather to the complex articulations of our human existence. A comparison with the prism will prove helpful. The invisible ray of sunlight is decomposed in a prismatic crystal and dispersed on a screen in all the colors of the rainbow. Something similar happens with divine grace. The prism, which breaks up God's simple Light and reveals the manifold riches of that Light, is human nature. But this is no reason why we should brush aside all distinctions, even though some textbooks are lavish in providing a few that are rather unimportant and, therefore, superfluous. We should be on our guard against the danger of taking our concepts and technical notions too seriously; otherwise the wealth of divine grace is analyzed and atomized to the verge of driving a normal man out of his wits. Unfortunately, we cannot be sure that such has never been the case in the history of theology; frequently, and under the influence of reigning rationalistic tendencies, theology has devoted its attention more to abstract notions than to the one living reality which those notions and definitions tried to clarify and defend against heresy.

The nature of sin

In Scripture, grace is opposed to sin, as life is opposed to death, light to darkness, good to evil. The French writer Gustave Thibon maintained that no proper insight into sin is possible without a profound understanding of God. Inverting the forms, we may say that a deeper insight into sin will enrich our appreciation of grace and, therefore, of God.

This chapter offers a further advantage. With the help of a more penetrating insight into the nature of our freedom, we have endeavored to refine the current conceptions of sanctifying and actual graces. The distinction we made between our basic will and our freedom of choice applies equally well in the domain of sin. The devil apes God; sin is a caricature of grace. Present-day teaching draws a parallel between sanctifying grace and mortal sin and, to some extent at least, between actual grace and venial sin. To speak more correctly, venial sin in a just man runs parallel, on the level of freedom of choice, to a sinner's good action done under the influence of grace. We may not forget that the Church has never taught that all the actions of sinners are unavoidably evil or sinful. The manner of dealing with the one problem can throw light on the manner of dealing with the other.

The word " sin " can have many meanings, called " analogical. " Unconsciously perhaps, we start from sin in its *complete* meaning; in other words, we start from the sinful action which verifies in itself the notion of sin in its most intense and radical sense. In comparison with such a deed, all actions and states are called " sins " in proportion to their resemblance in a lesser or greater degree to the deed which fully deserves the name of " sin. " In order to form our conscience and to come to a purer knowledge of the faith, it is important that we keep all those different meanings neatly apart. Our main intention here is to explain two terms frequently used in moral theology: mortal sin and venial sin. True to the method we have followed so far, we shall first inquire into the nature of sin taken in its fullest meaning, and then, in the light of that, try to see how it is verified in mortal sin and in venial sin.

The final sin

The sin which most radically bears out the notion of "sin" is the one that for all eternity separates from God. A life of selfseeking and egotism may bring it about that a man walls himself up in pride to the extent of closing himself till death to the love of God, of refusing to accept that love up to the end, and of fixing himself for all eternity in his rejection of God. This represents really the final choice, the irretrievable choice that cannot be made good, since it radically excludes all later conversion.

In order to understand this, we must learn to look upon freedom as a task imposed on life. We have dwelt on this subject in the previous chapter. Freedom is not delivered into our hands as a mature fruit. It is a task, an invitation to grow from freedom in freedom to a steadily increasing freedom. Further, true freedom is always positive, directed to what is good. We become truly free only when we freely become what we ought to be. Grace is freedom because it is love: love—coming from God and permeating us—gives birth to a new love in our hearts.

It is the tragedy of life that we are able to refuse freedom and love, to cripple and kill them—and this freely. For we are human persons, created in the image of God, and as such already endowed with a beginning of freedom. Sin, therefore, is that kind of self-destruction by which we freely let our freedom degenerate into "unfreedom." The definitive and final sin is the spiritual suicide of God's child absolutely and totally refusing the divine invitation to grace. Such a refusal is also called obduracy in evil. We point out that this final sin, occurring at the moment of death, seems to be unthinkable apart from a life-long persevering and ever more intense self-centeredness— "*incurvatio in seipsum,*" as classical theology would say. For it is probable that a dying man makes a choice which "sums up" all the previous choices made during his life. That single ultimate choice totalizes the past and surpasses all other choices in absoluteness.

Holy Writ mentions two kinds of sin that come close to the notion of final sin: the sin against the Holy Ghost and the sin against love.

Christ Himself gives us warning of "blasphemy against the Holy Ghost" (Mt 12:31-32). When He spoke thus, He had mainly in mind the Pharisees. These were the "pious" men of Israel. They knew the Scriptures better than the common herd of men. They studied the prophets who had borne witness to the Messiah. They were "pious"; they applied themselves to prayer, to fasting and to good works, but especially to the strict observance of the Law. Better than the simple people, they were able to recognize and thoroughly grasp the "signs" Christ wrought in their midst to prove His mission. They had the "light"; but they refused to see.

The sin against the Holy Ghost is the most dangerous kind of hardening of the heart. "No sin or blasphemy," says Jesus, "is beyond forgiveness for men, except blasphemy against the Spirit" (Mt 12:31). Most other sins are committed out of weakness and "ignorance," to use the words of Scripture. "Ignorance," in the scriptural sense, differs from the ignorance moral theology describes as a state of mind that frequently excuses from (all) guilt. It is true that ignorance of the latter type on occasion may admit of some degree of guilt; in that sense it is a sin, but a sin of weakness, because it occurs in a life wrapped up in earthly pursuits.

In a certain sense, the Pharisees could not be called "ignorant men." Their sin was not caused by weakness or disaffection from God; it was a sin deliberately committed. *They did not want to see.* And just because they did not want to see, they consciously distorted the import of the messianic signs. They said: Christ came from the devil; He was possessed; He was the son of Beelzebub (Mt 12:22-30). Christ, so they said, did the works of the devil.

This deliberateness of theirs sprang from "vexation," "scandal." They were filled with bitterness and resentment because Christ had torn the mask off their piety. More especially, they refused to admit that God would appear among men in the simplicity shown by Christ. They would not accept the idea of God acting at cross purposes with their own political, social and religious conceptions. They would not abandon their own brand of "justice," the kind of piety which they fondly imagined allowed them to treat God as an equal, to whom terms could be dictated. This sort of desperate tenacity to shut the door on love is the most characteristic sign of sin. That is how, finally, *they purposely deformed their conscience.* We may well ask: How can God's grace reach a man whose conscience is deformed, not out of weakness, but out of set purpose? Conscience after all, is but the door through which conversion, true faith and grace can find an entrance into the human heart.

Now, it so happened that that sin in Israel had to occur in men who, because of their manner of living, were looked upon as pious zealots for God's Law. A similar sin could possibly be found today in priests, religious and pious laymen, from the moment piety and religion serve as a cloak for a hard and pitiless pride.

There is no forgiveness for that sin. For grace must enter us through conscience. And in this instance, conscience shuts itself off from grace by giving it the lie. Religion, virtue, asceticism—everything becomes food for rigid pride. It is quite likely that this was the attitude of soul which the author of the Epistle to the Hebrews had in mind when he wrote that Christians who had fallen away from the faith cannot expect forgiveness (Hebr 6:4-6; 10:26-31). Of course, it is possible to lose one's faith through weakness and "ignorance." But the sacred writer was dealing with convinced Christians, recently converted from Jewry. A man who has enjoyed the pure light of faith is not likely to lose it, unless it be through deliberate bad will. One remark is in point here: it is not for us to judge whether or not someone has come to the state of obduracy. Nor are we in any position to do so. God alone can judge. It is important, though, to realize that such a sin is possible.

There exists still another sin almost like the final sin. It is the kind of sin which reveals the hidden core of all sin, that is, sin against love. St. John devoted to this sin the greater part of his first epistle. "Dearly beloved, let us love one another, because love is from God. Every one who loves is a child of God and knows God, but the unloving know nothing of God. For God is love" (I Jn 4:7-8). Like all genuine mystics, John remains sober and matter-of-fact. He does not trust a vague, sentimental and, therefore, illusory love for God. The one virtuous test of our love for God consists in love of the neighbor and in observance of the commandments (I Jn 2:3-11; 4:19-5:4). Unless this be done, we have no guarantee that we do really love God. Whenever and wherever fidelity to the divine law and brotherly love are missing, we have lost God.

St. Augustine vigorously summed up this fundamental truth when he wrote that throughout the entire world only two forms of love are to be had: love of self to the verge of scorning God, and love of God leading to trampling on self. [52]

Augustine's words reflect the pure teaching of sacred Scripture. As we shall see, in actual life we certainly come across, and possibly live in the midst of a variety of colorless, non-descript mixtures of human mediocrity. But absolutely speaking, whenever there is a question of the basic attitude that either leads to God or turns away from God, we have in Augustine's words the exact description of the final sin.

Both Christ and the apostles keep repeating: he who loves observes the entire law (Mt 7:12; 22:34-40, and parallel passages; Rom 13:8-10; Gal 5:14; 6:2; etc.). We shall never meditate enough on the one description which Christ, the Judge of all times and nations, has left us of the Last Judgment. We shall

---

[52] St. Augustine, *De Civitate Dei*, 14, n. 28, *PL* 41, 436: "*Fecerunt itaque civitates duas amores duo: terrenam scilicet amor sui usque ad contemptum Dei, coelestem vero amor Dei usque ad contemptum sui.*"

be judged by our love. Refusal to love, normally manifested and materialized among men under the guise of hardness of heart towards the neighbor—that alone brings about the final condemnation (Mt 25:31-46). Our Lord says exactly what Augustine wrote later; but Christ says it in Eastern imagery and popular parables. The essence of sin is refusal to love—to love men and, therefore, to love God.

We have thus far examined two sorts of mortal sin that come very close to the sin sealing everlasting separation from God. Something of this basic sinful attitude can be traced in all other sinful deeds. That is why any classification of sins must start from that principle.

Mortal sin and venial sin

Scripture seems unaware of this distinction which we learned from our catechism or from moral theology. It is true, though, that the Old Testament speaks of a "deadly sin"; and perhaps it is that sin to which St. John alludes in his first Epistle (I Jn 5: 13-21). However, it is by no means clear what is meant by it. Holy Writ knows of sins of weakness, of sins of "ignorance," of which we spoke before; those are sins that can be forgiven, which penance can expiate, which leave the door open to conversion. Scripture knows also other sins, forgiveness of which is more difficult; sins which of their nature exclude the guilty from the Kingdom of God. Of such, Paul has left some lists (cf. I Cor 6:9-10; 15:50; Rom 1:29-32; Gal 5:19-21, Eph 5:15).

The distinction between mortal sin and venial sin grew, in the course of centuries, from the Church's living experience of the faith, from the meditations of saints and theologians on the data of Scripture. Such a distinction has the advantage of offering a useful classification; it reminds us of the basic teaching of Holy Writ, and is of practical use for an examination of conscience. As such, it has its importance for receiving the sacraments within the Church. It is a stand-by for our conscience. That is why we spoke of a "useful classification"; in reality, matters are more complex. But the distinction offers something of greater import: by it, the Church teaches that some sins really do make us lose the state of grace, while others do no more than diminish and block the flow of grace into us.

It is very important for us to see the meaning, and also the limitations of such a distinction. But this is not always easy, considering that we are in the habit of simplifying our relations with God within the Church. Theologians, too, are liable to commit this fault, especially those who approach morals with a legalistic turn of mind. And it is all too evident that the legalistic slant has been increasingly prevalent in the Church in the course of the last centuries.

Wrong notion

Like everything else related to human activity, sin is a complex thing. Sin is an injury done to the divine majesty; at the same time it harms the Church, the neigbor and the sinner personally. In the sinner himself, sin is caused by wickedness of heart; but malice usually comes to the fore in combination with a medley of sentiments and intentions, not all of them bad. Once it has been committed, sin brings about all sorts of concrete acts or omissions—conscious, semi-conscious or almost wholly unconscious deeds. It brings about in the sinner blindness of spirit, and, alas, hardening of the heart, sin's most dire consequence.

There is also the sinful deed itself, its sinful sources in me and in others, the evil it does to others, and its sinful consequences in me. There is malice towards God, which is called *guilt* of sin. There is its further outcome, the state of sin. All these aspects we have to take into account with true Christian sincerity; for it is only then that we can speak of an adult, poised, well-formed conscience.

Such a well-formed conscience is often hard to come by. The human mind spontaneously tends to scale down all things to its own dimensions. Our shortsightedness shuts out all too easily the hidden mysteries of evil. We cut down sin to our own size through love of ease, through sloth, through shallowness, ignorance and " simplism "—also through fear of earnestness involved in a life of faith—finally, because we willfully shut out God. Other forces, too, may come into play, not all of them implying guilt; as instances we may cite: a primitive, infantile or immature mentality, insufficient religious instruction, and even some mental disturbances.

We should like to examine here two wrong notions, in direct opposition to each other. The first notion in practice fastens its attention exclusively on the external aspect of mortal sin, while the second takes such an absolute view of sin that the difference between bigger and smaller sins vanishes.

The first attitude is widespread, especially among people whose faith has not as yet struck deep roots. It is not so much a well-defined doctrine as a practical attitude. Those raised in traditional Catholicism can only gain from an earnest examination on this point.

This attitude reduces sin to the external sinful action. The distinction between mortal sin and venial sin then becomes a matter of very great importance. It provides people with a scale of values, perhaps their only one, for the guidance of their practical conduct.

In order to get a good grasp of this way of thinking, we shall start from one or other morbid form of "the sense of sin" that has nothing in common with sin. Where mental disturbances have promoted simplification and extremism, the case is unmistakable.

In anguished people, the sense of guilt is linked to definite stereotyped external actions which happen to fall within the field of vision of their misformed and morbid conscience. A few of those so-called "sins" are rather surprising; for instance, to tread accidentally on two pieces of wood lying cross-wise on the ground. Such a phenomenon may be met with in persons quite normal in other respects, but not possessed of a deeply religious spirit. It is striking to see how little attention such people seem to attach to sinful dispositions within themselves. As any priest may learn from the ministry of the confessional, the one preoccupation of such people centers on the external law; it appears immaterial to them whether the law is transgressed wittingly or unwittingly.

Not only is the external observance of the law their main solicitous regard, but even certain stereotyped instances of it: not to be fasting before communion, defects in the observance of Lenten regulations or of abstinence on prescribed days, omission of Sunday Mass, etc. Matters of impurity, or rather of unchastity, will of course stir up their anxiety, because in the domain of sex their emotions are heavily burdened. But even in this sphere, some points are attended to, while other points leave their conscience unperturbed.

They imagine God to be a hard task-master who commands some things to be done and others to be avoided. They nurture a secret dread that God is bent on taking vengeance on their disobedience. At bottom, they fancy God to be no more than a policeman. No one is molested for crossing a street. But no sooner does one transgress the traffic regulations than he is in trouble with the police. Naturally, the police are neither qualified nor instructed to inquire into the good or bad will of the people. Every citizen is supposed to know the law; and that is enough. The offense is blatant; warning or summons follow at once. Clearly, such a concept of sin supposes a very rudimentary idea of what God is.

In fact, it skirts magic. Magic has deep-seated roots in our instinctual behavior. There are some men who fear that the mere external act, committed with or without evil intention, automatically unleashes impersonal, direful, preternal forces. No wonder that for such people the distinction between mortal and venial sin is of paramount importance. Mortal sin spells ruinous consequences; venial sin is comparatively harmless. On the face of it, such a view is false. And yet, it frequently lies embedded in one or other more " advanced " state of piety and religion.

In all such people, the service of God has not yet reached the standard of being a personal task of life. It lies still buried under a mass of instinctual drives and superstitions. Religion serves the purpose of " insuring " against retaliatory measures from heaven, rather than of searching for the God of love and holiness.

One comes across another mode of externalizing sin, more subtle and, therefore, more dangerous. We shall call in the humdrum middleclass and pharisaic mode. It does not stem from a lack of faith, but from a deformed conscience and moral sense. People so afflicted are not prepared to accept the idea that God has a right to man's total surrender of heart in obedience and love. They deem themselves to be God's equals. They do their bit and expect God to fulfill His obligations toward them. That explains why they build up their religion almost exclusively on the strict observance of a carefully mapped-out law. This affords them the chance of knowing exactly where they stand, and eventually also of laying before God definite claims accruing to them from their merits.

This form of exteriorizing sin is to be traced back to a felt need of security. Man feels " insecure " and uncertain when facing God's majesty and eminent sanctity; or, more simply, when facing his own personal responsibility toward God. To live for God appears a fearful adventure: the closer one comes to God, the more exacting His demands. Fear clutches at the human heart when it is confronted by the leap toward God that real holiness involves, or when it has to face the unbeaten track leading to divine love. Hence, the desire of putting order into what looks like " romanticism "—of outlining what is expected and of clearly mapping out the obligations that bind us to God.

What comes under consideration, then, is not fidelity to God's will, and certainly not the service of God, but rather the need of feeling secure in our own personal moral and religious life. Nothing is as comfortable as an experienced sense of security, based on an awareness that we are in good standing with God and, especially, with ourselves.

Such an attitude is inspired by anxiety and by a lack of courage to live. We might dub it a *bourgeois,* or perhaps better still, a Victorian attitude towards sin, ranking sensibleness, moderation and orderliness above all else.

But the pharisaic conception goes one step further. From this sense of security there flows a feeling of pride. No one is entitled to blame us for anything, neither the neighbor nor God Himself. And that pride brings along with it a contempt for others whose life is not so carefully regulated by the rules of the prevailing fashion.

Implied in all these shades of meaning attached to the word "sin" is one common element: at bottom, there is next to no concern with God's person; the main concern is with self. Whatever happens, *I* must know where I stand; *I* want to settle my perfection and justice consist.

And here we have the source of exclusive preoccupation with external sin. It all amounts to this: I want to be in order with God and with myself. It is not hard to see why, with such people, the next distinction between mortal sin and venial sin is of decisive importance. Whatever is classified as mortal sin is not committed—at least not the coarser kinds of external sins. Elegant, refined, clever or disguised mortal sin is quite another matter. In such cases, conscience feels no qualms simply because no attention is paid to the interior evil dispositions of the heart. As to venial sin, it hardly enters into their reckoning; it presents no threat to their social and religious respectability; and conscience remains blind to the dangers it may entail.

Let those people lead lives outwardly ever so pious and decent, they remain unaware of the dreadful emptiness of their hearts. *They do not love.* Towards their neighbor they are hard and pitiless; they scorn the man who in their eyes is a "sinner," that is, one who commits gross "indecent" mortal sins; they despise whoever lets himself get caught. Nor do they forgive the faults of others. They stand on their rights, and hold it against God when He grants to public "sinners" the grace of conversion at death. Like the elder brother of the prodigal son, they feel slighted by such acts of mercy on God's part.[53]

We can never give enough thought to the dangers inherent in such a religious attitude of mind. It is *the* sin of "pious folk," of the respectable set, of the decent Christians, of the kind of man who kicks up a row because his wife has forgotten to order fish on Friday and yet feels no remorse of conscience for keeping up a long-standing, grim quarrel with some member of the family. They are offended when a pickpocket has been caught red-handed, but they injure society, or their neighbors, by under-handed crafty cheating, by falsified papers or crooked accounts. They advocate the death penalty for assassins, but they murder

<hr/>

[53] Cf. *Divine Grace and Man*, paperback ed. (New York: NAL, 1965), pp. 44-45.

the heart of their wives, of their children and subordinates by the unbending severity of their principles.

Our Lord has often spoken of such people. The history of the Church is there to show how necessary, and yet so frequently useless, His warnings have proved to be. He said, ' I tell you, unless you show yourselves far better men than the Pharisees and the doctors of the law, you will never enter into the Kingdom of heaven " (Mt 5:20).

We quote from the teaching of the Gospel two telling instances. St. Matthew begins his fifteenth chapter with an especially revolting example. In order not to be obliged to help his parents in their old age, a Jew could donate all his possessions to the Temple. He retained, of course, a full life-interest in it, and even ownership of it. But he could take his stand on the piety of his donation to the Temple in order to refuse assistance to his parents (Mt 15:3-7).

Whereupon Christ exposes publicly the real source of sin. To attract the attention of His hearers, He expresses His thought in a proverb, as was customary in the East. " A man is not defiled by what goes into the mouth, but by what comes out of it. " On hearing this, the Pharisees are " scandalized " because He dared to attack the rabbinical regulations, in matters of cleanliness, which in their formalistic code of morality were far more important than God's original law. The apostles themselves failed to understand the words of their Master. " Jesus answered, ' Are you still as dull as the rest? Do you not see that whatever goes in by the mouth passes into the stomach and so is discharged into the drain? But what comes out of the mouth has its origin in the heart; and that is what defiles a man. Wicked thoughts, murder, adultery, fornication, theft, perjury, slander—these all proceed from the heart; and these are the things that defile a man ' " (Mt 15:15-20).

True sin *proceeds from the heart*. In the Hebrew tongue, the heart stands for what is innermost in man, the very core of the person and liberty. And *it is from there that sin arises*. It is there also that we have to look for the true standard by which to judge the distinction between mortal sin and venial sin.

Before doing that, we shall throw some light on the second wrong notion of sin: the extremist view, which sees no difference between what is mortal sin and what is venial sin. According to it, there is no difference because all sin is grave, considering that all sin proceeds from the heart and does injury to God who has an absolute right to our obedience.

This is perhaps not an attitude actually lived up to by those who advocate it; for rigorists of this stamp do not dismiss all distinctions in the practice of daily life. It is rather a doctrinal position of principle, a rigid theological thesis. It has much truth in it. But it is wrong-headed because too narrowly conceived, too neglectful of the many-sidedness of human reality. As an expression of theological radicalism, it owes its origin to an impassioned opposition to pharisaical morality. As such, it is met with in many fanatical sects. It finds favor with a good many Protestant theologians. As we have seen earlier, the Reformation was launched largely in vehement protest against the moral degeneration rife in the Church of the sixteenth century. After the Reformation, a similar movement got under way in Jansenism.

The chief defect in all this lies in the fact that men mutilate the truth by positing one aspect of the thesis too absolutely and, consequently, lose sight of the various other aspects which ought to give poise to the first. For that matter, all heresies start in the same way: radicalization of a truth that ends by overwhelming its champions. At the end of our study we shall see how close the saints' awareness of sin comes to the teaching of the Protestants and the Jansenists; and yet how different the spirit with which the saints live up to their own kind of radicalism.

Correct notion

We begin by recalling a few principles learned from our catechism, and then proceed to look for their deeper meaning. This will be an instructive illustration of what religious reflection really is.

According to the teaching of the Church, mortal sin is a sinful action committed by man *with full knowledge and full deliberation*. It is a question, therefore, of a free act, such as any " normal man " is capable of. We like to stress this, in order to forestall all overstatement of the conditions required for a free act; for any exaggeration on this point would make it impossible for man to act with full freedom. When freedom is in any way impaired, there can be no mortal sin. In which case, the evil intention that may still be there produces no more than a venial sin. This much about the principal condition required for a mortal sin.

Venial sins are of two kinds. We have just spoken of the sin committed with an impaired freedom, whether the matter of the sin be grave or not. Those are venial sins of weakness—the more common kind of sin committed by men.

There is, secondly, the venial sin which, though committed with full freedom, remains *of its nature* a venial sin, and can never become a mortal sin. The catechism tells us that such a venial sin never becomes a mortal sin because the act is less grave, either on account of smallness of matter (as the saying goes)—for instance, stealing a little sugar—or on account of the nature of the act itself—as for instance, gluttony or lying. The deeper meaning of these precisions will appear a little later on.

The catechism teaches us also that the *act* of mortal sin causes in us a *state* of sinfulness so fundamentally in opposition to love that sanctifying grace is lost by it. In such a state of sin, we are no longer living members of the Church, but dead or dying members. Venial sin, on the other hand, does not take away sanctifying grace, though it diminishes it and, at the same time, constitutes a threat to our life as children of God.

All this is common knowledge; but an adequate explanation is rarely given. Nor is the explanation easy, for sin is a very complex thing, affecting our life in several of its dimensions. In order to arrive at a more mature and more responsible understanding, I propose to examine sin in three of its dimensions; we shall then see how from these three different perspectives we receive new light to realize what constitutes the difference between mortal and venial sin.

We shall examine the distinction between mortal and venial sin first on the level of the teaching of the Church—what is called sometimes the objective dimension; secondly, on the level of conscience and the personal commitment in life, known as the subjective dimension; thirdly, from the point of view of what sin is in God's eyes—the theological dimension. All along our inquiry, we shall do our best to avoid every form of legalism, the blight of moral theology for the last two centuries. The nature of sin is not made clear by the statement that for venial sin we are down in God's books for so many days in purgatory, and for mortal sin, for an eternity in hell. Willy nilly, that is the road leading to the magical conception of sin—or, if one prefers, to the "police court" idea where offenses are graded according to the penalty they deserve.

Sin in its objective dimension

In the Catholic Church it is not left to the individual to settle for himself what is and what is not grave sin. And it is by no means irrelevant to recall this glaring truth. Far too many errors have crept in, especially on the subject of conjugal morality. It should be plainly understood: a sin is grave or less grave because it is so before God. When speaking of sin, we are dealing with divine truth.

We know that Christ has given us the Church "to guide us into all truth," by the power of the Spirit. She has been entrusted with the mission of teaching us God's truth, of instructing us—to use a traditional phrase—in all matters pertaining to faith and morals. What we have to believe comes to us from God in the Church. What we have to do or to avoid in relation to good and evil, we also learn from God through the teaching of the Church. That is the objective order of things; an order independent of our personal views, of our likes and dislikes.

These days, we hear of opposition being raised on all sides against "objective definitions" of sin. We are indebted for that, to some extent, to our Western tendency to overrate individualism. The line of development, followed in the teaching of moral theology these last centuries, is also in part to blame for it. Many theologians of previous generations, attempted to map out God's objective law with an excessive self-assurance. They catalogued their findings, classified and grouped them with such exact precision that one wonders whether they did not fancy themselves to be infallible clerks of God's court. Like the truths of faith, the objective moral law is far richer and far more flexible than some textbooks would have us believe; for both the truths of faith and the moral order have their source in God, and belong to God. Influenced by the spirit of their age and surroundings, not a few moralists of a rationalistic cast of mind have yielded to their tendency to oversystematization, and have worn themselves out in the endeavor to force the divine law into their personal mental categories. Such a mistake, committed by a legalistic tradition in moral theology, is no justification for throwing overboard the principle that no individual man is free to settle for himself what is morally good or evil. One may not throw the baby out with the bath water, as some textbooks of moral theology seen to have done in the past.

How does the Church normally teach the faithful in matters pertaining to morals? Normally, she leaves this task to specialists who, for that reason, are called moralists. They are the theologians who specialize in the study of Christian morality. Like the teachers of dogma, they must base their conclusions above all on Holy Writ and on the living tradition of the Church; and they must be guided in their work by the Church's magisterium. Moralists are not infallible. Some are strict, some are broadminded, some are even lax. In cases involving doubt, discussions and disagreements are permissible. Wherever there is solid ground for discussion and disagreement, we are free to follow any one of the opinions that are publicly defended in the Church by men of authority.

When doubts arise in matters of grave importance, the bishops speak, they to whom has been committed more directly the authoritative mission of teaching the truth in the Church. However, they too can make mistakes. As a case in point: not so long ago, an American bishop publicly declared it was a mortal sin to vote for one particular candidate; and another bishop publicly denied it. However, that happens to be a matter of minor importance. On the main question of Christian morality, there is hardly any doubt to be had.

When all the bishops of the Church are unanimous in their teaching, no mistake is possible, especially when they speak to the entire Church and intend to bind the faithful in conscience for a relatively long period of time. Such unanimous secular teaching forms the basis of the Catholic moral code. In exceptional cases, the pope, or an ecumenical Council, can make a solemn pronouncement in condemnation of the sinful nature of one or other particular act. This happens very seldom. But the solemn pronouncement is infallible. It belongs to the well-known means used by the Church in the exercise of her teaching authority.

What is of greater importance for us here is to know what the Church has in mind when she pronounces a condemnation.

The Church has never passed a definite judgment on the sinfulness of a living person; she always judges the sinful *deed*. It is in that way that she condemns false systems of doctrine, as we saw in a previous chapter. She does not necessarily condemn the people who follow such false systems.

The Church can, indeed, treat a man as a sinner and subject him to definite sanctions proper to ecclesiastical law, such as excommunication. When she does so, she can only go by the external act of the culprit and by such visible signs as seem to indicate formal recalcitrance. But whether the man himself is truly guilty in God's sight, she can only guess. There appears to be little doubt that, since the Middle Ages, rebellion against the Church *(de " pertinacia")* and refusal of submission to the sentence pronounced by the Church *(de " contumacia")* have been dealt with from too juridical a point of view; the Inquisition, surely, displayed insufficient insight into the psychological complexity of the human conscience. Thanks be to God, we notice in the proceedings of both the Roman and the diocesam tribunals, a wholesome evolution in depth as regards the psychological factors involved in the cases submitted to them; in contrast to what happened formerly, greater respect is shown for the actual conscience of men.

The Church does not infallibly declare a person to be a sinner. Nor can she. Neither can the confessor in the confessional; he gives absolution when he has a reasonable certitude that the penitent has indeed sinned gravely and now repents. That is why the confessor does well in asking a penitent, who has confessed " sins " by nature insufficient for absolution, to include in his confession the sins of his entire past life; he does so in order to safeguard the meaning and purpose of the absolution.

What then is the real significance of the Church's pronouncement on the sinful nature of a particular deed? None other than to enlighten the conscience in the name of God. The human conscience is not just an obscure instinct. We may take it for granted that grace is at work within man, urges him to do what is good, promotes in him the desire of virtue and inspires him to turn away from evil. The spiritual sense to do good has nothing in common with a biological instinct. It remains true, however, that the desire for doing good is not immune to the warping influence of harmful education and of social surroundings; it is equally true that the actual presence of sin in man clouds the " heart " and turns it away from God.

Because of all this, our conscience has dire need of a *norm* to stand by, the law of God. We have dwelt at length on the religious and pedagogical values of the law. [54] In practice, the sentence pronounced by the Church amounts to this: when, in normal circumstances and with full knowledge and full freedom, someone has indeed done such or such an act, it must needs be that he really turned away from God. Aversion from God, freely committed, is a mortal sin, because it runs counter to the love befitting a child of God and, consequently, destroys the " state of grace. "

When the Church declares that the omission of Mass on Sundays is a mortal sin, it is not at all her mind to pronounce that all those who miss Sunday Mass are actually living in a state of aversion from God. Nor is she able to do so. *God alone can judge the sinner.* There are people who somehow have acquired the equally erroneous notion that whoever misses Mass on Sundays incurs the *penalty* due to mortal sin. Another example of the juridical—better perhaps, the " police "—mentality.

The Church judges of actual facts. Holy Mass is the principal act of religion binding on all the faithful as individuals and as members of the Christian community. The eucharistic celebration is the chief means for the faithful Christian to render to God due homage, in union with Christ, our High Priest. It is also the will of God that, both as individuals and as the people of God, we pay Him this homage at least once a week, on the Lord's day. The Church shifted the Lord's day from the sabbath to the Sunday, in remembrance of Christ's resurrection and of the first Pentecost, the two great days of our redemption. No one, in ancient times, thought of issuing a commandment on the

[54] Cf. paperback, pp. 161-168.

subject of having Mass on the Lord's day. Each of the faithful realized by himself the significance of the Mass as an act of homage, of adoration and religion, so much so that during the earlier centuries the most severe kind of punishment consisted in excluding guilty parties from the celebration of holy Mass. Public sinners, those at least whom the Church admitted to do public penance for scandalous conduct, were ordered to leave, together with the catechumens, the place of worship at the moment the offertory was about to begin.

When this spirit of the faith started cooling down, and especially when the significance of the eucharistic celebration lost its hold on the people, the Church felt the need of reminding the faithful that Sunday worship was not an accessory and merely private practice of devotion. She warned the faithful that any one who was fully informed concerning Mass and yet deliberately neglected it, turned away from God in matters of decisive importance for the life of faith, in matters which belonged to the essence of the Christian religion. It was thus to our shame that the Church should have had to remind us of such an all-important point. That alone proves the low ebb to which the Christian insight into the meaning of a life of faith had sunk, such as it had been initiated by Christ and the apostles. Conscience no longer urged people of their own accord to gather round the altar on the Lord's day. An authentic declaration of the significance of Sunday worship was called for; the Church did so by way of decreeing the *law* of Sunday Mass. The Church saw no other means of maintaining and safeguarding except by *external provision* that which was slowly withering *within* the hearts of men and was thus in danger of being lost.

What we said about Sunday Mass applies to the paschal communion as well. The eucharistic celebration loses its meaning unless holy communion is part of it. It ought to be the rule for all Christians attending Mass on any day, to receive communion. Various causes were slowly undermining the understanding of this truth. Those alone forced the Church to prescribe *as a minimum* requisite the obligation of receiving communion at least once a year, about Easter time. The purpose of this precept is not at all to impose a sanction, a punishment, on those who neglect it; its aim is to guard the faithful against the misguided notion of participating in the eucharistic celebration without receiving the divine victim of the altar in communion.

In that light, it is interesting to watch how, in their teaching, moralists themselves are susceptible of the influence of the prevailing spirit of the time, or of a faulty theology. The Middle Ages conceived of Christian worship too exclusively as a sacramental event through which divine grace was to be distributed. This conception led to the idea that the first part of the Mass was of minor importance. It was forgotten that the sacrament does not fully come into its own if unaccompanied by the word of God. It is the nature of the sacraments to confirm in us the true faith; consequently, the preaching of the word must go together with the administration of the sacrament. The word is not to be separated from the sacrament.

There we have the reason why the Second Vatican Council reminded the faithful and . . . the moralists that the "liturgy of the Word," as the first part of the Mass is called today, is hardly less important than the liturgy of the offering, which consists in the consecration and communion. Henceforth, it is no longer permissible for the faithful, through sheer carelessness, to enter the Church when the sermon is over. And this gives us occasion to point out that we have here an instance of how an ecumenical council redresses and corrects an opinion accepted by the generality of the moralists.

A moment of reflection suffices to show that the implicitly condemned opinion never made sense; that it was at best a sign that the spirit of religion was decaying and was in the process of being emptied of its content. Such a gross assumption can find acceptance only when a commandment of the Church is looked upon by the generality of the faithful as a "police regulation." It had come to mean that we could limit our assistance at Mass to just that part of it which let us escape the "penalty" by the skin of our teeth. Shame on us that such an observation had to be inserted into the *Constitution on the Sacred Liturgy;* and shame on the moralists who connived at such an erroneous practice!

Where liturgical worship is celebrated in a befitting, living manner, and when the faithful actively participate in the eucharistic celebration with renewed liturgical spirit, regulations, as described, are no longer needed. All are present from the beginning of the Mass, and no one leaves the church before the priest leaves the altar. Who would dream of behaving in such an uncivil manner when invited to some social or other function? But when God assembles His children on Sundays, such conduct does not seem to be unbecoming! Once again, such a thing can happen only when the religious conscience has grown grossly debased and when the one preoccupation is how best to escape the "penalty" of mortal sin. All one looks for is "to keep things in order." And meanwhile, God Himself is being forgotten.

Here we have matter for self-examination. There is still much in our religious conceptions calling for attention. We have to be schooled above all in a renewed outlook on the religious reality, on the realities of our faith, on the significance of Mass and Sunday, on the true worship of God. When we shall have

achieved that, many commandments of the Church will cease
to be necessary.

These last few centuries, some moralists have juggled exces-
sively with "mortal sin." However, when they do speak of
mortal sin, and have their teaching approved by the Church's
magisterium, they mean only that an act can be so central
for our life of faith, so momentous for our religious and
moral life, that unless we do it or omit it, we are *in very deed*
turning ourselves away from God. The moralists and the Church
take it for granted that the act, or the omission, is done or
accepted with full knowledge and full freedom; any catechism
will tell us as much. The legislative function of the Church's
teaching authority is, therefore, principally of *an educative,
instructional order.* When the Church intervenes in such matters,
her action has nothing in common with the nagging of a police
state. The important thing is not "that this or that be labelled
mortal sin," but that the Church point out to us how such or
such conduct *really* exposes us to the danger of falling away from
God and of losing thereby divine grace. The Church has no
power "to make a mortal sin" of something that does not
endanger our fundamental attitude towards God.

The Church acts still in another way, perhaps of little moment,
but yet not without significance. Every sin, in its deepest
dimension, is an injury done to God's majesty and sanctity;
and at the same time, every sin does harm to the Church.
And here we have the reason why the Church attaches to some
specified sins special ecclesiastical punishments. This is not
the place to enlarge upon the various ecclesiastical sanctions
contained in canon law. We confine our attention here to the
most ordinary—and, therefore, the least noticed—sanction that
truly affects an individual. The Church forbids access to holy
communion to any one who, with full freedom and knowledge,
has committed a sin ordinarily held to be mortal sin, and has not
previously confessed it. This precept constitutes in fact the first
and simplest form of excommunication.

The usual explanation of this precept is somewhat different,
because the canon of the Council of Trent, which mentions
the point (Denzinger, nn. 880 and 893), is not read in its
historical context. It is commonly said that he who has lost
sanctifying grace is not permitted to go to communion; which is
true enough. But, for one thing, the Church does not know with
infallible certitude that such or such a man has indeed lost
sanctifying grace; and for another, it is quite sure that the notion
of mortal sin, as we define it today, was unknown in the earlier
centuries; which proves that we have to do here with an
ecclesiastical sanction, founded on solid dogmatic considerations;
for, the reception of the eucharist, as the highest testimony

of our union with Christ, is by right reserved to the living members of the Church. There is no reason, though, why the order of things should be inverted.

We need not repeat that the man who, with a diminished freedom, has committed an objective mortal sin, is not considered by the Church to incur the sanction; for his sin is a sin of weakness, therefore, a venial sin. There are possible instances, however, when it is exceedingly hard to judge by oneself whether one has really acted with a diminished freedom. In which case, we had better submit to the sanction, even though in our eyes the sinful deed appears less grave. Conscience derives no benefit from uncertain and confused situations. On this ground, it is good to add in confession the formula: " Insofar as I am guilty before God. "

People often complain that moralists speak too little of charity in their teaching, that they do not sufficiently base their moral doctrine on the foremost principle of Christian ethics, namely, love for God and the neighbor. The criticism is in part justified, when addressed to rationalistic morality, or to casuistry. The reproach, however, conceals, as often as not, a great deal of sentimentality and ignorance of the moralist's true role. The Church has not promulgated any precept of her own on the subject of love; Scripture is explicit enough. Her function is to guide and to form our consciences concerning the manner in which we have to live up to love in the very complex circumstances of human existence. The principles are clear enough, especially as regards our attitude toward God: faith, hope and charity in complete obedience and surrender. Where we need the guidance of the Church is in the application of those principles in actual everyday life among men.

As a matter of fact, the Church speaks more of charity than is asserted by those for whom charity is far too much mixed with feeling and sentiment, a charity which lowers its flag as soon as it confronts the hard realities of life. No one could be more matter-of-fact than St. John when he wrote: " He who loves observes the commandments. " When the Church issues directions about just wages in a capitalistic society, she deals with charity, although her way of presenting matters may sound rather business-like and technical. Charity can but languish where justice is lacking, where the neighbor is not respected as man and as a person worthy of esteem. To want to solve all problems by distributing alms is to wander far from love; alms lower the neighbor to the rank of beggar. Is it not the romantic charity of the nineteenth century that did so much harm to the Church in the social sphere? In order that love may live, there must be honor, respect for truth, right and order, and even politeness and courtesy. It is the task of charity to seek and to expose the Christian standards that ought to rule the manifold, complex and ever-changing relations within human society—even though the sober matter-of-fact language of the specialist has nothing lyrical about it. Love is not lyrical; it is truth, esteem and justice.

The subjective dimensions of conscience

The Church thus offers us in the name of God *objective rules;* directives independent of our subjective arbitrariness; standards by which we may judge the moral worth of our actions. But, our actual deeds spring from *our conscience.* The Church is, therefore, commissioned to enlighten the conscience of man; she is no substitute for conscience.

Each time we turn our attention to the living deed, as it arises in man, we discern something original. No man is the precise fellow of another; no action is exactly like another. Each action has its source in the peculiar situation in which man is more or less freely engaged and sets out for a definite object. This applies to sin as well; though sin is, of its nature, more monotonous and more superficial than a genuinely free and authentic human act. The latter alone deserves to be called creative.

The teaching of the Church affords us important data by which to judge of sinful actions. But to size up their moral worth, we have to look, above all, for the personal stake of the sinner. We should know the sinful intent manifested in the action. Sin comes *from the heart.* In the heart lies the subjective dimensions of a sinful deed.

It so happens that the actual wickedness of the heart is frequently diminished because of the sinner's moral immaturity, his " ignorance " as Scripture would say. To take an illustration: the Church has for centuries held up to the faithful the grave obligation of attending Mass on Sundays. We like to hark back to this example, because it is a frequent matter of debate among the laity. As we observed in a previous chapter, such discussions commonly betray a formalistic conception of religion. Unquestionably, the Church stands on secure grounds when she imposes the " law " of Sunday Mass. But matters grow more complicated the moment we examine the conscience of the individual Christian. Many have only a vague notion of what Mass is, of what Sunday ought to be, of what Mass on Sunday ought to mean. All that depends on their education, on their social milieu. It depends also on the manner in which priests say Mass: the foreign tongue; the grouping of faithful and clerics, in an order suggestive of the theatre rather than of community worship; the absence of effort to adapt the architecture, the liturgy, sermon and instruction so that Holy Mass be a living, ecclesial, community celebration. Sunday Mass, especially, suffers greatly from slovenly routine, with plenty of " pastoral " excuses for it. Sunday Mass has come to be for many the supreme symbol of religious boredom. All, both priests and laity, bewail and bemoan the fact; but those that *do* something about it are still a minority.

How can a Christian brought up in such a liturgy, realize the gravity of their obligation *in conscience?* It is, therefore, a very ticklish pastoral query whether all those who miss Mass on Sunday do indeed commit a mortal sin. Many other illustrations are at hand. It stands to reason that a certain degree of maturity in religious outlook is necessary for people to commit greivous sin.

To be sure, no one contends that people do well by missing Mass. Considering the circumstances prevalent today in some countries, we had rather raise the question whether and to what extent people are still Christian. In any case, it is easy to see how an objective mortal sin—an action that of its nature is mortal sin—may in practice cease to be subjectively mortal sin, because of the absence of a sinful intention in the heart. The words of our Lord find here good application: " Forgive them for they know not what they do. "

On the other hand, the personal " ignorance " of the sinner is no excuse for making light of his case. There remains the teaching of the Church reminding him insistently of the fact that on this point he falls short of a grave obligation. Nowhere in the world is the guilty party accepted as a good judge in his own case, least of all in matters related to God. In the domain of sin and conscience, God alone is judge in the last resort. The Church is in duty bound to watch over and to promote the religious formation of her children. She fails in fidelity to that duty by bolstering up her " law " with threats; for then she merely intensifies religious formalism—as can be observed in Italy, for instance.

There remains a further question. Why, in the case of a real mortal sin, do we lose sanctifying grace? Not a few theologians answer the question along strictly juridical lines: the sanction for mortal sin is the loss of sanctifying grace; God withdraws His grace in very much the same way as the state deprives men of civil rights. This is indeed a poverty-stricken theology inherited from the Nominalists. The worst of it is that it misrepresents, lowers God to the status of a despotic, tyrannical judge. In sober truth, God is not out to take revenge. His punishments differ in kind totally from ours. They are not meted out high-handedly for the sake of avenging society, or of " putting the wind up the sinner, " or of protecting other men. All such reasons have their place and value in human justice. God's punishments are declarations of the truth. They arise from the very nature of sin itself; God always acts in conformity with truth. His punishments are expressions of what we actually want to be through and in our sinful attitude. Divine wrath is but another name for divine justice and divine love. God deals with the sinner as he is, as he freely wants to be. God respects His image even when it grimaces in sin.

But then, what is mortal sin? A sin, truly deserving the name of mortal sin is caused by a basic choice, proceeding from our total freedom, which fundamentally rejects God's love; it is a basic choice which, from out of our deepest personality, turns and organizes in principle the entire creation against God. Through mortal sin, we avert the whole of our person against God.

In order well to grasp the truth of our statement, we have once more to recall St. Augustine's aphorism: there exist only two kinds of love: love of God ready to trample on self, and love of self to the verge of scorning God.

Mortal sin is nothing but the existential option expressed in a concrete action belonging to the second kind of love. Mortal sin, therefore, is caused by a choice reaching far deeper than the simple decision of not attending Mass on Sundays. That free choice is to be sought for at the level of what the moderns designate by the fundamental option. The latter is not a separate act, but it hides in every action. It is the basic, dynamically tense and freely accepted orientation of the whole person, from out of the deepest self, from out of " the heart. " As Scripture often says: the heart is turned away from God. Mortal sin is but the expression, the materializing into a concrete action of that fundamental aversion from God, of that fundamental repudiation of love in a convulsive in-folding process of self-love. Just as a virtuous life arises from, and is borne up by a basic choice of love, so a life of sin is rooted on this one existential core: a fundamental, basic preference given to self-love and pride, away from God.

In that light, sanctifying grace is not a " thing " which God can arbitrarily take away or return. Ockham thought so, and the Nominalists after him. Sanctifying grace is precisely that same basic choice insofar as it is sustained and motioned by divine grace, God's love; it forms a permanent, dynamically tense orientation toward the good in obedience and love, in self-surrender. Such is the state of grace. It is not, therefore, something that has been stuck on to us, or has been grafted on to us as foreign element. It is always, to a larger or lesser extent—for our basic choice can wax or wane—love for God leading to despise self.

It should be plain why it is that mortal sin destroys man's basic choice of obedience in self-surrender, and how it replaces it by another that runs dead counter to it. The dynamic orientation of any life, caused by mortal sin, runs in diametrical opposition to the openness of surrender in love and obedience which divine grace brought about and *kept alive* in man.

Grace in me is not a " thing "; it is life and activity; it is the life of being that in its deepest ground is freedom and responsibility. Just as grace cannot sanctify me without transforming my deepest freedom, so sin cannot deform my life without distorting my deepest freedom away from its authenticity. Sin is the rejection of love, the disavowal of that love which from God comes down to us, permeates through us, and brings us back to God, our source. But sin can achieve this only because our basic option turns us wholly away from God and centers us on idols. The idol is mostly self.

The reader will want to know how we can fit all this into the teaching of the catechism, and how it agrees with what we said in previous chapters concerning the difference between the basic choice and the exercise of free choice, or concerning sanctifying grace. The answer is simple: an act is mortal sin when the actual concrete choice we make necessarily implies a fundamental option which runs counter to the basic choice grace had inspired, destroys it and converts it into a fundamental refusal of God, into a commitment of our person to a good that is not God. That is why we call it an " idol, " on the ground that this apparent good—usually, the " self "—is given an honor which by right belongs to God alone, namely, the total commitment of our person.

Evidently, there are degrees in this perverse commitment. In the first section of this second part, we have dwelt upon a few instances where the basic option has proved to be so fundamental and has so coalesced with the free commitment of the whole person that it grew into obduracy in evil. It is possible, however, to think of a mortal sin that has not brought matters to such a pass, a sin not many steps removed from a venial sin. This latter remark of ours goes to show how hard it may be in practice to distinguish clearly between mortal and venial sins. One state grown little by little into the other. Nevertheless, mortal sin as such is defined as a real and qualitative *breakdown* of the moral life. In venial sin, my life stays orientated toward God, though perhaps enfeebled. Venial sin forms a parenthesis in my existence; it is a failure in steadiness of purpose in respect of myself and God. While prefering God to all else, I admit in my life a sinful activity of my own. Such an anomaly is possible only in man, because here on earth he is as yet unable to attach himself utterly and definitively to his final end: his "heart" is divided. The heart is truly and sincerely directed toward God, and nevertheless, away from God in less decisive matters.

Mortal sin, as we said, is qualitatively a breakdown. From the moment of his grievous sin, man averts his entire existence from God. Thanks to a schizophrenia, inherent in mortal human nature, the sinner preserves power to do some good, enclosed so to say between brackets. But in fact, he has renounced all allegiance to God. By his fundamental option, the sinner has averted himself from God in principle and radically, and, in consequence, has made the state of sanctifying grace impossible in him.

Venial sin, too, can be committed by man only. In man alone do we meet with the division of heart, permitting him to love God while he is in pursuit of self in minor concessions to egotism.

It will be of profit to us to apply our doctrine to a concrete case. The illustration is chosen on purpose, because many confessors, spiritual directors and penitents lump together all manner of sins and condemn them *without further distinction.*

We are thinking of conjugal morality. Let us imagine a married couple who have made up their minds once and for all (making, therefore, a fundamental option) that they will not care a hoot for the teaching of the Church, that they live their married life as a "joint egotism," that on principle they will have no children and will resort to all available means not to have any. On the face of it, such people live in a state of mortal sin. We do not conceive how a priest could dream of giving them absolution: they show no sign of contrition, though they might possibly approach the confessor around Easter, moved by a remnant of religious formalism.

There is, then, another married couple who want children, who in fact have some already and are happy to have them. They desire nothing better than to live their married life in and with God. But they are the victims of the social pressure of the community in which they move. The woman may also dread another pregnancy, either because her physical strength is actually none too robust, or because the doctor has advised her against it. It may also be that for the time being they are in financial straits. Their situation is, therefore, widely different to that of the first couple; and it seems to us that it should be treated pastorally in a different way. Such people are liable to commit mortal sin; the full context of their life is evidence enough that their basic option is very unstable, hovering on the border line between venial sin of weakness and real mortal sin.

A third case may be thought of. The couple desire to have

children, but they are prepared to avoid a new pregnancy by all
the licit means at their disposal, because, for some reason or
other, children are not wanted for the moment. They live together, which is normal and sensible. They express their mutual
affection and love by means of the customary blandishments
without which their existence would be inhuman. And besides,
they have a right to do so; for between married people, love
normally manifests itself through mutual caresses which, as such,
belong to the meaning and content of a Christian married life.
On occasion, such mutual caresses sweep them off their balance,
draw them closer together than they had at first intended. And
maybe, at that very moment the dread of a new child may seize
upon them and prevent them from completing the marital act.
In this third case, again, it is clear that the required pastoral
direction falls along lines different from those called for in the
two preceding cases. Here, there is good ground for doubting
whether the question of mortal sin arises. This remark of ours
may startle some of the readers who, until now, were wont to see
in sin rather the material side and to judge of it from a purely
legalistic standpoint. Why not call to mind one of our former
illustrations? In the observance of traffic regulations, it is immaterial whether I am momentarily off my guard, or of bad will,
or can do no other: when I park my car in a prohibited area,
a penalty is pounced on me automatically. It is about time
we cease to look upon God as a police inspector. Infantile notions concerning our relations with God are unworthy of a mature
human being. In a priest, who has spent many years in the study
of moral theology, such shoddy notions are unpardonable. The
one excuse available perhaps—and is it an excuse?—might be
that a hard and fast rule is convenient; it takes no hard thinking.
The action is listed in the catalogue of sins, and there you are!
Meanwhile, a criminal love of ease and laziness throws into
disarray the religious and moral relations of the faithful.

We have spoken at some length about formal mortal sin and
deliberate venial sin. There remains now the venial sin of weakness. When the latter happens, we meet with plain signs that
the fundamental option—and therefore, the state of grace—is not
done away with, but only threatened.

The theological dimension of sin

From what we have said so far, it is possible to make out that the
distinction between mortal sin and venial sin is qualitatively very
great, though in practice it may not be easy to tell offhand the one
from the other. On deeper reflection on the sinfulness of venial

sin, especially a fully deliberate venial sin, we reach the conclusion that, existentially, the distinction is no longer so very great. As soon as I discover evident symptoms of an incipient cancer, I shall be as worried as when the doctor warns me that the disease has spread throughout the body. It remains true, however, that while in the first supposition I entertain some hope of a cure, in the second, the probability of recovery is more than doubtful.

We may apply this to the voluntary venial sin, above all if it has entered into my life as a confirmed habit. By deliberate venial sin—I mean an actual malicious venial sin—I do not definitively shut the door upon grace; yet, I freely allow in me the growth of a basic will whose normal outcome must be a fundamental refusal of God A deliberate venial sin—more so, the sin freely accepted as a habit—is the immediate preparation for a mortal sin. On no account may we forget that our actions are linked with each other: the past lives in the present, and the present prepares the future. Every sinful deed enfeebles the fundamental basic option we made under the influence of grace. Every venial sin fortifies in me the self-love which, one day, may grow dominant and turn into " contempt of God. "

One more consideration. What shall I think of mortal sin and of venial sin when I realize that I am actually in God's presence? That, after all, is the all-decisive way of looking at sin.

Gustave Thibon wrote that to grasp what sin is, one would need to know what God is in His reality. Thibon's remark strikes from us the arguments we might use in answering the raised question, important as it is. We do not know God! To us, here on earth, God is too unreal, too much an ethereal idea, a truth too far removed, an impalpable presence; to us, He is not the living God of majesty and holiness. In our helplessness, we turn to the saints for an answer. In their life of faithful love and prayer, they stand so much closer than we to God.

When we observe the saints, we soon perceive that their reactions differ from ours. We are inclined to mistake their ways of speaking for expressions of pious exaggeration. It is noteworthy, though, that identical reactions are to be observed in very level-headed, virile and totally unhysterical holy men. To the saints, any and every sin is a serious matter. All their lives, they bemoan even the minor sins of their youth. And why? Because they realize so intensely who God is and what are His rights to our undivided devotion and love. God's sanctity should not be offended; yet, sin in all its forms is an abomination in His sight. The saints do not demur to the Church's teaching on the distinction between mortal and venial sin; they even put it to use in their sacramental and spiritual life. Their conduct here is in sharp contrast with Protestants and Jansenists alike. At the same time, more than the average faithful, they are sure of God's forgiveness, of His great mercy toward sinners. They are free from anxiety and despair; they make no secret of their soul's serenity. More than we, they share in God's joy and consolation. Yet their life is overshadowed by a subdued sadness that God is not loved as He alone deserves to be. Their consciousness of repentant love is the hallmark of a faith nourished by familiarity with Holy Writ and by the realization of God's infinite purity. In heaven, we too shall have full experience of repentant love; for in heaven, we shall be sinners to whom out of sheer mercy pardon has been granted.

In the face of God's love, in the face of God's mighty majesty, in the face of His inviolate sanctity, in the face of His inalienable and total right to a return of love, to fidelity and obedience, every shortcoming is serious. When all is said, there is but one sadness in this world: God is not loved as He should be. The sadness of the saints goes hand in hand with an unimpaired trust in His forgiveness and love, with an unmixed joy in His glory. We are not likely to grasp this yet. But we shall realize it when we stand face to face before Him, or rather, on the threshold of His glory. At any rate, that will be the great grief and joy in purgatory.

Grace and psychology

While treating of grace, we had repeated occasion to mention freedom. Most of our attention rested on " theological freedom, " the freedom of the children of God. As witnesses, we cited John and Paul. Any argument about freedom which neglects this aspect stops halfway; which is surely the case when we deal with the relationships between grace and freedom.

It remains that most difficulties, connected with the influence of grace on human freedom are of a philosophical nature. In the chapter on election, and again in the chapter on sanctifying grace and mortal sin, we touched on the problem.

On the subject of human freedom, we come across a third series of objections and queries. They are of a more practical kind. They have their source in the methodical presentation of the problem of psychology with which we are familiar today. In the field of popularized science, paperbacks have brought to the masses a closer acquaintance with psychological questions. It may very well be that such glimpses into the human psyche remain unassimilated by most readers; they have at least made modern man alive to the objections thrown up by scientific psychology.

We have one more reason for writing this chapter. For three centuries, the theological school of Suarez has denied the possibility of a psychology of grace. This theology, which inherited, so we think, some of the pre-Tridentine Nominalism, did much harm to the life of the spirit, to spirituality and asceticism. Mystical theology, too, has suffered from its impact. And so, reasons are not wanting for a deeper investigation into the subject.

We have to forget a past which weights heavily on us, in some countries more than in others. We are facing an era intensely interested in psychological problems.

Basic option and freedom of choice as psychological problem

Every free action, taken in its totality, runs its full course on a twofold level: the deepest level of our personal basic option, and the level of the concrete choice of action lying more closely to the surface and within reach of our immediate experience.

Our commitment on the deepest level is not so subject to variation as the commitment on the second level. This first aspect of our freedom is marked by a slow maturing process, a development toward an ever-increasing authenticity and inner truth—or toward an ever-expanding hollow lie. On the deeper level, we are only free to grow and develop. In other words, freedom is given us as a task to be fulfilled: it gropes its way toward clearer and firmer self-realization.

Freedom on the second level adapts itself progressively to the new problems constantly raised by the changing situation of place, age, profession, responsibility and individual history. The two combined levels make for the continuity of our freedom, its extremely supple mobility, its creativeness and power of adaptation.

Both aspects of our freedom should normally work together in perfect harmony and mutual dependence. But, in fact, they fail to do so on many counts. For one thing, we are persons in matter. For another, to speak more theologically, our freedom itself is, in both aspects, impaired in its purity and integrity by the state of estrangement from God and the state of perdition in which we all are jointly born, and which we assent to and actualize by our personal sins. A twofold resistence retards the normal unfolding of the healthy and praiseworthy free action of our person. Simone Weil called this restraint *la pesanteur humaine,* our creaturely condition and our materiality with all its determining forces and impeled inhibitions *(Hemmungen),* not to mention our sinfulness.

It is not hard to see how our sinfulness acts as a brake on the smooth progress of our free action toward its befitting development. The freedom of our all-embracing choice, together with the basic surrender, imply a stand taken in respect of total reality. On this plane, it is always a question of " all or nothing "; the " more or less " lies in the growth, but never in the initial choice itself. Either I surrender myself utterly to God as He truly is, i.e., the source and ultimate goal of my whole being; or I refuse to surrender and lock myself up in myself. As St. Augustine remarked long ago, there is no other alternative. A sound Catholic theology draws the practical conclusion that a man is either in a state of mortal sin or in the state of grace. Confused, undecided situations, so well known to human vacillating mediocrity, are to be traced back to the want of resolution with which the fundamental option is generally made; they are to the fore on the level of our concrete experience, on the level where the basic choice presents itself in everyday life. We know all too well from daily observation how ambiguous life can be:

the sinner keeps looking for God and the religious man goes on seeking self-satisfaction in disobedience and self-will.

The one alternative open to man is thus the choice between God and self. Now, it happens that on the level of actual daily life, God must habitually be discovered in our dealings with the neighbor; and that is why true love is endowed with a high degree of sacramental value the moment it becomes disinterested, pure, self-forgetting surrender to another person. Keeping this in mind, we may repeat with St. John that all true love is born of God and leads to God (I Jn 4:7-12); a truth which applies in the case also of those who, for the time being, fancy they have to deny God's existence. God is love. We understand better why St. John is so emphatic when he declares: " If a man does not love his brother. . . .it cannot be that he loves God " (I Jn 4:20).

Our state sinfulness, whether it be the state of perdition inherited through original sin, or the consequence of personal actual sin, can always be shown to have its roots in some form or other of self-love and self-indulgence; the instance of hardened pride in the ultimate *mortal* sin makes no exception. But any and every kind of self-love, which shuts out God, is at the same time the most thorough going existential lie of our life. For it is the most thorough going existential lie of our life. For it is the refusal to acknowledge ourselves for what we really are: the refusal to recognize that our being is God's possession because it flows out from Him and is bound to return to Him.

For the same reason, when sinning we deliberately attempt to destroy our freedom. Herein lies the paradox of sin: it is a wilfully sustained crippling denial of what is essentially our freedom. The good action is the one thing that makes us truly free. This is why sin is so monotonous, as the priest soon learns from the ministry of the confessional. It explains also why genuine sanctity, so different from the counterfeit holiness set forth in some pious books, reveals itself so original, always new and arresting; it resembles God's own creative freedom.

We mentioned just now that the normal unfolding of our freedom is powerfully checked by the material side of our being. We did so with the intention of pointing to the primary fact that we are not pure spirits, but actually spiritual bodies, or better, embodied persons. There is no denying that we are free, but free in the midst of struggle with an odd assortment of restraints. Much thought has been given in our day to the many forces and influences which either completely evade the ruling of our free choice, or can be subdued only indirectly by a wise diplomacy and trained self-assessment. Whatever the history of men and peoples, whatever a healthy psychology has to teach us on this point, is true. The exercise of freedom in this world supposes a rare art of living, a spiritual hygiene and a mental balance which few men can boast of.

Long before we get a chance to use our freedom, we are caught in the coils of determining factors which we are simply undergoing. Think of our birth, our heredity, our education at home and at school, the spiritual climate of our time, race and country; think also of the caprice of events, such as sickness, failures, accidents, favorable or adverse conditions of life—in a word, the whole concrete situation which we, men of earth, have to face moment by moment.

In this connection, we should like to call special attention to all the forms of psychic weaknesses and ailments. Medicine is increasingly aware that the so-called organic diseases are closely linked to our psychic states. Whatever the origin of a psychosis, whether it be fatigue, heredity or sickness, the tragedy of such a state is that human dignity and freedom, thus also the life of grace, are endangered.

Let it not be overlooked, though, that such illnesses do not attack what makes up in us the central core of the life of the spirit. In other words, a mentally sick man does not *really* lose his dignity as a human being; we, Christians, have to stand by, and defend the rights which, as a human person, he possesses even when he becomes a burden to society. The sickness affects only the faculties, the powers and mechanisms, or whatever is necessary to give the fundamental personal option its fitting human unfolding in actual deeds.

In order to perform a concrete action, man has, from within his fundamental self-surrender, to call upon all his powers and aptitudes which lie in the no-man's land between the deep-seated spiritual personal core and the body. To act freely, we must in the first place think, therefore understand and grasp, a variety of things; we must, further, exercise our will and, therefore, dispose of a will-power normally developed, fortified and assisted by the emotions and the imagination. It is the whole man who acts, with heart and soul, with will and emotions, not excluding the bodily forces, such as health, muscular strength, etc.

Grace renews and raises in Christ the whole man; the whole man is reborn by grace. This completely " new creation, " as Scripture calls it, will be fully manifest in the " new heaven and on the new earth, " when all men will be one in Christ. Until that day, God works in us " from within outwards. " The spiritual dynamism born of grace, the infused charity which God's initial love has set up in us, has thus from within to permeate our entire being. Since God respects our human nature, every aspect of it—as we described in the preceding pages—will come into its own. The gift of freedom in Christ must now grow in our lives and express itself in our ordinary daily actions. Our emotions and all that belongs to our bodies has gradually to come under the influence of the higher love born in us. Men generally fail to notice this process, because they don't give God a free hand. The saints alone can, and do bear a shining witness to this transforming operation of grace.

A provisional conclusion must do here. A long list of terms could be prepared to indicate the many ways in which grace, from within, draws and attunes us to God; theologians have done so in the past. The reality of grace, however, remains always essentially one and the same thing: *an ever purer love for God, offspring of God's own love for us.* It is of the utmost importance to us to realize this. Only in this light will our religious life assimilate the theology of grace technically expounded. And at the same time, theology will gain in meaning for our personal life.

Life of grace, moral conduct and psyche

Someone might think that in the preceding pages we have accumulated abstractions, perhaps futile considerations, to reach a fairly obvious conclusion. Be that as it may, let us not forget that the simplest truths are most easily overlooked. While writing these pages, we kept before our eyes especially the many priests and religious men who finished their study of the treatise on grace with an impression of disillusionment and discouragement; we wanted to be of some help to them. And we hope that our explanations will prove of some use to the lay people who dare to tackle a technical book on grace. A very courageous undertaking, indeed.

We had still another purpose in view, one that is of capital importance for the practical life of a religious man; a purpose, too, which is suitable to the layman in search of a deeper understanding of his faith. In pursuit of our purpose we shall mark the distinction between life of grace, moral conduct and psyche.

What constitutes the secret well-spring of our life of grace has been given us directly by God alone; it has to manifest itself in our fundamental self-surrender to God in the three theological virtues of faith, hope and charity. Moral conduct is not quite the same thing; its ruling principles are the natural law, the laws of the Church, the civil and social directives necessary for our human activity here on earth. As to psychic deportment, we have seen that it may be subject to compulsions; it may be determined by normal healthy instincts and possibly also by more or less neurotic states.

Neither moral conduct nor psychic deportment lie outside grace's sphere of influence. But this does not mean that the immediate contact of grace pervades and imbues their every part in the same way and in the same measure.

A typical example will bring home the main burden of the question we want to consider. It is rather fashionable today to compare psychoanalysis with confession, or vice-versa. Some unbelievers admire the Catholic Church for achieving an insight into the therapeutic value of self-manifestation of man to man, long before Freud, Jung and Adler found that out. And some Christians, ill-informed on their faith, are heard at times to agree with this view. But it is a wrong view.

Confession is a sacrament, instituted by Christ, entrusted by Him to the Church to grant in God's name through the words of an ordained priest, remission of all sins committed in the sight of God. Obviously, the sacrament of confession belongs strictly to the divine plan of grace. God alone forgives sin and restores His love to man; the Church and the priest are His appointed instruments. That is all.

We are also acquainted with spiritual direction. Spiritual direction may be given in or outside the confessional. Its object is not only sin, but the guidance of a particular man's concrete life. In our own days, direction is usually confided to a priest; in the past, especially in the East, it was entrusted to laymen as well. Spiritual experience and piety are valuable assets; a spiritual director should be a man of God. From his human experience, from his theological knowledge and his personal experience, he draws what is of help in word and deed to his " spiritual child. " In case the director has also some ecclesiastical authority, he can, in the name of God, lay down a definite line of conduct; it is God who then acts through men. In general, though, it is an established principle that direction should be as discreet as possible and leave the door open to those inspirations and designs of God which lie outside the initiative or anticipation of the guide. For, his role consists more in helping the neighbor to find by himself the will of God than in obtruding his own views.

A healthy, Christian-inspired psychoanalysis has nothing to do with sin; it deals with psychic illnesses and reverently stops at the threshold of religious conscience.

Absolution, spiritual direction and psychoanalytical treatment could very well fall to the charge of one and the same man, though it is not desirable. A medical man has no authority over conscience; and it is not good that priests should try an amateur hand at delicate and dangerous methods in which the psychiatrist is specialized. These three therapeutic methods resemble each other in some respects, but only superficially. It does happen that a man experiences in confession a beneficial sense of psychic relief; or that an allayed anxiety proves to be for some others an excellent preparation for a truer knowledge of their sins, thus also for a good contrition. Nevertheless, the fact remains that we have here three different ways of dealing with men. To mix them up would inevitably result in levelling down the highest to the rank of the lowest: everything would be psychology! An unfortunate tendency much in vogue today.

We shall, then, carefully distinguish between the divine life of grace, moral conduct and psyche. Let us start with the difference between the state of grace and moral conduct.

The difference is best seen in the light of what we have already indicated in the preceding pages. We perceive it easily enough in some instances. An obvious one is the case of the baptized children: they have already received grace, in the measure possible to children; but they have still to learn a great variety of things before they can lead a moral life as it should be. Another, equally clear instance can be taken from the experience in the foreign missions; some impatient missionaries are apt to make mistakes in this respect. It amounts to this: adult Christians, and even ordained priests in Africa, really believe in Christ and live in the state of grace. Yet, it is a fact of experience that they have great difficulty in freeing themselves from the pagan mentality in which they have been brought up. The suggestion is not that they should adopt all our Western habits! We have in mind the basic Christian principles taught by the Gospel and the faith. Is it so certain that, after their conversion in the seventh and eighth centuries, our forefathers lived up to the pure Christian doctrine overnight? A friend of mine, specialized in missiology, spoke one day of what he had learned from an attentive study of the *Monumenta Germanicae Historiae,* concerning the decrees and statutes promulgated by the German Councils. For four centuries, the Church had to be insistent with the German peoples, that magic and superstition, vendetta, divorce and polygamy (especially in the upper classes) were contrary to Christian principles; that dukes and rulers had no right to interfere in Church matters; and so on.

We ourselves, dare we be sure that after so many centuries all trace of paganism has disappeared from our civilization, especially today when our modern world is so severely exposed to the onslaught of modern brands of heathenism? An enlightened, balanced conscience, a correct appreciation of what an authentic Christian morality demands are fruits that grow only in the seed-plot of a thoroughly Christian family. Naive rationalism alone will say that to lead a Christian moral life it is enough *to know* what is forbidden, to have read or heard once what is recommended. Like so much else, moral insight is held subject to the law of time. For nations and individuals alike, the development and ripening process of the moral sense are slow.

A defective moral conduct does not surely imply that man is excluded from God's love, deprived of grace and, therefore, in a state of mortal sin. When such "sinners" do objectively sin against Christian precepts, we have no certainty about their actual guilt in the sight of God. Rather than condemn them out of hand, we had better ask the question: What has been their education, their youth, the moral and religious climate in which they grew up, the false principles imbibed? Quite possibly, their spiritual balance has been upset by some factor or other, so that their conscience has lost "the feel" for what is wrong—though, in the abstract, they may "know" that this or that is forbidden.

Morality, thus, is not always synonymous with grace. Grace moves in the depth of the heart, while morality belongs to the domain of our "freedom of choice." As we saw, it is no easy matter to pass smoothly and effortlessly from the basic self-surrender of the heart on to the sphere of an actual life in which morality finds its outlet in concrete deeds.

It remains to be emphasized that, normally, a life of grace, demands a moral life conforming to Christian standards, and, further, that its aim is high perfection. Our Lord Himself is categorical: "If you love Me, keep My commandments" (Jn 14:15). St. John, more than the other apostles, underlines the Master's teaching on this point. In him we recognize the level-headed, practical realism so characteristic of the great mystics who, one and all, are violently adverse to pious verbiage and emotional moonshine. The reader who wants to be convinced of this should read the whole of John's first Epistle. We have already quoted several texts in which the sacred author speaks so tersely of the all-pervading mystery of God's love; they all end with the unrelenting, practical conclusion: "*To love God is to keep His commandments;* and they are not *burdensome,* because every child of God is victor over the godless world" (I Jn 5:3).

God's commandment is, in the first place, love of the brethren; John never makes light of it. By way of introducing the lines just cited he poses the principle in plain and absolute terms: "Every one who believes that Jesus is the Christ is a child of God, and to love the parent means to love his child; *it follows* that when we love God and obey His commands, we love His children too" (I Jn 5:1-2).

A little earlier in his Epistle, St. John had enlarged on the same theme: "Beloved, let us love one another, because love is from God. Every one who loves [notice how unqualified the statement is!] is a child of God and knows [i.e., serves Him and believes in Him] God; but the unloving know nothing of God, *for God is love....* Beloved, if God thus loved us, we in our turn are bound to love one another. Though God has never been seen by any man [thus, illusions remain possible when we pretend to love God], God Himself dwells in us if we love one another; for His love is brought to perfection within us.... We love because He loved us first. But if a man says, 'I love God,' while hating his brother, he is a liar. If he does not love his brother *whom he has seen,* it cannot be that he loves God Whom he has not seen. And indeed, this command comes to us from Christ Himself: that he who loves God must also love his brother " (I Jn 4:7-21). Such texts belong to the finest declarations of Scripture on the subject of what we have called the sacramentality of brotherly love. An authentic love for men is the one guarantee we have of attaining to and of meeting God.

We may conclude. It is abundantly clear that a life of grace insistently demands morality and even holiness. It is no less evident that in the concrete conditions of life of most men, a great deal has to happen before their Christian moral life is actually up to the standard of their election to grace; lack of good will and tepidity are not necessarily involved. In actual life, a tension—and therefore, also a practical difference—may be experienced between the life of grace and moral conduct. As a rule, such a tension is gradually eased and overcome by grace's own motive power, identical with the dynamic power of love. In some individuals, the tension may endure for life, not necessarily through any fault of theirs. God judges.

Anyone with any knowledge of men knows of further possible tension in man: a strain between the life of grace and the psychic urges. Not to put too fine a point upon it: a harmonious, psychic health does not prove that God had given us His grace; but it is a sure indication that God will exact more from us, the healthy ones, than from others less favored.

Let us take an extreme case to establish the latter proposition. Every man, even though he be subject to serious mental deficiencies and affective disorders, is called to holiness. For, what is holiness? Basically it consists in this: that, with the help of grace, we accept unconditionally the situation in life as foreseen for us at every moment by providence, and that we, as true children, answer the call of the Father, in imitation of and in union with Christ. A man's condition may ever be so pitiable; he may be smitten with irrational anxieties, scruples and obsessions; he may have his moral conduct crippled by them; as long as he perseveres, humbly and lovingly, to do all he can to accept his life as it is, he is striving after real holiness: all the holiness within his reach under the given trying circumstances.

Our assertion is likely to scandalize those who know of

Christian life no more than some external conventions and proprieties, people who are spared all problems. Such staid temperaments, too staid perhaps in the sight of God, have still to learn to appreciate their less fortunate brethren. To an inveterate kleptomaniac, the difficult commandment is, of course, the seventh; his infirmity, though, is no excuse for not trying his level best to correct his bad habit. Do what he may, a complete cure for him seems problematic. In his case an expert doctor will prove of greater use than a pitiless spiritual director. His sanctification will lie in the patient enduring of his shame and misery. Since holiness consists mainly in the love of God, fruit of God's initial love, a kleptomaniac's perseverance in humble submissiveness to and love for God gives more joy to heaven " than the ninety-nine righteous people *who do not need to repent*" (Lk 15:7).

To make our point, we have cited instances where no doubt is possible. Other examples could be produced which do not usually receive sufficient notice. Here is one. Difficult young people, during the critical period of puberty, are not so " good " as the " nice boys and girls " whose praises are on everyone's lips, both at home and at school, and who are cited as models for others to imitate. But, instead of praising or blaming an external conduct, would it not be better to ask the question: which of the " difficult " or " nice " young people stands closer to God? It may be with them as with Christians of high moral standard who show themselves so hard to please that they vex everyone around by their nagging " selfishness, " from the moment a serious sickness, or " old age, " overtakes them. Is their aggravating conduct to be blamed on a sinful, self-opinionated will? Should it not be blamed rather on the nature of their sickness or senile decay?

Whatever we have said so far aims at making it definitely impossible to lower the glorious mystery of God's love in souls to a level where it can be measured by the yard stick of human reason. God's grace in me has nothing to do with fashion, conformism, good table-manners, refined language, though these may contribute their share to an increase of respect on the part of the neighbor. Grace has not even anything in common with what we think goodness and righteousness ought to be. In sheer richness, simplicity and ever-surprising divine freshness, grace surpasses all our dreams of beauty.

Is experiential knowledge of grace possible?

One more point remains to be examined. It will serve both as a conclusion to what precedes and as a preparation for more positive explanations that are to follow. The reader has surely gathered that the divine attraction in grace, the God-given dynamism operative in our existence, connotes a new element, different from the natural impulses, tendencies, different also from spiritual aspirations. Grace is called supernatural on no other grounds than that it is something divine in our life. Here the question may be asked: granted that this new dynamic force forms an additional factor in the complex reality of our activity, and granted that because of its divine origin it is of an essentially different nature: does it follow that we can have experiential knowledge of it, and that we can recognize it as such? Can we have conscious certitude of the presence of grace in us? Can we make out that grace is really divine grace?

At first sight, we would expect an affirmative answer. Closer attention, however, suggests a more prudent reply. To begin with, we have a first, rather superficial reason for caution: the very complexity of our psychology. The numerous lines of force in our biological, psychic, rational and spiritual functions are so mixed up together, so interwoven and tuned to each other that it seems impossible, even on the natural plane, to unravel a single strand from the entangled skein. We know very well how hard it is, in our moments of greatest sincerity, to hit on the determining motive of any one of our actions. As the saying goes: " Every man has many reasons for what he does: the good reasons, and the real one. " Those familiar with the practice of the examination of conscience have learned how difficult it is to tell the " real reason " from all the " good reasons " that crowd into the mind. Psychologists are well acquainted with this process. Each one of our actions is automatically followed by the complicated play of " rationalization " that serves to defend our conduct against the contradictions coming either from the others or from ourselves. In that process, the " real reason " habitually disappears behind a massive screen of motives, all of which may seen to be quite laudable, but are not in each case to be trusted.

On the level of conscious motivations, a man can practically never single out one unmixed " real reason. " The human mind being what it is, there is always at hand a host of inducements of varying quality which, at the moment an action is decided upon, have come to a diplomatic and political agreement not always to be proud of. The " real reason " lies hidden deep down on the level of our fundamental will and its option. And these, as we saw, are not within our immediate awareness, and, therefore, cannot be genuinely experienced by us.

The substructure of all this betrays itself, nevertheless, in an indirect way, through the general trend of our behavior; and this only in the case of normal, balanced people. When psychic integration is impaired (as may happen to any one of us at moments of sickness, depression, fatigue or shock), the numerous psychic disturbances on the surface make it often impossible to form a distinct and complete picture of the deeper meaning of our conduct.

The divine presence urges us on Godwards from within and increasingly energizes our conduct, in the measure we, as persons, yield more and more to the pull of the divine appeal. In the last analysis, that is precisely what we call "sanctifying grace": a fundamental, interior and actively intense orientation of our innermost self toward God; a steady, dynamically decisive opening of the heart to God in faith, hope and charity.

Let us repeat: this dynamism, as such, escapes our immediate and clear consciousness. A first reason is that the dynamic commitment is of a nature that cannot be the object of immediate experience.

There is a second reason as well: God's considerateness. Grace never means coercion. Grace is not thrust into the delicate fabric of our psyche as would a hard body in another substance. It rather adjusts itself to the internal quality of our person; we have evidence of this in the great diversity and wealth displayed in the lives of the saints. God respects our freedom, the reflection of His own. Besides, God is not exterior to us. He is no foreigner. In the words of St. Augustine, He is "*intimior intimo meo,*" "deeper within me than my innermost self." Not for a moment can we be disconnected from Him. Rather, what is most ourself rests in and utterly depends on God's creative hand. And this is the ultimate reason why God, and God alone can from within—we stress this point!—exert a penetrating and decisive influence on our free will, and yet not coerce it, still less destroy it.

There remains a last reason why the divine action of grace lies outside experiential knowledge. It is founded on religious grounds, and is frequently lost sight of. The reason is this: grace is, on our side, a divine way of acting under the influx of the Spirit. Action under grace is *ours* in the vigorous sense of the word; at the same time, and in a still more vigorous sense, it is *God's sovereign action in us.* In one and the same identical action, two freedoms converge and blend, each one preserving its peculiar distinctiveness. There is first the sovereign, transcending freedom of God Himself; and secondly, there is our own human freedom, reflection of the divine freedom, given in creation, healed and raised by grace. It stands to reason that God cannot suffer Himself to be experimented upon by man. He may not become the object of our brash psychological inquisitiveness. Faith, and faith alone, reaches God, in deference to what we are and to what God is. This last reason is the clinching argument why we may not expect to draw God's action within the field of psychological and anthropological tests.

Have we then to give up the idea of attaining to any knowledge that grace is at work in us?

God's evidence in our conscience

We have dwelt at some length on the reasons for showing caution when we speak of experiencing grace in us. Self-deception is so easy, as is evidenced in the history of the Church. Numbers of people are persuaded that the Holy Ghost has spoken to them directly, or that the ideas haunting their brain are divine inspirations. From the early beginnings, right down to our own technical world, Christendom has known strange " spiritual " movements; most of them have cut themselves adrift from the Church. And we shall do well to keep in mind this unmistakable mark: division and isolation. On these sectarian aspects we shall come back presently.

When enthusiasts of this brand assemble, it is a forgone conclusion that hysterical or paranoiac zealotry is passed off as an inspiration of the Holy Ghost. Hysteria and paranoia have a marked preference for religious themes; for, of their essence, religious matters are absolute; their absolute character provoke " absolute " assertions and, of course, the spectacular—like a magnet attracting iron.

The liturgical movement has greatly suffered from this excess. Competent liturgists have all the trouble in the world to expel extremists from their ranks. In liturgy, more perhaps than in other domains, it is typical to try to associate the spectacular with the absolute.

In matters like these, we can look to St. Paul for safe guidance. It had not escaped his vigilant eye that the Corinthians tolerated a strong dose of hysteria in their community. The " gift of tongues, " above all others, had an undoubted vogue among them. This charismatic gift manifested itself in spectacular utterances, accompanied by " sacred " distinctive transports of mind. As far as we can judge, the " gift of tongues " has to be classified as a variety of ecstasies. Those who had it and were in their trance, uttered loud exclamations of delight and enthusiasm, words and sounds that for the most part were unintelligible. That seems to have been the reason why this particular " gift of the Spirit, " one of the many known in the early Church, was so avidly desired by all those who had a streak of hysteria in their mental composition.

Though Paul was keenly aware of, and greatly feared this sort of abuse at Corinth, he never dreamed of smothering the voice of the Spirit. He did not think that such a step would be the safest solution. Unfortunately, later centuries have not imitated Paul's wisdom. The latest flare-up of unbridled mysticism in the seventeenth century caused in the Church, especially among the Church authorities, a fear that has not been mastered even today. Rationalism stiffened still further the distrust of things disorderly and " unreasonable. " Thanks be to God, we are recovering from the anxiety-reaction.

Paul was not to be checkmated by anxiety. He devoted to the charisms at Corinth three chapters of his Epistle (I Cor 12-14). He solves the problem by giving good advice on how to sift the wheat from the chaff. He makes no mistake about the sovereign freedom of the Spirit within the Church. He seeks to awaken in the Corinthians the sense of personal responsibility. The criteria he proposes are supremely simple and, therefore, most efficacious. This is in effect what the Apostle says: The Spirit is one, just as the Father and the Son are one; He can only promote unity within the Church; He sows neither division nor sectarianism; and therefore, granted that the Spirit is the Spirit of unity, His highest gift is the gift of charity (I Cor 13). Those " gifts " alone which make for the " building-up of the Church " should be considered as undoubted favors of the Holy Ghost (I Cor 14).

We shall be well advised to adopt Paul's attitude. We, too, have shown deference for the absolute freedom of the Spirit Who works in the souls when and in what manner He chooses. When His influence is neglected, the Church hardens into an authoritarian, legalistic organism. We ought always to put our trust in the Spirit, to seek to recognize His action in the Church, and to distrust whatever causes division, rivalry and absence of love.

If it is true that the presence of grace cannot be denied in the good inspirations which urge us on, it is truer still in cases when God really does speak in us, attracts and brings us to Himself. In previous pages, we have spoken of the freedom which is our privilege as children of God. But it is sure that we shall fail to exercise this freedom as long as we have not learned to listen to the voice of God in us. All have to acquire the art of " discernment of spirits, " as the consecrated expression has it. We all have to learn how " to test and interiorly to taste " what has the flavor of God, what comes from Him. On all sides efforts are being made to renew Christian morals, in conjugal matters especially; strong appeals are being made to personal responsibility and to conscience. The hoped for renewal will not be forthcoming as long as we do not teach the faithful how to listen to the voice of God in their hearts, as long as they do not possess the art of recognizing with satisfactory certitude the interior guidance of the Spirit.

For divine grace does fall within the range of our awareness. All we have to do is to lend keenness to our spiritual senses, to train them to tell the " tone " of the divine from all other sounds that ring false because they are more or less suggested by self-love. Paul was not blind to the danger of possible mistakes. To the simple Galatians, he had announced the freedom of the children of God. At the end of his daring chapter on freedom (Gal 5:1-12), he takes pains to guard the flock against spurious forms of freedom. Spurious freedom springs from self-seeking and, as such, cannot proceed from the Spirit. " Brothers, you are called to be free men; only, *do not turn your freedom into licence* for your lower nature, but be servants to one another in love. For the whole law can be summed up in a single commandment: ' Love your neighbor as yourself. ' But if you go on fighting one another, tooth and nail, all you can expect is mutual destruction. I mean this: *if you are guided by the Spirit,* you will not fulfil the desires of your lower nature. That nature sets its desires *against the Spirit,* while the Spirit fights against it. *They are in conflict with each other,* so that what you will to do you cannot " (Gal 5:13-17).

What are the criteria, the signs by which to judge of divine grace? The first is an indirect one. It is based on the principle set down in the Gospel: " You will recognize them by the fruits they bear " (Mt 7:16). We rightly infer that grace is present in us when the main direction and the general tone of our life are as they should be. Considering that the primal effect of grace is the basic option which turns us dynamically toward God—its name is sanctifying grace—and considering that the basic option normally comes to the fore in the countless daily actions, it follows that the global orientation of our life affords a reliable picture of our real position before God. Misapprehensions here are not necessarily ruled out; these can happen in all things involving self. Some indications, however, are unmistakable.

The indirect method for recognizing in us the presence of divine grace has its value. Too many people are plagued with periods of depression, discouragement and doubt, to such an extent that they are gripped by the fear of being on the wrong track. There are others who feel aversion to God, repugnance against all religious practices, or who imagine that they are condemned by God. Let such souls quietly get on along the road they started upon; let them persevere in their struggle against self-seeking and all forms of egotism; let them, in spite of " feelings " of aversion and impatience, hold on bravely to the law of love. As long as they do what they can and help others, they are on the right path: God's grace is in them. That is what Holy Writ teaches; its testimony can be utterly relied upon.

St. Paul frequently mentions the *signs* of the Spirit. He calls them the " fruits of the Spirit. " " The harvest of the Spirit is love, joy, peace, patience, kindness, goodness, fidelity, gentleness and self-control. There are no laws dealing with such things as these " (Gal 5:22-23). In this Epistle to the Romans, he writes: " Those who live on the level of our lower nature [i.e. man's sinful nature] have their outlook formed by it, and that spells death; but those who live on the level of the Spirit have the spiritual outlook, and that is life and peace " (Rom 8:5-6; 7:4-6). " For though you were once all darkness, now as Christians you are light. Live like men who are at home in daylight; for where light is, there all goodness springs up, all justice and truth " [this latter remark of Paul's indicates fidelity rather than insight] (Eph 5:8-9).

In the first Epistle to the Corinthians, Paul devotes his first four chapters to the spirit of division rife in that Christian community (I Cor 1:10-17). Corinth was a Greek city. Division among the Christians had its source in intellectual snobbism. One of the questions agitated was: Who possesses the highest wisdom? To vain " wisdom " Paul opposes the " folly of the cross, " the true wisdom before God (I Cor 2:6—3:4). Divine wisdom is a gift of the Spirit. " The Spirit explores everything, even the depths of God's own nature. Among men, who knows what a man is but the man's own spirit within him? In the same way, only the Spirit of God knows what God is. This is the Spirit that we have received from God, and not the spirit of the world, *so that we may know* all that God of His own grace gives us; and because we are interpreting spiritual truths to those who have the Spirit, we speak of those gifts of God in words found for us not by our human wisdom but by the Spirit. A man who is unspiritual refuses what belongs to the Spirit of God; *it is folly* to him; he cannot grasp it because it needs to be judged in the light of the Spirit. A man gifted with the Spirit [i.e. a man led by the Spirit] *can judge the worth of everything,* but is not himself subject to the judgment of his fellowmen. For, in the words of Scripture, ' Who knows the mind of the Lord? Who can advise Him? ' We, however, possess the Spirit of Christ " (I Cor 2:10-16).

We now come to the direct signs of God's presence in us. And first the divine presence in our conscience, the interior voice whispering to us what is good and what is evil. To avoid explaining things in abstract terms, we shall show how the presence may be experienced in a concrete setting; we mean: in today's great problem of conscience, the problem of birth-rate in a Christian family. How are husband and wife to know what

God expects from them, what grace prompts them to do in their actual situation, what is allowed, what is better or best? God is wont to leave several avenues open to our love (Cf. Mk 10:17 ff).

The first thing a married couple have to do is to rid themselves of any inhibiting, cramping factor in them that could prevent the voice of God from coming through to them. They should rid themselves of: rebellion against the directives of the Church, an excessive seeking after comfort and unhindered freedom, fear of effort and responsibility, anxiety, obstinacy and aggressiveness. That is a prerequisite; what is at stake is the exercice of our highest freedom, our freedom as children of God. We shall be unfit for it unless we throw off all prejudice and passion. *Self-liberation,* disengagement from the secret ties that bind us to self-love are the first step to freedom. As long as we do not have the necessary " openness "—which the French today call " *disponibilité,* " or " availability " in English—we shall not perceive God's voice. The voices we claim we hear are just echoes of our desires resounding through the solitude in which self-indulgence seeks to confine itself.

The second step follows. Prayer and quiet meditation allow us to " test and interiorly to taste " what God wants from us. An attentive reflection on what we intend to do will soon enable us to notice that some of the things we plan to do leave us interiorly dissatisfied, make us uneasy, disturb our inner peace. We shall experience this when, at moments of great sincerity, we turn to God with a liberal heart, and place ourselves before Him. And we shall observe that other decisions procure to the heart a relish of peace, of rest and quiet joy, of generosity and assurance.

To take a rather commonplace illustration: when we turn on the radio, or the TV, to the correct wavelength or channel, we get a pure sound, or a distinct picture on the screen, provided our apparatus is in good condition from the antenna down to the contact. Something similar happens to our hearts as soon as we are attuned to God. When everything within us is in order, God's peace comes through, together with His joy and strength. We breathe more freely, we are sure of ourselves, and yet entirely and truly humble, ready to do what is right. As soon as we attune our hearts to God, divine love streams into us and fills us with the wealth of God's abundance.

The moment, however, we adjust ourselves to false values, peace and interior joy are quickly disturbed. Curiously enough, the hardened sinner, the man willfully firm in his aversion to God, undergoes the opposite experience: a murmur of God's voice starts up a salutary disquiet in a heart that so far had satisfied itself with a false peace.

We apologize to the reader for indulging so freely in figurative speech. The experience of God in our conscience does not consist in " seeing, " or in clearly beholding something or other. To express their awareness of God, the mystics were reduced to speak in metaphors not borrowed from the sense of sight. We, like them, speak of savoring, of tasting, feeling and listening. Images taken from the sense of smell are rarely used, except in Paul's well-known quotation: " Thanks be to God, who continually leads us about, captives in Christ's triumphal procession, and everywhere uses us to reveal and to spread abroad the fragrance of the knowledge of Himself! We are indeed the incense offered by Christ to God, both for those who are on the way to salvation and for those who are on the way to perdition: to the latter, it is a deadly fume that kills, to the former a vital fragrance that brings life " (II Cor 2:14-15).

We make use of such metaphors not for lack of insight into what actually happens. Nor are we induced by specious sentiment, sickly romanticism—as some hardheaded rational temperaments might suspect us of. Our one reason for doing so is that the experience of God's grace in us is properly inexpressible and can be perceived by those only who have generously opened their minds to spiritual influences. We are aware that most laypeople, religious too and priests, have rarely, if ever, been trained to acquire for themselves the interior habit of ready openness before God. That is why we try to couch our explanations in simple language and at length; we do not want to be misunderstood. When all is said and done, the best we can do here is to invite one and all to get started on the way. *No one but he who has some experience of it will understand what I write.*

We have no mind to maintain that neither our intelligence nor our judgment have any part assigned to them in the spiritual life. Our reason may not be cast for the principal role; but it remains irreplaceable. There is always need for serious reflection, for using sound common-sense. In the example, chosen a moment ago, the example of birth-rate in the Christian home, it is highly desirable that we keep level-headed, businesslike, that we take into account the health of the married couple, their finances, their social and political duties, and so on. Therefore, it is good for them to consult other men who proved themselves trustworthy because of their thorough Christian manner of life and because they share our religious convictions. Their advice will assure us that we are not seeking to " rationalize " a warped conception of life with sophisms and self-excuses. An appeal to those we can trust, whether it be a doctor, a faithful friend or, eventually a priest, will save us from mental strain or personal delusions that breed in moral solitude.

Nor should we neglect to draw inspiration from the directives of the Church. The Spirit who speaks to us in our hearts is *the same Spirit* who guides the Church and preserves her in the truth. We should address ourselves preferably to wise, sober-minded men conversant with the Church's teaching and able to expound it. Most laymen will not draw great profit from the official texts of the Church; such documents are written in a style all their own, in a language with which one needs to be familiar before one can correctly interpret what is said. The Roman Curia has developed, in the course of time, a delicately shaded specialized style, in which words and expressions have a definite meaning. Some of our contemporaries take offense at this; they declare it hackneyed phraseology. There is no doubt that such specialized language may lead to legalism and Byzantinism. But it cannot be denied that it possesses also many advantages. Important ecclesiastical declarations are always addressed to the entire Church in which are gathered a great diversity of nations, each one with its own civilization, its own tongue and customs. In documents of great weight, the Church tries to take into account as many facts as possible. Herein lies the reason why the Church's declarations are couched in fairly abstract language, somewhat above the level of the concrete domain where our consciences have to take decisions. Another reason for consulting competent people is that, in general, our Catholic daily papers do not think it an honorable task to reproduce the correct texts. They satisfy themselves with summaries received from international press agencies that thrive on sensational news items; and these are utterly unsafe.

For all that, in the end, it is *we who in our personal conscience have to come to the final decision.* In whatever concerns our responsibility toward God, no one, not even the Church, is a substitute for us. Our neighbor may enlighten us as to the choice to be made; he may help and assist us with sound advice. But I alone am responsible to God for my action. Such is the freedom conferred upon us in Christ, when grace was given. A great responsibility indeed! Not a few will look with nostalgic regret to the time when they could content themselves with the mere carrying out of what was prescribed. But such an attitude belongs properly to the underdeveloped, the child. If we care to stand before God as true adults in the Church, we have resolutely to take our personal responsibility in hand. The task is momentous; but nothing is more liberating.

At that moment we stand alone before God's majesty. It is the moment of prayer, the sacred instant when we have nothing else to do than to listen to God's voice, with hearts attuned to divine grace. The ultimate sentence pronounced in the inner court of our conscience must rest on the immediate inspiration of the Spirit. We shall recognize it by the sense of peace and joy, of a deep longing to be good toward the neighbor, to share with others what we have received. This is precisely what the Spirit tries to work out in us.

Need we mention that, in order to exercise this highest form of freedom in grace, there ought to be self-command, self-discipline, " openness " and interior peace? The least we can do is to guard against pride and self-love whose roots seem to be indestructible. And, of course, we should not have the audacity to say that the Church is of no use to us, that she has nothing to tell us in the name of God. It is the same one Spirit who speaks through her and in our conscience. It remains that the ultimate decision is ours exclusively. We shall be able to decide " according to God " when realizing that God dwells in us and speaks to us. Prayer grown out of this listening attitude: " Lord, what do You want me to do? " His voice is always in the nature of an invitation; no one shows greater deference for our freedom than God. His fidelity is unwavering, in spite of our sins. The moment we open our heart, we shall hear Him; and He will guide us along the path of peace, the surest guarantee of His presence.

God's evidence in our faith

Priests and laymen, brought up on the now outmoded rational apologetics, may keep from this teaching the impression that faith is the outcome of a long and intricate, historical and philosophical argumentation. This is surely a dangerous notion; for it is a false one. It is also an unjust one, since it would imply that a thorough faith is reserved to those intellectuals who are capable of following strings of elaborate reasoning. Some men are unfortunate: as soon as one or other historical or philosophical argument has been disproved, they fancy that the faith has fallen with it. They are indebted for that impression partly to an anxiety-complex quite common today in the face of the many switches taking place in the Church. " *On nous enlève notre religion* "—" we are being robbed of our religion, " cried a well-known French Dominican a few years ago.

Historical arguments about the life of Christ, His teaching, His miracles and resurrection; arguments, too, about the origin and the spread of the Church, can, of their very nature, yield no more than well-founded probabilities; in this they resemble all other historical arguments. Humanly speaking, we possess solidly positive data on which to found a " moral certitude " regarding the events from which our faith has sprung. " Moral certitude " must do in a life in which our most important decisions rest on greater or lesser probabilities. Faith, however, is more than that.

Philosophical arguments, too, may strengthen our convictions regarding truths connected with revelation, such as: the existence of God, the immortality of the soul, the personal freedom and responsibility, creation, etc. All such arguments derive their ultimate vigor from faith.

These arguments belong to what is called rational justification of the faith. Faith is not blind. Human intelligence has a right to a certain measure of insight and grasp. But insight, here, rarely goes beyond probabilities. We satisfy ourselves with much less for the solution of problems in other fields. Faith is more exacting because the commitment of a whole life is at stake. At times we ask for what reason cannot give. We ask too much because we do not know the nature of faith. Above all, we do not know what God is. We cannot conceivably encompass God within the narrow limits of human demonstrations. God's plenitude escapes from our mental grasp. Unless we realize this clearly, we shall expect from reason what faith alone can give.

True certitude, rooted in faith, is derived from God alone who dwells in us and speaks to us. It is His voice that converts into absolute certitude what otherwise remains a certitude that is humanly valuable but imperfect. For absolute certitude we are indebted to God alone; it can come from no one but Him.

This doctrine concerning faith is of great relevance to our personal spiritual life. At critical periods, like puberty, early adulthood, menopause and old age; in periods also of sickness and exhaustion, in times of war or of momentous upheavals in civilizations—as we witness today—we are liable to the impression that faith slips through our fingers. Trusted arguments lose their hold, doubts set in. Former evidence now seems senseless and dark.

At such critical moments, the *rational justification* of the faith crumbles. For some men it is a painful experience, periodically recurrent. A justification of the faith, suitable to a child, is not the same as that of an adult; nor is that of the farmer, the worker, the shopkeeper, the citizen of a large city the same as the one of the scientist, the artist and the philosopher. Each category of men is amenable to a set of arguments that have small meaning for others. What carried conviction yesterday, leaves in doubt today. But it is good to remember that any number of doubts do not make up a single act of unbelief. We have forever to look for a better justification, suited to our actual situation and growing powers of understanding.

Faith shoots deeper roots; and this is a fact hard to realize for those who, from childhood, have been brought up in Catholic surroundings; faith for them belongs to the category of things that make up the familiar pattern of life; faith grew up with them, matured with them. If faith is accepted as a hereditary and traditional mode of life, it acts as a screen to a faith that shelters at greater depth where it rests only on God and our personal conviction.

A convert realizes more keenly how God intervenes to confirm the faith in him. A special instinct, if we may use that word, makes him aware of something he did not possess before; and the unusual character of this awareness alerts him all the more to what is peculiar to the experience of faith.

There are other moments when an experience of faith stands out sharp and clear. For instance, the days of generosity and consolation, the times when God's truth floods the soul with light, lends meaning and reality to all things. Such moments should be gratefully remembered and treasured up against the days of darkness and trial. The chief standby in a life of faith is the occasional experiential proofs in us of the divine reality and truth.

How does God bear witness to the truth in our faith? God's ways are wonderful. The lives of the saints and of the more illustrious converts are there to show that God does not need our advice. The *normal* way is the Church, God's visibility on earth. It is in the Church that we have His Word. We see and listen to it in the sacraments that nurture our faith to full life. It is within the sphere of this visible testimony that the invisible divine truth communicates itself to us, that it witnesses to itself and its own veracity within our souls, that truth draws the heart and stirs up in it a deep longing for what is real, perfect and sure. The words of the liturgy—expression of the Church's perennial faith—the gestures of the priest, the preaching of God's truth become alive to us when the divine reality manifests itself to us without intermediary; and this happens precisely in grace.

God's evidence is partly mediate, insofar as it comes to us through the medium of the Church. At the same time, it is immediate insofar as *within* the ecclesial intermediation God Himself is speaking to us and grants us a taste for the truth, which is Himself. We taste God mostly in the reading of Scripture. Scripture demands to be read prayerfully, meditatively, in union with the Church, the Bride of Christ who preserved for us the sacred words and today meditates on them, rehearses them in the liturgy for the benefit of all.

It is after this manner that God sets up in us, as it were, a new organ, the sense of faith. It consists in a spontaneous taste and recognition of what is authentic, what does really come from God. It is comparable to a spiritual "instinct"—to use a daring metaphor—permitting us effortlessly to know whether what we read or hear bears the divine stamp and has the ring in it of God's voice.

What else have we done while writing this book? We have constantly listened to Scripture, to the Church speaking in the Councils, to the Holy Ghost bearing witness in theology and in the " feel for faith " granted to the members of God's people. By itself, though, this is insufficient to achieve a reflective understanding of the faith. True theology—" speech about God " —is had when, in this conversation with Scripture, with the liturgy, the theologians and the living Church, a third factor comes in: my personal sense of the faith together with the sense of the faith in the others. The conversation should be a real dialogue, an actual exchange of views.

The contribution of my sense of faith alone is insufficient. True, of itself it is infallible insofar as it is God's immediate evidence in my heart. But its sound can be drowned in the noise of human passions, or deformed by the cramping limits of a narrow mind. Its voice is so faint, so subdued, that in the absence of interior freedom, it is soon misinterpreted. Yet, without the echo from my believing heart, the texts of Scripture or of the Councils remain a dead letter; they can serve the purpose of scientific work, but not of faith and prayer. Whenever in this book we have rejected notions about grace, we did so Very much as an animal instinctively bypasses harmful plants, we have followed the spontaneous reactions of our instinct of faith. And, of course, we found confirmation for what we did in the teaching of both Scripture and the Church.

We fear that our descriptions and images must appear rather woolly to some of the readers. They have yet to learn how to avail themselves of the " feel for faith, " with which God endows us all through the gift of faith. And this is the right moment for proposing an example belonging to our own day and known to all: the person of Pope John XXIII. We have seen him live; we have seen him die. No man in this age has so thoroughly won over the hearts of millions of both believers and unbelievers. And why? Other persons are not wanting whom we value for their simplicity, their sense of humor, their warm humanity. These qualities lent Pope Giovanni no more than external charm. He impressed men because of something far deeper in him, something we all have sensed in him.

Some authors try to puzzle out the " mystery of Pope John " by speaking of a kind of intuition, a personal vision guiding him, a very original inspiration driving him. In fact, on one or other occasion, he himself alluded to that. Greater writers remain perplexed. Pope John manifested two faces before men; he lived on two planes. And that is the Roncalli mystery!

Before his election to the papacy, he was known to those around him as a worthy priest from Bergamo in the mountains, a fluent Italian prelate, a devout and conscientious prince of the

Church, a very humble man of unaffected simplicity and charm. He looked the ideal interim pope; he was just old enough to give the Church sufficient time to look for a successor worthy of Pius XII. As Pope, he remained what he had always been. That is how, during the Council, he displayed now and then typical "Italian" reactions which disappointed his admirers; for these seemed to contradict the genius, the prophetic spirit so much revered in him.

He was no great theologian. The new progress in contemporary theology and exegesis was too complicated for him. He abandoned it to learned specialists; that was their "job," not his. It is admitted, though, that as a Church historian, he was better acquainted with the rich and many-sided historical past of the Church, and, in consequence, was not the prisoner of the present, or rather of the "present of yesterday," as could have been a jurist or a scholastic theologian.

At the same time, he had a vision of the Church suited to the present day, so novel, so authentic and so bold that, old genial grey man though he was, he outstripped the best theologians. That was then called an "intuition," a genuine "feel" for the message of the Gospel, an unerring insight into what God expected from the Church today. On one occasion, he set to the Council the task that the Church show indeed an *evangelical countenance*. Now, that gives us the key to the so-called Roncalli mystery; it is nothing else than the unerring *perception* of what is in perfect conformity with the teaching of the Gospel. We shall never understand him unless we pay due regard to a sense of the faith so powerful, so pure and so true that it throws into the shade all our theoretical considerations.

Faith achieves this in a man who once and for all allowed God to speak in his heart and now listens to God's voice with the docility of a second nature. The Roncalli mystery hides in the pages of *Journal of a Soul*, in the unobtrusive history of a soul whose guiding rule in life was ever the divine interior voice. [55]

Faith is given to the learned and the ignorant, to the poor and the rich, to theologians and to the simple faithful. God lives in their souls, speaks in their hearts. Profound humility and self-forgetfulness are pre-requisites for hearing the voice and for conforming to it.

Luke relates the story of the mission of the 72 disciples. When they returned, flushed with what they had done in the Master's name, Christ addressed His Father in a prayer which is one of the summits of Luke's Gospel. "At that moment Jesus exulted in the Holy Spirit and said, 'I thank Thee, Father, Lord of heaven

---

[55] *Journal of a Soul*, paperback (New York: NAL).

and earth, for hiding these things from the learned and wise, and *revealing them to the simple*. Yes, Father, such was Thy choice.' Then turning to His disciples He said, 'Everything is entrusted to Me by My Father; and no one knows who the Son is but the Father, or who the Father is but the Son and those *to whom the Son may choose to reveal Him*.' Turning to His disciples in private He said, 'Happy the eyes that see what you see! I tell you many prophets and kings wished to see what you now see, yet never saw it; to hear what you hear, yet never heard it'" (Lk 10:21-24).

Earlier in these pages, we have quoted an inspired text of Augustine commenting on the well-known Johannine words, "No man can come to Me unless he is drawn by the Father who sent Me, and I will raise him up on the last day. It is written in the prophets, 'And they shall all be taught by God' (Is 34:13; Jer 31:33). Every one who has listened to the Father and learned from him comes to Me. I do not mean that any one has seen the Father. He who has come from God has seen the Father and he alone. In truth, in very truth I tell you, *the believer possesses eternal life*" [56] (Jn 6:44-47).

St. John comes back upon this idea in his first Epistle. "With you it is otherwise; the Holy One has anointed you ["anointing" here means: you have received the Word with which Christ anoints and vivifies the faithful, i.e. initiates them into the faith], and *now nothing is hidden from you*. It is not because you are ignorant of the truth that I have written to you but *because you know it,* and because lies, one and all, are alien to the truth.... *You therefore must keep in your hearts* that which you heard at the beginning; if what you heard then still dwells in you, you will yourselves dwell in the Son and also in the Father. And this is the promise that He himself gave us, the promise of eternal life. So much for those who would mislead you. But as for you, the unction which you have received from Him stays with you; *you need no other teacher,* but learn all you need to know from His unction, which is real and no illusion. As He taught you, then, dwell in Him" (I Jn 2:20-27).

John has here in mind the Gospel preached by Christ "from the beginning." To His teaching we owe fidelity. The Apostle, however, knows well that fidelity is impossible unless we remain observant of the interior voice of the Spirit. "There is still much that I could say to you, but the burden would be too great for you now. However, when He comes who is the Spirit of truth, *He will guide you* into all the truth; for He will not speak on His own authority, but He will tell you only what He hears;

---

[56] Cf. paperback, pp. 169-170.

and He will make known to you the things that are coming. He will glorify me, for everything that He makes known to you He will draw from what is mine. All that the Father has is mine, and that is why I said, ' Everything that He makes known to you He will draw from what is mine ' " (Jn 16:12-15).

This Gospel passage shows the fulfillment of the promises made by the prophets for the messianic times, the era, " the hour " of the gifts of God's Spirit. " And I will give you a new heart, I will put into you a new spirit; I will take from your flesh the heart of stone and will give you a heart of flesh. I will place My Spirit in you and will see to it that you walk according to My laws and that you observe and follow My ways " (Ez 36:26-27; 37:14). " I will put My law *in their innermost self,* and I will write it *in their hearts* [therefore, no longer on slabs of stone]. Then I shall be their God and they shall be My people " (Jer 31:33).

On Pentecost day, Peter announces the message of the new Church to the surrounding multitude: " This is what the prophet Joel spoke of: ' God says, This will happen in the last days: I will pour *upon everyone* a portion of My Spirit; and your sons and daughters shall prophesy; your young men shall see visions and your old men shall dream dreams. Yes, I will endue even my slaves, both men and women, with a *portion of My Spirit, and they shall prophesy* ' " (Acts 2:16-18).

The text of Joel, quoted by Peter, must be well understood. The prophet's poetic language multiplies marvelous signs just to indicate that *all* will receive. The words " they shall prophesy " do not mean " they shall foretell the future, " but rather " they will speak through the power of the Spirit. " And in this precise sense, Pope John was outstandingly a prophetic man. Anyone who hears God's voice in his heart, chooses it for his guiding rule and thus allows his faith to burst into full bloom: he will share in the promises of the Spirit. His life becomes prophetic, because his faith is borne along by the interior voice of the Spirit who reveals to him what is the will of God in his regard and what has to be done with life in imitation of and in union with the Son.

God's evidence in our hope

Hope is nothing but a more thorough living—up to the faith. Hope, so say the theologians, is an initial love for God, our highest good; it is an assured looking-out for God, our ultimate reward. Hope enables us to bear up against the trials of life with becoming courage and fortitude.

Hope is offspring of faith and parent of true love. It looks to eternity, derives its assurance from the past and proves its strength in the present. Hope looks to God alone, while yet energizing life here below. Hope is not a strictly personal affair: it expresses the expectation of God's people and causes all mens with and for each other, to look forward to " the day when God will be all in all. "

It is eminently the virtue of the faithful during the mundane time, the virtue of God's people still on its pilgrimage through the desert of human history. Behind us, we have our deliverance from Egypt and our Sinai: Golgotha, the cenacle, the empty tomb of the risen Lord, combined with the first Pentecost day. Ahead of us, on the distant horizon of our history, in the rosy dawn of eternity glows the heavenly Zion as described by St. John.

" Then I saw a new heaven and a new earth, for the first heaven and the first earth had vanished, and there was no longer any sea. I saw the holy city, the new Jerusalem, coming down out of heaven from God, and made ready like a bride adorned for her husband. I hears a loud voice proclaiming from the throne: ' *Now at last God has His dwelling among men!* He will dwell among them and they shall be His people, and God Himself will be with them. He will wipe every tear from their eyes; there will be an end to death and to mourning and crying and pain; for the old order has passed away.... I saw no temple in the city; for its temple was the sovereign Lord and the Lamb [Christ]. And the city had no need of sun or moon to shine upon it; for the glory of God gave it light, and its lamp was the Lamb.... "

Here follows a poetic description of the Holy Ghost, in terms of images borrowed from the Old Testament: " Then He showed me the river of the water of life, sparkling like crystal, flowing from the throne of God [the Father] and of the Lamb down to the middle of the city's street. On either side of the river stood a tree of life, which yields twelve crops of fruit, one for each month of the year. The leaves of the trees *serve for the healing of the nations,* and every accursed thing shall disappear. The throne of God and of the Lamb will be there, and His servants shall worship Him; they shall see Him face to face, and bear His name on their foreheads. There shall be no more night, nor will they need the light of lamp or sun, for the Lord God will give them light; and they shall reign forever " (Apoc 21:1-4; 22:1-5).

We notice that John describes heaven as the mystery of God's indwelling—the theme of this book—as the mystery of the radiant presence whose glory dispels all darkness and night. Such a heaven is possible because *we have it already,* though it be in the stage of slow growth, of an expectation that is none-

theless a possession conferred on us by grace. For grace is the
" pledge of heavenly glory"; from now on it is a hidden
beginning of what we shall be later under the light of God.
Already now, we live by the presence we move in it, while
the history of salvation is in progress. We live at present—
to use a German expression—" *Zwischen den Zeiten,*" in between
the day of Christ's first revelation and the day of His final
revelation at the end of time. The main burden of this revelation
is that Christ will prove Himself to be our " Emmanuel," the
Hebrew for " God-with-us." This is surely what John alludes to.

The distinctive mark of hope is that *we expect because we
possess already,* though imperfectly on account of our sinfulness
and the night of our earthly condition. The future will disclose
what in fact we are already. " How great is the love that the
Father has shown to us! We are called God's children [another
image for grace], and such we are.... *Here and now,* beloved,
we are God's children; *what we shall be* has not yet been
disclosed; but we know that when it is disclosed *we shall be like
Him* [children with the Son], because we shall see Him as He is.
Everyone *who has this hope* before Him purifies himself, as
Christ is pure " (I Jn 3:1-3).

Paul teaches an identical doctrine. " Not only they [the cosmos,
the entire world], but even we, to whom the Spirit is given as
firstfruits of the harvest to come, are groaning inwardly while we
wait for God to make us His sons and set our whole body free.
For all who are moved by the Spirit are sons of God. The
Spirit you have received is not the spirit of slavery leading you
back into a life of fear, but a Spirit that makes us sons, enabling
us to cry ' *Abba!* ' ' Father! ' In that cry *the Spirit of God joins
with our spirit testifying* that we are God's children; and if
children, then heirs. We are God's heirs and Christ's *fellow-
heirs,* if we share His sufferings now in order to share His
splendor hereafter.... For we have been *saved, though only in
hope.* Now, to see is no longer to hope: why should a man
endure and wait for what he already sees? But if we hope for
something we do not yet see, then, in waiting for it, we show
our endurance. " Paul does not mean to say that the reality our
hope aims at is not present already in us, one way or another.
On the contrary, it is *because* it is present that we may look
forward to its perfect realization. In this strain, Paul continues
writing: " In the same way, the Spirit comes to the aid of our
weakness. We do not even know how we ought to pray, but
through our inarticulate groans the *Spirit Himself is pleading for
us,* and God [i.e. the Father] who searches our inmost being
knows what the Spirit means; because He pleads for God's own
people in God's own way " (Rom 8:14-27).

No satisfactory explanation is as yet available of what Paul

wants to convey to us by "inarticulate groans." Some modern
exegetes see in them effects of the gifts of tongues: the "inarticulate" ecstatic inspiration of the Spirit wrung from the faithful
in their trance, loud "groans" and cries of joy and delight.
Classical exegesis explains the text as applying to prayer; but
this opinion, too, has its difficulties. Whatever the explanation
adopted, it is plain enough that our hope derives its firmness
from the Spirit of the Father who, in our hearts, "comes to the
aid of our weakness."

The first Epistle of Peter has often been called the Epistle of
hope. It was written at a time when the first persecutions befell
the Church. It had become dangerous to accept Christianity.
It is all the more interesting to note that most modern exegetes
are of the opinion that this Epistle was written in connection with
pre-baptismal instruction. It would be a typical example of the
earliest instruction, outlining what is distinctive of an earthly
condition that has been oriented toward God by baptism.

The opening lines of the Epistle bring us at once to the main
problem discussed in this chapter. "Praise be to God and Father
of Our Lord Jesus Christ, who in His mercy gave us new birth
into a living hope by the resurrection of Jesus Christ from the
dead! The inheritance to which we are born is one that nothing
can destroy or spoil or wither. It is kept for you in heaven, and
you, because you put your faith in God, are under the protection
of His power *until the salvation comes*—the salvation which is
even now in readiness and will be revealed at the end of time.
This is cause for great joy, even though now you smart for a
little while, if need be, under the trials of many kinds. Even
gold passes through the assayer's fire [a classical image of the
Old Testament to indicate God's purifying action], and more
precious than perishable gold is faith that has stood the test.
These trials come so that your faith may prove itself worthy of
all praise and glory and honor when Jesus Christ is revealed."
Now follows the description of the interim time: *"You have not
seen Him,* yet you love Him; and trusting in Him now *without
seeing Him,* you are transported with a joy too great for words,
while you reap the harvest of your faith [already possessed
through hope], that is the salvation of your souls" (I Pt 1:3-9).
Some lines further, Peter concludes: "The price [of your freedom]
was paid in precious blood, as it were of a lamb without mark
or blemish [an allusion to the exodus from Egypt and to our
Pasch], the blood of Christ. He was predestined before the
foundation of the world, and in this last period He was made
manifest for your sake. Through Him you have come to trust in
God who raised Him from the dead and gave Him glory; *and
so your faith and hope are fixed on God."* Anticipating on our
next chapter, we shall quote further lines in the Epistle: "Now

that by obedience to the truth you have purified your souls until you feel sincere affection toward your brother Christians, *love one another wholeheartedly* with all your strength. You have been born anew, not of mortal parentage but of immortal; through the living and enduring word of God. For, as Scripture says,

" All mortals are like grass;
all their splendor like the flower of the fields;
the grass withers, the flower falls;
but the word of the Lord endures for evermore " (Ps 103:15f).

And this " word " is the word of the Gospel preached to you " (I Pt 1:19-25).

The elevated opening of Peter's letter ends with a glorious summing up: " You are a chosen race, a royal priesthood, a dedicated nation, and a people claimed by God for His own, to proclaim the triumphs of Him who has called you out of the darkness into the marvelous light. You are now the people of God, who *once were not His people; outside His mercy once,* you have now received His mercy " (I Pt 2:9-10). All these texts put it past dispute that our faith and hope must be lived up to within the Church, and that too personal, too individual an expectation is not in conformity with the perspective of Scripture, or of the Church in her liturgy.

We take it then that hope implies an inchoate possession of what it looks forward to; we have already the firstfruits of the Spirit. Nevertheless what we do possess now is but an incentive to long for the revelation of what we are in the Spirit, and have still to become.

Like faith, hope grows through the actual presence of God in our hearts, through His actual indwelling in us. Unless we had some sort of experiential foretaste of " how sweet the Lord is, " we neither would nor could look out for Him. Nor would we live in expectation unless consolation were present in us to keep us going until the moment we meet Him face to face. The greater our docility to the stirring of the " inarticulate groans " of the Spirit, the more intense will be our longing to encounter Christ; and the firmer also our steadiness during this interim earthly life, so beset with trials and darkness.

This explains why John ends his Apocalypse with a prayer borrowed from the primitive liturgy, the " maranatha. " That short prayer, made up of only two words in ancient Syriac is susceptible to two translations according to how one chooses to divide the syllables. It may mean either " The Lord has come, " or " Come, Lord "; a twofold meaning which satisfies us as to the paradoxical nature of our hope and, in general, the dialectic tension implied in all expectation. In hope, we possess, yet do not possess, but look forward to the complete fulfillment of what in fact we are already.

With this theme, John ends his book. He lets Christ speak first: "Remember that I am coming soon...and bringing My recompense with Me, to requite everyone according to his deeds! I am the Alpha and the Omega, the first and the last, the beginning and the end." The Church replies in the Spirit: "Come, say the Spirit and the Bride. Come! let each hearer reply. Come forward, you who are thirsty, accept the water of life, a free gift to all who desire it." The final ending is John's own prayer: "He who gives this testimony speaks: 'Yes, I am coming soon!' Amen, Come, Lord Jesus! The grace of the Lord Jesus be with you all" (Apoc 22:7-21).

God's evidence in love

"There are three things that last forever: faith, hope and love; but the greatest of them all is love" (I Cor 13:13). And there are many gifts of the Spirit (cf. I Cor 12:4-11); one stands out above lal the others, love, "the best way of all" (I Cor 12:31).

These three aspects of a Christian existence are spoken of together in the Epistle to the Romans: "Now that we have been justified *through faith,* let us continue at peace with God through Our Lord Jesus Christ, through whom we have been allowed to enter the sphere of God's grace, where we now stand. Let us exult *in the hope* of the divine splendor that is to be ours. More than that: let us even exult in our present sufferings, because we know that suffering trains us to endure, and endurance brings proof that we stood the test, and this proof is the ground of *our hope.* Such a hope is no mockery, because God's *love* has flooded our inmost heart *through the Holy Spirit He has given us"* (Rom 5:1-5).

In this book we have consistently described grace in terms of love. Grace can truly flourish in love only. No need to go over this ground once again.

Most people will spontaneously think here of love for God. Well and good. It is a pity, though, that so excellent a description of what Christian life is should not be free from danger. What cruelty has been displayed in the name of "the love of God!" Last century, when industrialization set in, Christian charity became a cloak for sentimental benevolence and social injustice. The young Marx could say: "It is not hard to become a saint, if one need not be a human being." We have so misused and debased the word that in some countries "charity" tastes sour in the mouth. Other words must do duty for it, now that through our fault the word used by Scripture repels many men. What St. John wrote in the first century remains true nineteen centuries later: "If a man says, 'I love God,' while hating his brother, he is a liar" (I Jn 4:20). Alas, that lie has caused "love for God" to be a source of hatred among men.

To narrow down the idea of love to "love for God" is not only dangerous but inexact. Scripture is emphatic: from Christ's own description of the Last Judgment (Mt 25:31-46) right down to the impassioned declarations of Paul, John and James (cf. James 2:1-4, 13, 15-17; 4:1-3), everywhere we are made to face the paradox: love for God and love for the neighbor are one and the same thing.

Whenever either of these two loves is cut away from the other, it lapses into a caricature of itself; love for God becomes pride and haughtiness; and love for the neighbor turns into a vague sentimental philanthropy, into "fellow-feeling," as Max Scheeler characterizes it so aptly. The lowest ebb of "fellow-feeling" is reached when love for animals crowds out love for men.

Love for God is greatly threatened when the neighbor is not loved. Some "pious souls" drink avidly the cup of maudlin devotions while indulging their own sweet will, and shutting their hearts upon the neighbor. A companion of St. Ignatius, and for many years his secretary, vented one day his long experience in the government of the religious in the sarcastic remark: "Why must 'pious' religious be those who are the most intractable, the most wayward and self-willed men? "Piety" meets with scant sympathy on the part of many outsiders, not because these people foster an aversion to fellowmen who consecrate themselves to God, but because such a consecration seems to serve for a cloak for hardheartedness, indifference and inhumanity. In their eyes, "love for God" appears either a pretext for grim severity, or a form of escapism from real life, a flight from the simple solid human virtues, such as courtesy, tact, sincerity and honor. The wars of religion, religious persecutions, the Inquisition, suspicions, social injustice and veiled slander: all these in turn have been vindicated in the name of love.

Nor could it be otherwise. "We love because he loved us first" (I Jn 4:19). "And indeed this command comes to us from Christ Himself that he who loves God must also love his brothers" (I Jn 4:21).

But how is this possible? Classical theology, followed by most catechisms, says that we must love the neighbor "for God's sake." This explanation, of course, can be, and has been, rightly understood; however, the nature of love is such that it never loves anyone *because* of another. Nor does anyone care to be loved *because* of another; he wants to be loved *for his own sake*. Such a demand is perfectly justified; it conforms to the very law of love. For love is based on immediate reciprocity between persons.

True enough, of God we cannot possibly say that He is " another, " at least not in the ordinary sense of the word, as if He were one of the many persons we can eventually love. God is the ultimate source of all existence; He is the deepest ground of our persons; He has made of us His children. To love someone " for God's sake " should mean that we love him *in* God, and *God in him*. John said so.

History tells us that this is liable to misapprehension. " To love someone for God's sake " is easily mistaken for a " good work " of ours—a self-regarding thought, if anything. The neighbor affords a favorable *occasion* for us *to practice* " love. " The next stage could be that we love the neighbor *at his own cost*. The latter stage is best exemplified in the persuasion that the problem of social justice is solved by " charitable " action. Charity balls are held; by dancing people fancy that they lay up treasures in heaven, while the neighbor is leveled to the rank of beggar. The neighbor does not ask for alms; he asks for his right, therefore, for esteem. During a famous march from Manchester to London, the strikers carried before them a banner bearing the inscription: We are fed up with your charity! We claim our rights!

Too much injustice has paraded under the slogan of " God wills it. " We have had the crusades; we may have an unrelenting father chasing his child from the home; we meet with the inexorable " justice " of the priest who throws the sinner out of the Church and refuses all further dealing with him.

In our view, we stand on surer ground when we propose to love the neighbor with the love *which Christ Himself bears him*— with a love which, like grace, is lived " in and with and through Christ. " Not only is such a concept more secure, but it is truer.

It is truer because the love with which we love the neighbor is not our own. It is, above all, grace, divine life. " God's love has floded our inmost heart through the Holy Spirit He has given us " (Rom 5:5); Or more profoundly: for St. John, love is conceivable only when bound up with the divine essence. " For God is love " (I Jn 4:7-16).

In Kittel's standard *Theologisches Wörterbuch zum Neuen Testament* [57], E. Stauffer remarks that John describes the divine

---

[57] *Theologisches Wörterbuch zum Neuen Testament,* HRSG von Gerhard Kittel (Stuttgart: W. Wohlhammer, I, 1933), " agapè " by E. Stauffer, especially pp. 53-54. Stauffer's article has been translated by J. R. Coates, in *Bible Key Words from Gerhard Kittel's Theologisches Wörterbuch: Love* (London: Adam and Charles Black), especially pp. 61-63.

agapè, love, in two ways.   On the one hand, one gathers the impression that, when not further specified and, therefore, conceived purely as love, *agapè* is characterized as a "cosmic" reality.   God—in the New Testament, the Father—possesses love as the deepest trait of His personal being.   He communicates it to the Son who, in His turn, reveals it to us.   Or, in other words, love is made visible in the act of redeeming, in the fact that Christ gave His life for us all.   Christ Himself said that "there is no greater love than this, that a man should lay down his life for his friends" (Jn 15:13).   Love became incarnate with Christ.

The Spirit distributes and establishes that love, through interior testifying, in those who believe in Christ.   He gathers them all together in the "*koinonia,*" the fellowship we have with each other and, thus, with the Son and the Father.   This is in essence the new life in Christ.   We know of no grander theology of grace than the doctrine of *agapè* as mapped out in St. John.

Endowed with love, the faithful are now entrusted with the task, the "command" to carry *agapè* to all men.   "It is by this that we know what love is: that Christ lay down His life for us.   And we, in our turn, are bound to lay down our lives for our brothers" (I Jn 3:16).   "This is His command: to give our allegiance to His Son Jesus Christ, and love one another as He commanded.   When we keep His command, we dwell in Him and He dwells in us: *we know* it from the Spirit He has given us" (I Jn 3:23-24).

To summarize: the divine *agapè comes down upon this earth* like a "cosmic" power from the Father, is manifested in the Son, and firmly planted in our inner self by the Spirit.

We quote here St. John's testimony, as we read it in the lofty prologue of his first Epistle:

" What existed from the beginning,
what we have heard, what we have actually seen,
what we have closely observed and held in our hands
was something of the very Word of Life Himself.
For it was *life* which appeared before us,
We saw it, we are eye-witnesses of it and now are writing to you about the *eternal life*
that was with the Father and actually became visible in person to us.
We repeat, we really saw and heard
what we are now writing about to you,
so that you and we together may share in a common life,
that life which we share with the Father
and with Jesus Christ His Son.
And we write this
in order that the joy of us all be complete " (I Jn 1:1-4).

The noted Hebrew scholar, J. Bonsirven, calls the Johannine concepts "light," "life," "*agapè*" three divine categories. According to Bonsirven, the three concepts stand for different aspects of one and the same divine reality that came down to us from the Father. St. John wrote: "God is light, and in Him there is no darkness" [darkness means sinfulness] (I Jn 1:5). In his Gospel, he had said: "As the Father has *life-giving* power in Himself, so the Son by the Father's gift" (Jn 5:26). Christ's long discourse on faith and "the bread of life," ends: "As the *living Father* sent Me and *I live because of the Father,* so he who eats Me [by faith and the Eucharist] *shall live because of Me.* This is the bread which came down from heaven; and it is not like the bread which our fathers are [manna]; they are dead, but whoever eats this bread shall live forever" (Jn 6:57-58).

In the "light" which the Father is, and still more in the "life" which He possesses in Himself, we recognize the same characteristic traits we noted in the divine *agapè*. These three realities come down from heaven and instil in us a new life that endures forever.

The "cosmic" aspect of *agapè* is not to be overstressed, otherwise it might suggest notions of magic, or at least a more or less impersonal, mechanical form of Christian life and redemption. We stigmatized earlier such a misrepresentation of the truth as an abortive attempt to make of grace a "thing," notably in the sacraments.

John does not succumb to the temptation, as Stauffer is well aware. While he develops his near-cosmic symbolism, the Apostle expatiates on very personal—intensely existential—categories proper to *agapè*. "Light," says John, purifies us of sin. "If we claim to be sharing in His life while we walk in the dark [Jewish expression meaning a life of sin], our words and our lives are a lie; but if we walk in the light as He himself is in the light, then we shall share together a common life, and we are being cleansed from every sin by the blood of Jesus His Son" (I Jn 1:6-7).

The same with "life." Without doubt, "life" is connected with the eating of Christ's flesh and the drinking of His blood (Jn 6:54). But no automatic, near-magic divine operation. "Eating" and "drinking" cannot be separated from faith. "In truth, in very truth I tell you, the believer possesses eternal life" (Jn 6:47).

And so also with *agapè*. We have quoded abundant texts which plainly and ceaselessly affirm that *agapè* in us remains closely linked to the observance of the commandments and to the love of the neighbor. "*It follows* that when we love God and obey His commands, we love His children too. For to love God

is to keep His commands; and they are not burdensome, because
he who is born of God [image for grace] is victor over the godless
world. The victory that defeats the world is our faith. For,
who is victor of the world but he who believes that Jesus is the
Son of God?" (I Jn 5:2-5). Let us not forget that for John the
"world" means the fellowship of men living in sin, "who walk
in darkness," "do not do the truth," and refuse to believe in
Christ's mission.

In this summary of four or five leading Johannine themes, we
discover still another theology of grace, expressed almost entirely
in images and notions proper to John. This theology of grace,
expressed by "child of God," "born of God," "light" and
"life,"culminates unmistakably in *agapè,* the divine love that
came down to us.

We may now return to the criticism of the classical notion of
"love" for the neighbor "for God's sake." We repeat: the
formula is susceptible of an understanding consistent with faith.
Therefore, it is not necessarily wrong. In our opinion, however,
it is not a felicitous formula; so experience tells us.

We propose another concept to correct and to fill out the former. As we proceed, we shall broadly outline the doctrine of
grace we have developed so far in these pages; and we shall
apply it to the subject of our love for God and of our love for the
neighbor.

We receive grace because the Father dwells in us, recognizes
in us His Son's countenance brought to life by the Spirit. The
holiness we acquire through grace consists in living—as says the
solemn ending of the Canon of the Mass—"through Him and
with Him and in Him." We have expressed that idea in other
words: our new life is a life *in* Christ. Which means that
through grace we have become servants in union of obedience
with the Servant, and children in union of love with the Son.
We enlarged on the idea earlier in the book. It is all established
in us *through* the indwelling, *in* the indwelling, *in view of* an
ever more intimate indwelling.

From this capital vantage point, we can see more deeply into
the nature of love. We love God with the love which the Son
has for the Father; we are taken up and borne along by the
personal love of Christ Jesus; so that—to repeat the words of the
end of the Canon—"through Him and with Him and in Him
is given to you, the Father almighty, in the unity of the Holy
Ghost, all honor and glory, world without end. Amen."

We love the neighbor as Christ loves us, namely, *for his own
sake,* as child of God and brother in grace. Love, of its nature,
demands that we love man for what he is. We love him as he is,
whatever be his condition, in whatever situation he may find
himself. We do not love him in the abstract, so to say, according

to a fancied picture of him. On one point our mind may be at rest: God's love and Christ's love for any one man is intensely actual. What we have to do is to let our love be directed by Christ's purpose and impelled by the impetus of the Spirit. Then, we shall *never* humble the neighbor by what is often labelled " love "; we shall not outrage, ill-treat him. By looking upon the neighbor in that light, we prepare ourselves for an existential commitment manifesting itself in an attitude of humble service. Service is twofold. On the one hand, we promote Christ's love by letting it shine forth in our own love for the neighbor; Christ prolongs His love for men through the brotherly love He awakens in us by grace. And on the other hand, our love for the neighbor remains a love of service and not a love which obtrudes itself, or condescends or seeks its own interested ends. Neither will it be a love that takes more interest in the picture we form of the neighbor than in his real state and needs. Man's greatest need is one of esteem, respect and appreciation, for his own sake and not for the sake of another. We shall never acquire a genuine appreciation for the others unless we let our love be permeated with Christ's love through the power of the Spirit.

And thus " Christian charity " will no longer be mocked by the world at large, as an expression of servile cowardice, as Nietzsche did; nor as an unbending pride, as Dostoevski so grippingly described in his " Grand Inquisitor. " The poor will no longer speak of it slightingly, since such love does not humble them. Sinners will no longer scorn it, since it does not condemn them, but, on the contrary, seeks forgiveness and trust, in view of bringing them back to Christ. Such has been the love Pope John wanted to show to the world. His behavior was not understood nor followed by the Catholics with the respect it deserved. A proof that we have still to learn much.

If we do not want to follow Pope John's example, we should at least listen to the teaching of St. Paul. " Love is patient; love is kind and envies no one. Love is never boastful, nor conceited, nor rude; never selfish nor quick to take offense. Love keeps no score of wrongs; does not gloat over other men's sins; but delights in the truth. There is nothing love cannot face; there is no limit to its faith, its hope and endurance " (I Cor 13:4-7).

Now that we have explained the true nature of love, we are in a position to reply to the question raised in this chapter: How can we actually experience grace in the practice of love?

As we said a while ago, we can but refer the reader to his own experience approaching in kind what we are speaking of here. Experience cannot be shared with others as easily as, for instance, insights and ideas. And this may be owing to the climate of our civilization. To grasp another man's ideas, we have to start from our own experience and from the knowledge stored up by society. In a civilization like ours, schooling and training are mainly based on the transmission of ideas of a rather abstract nature; we all possess a common fund of established truths, acting as foundation and starting point for the transmission and spread of new insights.

Purely individual experiences cannot be transmitted like abstract ideas. Symbolic language, whether it be plastic arts or music or poetry, is better adapted to express and, therefore, to communicate what is most personal. Experience, though, must always preserve the strictly personal aspect which, as such, is incommunicable. And so, if we want to understand one another, we have to resort to analogous experiences. To someone who has never lived in the mountains I cannot possibly convey what it means to watch and admire an ever-varying play of light and seasons in the mountains. Nor can I myself begin to understand musical masterpieces, like the "Passion According to St. John" by J. S. Bach, the "Deutsche Requiem" of J. Brahms, "The Messiah" of J. F. Handel, unless I have listened to them often, know them almost by heart and have soaked myself with them.

All this applies *a fortiori* in the matter of spiritual experience. We are forced to resort to images and comparisons in order to help another man discover in his own interior something analogous. That is the reason why we dwelt at length on love authentically given to us in grace. A love which is not genuine cannot yield the slightest experience of what is the operation of the Spirit; the Spirit is absent. We are apt to believe that we are led by the Spirit, when in fact we are the victims of personal prejudices, opinions and fancies, falsely mistaken for inspirations of the Holy Ghost.

We have already mentioned that one of the characteristic marks of spiritual consolation is *growth in generosity* toward the neighbor. For then, we stop folding-in upon ourselves; we are rather impelled toward the others. Our desires, henceforth, are to make them happy, to see them as happy as we are.

We experience then something of the stream of life that comes down to us from the Father and, in the Son through the power of the Spirit, flows on to the neighbor. From where comes a deep peace and joy, a plenitude, a liberality, a discovery of beauty and goodness unsuspected formerly. The stream of life carries us effortlessly toward the others, toward creation as a whole: nature, animals, mountains; even the light and the clouds partake of the new glory that suddenly transfigures all things; they all share in the hidden glow newly perceived in things and men. Such an experience can also be described as the awareness of a fundamental bond of brotherhood which links us all together and makes us live for one another.

Something further arises from this experience: the open-mind-edness, the *parresia* of which we spoke before. As St. Paul writes: " There is nothing that love cannot face; there is no limit to its faith, its hope and its endurance " (I Cor 13:7). And this is not foolish naiveness, nor silly ignorance of the world. The simplicity of " pious folk " jars us. Enlightened people know quite well how things are, and yet they believe, hope and endure all things, because they dare undertake all things and feel equal to them. No question here of violence, display of muscular energy, grim fanaticism, though such feelings may at times come to the fore. It remains that the awareness of competence grows out of God's power which does not lose its might in small matters. " Divine folly is wiser than the wisdom of men, and divine weakness stronger than men's strength " (I Cor 1:25).

Often in this chapter we have had to deal with the ineffable. The words we used could call up associations deforming our meaning. Other words that have kept the purity of their original sense suggest far less than what we want to express. This is a clear indication that our spiritual experiences reach planes both deeper and higher than daily experience for which current language is the apt medium.

Let us not think that the term " experience " refers only to feelings that flit by and fade as fast as they show up. The authenticity of the experience we speak of here may be gauged from its draught in human existence. Basically, it is not feeling; it is of the nature of a life which it is destined to foster; and when it achieves precisely that, we may take it for granted that it is a genuine experience coming from God. But so long as it does not urge us to action, it stays on the level of mere sentiment.

In this domain especially, we should look for confirmation in lives of the saints, the men and the women who allowed the Holy Ghost to work in their hearts unhindered and powerfully. Where did they draw their daring from? their spirit of enterprise, but above all that astonishing patience which could face all things, believe and hope and endure all things? (Cf. I Cor 13:7).

St. Paul provides the answer: " God's love has flooded our inmost hearts through the Spirit He has given us " (Rom 5:5).

" With this in mind, then, I kneel in prayer before the Father, from whom every family in heaven and on earth takes its name, that out of the treasures of His glory He may grant you strength and power through His Spirit *in your inner being,* that through faith Christ may dwell in your hearts *in love.* With deep roots and firm foundations, may you be strong to grasp, with all God's people, what is the breadth and length and height and depth of the love of Christ, and to know it, though it is *beyond*

knowledge. So may you attain to fullness of being, the fullness
of God Himself " (Eph 3:14-19).

Life and death

By way of conclusion, we propose a final description of the
experience of grace. Grace is night and day, darkness and light,
pain and joy, disquiet and peace, all at the same time. Grace
is death and life.

However, before we enter into this subject more deeply, we
want to recall to mind the teaching of the Church on the effects
of grace. By infusing into our souls His living and re-creating
grace, God *heals* and *elevates* our human activity. He heals by
mitigating in us the consequences of sin, both original and
personal sins, extinguishing them little by little. How this is
done is not hard to understand. For sin can always be traced
back to some kind or other of egotism, self-satisfaction or pride.
Against the latter, grace is power to build up a self-forgetting
love. As the newly given love grows in strength, self-centered
love loses its motive power.

Grace does more: it " elevates. " Through grace we share in
the love of the Son for the Father by the power of the Holy
Ghost. No question here of man merely surrendering himself in
love, but of man sharing marvelously in the eternal and total
surrender of the Son to the Father. *We are " sons " in and with
the Son.* For a full realization of this, grace has to be understood
for what it is in its actuality: a participation of the divine life,
something divine, or, in technical terms, something supernatural.

The " healing " and " elevating " process through grace cannot
possibly be carried on in our person in its concrete setting without
starting up simultaneously a strong countercurrent, a resistance.
We, men, are not easily persuaded to give up ourselves; we behave like the drowning man who, dazed and paralyzed by fear,
does not dare to jump off the sinking wreck. Our speculation,
though, should take care not to turn the mystery of grace into
a mere interplay of psychological reactions. Nevertheless, we
admit that since grace sets up a tension in our soul, our ordinary
psychological experience can give us an image, a vague reflection
of what takes place in our inmost hearts from the moment it
intends, under the influence of grace, to yield to grace; or as
Ruysbroeck puts it pithily: " through God to God. "

The surrender grace wants to lead us to is nothing short of a
total surrender to God, sealed with the absoluteness of Christ
Himself; for it is that which He seeks to effect in us through His
Spirit. Face to face with the uncompromising glory of God's

majesty, our mediocrity, our diplomacy and endless capacity for striking a mean between " God and mammon, " lose countenance. Man senses that his " self " is being threatened at the roots, right at the center of his painfully gained petty human sureties. His " self, " the " self " of this world, had organized all things neatly and comfortably around its own interest, and had found delight in this achievement; and now, that very " self, " with its well-known lies and daily dreams, must die. In the final decisive choice between God and ourselves, we have to jettison everything. We are like the diver before the plunge. He has to dare to leap into the menacing ocean of God's all-exacting love. Life appeared to him so safe and reliable in its puppet-show of narrow-minded personal security. And now, before him, there opens a world of unknown breadth, extent and depth in which there appears no end to hardship, struggle and death to self. The God of love discovers Himself to be also a God of awe, of consuming fire and all-devouring holiness. In the face of His absolute truth, no lie can stand, no pretext or compromise, no cowardice or artful dodge. In sheer truth, grace is a smarting death, an agonizing dying. The death of the body affords but a pale image of it.

The saints, for whom grace and love of God were matters of extreme importance, have told us of the " dark nights, " in language which may leave us skeptical, perhaps even suspicious of hysterical neurasthenic delusions. Their witnessing, however, is too strong, too unanimous for us to shake it off with a superior shrug of the shoulders. Besides, it is a well-established mystical doctrine to explain in this way the passive purifications undergone by a soul who, under the guidance of God's grace, passes from acquired to infused contemplation. When infused contemplation takes over, the soul is no longer steering by her own compass; the Holy Ghost is henceforth at the helm of the ship and sets the course to the port of higher calling. Riddance of self, or better, decentralizing from self to God alone, causes such a sundering right down to the lower psychic regions, that the mystics have found no expression better suited to describe their experience than an exceedingly bitter death, a " dark night " for both the senses and the spirit.

We, who form the undistinguished general run of Christians, rarely reach far enough to attain to, and to go through such an interior death struggle. To most of the faithful, this deep spiritual agony occurs, perhaps, around the time of the death of the body, or otherwise in purgatory. A dying man, realizing that he is being robbed of all the earthly values he could till that moment rely upon—such as health, money, power, honor—gets at long last a chance to throw himself into the arms of God, and to risk the leap into love. Without this leap of surrender away from self and into charity, no one is safe to appear before God. That might be called the " sacrament " of our death.

The sense of losing self, with its inner severance, goes always hand in hand with an incomparable joy and delight. The self is lost yet found again on a superior level. Just at the moment when we feel utterly alone in the darkness of the night, there dawns the morning. Grace is both death and life, suffering and joy, disquiet and peace. Grace bears out in a unique way what Our Lord Himself underwent on the cross, and what He foretold in the metaphor: " The hour has come for the Son of man to be glorified. In truth, in very truth I tell you, a grain of wheat remains a solidary grain unless it falls into the ground and dies; but if it dies, it bears a rich harvest. The man who loves himself is lost, but he who hates himself in this world will be kept safe for eternal life " (Jn 12:23-26).

Both experiences, of disquiet and peace, remain inseparable from each other all through life on earth. One of these prevails at one moment; at another moment, the other. At times, one of them may almost completely eliminate the other. A human existence, in which grace lives and rules, bathes in deep peace, in spite of the bustle of work, in spite of hardship and sickness, and even sometimes in spite of " *angst* " of life. Peace forms the fundamental tone of life and may be compared with the reposeful, soothing " *basso continuo* " that lends cohesion and restfulness to Bach's most intricate fugues.

To end this section, let us examine the case of a man unfamiliar with religious language, still less familiar with the pious platitudes which often make the conversations of the priest and pious lay-folk so vapid and unconvincing. For there exists a clerical " unctuousness " that often mars the allocutions and writings of bishops and other religious authorities, gets under our skin and, alas, has nothing to do with the experience of grace.

M. Khoriakoff is a Marxist, brought up in atheism. He has no knowledge of pre-communistic days in Russia. We have told in another place how he sensed for the first time the presence of God during the battle for Moscow in 1941.

We are now back on Sunday, May 21, 1944. The Russian armies have driven the Germans back beyond the Berezina. Khoriakoff is now a war correspondent with the air force, and a captain. Since 1941 he has thought much over religion and God. He has begun to pray quietly by himself.

On that fateful May 21st, he stands in the pressbureau, looking absentmindedly at a Moscow message ticked off on the telex, that reads: " Sergios, the patriarch of Moscow and of all Russia is dead. "

He has never met the patriarch. In the past he had admired a portrait of him painted by Arseniev. His sister, an atheist like himself, had gone, in the beginning of the war, to listen to one of the patriarch's sermons, and had spoken about it. A little later, a moujik had given him a soiled, well-thumbed letter with the text of a prayer composed by the patriarch at the outbreak of the war. He had recited it every day. The sudden death of a man he had never seen, but had slowly come to regard as the living symbol of his hunger for God, was the last impact he needed to be bowled over by grace.

He was able to describe so realistically this experience of his because he had no ready-made *shablonen* at his command. He did not know of any. All he could do was to describe what he felt. " What is *this* to me? Why must I learn of this in Wolynia? Who orders me to do that? Where does it drive me to? There I stood, next to the printing machine, speechless, holding a freshly printed newspaper in my hand. The sudden realization of the immense role Sergios had played in my life threw a burst of light on my consciousness and pierced me to the heart *like a sharp pain*. The pain did not abate, but blent with another awareness, more intense still and unalloyed, the feeling of a fulfillment, a somersault overwhelming me *with joy*. " [58]

He goes out, enters a church and there asks the priest to conduct, after Sunday Mass, a religious service in memory of the deceased patriarch. He assists at the service in his officer's uniform, and leaves the church in the sight of all present, well aware that a public action performed by one who is reckoned among the elite of the Soviet army must unavoidably entail costly consequences. And so it happened to be the case with him.

Wolynia is situated close to the frontier between Poland and Russia. The church belonged to the Eastern rite. As he left, he received like all the other faithful a small piece of bread, the *prosforka*, distributed at the door of the church.

" Frankly, I did not know what to do with it. ' Make the sign of the cross and eat it, ' the sacristan told me. I broke the *prosforka* in two halves and leisurely ate it in the porch of the church. That done, I went to a meadow full of flowers. I felt that my life lay *broken* in two parts, just as one snaps a stick in two on one's knee. " [59]

We have quoted this unadorned tale of a conversion as a fitting ending to this chapter. It shows us plainly how the " leap " of faith—which we designated by the name of fundamental option— is embodied in a concrete individual action in life. The trifling action assumes at times the value of a symbol; and so it was in the eating of the *prosforka* in the porch of the church in view of the bystanders. We notice also how the choice of life, under

[58] *Je me mets hors la loi*, p. 40.
[59] *Ibid.*, p. 41.

the influence of grace, provoked in him an inner pain and, much deeper still, an ineffable joy: life and death mixed together.

Grace and the body

An old student and friend of mine in England reproached me for not mentioning a word in my first book on grace about the significance of grace for the body.

The reproach is deserved if we refuse to see man as a more or less awkward amalgam of the spiritual and the corporeal. In grace, *the whole man* is renewed by God's presence. The idea of the divine presence we borrowed from the Bible. Paul speaks of the body as a temple. " He who links himself with Christ is one with Him. Shun fornication. Every other sin that a man can commit is outside the body; but the fornicator sins against his own body. Do you not know that your body is the shrine of the indwelling Holy Spirit, and the Spirit is God's gift to you? You do not belong to yourselves; you were bought at a price [allusion to a slave sold on the market]. *Then honor God in your body* " (I Cor 6:17-20).

We have pointed out that Hebrew thought, therefore, biblical thought in both the Old and the New Testaments, does not know of the distinction between body and soul. At any rate, the distinction is rarely mentioned. The Semite, though, recognizes within the unity of the living man different depth-levels and designates them in concrete terms. " Man " is synonymous with his " face, " his " name, " his " loins, " above all his " heart, " the inmost core of his person. The " bowels, " too, and the " liver " indicate sources of human activity emerging above the purely animal. The best known description of man—and sometimes of all and any living being—is " flesh ": man in his creaturely weakness and limitations and, especially in Paul, in his sinfulness. Opposed to it, is the " spirit ": the same man insofar as he is filled with the power of God.

Neither did the Semite realize clearly the distinction so familiar to the mystics: spirit, soul and body. Scripture does not often allude to it. This explains why the Semite could not form an idea of either death or resurrection without reference to the body.

Ancient Hebrew thought did not move in the field of speculative philosophy; it prefered symbolism. For all that, the Hebrews were convinced that God never operates in man without producing some effect on, or transformation of the body. In our opinion, this fundamental insight of theirs is exact.

The theology of the first centuries, too, was aware of that

fact, even in circles removed from the Jewish sphere of thought. The Greek Fathers describe grace in terms of bodily attributes. For instance, grace is " immortality, " " incorruptibility "; two notions devoid of meaning apart from a real reference to the body. According to the Byzantine tradition of Gregorius Palamas, the light of Thabor will, through grace, permeate the whole body like a divine " energy "; a dogmatic idea that passed into the hard and fast rules to be observed in the painting of holy icons.

For several centuries in the West, Extreme Unction was given to all the sick and not only to the dying. It is clear from the Epistle of St. James, and from the ritual prayers of the liturgy, that the sacrament not only confers grace and forgiveness of sins, but is beneficial to the body: " Prayer offered in faith will restore the sick man, and the Lord will give him relief " (James 5:15). That is why it is the sick limbs that are anointed by the priest.

Under the influence of a certain Platonism and of a debased version of Aristotelian thought, we today draw a neat distinction between soul and body; with the result that ancient Christian practices and insights have become unintelligible to us. Small children and lay-people are taught that grace sanctifies the soul and has little to do with the body. Or at any rate, this point receives but scant attention. As to the Christians of the Reformation: they did not borrow our doctrine of grace; yet, their way of tackling the problem suffers from an outlook inherited from the theology of the Middle Ages. And that outlook colors their views so much that, in spite of a remarkable familiarity with biblical thought, they have not yet raised the theological question which we are considering here. At least, we know of no author who deals with the question explicitly.

The view, adopting a sharp distinction between body and soul, is not entirely false. For, there are purely natural forces that act upon the body and not upon the soul. Good health and bodily forms of beauty cannot be relied upon as sure signs of the state of grace. Our body belongs to this world and, from the first day of its coming into existence, is caught up in the interplay of causes and effects: heredity, germs of sickness, biological and chemical factors, physical and human climates surrounding us.

Nevertheless, on this topic, modern medicine and psychology have drawn ahead of us. They start from the body; they show that intra-world influences and forces do not leave the " soul " untouched. From the first hours of its life, an infant has greater need of affection than of food. Some sicknesses, like cancer and T. B., can be conquered or slowed down by optimism and zest for life.

On these grounds, grace must needs enter into the sphere of our psychological activity and, further still, into the region of our bodily substance. It remains, however, that we are unable sharply to mark off the effects of grace from other influences; we cannot clearly determine—on an experimental basis—what grace precisely does or does not do. This inability of ours in this domain has been touched upon in the chapter on *Psychology and Grace.*

One of my former professors of philosophy dropped the remark one day: "Gentleman, at forty years of age, a man is responsible for his face." Those words were greeted with general hilarity, all the more because the speaker's face had not been molded by Phidias. The remark, and the merriment of the audience, were basically justified. It is true that, as a rule, grown-ups wear the faces their past entitled them to. But as other influences play their part—in the case of the professor, a marked baldness— sweeping statements can be rather embarrassing at times.

It is sure that the renovating power of grace thrusts its rays in every part of a man's body, and shines in face and eyes. The experience of each one of us bears this out. Who, among us, has not met a person, a true man of God, radiating in his countenance the profound peace reigning in his heart?

The question might be asked: Does a man, who thoroughly lives his grace, enjoy better health? We are inclined to think so, were it only on the ground that trust in God immunizes him against any disquiet that can threaten health and psychic poise. In point of fact, though, grace is no remedy against infectious diseases or against sclerosis. For all that, the first thing a doctor or a psychiatrist seeks to produce in their patients is peace of mind, confidence. What then must be the all-surpassing peace that comes from God? In the first part of this book, we cited the example of St. Teresa of Avila, as seen by Walter Nigg, the well-known Protestant Church historian. Many saints made a profound impression by their mere physical presence. They literally radiated God.

But, to take our inquiry a step further still, let us begin by ridding ourselves of the idea which we have of death and resurrection, of the generally accepted notions that have sprung up from the concept of a dual human nature we criticized a moment ago. When we conceive of body and soul as two elements loosely joined together, death is nothing more than the soul being freed from the "earthly bonds." The body stays behind and perishes. Later on, on the day of the resurrection, soul and body are to be re-united, though in a "spiritual" manner. Between the moment of our death and the day of the resurrection, our soul hovers about, no one knows in what condition.

The least that need be said of such a concept is that it lacks good logic. For, if the concept is true, the disembodied state of the soul, occurring between death and resurrection, ought to be the "noblest" state of human life. The resurrection has to tie us once again to the body. It serves little purpose to say that the soul will have been " spiritualized. " Pushed to its logical conclusion, this concept implies a negation of our true corporeity; in other words, the body is not so essential to man.

Some theologians would have us believe that this concept binds us in faith, in virtue of the definition of the ecumenical Council of Vienne, in 1312 (Denzinger n. 481). They assert too much. An inquiry into the history of this ecumenical decree shows that the Coucil does not impose as an article of faith the rather primitive description of man's condition, of his death and resurrection, set down by some theologians. The Council does, indeed, propose as " belonging to the faith " the Aristotelian teaching of the soul as " form of the body ": " Whoever teaches in future, defends and dares obstinately to hold the doctrine that the rational or intellectual soul is not by itself and essentially the form of the human body, must be considered as a heretic " (Denz. n. 481).

The conciliar declaration calls for some interpretation.

Theologians who take the trouble of keeping in touch with the historical studies concerning the meaning of the Latin terminology used by the Church during the Middle Ages, up to and inclusive of Trent, are aware that the terms " faith " and " heretic " had a broader connotation than now. Today, " faith " and " dogma " designate a truth directly revealed by God; no man can deny such a revealed truth without lapsing into heresy in the strict sense of the word. But no one will accept the idea that the Church has ever declared a philosophical system to be a dogma. Consequently, we have to interpret the definition of Vienne as a corrective of the teaching of Petrus Olivi, O.F.M., from the point of view of what was then the *unanimous by* accepted doctrine in the Church. To this doctrine, Olivi submitted with exemplary willingness.

Modern biblical theology and contemporary philosophy have come forward with a number of new queries demanding appropriately shaded answers. I do not at all suggest that adequate and mature answers are to hand now, ready to meet all questions. All we can do is to hold out some prospects. [60]

[60] May be consulted: Karl Rahner, S.J., " Auferstehung des Fleisches, " *Schriften zur Theologie* (Einsiedeln; Benziger, 1960, II. pp. 211-225, translated into English by Karl H. Kruger, in *Theological Investigations, The Resurrection of the Flesh* (Baltimore: Helicon; London: Darton, 1963), II, pp. 203-216. Also: *Zur Theologie des Totes (Quaestiones Disputatae,* Band 2; Freiburg: Herder, 1958); English translation: *On Theology of Death* (Freiburg: Herder; Edinburgh, London: Nelson, 1961). May be consulted also R. Troisfontaines, S.J., *Je ne meurs pas* (Paris: Editions Universitaires, 1960), translated by Francis E. Albert, *I Do Not Die* (New York: Desclée, 1963).

We note first that the notion of " body, " which until now we have been consistently using for convenience sake, is in the process of being reconsidered. Bluntly put: Is our body confined to the limits of our skin? Unquestionably, the skin encloses a clearly delineated biological and organic unit. Parapsychology, however, suggests that this is by no means so evident on the psychological level. Even though it be taken as a biological unit, the body cannot be conceived of as separate from the surrounding cosmos. The personal core, which commands our corporeity and actualizes itself by means of that corporeity, remains still engaged in the cosmos as a whole. What is more real for a man: that he possesses a head, two legs and arms, and whatever else goes together with them, or that, as human person, he actualizes himself within the cosmos and thus belongs to the cosmos? Outside of the cosmos, he is no longer a man! He pertains to the cosmos and, at the same time, transcends it. He is from within motioned toward a complete possession of self, toward a complete and perfect " presence-to-self " of the spirit. That much has been made sure of by philosophy. And theology explains further that the " presence-to-self " issues, through grace, in a " presence-to-God. "

A man's body, distinctly perceptible in space, is thus really his own, though not in a manner that absolutely excludes the others. How else could we have been created by God as a unity, renewed by grace as the society of God's children in the Son? It is time that we break with the atomizing view of our existence, which looks upon men as incapsulated monads, held together by God with external bonds after the fashion of figures, in a puppet-show controlled by the wires in the hand of the manipulator. The body is indeed each man's own, yet belongs to the cosmos outside of which it can neither exist nor be conceived of as existential actuality. The *visible* body forms the bridge between the person and the cosmos.

It is high time we learn to *realize* that our actual existence ramifies at greater depths than what is *perceptible* to the eye.

" There are more things in heaven and earth, Horatio,
Than are dreamt of in your philosophy, "
said Hamlet to his friend.

Of death we may say that it puts an end to our *present* manner of existing and behaving inside the cosmos. Our present manner of existing is cut short when and because the bond with our corporeity, visible in our concrete body, is snapped.

But then, at death, do we sever all living and existential connection with the cosmos? We are inclined to think that we do not. If we did, we would repudiate our human nature. Unfortunately, we do not know how to translate this relationship in terms of life. After death, we shall know it from experience.

Seen in this light, the resurrection is a partaking in the relationship with the cosmos which Christ achieved by His death. No dogma of the Church prevents us from thinking that there is a kind of resurrection awaiting us soon after the death of the body. When the Church, in 1950, defined as an article of faith that Mary had been taken up, body and soul, into heaven, she did not say that it was Mary's exclusive privilege. Mary's privilege rather consists in this: that, because of her unique personal role in the Redemption, both as Mother of God and model of divinization, her resurrection testifies to the reality of the grace of us all. Whether we know or do not know that Mary has been taken up with her body into heaven, is dogmatically of no great significance. What is of great importance to us, dogmatically speaking, is that in virtue of her singular election, she has become the visible and perfect guarantee of our own resurrection. She has been exalted as a token before all nations; in her we recognize our own personal grace and divinization.

In the words of Fr. H. Schillebeeckx, O.P., Mary is the " most perfectly redeemed " among the members of the human family, [61] and, therefore, the living sign, the shining symbol and, at the same time, the visible guarantee of our own resurrection. It goes without saying that Christ's resurrection is the highest, even the sole guarantee of our resurrection. But Christ gave to the Church the resurrection of His Mother as a reflection of His own, as a tangible proof that His resurrection has been conferred already on *men*; that His resurrection does not belong to Him as God-man, but has been won by Him *for us all*. Mary is to be regarded as the New Eve standing before the New Adam. Her glory is not founded on any perfection of her own, independent of divine grace. She is a human being like us all; as she rose, so shall we one day. She represents in her person the visibility of the grace attested to in her and given to us, too. She is the model faithful and thus also the model of man raised from the dead by sheer divine benevolence. Christ rose through the power of the Father in the Spirit, and also through His own divine power. The resurrection belongs to Christ by right; it is the revelation of His sovereignty over the cosmos. But in Mary, resurrection is a grace, and sign of our grace.

After these explanations, we realize that nothing prevents us from admitting that somehow our resurrection begins after our personal death. The Last Judgment simply means that mankind shall appear before God's majesty, not as individuals casually called together, but as one whole, whose history

---

[61] H. Schillebeeckx, O.P., *Maria, Christus' mooiste wonderschepping* (Antwerp: Apostolaat van den Rozenkrans, 1954).

is due for judgment by God. Scripture pictures this ultimate scene in apocalyptic metaphors. At the sound of the angels trumpet, the dead will awaken and leave their tombs. But, such language is figurative, inviting us to seek for its underlying meaning. Very little thought is necessary to convince us that such imagery, if taken at its face value, is unintelligible.

If we grant—and grant we must—that our resurrection is to be a partaking in the new sovereignty over the cosmos, both from within and from outside, which Christ as Mediator and Redeemer has merited first for Himself and then for us, a dominion which He, as God, exercises in union with the Father and the Spirit, then it becomes clear how grace prepares us already on earth for this resurrection. The early Fathers of the Church spoke of grace as seed of immortality and incorruptibility conferred on us by the Eucharist. The chalice of Christ's blood, says St. Ignatius of Antioch, gives us " the medicine to restore immortality. " Sentences like these have, in the course of time, grown obscure to most Christians; the tendency is to see in them poetic licence. But, if our interpretation is accepted, they recover their rich significance. We mean: if grace is what we say it is, it follows that our person, sharing in the life of Christ and of the Spirit, acquires a new relationship to the cosmos *from now on,* and thus possesses the *seed* of immortality.

Existentially, then, grace does not withdraw us from this world neither in this life, nor at death, nor at the resurrection. On the contrary, grace strengthens and enhances the bonds with the cosmos in which God willed us to have our being, and apart from which He never conceived us. Through grace, we become more thoroughly, more profoundly men, insofar as our personal core has to actualize itself by sharing in the Kingship of Christ. Simultaneously, with Christ we transcend this present world. We are not buried in it; we do not perish with it; we do not fall apart on the current of the centrifugal forces concealed in sin; and all this because in Christ and His Spirit we already partake in this world of His Kingship.

From now on, the " image of God " in us is restored. According to the exegetes, the old texts of Genesis, which say that man is created " in the image and likeness of God " (Gen 1:26-27), refer principally to man's lordship over the cosmos. It is man who gives animals their names (Gen 2:19-20), an Eastern way of expressing the idea that man assigns to the animals their significance and place in the cosmos.

The glory of man is extolled in the eighth Psalm. It is noteworthy that the Psalm opens and closes with a hymn of praise to the glory of God, Yahweh, of whom man is a reflection in this world, " the image and likeness. "

" O Lord, Our Master,
How the majesty of Thy name fills the earth!
Thy greatness is high above heaven itself.
I look up at those heavens of Thine, the work of Thy hands,
The moon and the stars which Thou hast set in their places.
What is man that Thou shouldst remember him?
What is Adam's breed that it should claim Thy care?
Thou hast placed him a little below the Godhead,
Crowned him with glory and honor,
And bidden him to rule over the works of Thy hands.
Thou hast put them all under his dominion,
The sheep, the cattle,
And the wild beasts besides;
The birds in the sky and the fish in the sea,
All that travels by the sea's paths.
O Lord, our Master,
How the majesty of Thy name fills all the earth " (Psalm 8:1-
   10).

The early Christians saw quite correctly that to die is to
" fall asleep. " Scripture's way of speaking agrees with this
view. Our death is, indeed, a " falling asleep, " a goodbye
to the manner of existing we are so familiar with. Yet, to die
means also to rise to a new life which, in the event, does not
snatch us away from our human destiny, nor from the cosmos
our home. United with Christ, we shall then recognize, from the
outside, so to say, the cosmos as it issues from God's eternally
creating hand. In and through grace, we share in Christ's
Kingship, as the early Christians understood and expressed it by
the word " Lord. " It is by His resurrection that Christ became
the Lord (Phil 2:6-11). The nascent Church summed up her
confession of faith in the formula " Jesus is Lord " (Rom 10:9),
a confession which we can neither profess nor believe " except
under the influence of the Spirit " (I Cor 12:3). By grace, we
share in the Lordship of Christ. In grace, we posses the seed
of that Lordship *already in this life,* the seed of immortality
and of incorruptibility. " As we have worn the likeness of man
made of dust, so shall we wear the likeness of the heavenly
man " (I Cor 15:49). " Thus we shall always be *with* the lord.
Console one another, then, with these words " (I Thes 4:17-18).

Diverse and complex, and yet so much one

We shall conclude this part of our book with a last comparison.
   We may liken man to a mountain lake. Out of the depths
of massive rock formations, powerful streams of crystalline water

well up to the surface. The clear and mighty waters spread out over the entire face of the lake in broad, smooth currents. Other factors, too, enter into play: the nature and structure of the encircling rock formations, the rhythm of the seasons, the sun and the nights, the wind and the rain, the fauna and flora. The later could not maintain their existence in the peaceful waters without the hidden well-spring which, from within, feeds, cleans and makes the lake what it is. It is the source which feeds the mighty currents moving quietly through the waters, determines the luminosity and purity of the water under the play of light and clouds.

Man is a deep lake. God placed him in the concrete situation which, for the most part, is not of man's choosing: family, nation, race, culture, hidden heredity and the more superficial gains from education and individual experience. But all this cannot ripen into a noble human existence, into a life of a child of God, unless man possesses, in the depth of his heart, " streams of living water, always welling up for eternal life " (Jn 7:38; 4:14), the secret dynamism, the creative force promoting life and self-surrender. God is love. Man, made in the image and likeness of God, transformed into Christ, the effulgence of the Father, is primarily love, reflecting that first love which Dante speaks of in his great poem on heaven: " *Amor che muove il sole e l'altre stelle* "—" love which moves sun and stars. "

PART II

What may we expect from grace?

The question sounds businesslike, rather cheering perhaps. We need to be cautions. Where God is involved, the question should not be: What can we get? but: What does God expect from us? The correction is not out of place, today especially when we witness a certain "humanizing" tendency in religious apologetics. Besides, who in his senses dares ask from the one he loves: What can I get from you? A true lover seeks the good of the beloved, not his own gain.

Grace is love; it is love for God. Consequently, the question: What may we expect from grace? is bound to raise objections; nonetheless, we formulate it; *after all we have said so far*, it has a real, if secondary sense. *Taking into account all that precedes*, we are justified in examining the contribution of Revelation and theological thought to the general study of man. More precisely, perhaps, we may ask: What does grace change in man? The reply is: Nothing and everything. This final part undertakes to give nuance to such a bold answer.

Grace changes nothing

To begin with, we say that grace adds nothing to man's earthly nature and situation. Can we maintain this contention, and to what extent?

We said "nothing," for grace affects *directly and immediately* only the spiritual core of our person; it affects the rest insofar as it follows up the spiritual lines of force which emanate from that core and spread through the whole of our activity. Actual grace (as, for instance, in connection with good example, an inspiring book, etc.) opens the mind to divine things and awakens in the will a spiritual taste for them. But all the rest *remains what it was*.

There remains the world with its laws and its inevitable sequences of cause and effect. Storms and spring tides shatter the dikes on the coast, though baptized men and women are residing there. Cloudbursts cause rivers to break through their banks. Earthquakes lay waste whole cities. Historical laws continue to rule the destiny of nations, races and societies. Political mistakes must provoke reaction. Catholic states, parties or banks fare no better than others. It matters not a whit whether I am in a state of grace or not when my automobile hits a tree; the consequences are disastrous for the automobile, the tree and possibly the driver.

There remains also my body with its health, its illnesses, weaknesses and habits—and, unfortunately, its unmannerly tricks increasing with age. Grace has nothing in common with antibiotics. Each winter I shall run up my usual score of colds. The surgeon who examines my case does not need to inquire whether I am in a state of grace; he may safely diagnose my condition and be satisfied that a resection of the stomach is necessary.

There remains further my psyche with its inborn or acquired urges, complexes and disturbances. Grace has nothing to do with leptosomes; it will not change my primary characteristics into secondary ones. The sacraments as such will cure neither neurasthenia nor schizophrenia; they leave a free hand to the psychiatrist, whether he advocates the method of Freud, Jung, Adler or the behaviorists.

There remain, too, my reasoning faculties and the peculiar nature of my will power, at least in their psychological and functional characteristics. Grace does not improve my memory or sharpen my wits or strengthen my volition—not directly, at any rate.

Why mention such obvious truths? Because these truths, so absurdly evident in the abstract, often lose their plainness when they affect us personally in the concrete. The time is past when professors at the Sorbonne in Paris could come out with " *Je n'ai jamais trouvé l'âme au bout de mon bistouri*" ("I have never found the soul under my scalpel") without even provoking a smile at their dreadful nonsense. But one still meets with scientists who fancy they can annex grace and the life of grace to the domain of their research, if only to deny their existence. Believing Christians, too, fail in logic when they hear of a fatal automobile accident and exclaim, "How is it possible! Such a good man!" Driving an automobile involves equal risks for all, good men or monsters.

Each science enjoys its own peculiar method. That method is conditioned by the specialized object of the science. We now add that it is of the utmost importance to remember that the specialized objects are not affected by grace either in their inner structure or in their functional relations. Consequently, the sciences remain undisturbed by the theology of grace as long as they keep to the investigation and ascertaining of fixed laws and relations among the *same specific phenomena*. One exception might be made here: philosophy takes up a privileged place as the "handmaiden" of theology—to use a metaphor, dear to the Middle Ages, for something that is no more than a half-truth. All the other sciences, as far as they move and operate within the limits of a clearly delineated field, need not worry about the question of grace; they enjoy an inalienable freedom of research and action within the framework of their speciality. This does not mean, however, that a man of science, as a human being and particularly as a Christian, has a right to remain indifferent to the reality of grace. For instance, a specialist will owe it to his faith not to fall prey to out-and-out materialistic hypotheses; his belief in grace will serve him as an alarm. But it will never interfere with matters belonging to his domain and method. We should add the remark that a surgeon would be an unworthy Christian if, before a dangerous operation, he showed serene indifference to the state of the patient's soul. His profession may indeed demand a great deal of discretion and objectivity, but never indifference to essentials.

Redemption through the incarnation

More remains to be said. We are coming to a second conclusion, the premises of which lie in deeper truth, and which will afford us fresh light on the full salvific significance of grace. We shall not satisfy ourselves with a ready-made, pedantic distinction between the downward trend of nature and the uplifting energy of grace. We have to dwell upon some theological aspects of redemption and grace, some points of considerable speculative and practical importance.

As we saw, grace and redemption are, more than anything else, God's creative, loving way of speaking to each one of us individually in Christ and in the Church. Now, the divine word does not find us located in the rarefied regions of a stratospheric spirituality where the trifling though very real cares and responsibilities of this puny world are lost to sight. God speaks to us *in the very concrete situation which is ours*. The essential message of redemption and grace is that we must surrender ourselves to God in faith, hope and charity here and now, on this earth, in the spot to which providence has consigned us and in which He wills us to dwell provisionally. As Roman Guardini wrote, it is planned by providence that God should speak to us really through the details of a determined situation. God is present in the daily events of our lives, calling us to His love. It is precisely this divine presence which gives our personal existence its deepest significance.

In God's design, our earth is entrusted with its own commission, a positive religious function. More will be said about this later. For the present, we should know that Revelation mentions another role our earth has to play, a negative religious role: the role of " world, " in the sense frequently met with in Scripture, especially in St. John. The world in this role means the realm of wickedness, the kingdom of the evil one, the place, too, of God's patience, the historical space abandoned for a while to its own determination while the divine wrath bides its time in silence. Into that world Christ came in order to save it. And in the midst of that same world He planted His Church. Some of His followers may, in fact, belong to this world, though He Himself is " not of the world " (Jn 17:14). However, taken in the aggregate, they all have in common with and in Him an inescapable task regarding this world of sin and evil. In His sacerdotal prayer after the last supper, Christ addressed His Father: " I pray not that Thou shouldst take them out of the world, but that Thou shouldst keep them from evil. They are not of the world, as I also am not of the world. ... As Thou hast sent me into the world, I also have sent them into the world " (Jn 17:15-18).

The world, where sin and its consequences hold sway, is thus the *place* where grace comes to us, where God speaks to us of love and reconciliation, where, with the Son and through the power of the Spirit, we return to the Father in faith and charity. We do so with and in Christ *because Christ Himself has done so.* And here we meet with the deepest significance of redemption.

Redemption denotes a divine gesture, one and perfect: God's only begotten Son coming down into the world of our perdition and thence returning to the Father, not alone, but *with all those* who share His Sonship on the ground of their first election by the Father and of their own individual self-surrender in grace. "I came forth from the Father and came into the world. Again I leave the world and go to the Father" (Jn 16:28). The value of the redemption is not to be measured by the sum of sufferings and humiliations undergone by Christ on the cross; it is to be gauged by the perfect acceptance, from the hands of the Father, of the situation Jesus freely assumed in the world. His messianic appearance in the world could not but cause a formidable avalanche of hatred, jealousy and scandal. And Christ accepted it all for us, in our stead, but also to teach us by His example how to act in like manner in our respective callings. St. Paul brought out in a unique way what the essence of redemption is when he wrote his celebrated text to the Philippians, a text which is still the basic theme running through the paschal liturgy: "He humbled Himself, becoming obedient unto death, even to the death of the cross" (Phil 2:8). The cross is the culminating point, the supreme expression and therefore the highest visible symbol of Christ's obedience. Beyond dispute, the sum and substance of the redemption must be sought for in the love of the Messiah, the Son of God and the most beautiful of men, which caused Him to surrender Himself totally in humble obedience. Indeed, that was the only way to defeat sin; for sin, at bottom, is pride, rebellion and disobedience.

Christ's sanctity lay in His obedience to the Father. The grace He merited for us must consist in repeating, through life and till death, the Son's everlasting "Yes, Father," in loving obedience and surrender.

Grace in this "world"

As it was with Christ, so it is with us. Our holiness, the call of grace, lies in an ever-growing, ever more complete and humble acceptance of our life. And in this we can never be level-headed or businesslike enough. It is this life on this earth which is in question, this actual situation, here and now. The cross which we as Christians have to carry daily consists of our ailments, our failures, our discouragements, our sufferings, our weaknesses, our shame, our loneliness—all borne in humble obedience, like, with and in Christ.

Here again, but from a higher religious standpoint, we perceive that grace does not alter, remove or mitigate the consequences of sin on this earth—not directly, at least. The world will remain what it always was: the place where God is silently patient, and for us, a place of exile. Grace in this life attacks sin in its marrow of pride and disobedience. All the rest stays. The seed of sin is to be destroyed on the exact spot where sin strikes its root: in our fundamental personal option, in our deep-seated, proud rebellion against God. St. Augustine had this all-important issue of our lives in mind when he wrote, " Two societies have issued from two kinds of love:... selfish love which dared to despise even God,... love of God that is ready to trample upon self " (*De Civitate Dei,* 14:28). We are now able to grasp the sense of " self-contempt. " The self to trample on is the self inasmuch as it is in league with the world, as it takes sides with sin and evil and goes against God.

At this point in our considerations, we may mention one or another exceptional occurrence. Grace sometimes erupts palpably into our impious world when God works miracles. Looking at miracles with the eyes of simple faith, we understand that, according to the well-worn tag, " the exceptions confirm the rule. " For miracles and, to a lesser degree, special instances of heard prayer are given no meaning by God other than that of being signs of the divine presence and thus also signs of divine grace.

Of their nature, miracles are not so exceptional as we tend to believe. Let us recall that, in spite of His silence, God is ever present in the world and speaks to us of His love in the intimacy of our hearts; further, from the religious standpoint, God's mysterious providence has no other purpose than to " stand by " us in whatever situation we may have landed in. Miracles and answers to prayer stand out as highlights of God's loving presence in our history. Far above the somber, low-banked clouds of sin, God's presence shines pure and glowing; in a miracle, the divine radiance breaks through.

In other words, to the eyes of faith the world remains always open to and charged with divine power. In the event of a miracle, this becomes momentarily perceptible in a divine sign. [1]

On occasion the Father breaks His patient silence and dis-

---

[1] Cf. L. Monden, *Le miracle, signe de Salut* (Bruges: Desclée de Brouwer, 1960); Eng. translation: *Signs and Wonders* (New York: Desclée, 1966), pp. 99 à 105.

creetly drops His children the hint that He is there. Those
delicate, unobtrusive signs of consolation, fidelity and love have
the sole aim of stimulating us in the performance of our ordinary
task. No other task has been entrusted to us than that of
accepting this life just as it is, in humble, obedient love, holding
fast to the one irreplaceable mainstay, which is faith in Jesus
Christ, Who is the personal manifestation and presence of God
in this world of sin and evil. His Church will endure till the end
of time as His sanctuary, His tabernacle of the covenant, the
visible pledge of His love. The other tokens God gave to mankind in the past become intelligible and are guaranteed in the
light of God's manifesting Himself in the incarnation; all are
evidence that God is discreet, even when testing us by His
" obscurities. " Like a soft halo, they enshrine the one radiant,
tremendous event on earth: Christ's rising by His own power from
the dead and becoming the " Lord, " God in our midst. [2]

Secularization and religion

Hard upon the first edition of our book *Divine Grace and Man,*
published in 1962, there appeared a work which created quite a
stir in many quarters, in England first and later in north-western
Europe. We mean *Honest to God,* from the pen of J. A. T. Robinson, Anglican bishop of Woolwich. [3]

We shall say nothing here of the technical, sometimes pedantic,
objections raised against the book by professional theologians.
In a subsequent article, Robinson frankly pleads guilty of numerous historical and theological simplifications found in that work.
A paperback is not a " compendium " in several volumes. In
the same article, he clarifies the purpose he had in view while
writing his pastoral " intention. " [4] In the present section of our
book we shall mainly concern ourselves with some practical
questions.

As we said, Bishop Robinson did not write a dogmatic treatise. His Christology is, to put it mildly, rather weak; read
outside the context, it is unsatisfactory. He admits that the
publicity-explosion around his book, *Honest to God,* frightened
him; he had anticipated nothing of the sort. His fright has had
at least this advantage that, in later articles, he wrote more
carefully, attempting to state unambiguously what he had really

---

[2] Cf. *ibid.,* pp. 107-130.

[3] J. A. T. Robinson, *Honest to God* (London: SCM Press, 1963).

[4] *The Honest to God Debate,* edited by David L. Edwards, with a
new chapter by its author, John A. T. Robinson (London: SCM Press,
1964): Chapter IX, *The Debate continues.*

wanted to say. Robinson has no mind to break with the old faith; he is no " godless bishop " as one or other English newspaper made him out to be. He accepts the decrees of the early Ecumenical Councils of Nicaea, Ephesus and Chalcedon; but he holds that the decrees and dogmas, issued by those Councils are couched in a language and conceived from an angle of worldview completely unintelligible to modern man. Robinson does not undermine the faith: his purpose is rather to preach the faith in an idiom acceptable today. It is a preoccupation he shares in common with R. Bultmann and D. Bonhoeffer; he makes no bones about that. What has been less noticed is that in this he agrees also with John XXIII.

His intentions and writings have been misconstrued in many quarters. He owes that, perhaps, to the fact that his *Honest to God* is composed in a spirit of sporting unconcern which an Englishman affects when dealing with abstract ideas. But we think that most of the blame for the numerous misunderstandings lies with those who have read the volume as a manifesto, or as a complete considered exposition of the Christian faith, or as the definite final answer to all queries, rather than as an invitation to discussions—the author's real intent.

For our part, we shall dwell preferably on what he wrote and added as Chapter IX in his *The Honest to God Debate,* " to mark out afresh the area in which ... the discussions could with profit move forward. " [5]

Robinson does not write for the " Church people. " They are on their home ground in the language and " the presuppositions of the accepted categories. " They experience no difficulty in thinking out their Christian faith in the " Church perspective. " Let them do so by all means; it is their right. He has nothing to tell them.

He feels for the thousands of people to whom both the language and the " accepted categories " are as strange as is to us any medieval author. Modern man's spontaneous thought and sentiment, he says, are marked with *secularization*. What does Robinson mean? It is here that he has been most frequently misunderstood.

To begin with: modern man is attracted by science and technical progress. In former days, the theologian, the philosopher, and even the artist had some influence on the course of world events; today, the scientist and the technician hold sway and are looked up to. One of the signs of this shift of interest is that in the educational domain the classics are gradually yielding ground to the sciences.

Now, it is a basic axiom in the sciences that the world has a

[5] *The Honest to God Debate*, p. 232.

meaning. This meaning can be discovered *within this world* on condition that we look for it with assiduous diligence. The use of scientific methods of work create little by little a diffused mentality, a sort of intellectual climate; it develops in the mind definite hard and fast habits of thought. Not unnaturally, modern man has come to disapprove of any attempt to explain the things of this earth by hidden causes that seem to him to be inserted into the world *from the outside*. All such attempts run dead counter to his sense of intellectual honesty. He cannot help looking upon any sort of extrinsicalness as an instance of intellectual and moral convenience, sloth, dishonesty. He feels that no problem can be truly attacked by men who do not have both feet firmly planted on this earth.

Robinson sees a second reason for this outlook in psychoanalysis, a branch of learning closely allied with modern science, widely spread and popularized in Anglo-Saxon countries. Psychoanalysis, as a scientific method, seeks to account for human conduct, and eventually to cure it, by bringing to light the unconscious and subconscious mechanisms which each man builds up for himself from his earliest hours. Here, too, attention goes to what happens *inside* man, to what is manifested in his active attitude or aversion to the surrounding world. As a scientific technique, psychoanalysis refuses, of course, to admit that man is a psychological entity subject to influences *external* to this world.

And there is a third reason: a school of philosophy typically English and not widely known on the continent. It forms a tradition endemic in the British Isles and reaching back to the Christian Middle Ages. This philosophy is called "logical analysis." It has developed a subtle logic, built on mathematical lines; it claims to offer a philosophy of reality as well. The great axiom of this philosophy is that no concept may be conceded a positive mental content unless it can be traced back to *a concrete experience*.

In the light of these reasons, it is easy to understand why Robinson wants to build his conception of God and his theological vision of Christ on experiential grounds of love. Let us not imagine anything romantic connected with this; for it is just a typical English attitude reinforced by the influence of the philosophy of logical analysis. A "continental mind" desirous of forming to himself an idea of the peculiar language of such people, should sample their mentality at close quarters. Some years ago, we were present at a Roman Catholic Congress of English laymen gathered in France for an exchange of views with French and Belgian theologians. Among those laymen, there were several disciples of the Austrian L. Wittgenstein, founder of the Oxford school of philosophy. No one who has not taken part in such gatherings, or is without firsthand experience, can have an inkling of the difficulty for a "continental" to follow those English philosophers—and vice-versa; and this in spite of a religious persuasion shared in common. One realizes on such occasions how profoundly some intellectual methods and schools of thought affect the mentality of a man and, therefore, of a whole society. In their appraisal of Robinson's book, continental writers failed to pay due attention to such insular traits.

There is still a fourth reason. Robinson frequently mentions the "coming of age of man." In juridical language, the expression signifies that "man is emancipated." But what he really means to convey to the reader, Robinson does not tell. He uses the phrase while replying to some of his critics and making a point that, in his view, "the coming of age" has not improved mankind. Nor is there relevance for greater precision, he says; one could just as well speak of "adolescence." I think that the latter word expresses better his intuition; for it fittingly describes a development actually in process in the structures of our civilization.

It is natural that man should picture to himself the spiritual world on the model of what he notices and meets with here on earth, and in particular on the model of the social structures into which he has been born. Most civilizations—ours too—have known feudal structures, offspring of earlier patriarchal or matriarchal structures. It is characteristic of such, or similar, structures to grade men, already before birth, in a hierarchical order of social strata. This characteristic trait is so deeply rooted in family and tradition that it is mistakenly thought to belong to human nature itself. There have been critical periods—the nineteenth century was one of them—when such a hierarchy of social conditions was looked upon as of divine institution.

The standards of measurement for such a storeyed hierarchy are not based on the worth of the human person, but on *outside* factors: birth, race, social standing, caste. The greater part of mankind is born into a state of *tutelage*. Rights of the individual man, such as private property, right of marriage, rights of self-defense, many social and political rights too, are in large measure given in custody to a small minority who enjoy full use of those rights from birth onwards. K. Brockmoeller calls such structures *Agrarkulturen*. To these he opposes the structures which today are spreading throughout the world, and calls them *Industriekulturen.*[6]

[6] Klemens Brockmoeller, S.J., *Industriekulturen und Religion* (Frankfurt am Main: Josef Knecht, 1964).

It matters little in what terms we analyze this evolution in our history. In our present new world, the merits and rights of the person are the primary determining factors. Complexion, birth, titles of nobility and caste are given fewer and fewer privileges.

This is no ground for thinking that modern man fails to feel the profound significance and the need of authority—as is contended by those who cannot read the signs of the time and who hanker after the old order. Circumstances have compelled modern man to concede to governments or to international organizations, competences undreamed of in former days. In our era we have witnessed powerful currents of the *Führer-cult.* Authority, however, is no longer regarded as the privilege of a family, of a class or a race. The men who bear authority today are chosen by the people. They are judged by public opinion. They are subject to the law like every one else.

It is but natural that these " new men " should in their turn try to arrogate to themselves personal privileges. But modern man is averse to concede them. No privilege is countenanced unless it is used with great discretion. The moment it obtrudes itself, as was formerly a matter of course, it starts social unrest and revolution.

What is of fundamental value in the eyes of modern man are the relationships between individuals among themselves and considered as equals, and the relationships between the individuals and society. This fundamental attitude has started in the Church a crisis of authority of a peculiar nature. There survive in the Church many feudal customs and symbols, very traditional though they do not belong really to the authority as instituted by Christ. Modern man looks upon authority as a service, and not as a privilege. No one who reads Holy Writ attentively can, in principle, have any difficulty on this point. There is perhaps no truth connected with authority, as instituted by Christ, that is more often repeated and stressed in the Gospels than the principle of service. The word most commonly used in Scripture to designate authority is *diakonia*—the term meaning service. In that sense, it has been incorporated into many European languages; strangely enough, Engels adopts it and speaks of the " ministry. " That is why in the Church men today will tolerate no privilege, whether social or allegedly " spiritual. " They do not accept that *only* the people in authority form the Church, that they *alone* are under the guidance of the Spirit, that they are of a finer quality than the other baptized. All such notions are corruptions of the concept of authority preached by Christ in the Gospel.

The modern mind takes exception to authority as formerly exercised within the framework of the feudal system, when king

and emperor were surrounded with a religious aureole; it objects
also to what seems to be a survival of this notion under the
guise of colonialism, paternalism, autocracy.

Modern man will hear of no tutelage which chains or disregards
the rights of public opinion, the rights of science, of genuine
thought, of freedom of conscience; in a word, all the basic rights
of the human person.   Any one who paid attention to the
currents within the Second Vatican Council, will have noticed
how powerfully the Church was being stirred from within to adapt
herself to the modern conception of life.   John XXIII's suggestion
of *aggiornamento* purported nothing else; it was the task of the
Council.   That is why the conciliar debates were freely com-
municated to the press.   It is also the reason why schemas have
been prepared, such as those on the Jews, on the freedom of
conscience, on the more adequate notion of the Church as the
People of God, on the concept of Primacy, on the episcopate and
the Roman Curia at the service of the Church, the much talked
of 17th—now 13th—schema about the task of the Church in the
world today.   It is significant that most of those themes came
into the open while the Council was on; they were not drawn
up by the Preparatory Commissions; they arose from the consciousness felt by the Church of the needs of our era.

We have spoken at some length of the emancipation of modern
man because Robinson himself has not analyzed this historico-
social evolution.   Yet, it is what he calls " secularization. "   One
may question the aptness of that word.   Its content is more important.   The word is there nevertheless; it has come to stay.

All this is further evidenced by another word of Robinson's:
" religion. "   In the wake of D. Bonhoeffer, he says that modern
Christendom should forgo all forms of religion.   He places
" religion " in direct opposition to " secularization. "

" Religion " is—to say the least—an ambiguous term.   An
Indian priest confessed to me that in his country one had better
avoid calling Christianity a religion.   For, in India—also in
Japan, I am told—the word is associated with fanaticism, intol-
erance, forced conversions and wars of religion.

In modern Lutheran theology, strongly influenced by S. Kierkegaard, " religion " means mainly man's organized endeavors
to attain to the divine by his own unaided strength, and to annex
it.   In those circles, the word is frequently used as a synonym
of " mystical "—exactly the opposite of what " mysticism " ought
to stand for!   Magic, therefore, is the typical example of " religion. "   In this sense, " religion " is the original sin of human
society which refuses to recognize God for what He is, and
foolhardily seeks somehow to bring God under its dominion.

The science of comparative religion betrays a similar tendency.
It will often designate by the word " religion " what is of human

initiative, and oppose it to the divine initiative of grace. Philosophy, too, is liable to use the word " religion " in a depreciatory sense, or at least in a more neutral sense, as the visible shape given in this world to an actual or . . . non-actual relationship to God.

In Robinson's writings, some of these meanings crop out here and there, vaguely. When he clearly outlines his idea, he opposes " religion " in sharp contrast to " secularization. " By doing so, he defines " religion " in a manner peculiarly his own, namely, as the form of reaction by which man, facing an insoluble problem, fastens on the idea of God to fill a vacuum. And then, God is no more than a " stopgap, " filling any hole when man is at a loss.

No need to point out that such a definition is not very philosophical; it is typically English, inasmuch as it rests on experience. Similar reactions can be instanced in common life. Here is an example: the university student who, during the year, feels competent to deal with the studies and neglects somewhat his religious duties, falls suddenly victim to anxiety as soon as the examination is in sight; at that moment, he feels strongly impelled to pray and to go on pilgrimage. In like manner, the sick man calls for the doctor; if the latter fails to comfort, the priest is sent for.

On the speculative level, we have a very telling illustration of this mental attitude in scholastic theology. After death, the theologian says, the soul is separated from the body. But, apart from the body, the soul can neither think nor will. This anomaly need not worry us: God takes care to infuse all the opportune ideas. This opinion could be read some years ago, in a book by a fairly well-known German theologian.

Such an attitude, it seems to me, is at bottom dishonest, unworthy of God. Robinson does not want to hear of praying to such a divinity. And, obviously, he is right: that is not the true God. It is an idol, the projection of a symbol that serves to make up for man's own impotence; pure illusion, of course.

We add that it is a dangerous attitude for the mind to adopt. The sphere of action of such a " divinity " keeps shrinking in proportion as the sciences progressively account for what in days past was mysterious. As long as astronomy was in its infancy, people prayed for a sunrise on the following day. No one does that today. But we still pray for rain or good weather. In the foreseeable future, when atmospheric factors are better known and the state has instituted services regulating the distribution of rain, there will be no further need for such prayers. Far from us the idea of belittling all prayer of petition. But it is worth while discrediting a fairly widespread *motive* underlying this sort of prayer. We may believe that God is infinitely patient with our weakness. Perhaps He makes use of primitive reactions to head us gradually to a purer representation of what He is, and also to a more authentic prayer-life.

In a later conference, held in Holland, [7] Robinson proposes of the word " religion " a still broader meaning that agrees in good part with the notions we summarized above. " Religion " is the form of organized church life, the ways of thinking and speaking and acting which, on account of their esoterism in the eyes of the world, have lost all contact with actuality. It is indeed possible to come across people who believe in God, pray to Him, follow the dictates of their conscience, but who will not entertain the thought of joining any organized religious community. There we have the nemesis of the ghetto mentality prevailing within the Churches! It is characteristic of the ghetto to raise walls around it such as to prevent the inmates from looking outside, and to deprive the outsiders from all desire to know what happens inside: a phenomenon more frequent than is generally believed in countries that have been Catholic from time immemorial. It is interesting to notice that the Anglican Church is confronted with the same problem we are grappling with. From our tours in Germany, mainly the north, we have learned that in the Lutheran regions, too, many people look upon the Church as an antiquated artificial milieu, estranged from the world. And so, nothing in them feels tempted to join any Church communion *where* they may live up to the craving for God which they experience and want to be faithful to.

This is the class of man Robinson is concerned with. He met him at Cambridge and in the London slums. And this man must be evangelized; he must be taught the doctrine of grace. The strong reactions stirred up by *Honest to God* in many readers, Protestants as well as Catholics, priests and laymen, are proof that Robinson suddenly made articulate in them what their religious—or better, their Church-conformist—conscience strove anxiously to drive under. And repression is always a dangerous procedure. It is far more healthy to dare to look in the face the problems of the times, to discuss them honestly and to take account of them in our theology.

When in the first edition of our book, we began the third part with the section *Grace changes nothing,* we were spurred on by the identical preoccupation which moved Robinson to write his first paperback. We wanted to put a stop to the misure of grace as a *deus ex machina,* a sort of magical term to get out of the

---

[7] *Waar kan ik Hem vinden?—Where can I find Him?* a paper read at a meeting for promoting ecumenism, on February 29, 1964. Available only in cyclostyled form.

sore straights we were caught in today. " Grace " is not to be used as a knock-out argument each time a problem of real life comes to the fore. We wanted above all to replace the life of grace where it belongs, namely, in the full setting of human existence of every day and of every moment. Grace is not a commodity of which we have a snack at stated times and places; nor is it something relegated to a special sealed-off compartment of our life—something we decorate with the name of " religion, " and eventually also " church life. "

Christianity is by no means a " religion " in the narrow, world-estranged meaning we have described. This ought to be evident from the nature of the incarnation, from the biblical teaching about the redemption, from the conduct of Christ and the apostles, from the task devolving upon the Church in the shaping of history. All this has been shown in preceding pages. *It is evident especially from the doctrine of grace.* Grace is the fruit of the presence of the living God in us. The Triune God is not an abstract doctrine; it is a reality, *the* reality deeply involved in our personal life. He has wanted to enter into our world, to come within our experience. He is the deepest ground of our being. He is the love that dwells in us and seeks to reveal itself in our love. He is neither " up there " nor " out there "; and yet He is *Der ganz Andere,* " the totally other, " so radically different to the temporal in us, so transcendent that He alone can be truly immanent in our life. His presence is so total, so loving, so intensely personal that it reaches us in whatever situation we may find ourselves, and yet does not shape our existence nor cut it up into sections. Grace does not partition our lives into religious moments and non-religious moments; nor does it divide mankind into religious souls and non-religious temperaments. Our human life in its entirety is borne along by it and energized.

Pessimism?

Some readers who have followed us this far may have gathered the impression that the role assigned to grace here on earth cannot fail to lead to fatalism or pessimism. But let me be well understood. From Revelation we do indeed learn that the true purpose of redemption is to bring us to accept fully the divine will regarding our concrete situation here below. This is far from suggesting fatalism of any kind, not even the kind pre-vailing in Islam; for it is God's will also that we do all we can to make the sufferings and disorders of this world as bearable as possible, both for ourselves and for our neighbors. A true son of the Church knows, as Christ did, that until redemption reaches its full perfection on the last day, he dwells in a world where vanity, egoism, the brutal will to power and pride will always endeavor to undo all medical, social, economic, technical and psychological progress. Did not a pagan say of old, " *Quid sunt leges sine moribus?* " (" What are laws without morality? ")? No reform devised by human brain, *a fortiori* no dangerous mirage of an absolutely certain and irresistible human progress, can save man from the world where evil holds sway. The grace of Christ Jesus alone can do so by persuading us to follow in the Lord's footsteps, practicing humble obedience in faith and charity. God's Kingdom is not of this earth.

The Church, too, lives in exile in this world. It is a common weakness of ours to give way to the daydream that the Church, or at least some Christian social and political reforms, could definitely establish God's Kingdom in this world. The Middle Ages were haunted with this illusion, which we still have great trouble with today.

Everything is grace

Let us sum up what precedes. On the one hand, grace does not abolish the regular natural functioning, the structures and interrelations of this created world. On the other hand, during the interval separating Christ's resurrection and ascension from His return in glory on the last day, the divine power of grace attacks the roots of sin in every free person. In the sinner, and notably in the one who deliberately shuts out God, sin with all its evil consequences is in the ascendant. But the man in the state of grace is *in* the world though not *of* the world, as our Lord Himself says. Redemption and grace enable us to accept in humble obedience, like and with Christ, the concrete situation allotted to each one on earth by providence; this is the way to engage in a head-on conflict with sin, to overcome sin and destroy it in its essence. This is also the way to meet and possess God.

But faith tells us that, besides its somber aspect, life has also its bright side. The complete Christian picture of life has always eluded colorless, oversimplified formulas. Man's mind is so very limited, its conceptions are so unavoidably infirm that they often lead to heresy and sectarianism. Do what we may, we shall never cramp within the confines of a human concept God and His all-encompassing actuality. And so, in spite of a legitimate dose of pessimism, the true Christian should be radiant with an all-pervading optimism. For *grace means everything to him, even in this world.*

Everything is grace: the last point we want to consider now.

The positive religious value of the world

First, let us give a corrective as a pendant to the preceding considerations. The universe in which we live also displays a positive religious aspect, and this, too, for and through Christ. By the mere fact that Christ entered into this world, the All-Holy into the realm of sin, His humanity has affected the world to its very foundations. Because He was not only man but also God, the world has found in Him a new center, a new basic principle and unifying law. In Christ's humanity and body, the material world as a whole has been blessed; in germ it has been freed from its curse and once again oriented Godward. That is why, from now on, nature and this earth are fit to serve as signs and instruments of God's grace in a rich symbolism, archetypes of which lie hidden for the most part in the human psyche. The sacraments especially are evidence of this; so also to a lesser extent is the Church's liturgy. Ambivalently and by way of suggestion, the rites and symbols of other religions bear the same witness.

There is more. God has decreed that redemption and thus grace should come to man through the cooperation of other men. As we are mutually dependent on each other in regard to good and evil, Christ's great mercy has willed that no man should be saved without the cooperation of other men. To put it differently, we can and must work out with Christ the salvation of the world. It does not follow, though, that in this cooperation—or in any other capacity—we take up our stand next to Christ as His equals, as associates on a par with Him. Etymologically, the term *cooperation* here is too crude. We are allowed to work *with* Christ for the salvation of the world as far as we let ourselves be borne along and used by the one *Savior* to bring all men to Him, and inasmuch as Christ's life and action in our lives radiate His influence on our neighbors.

Every man, on receiving grace, has this duty imposed upon him. And this holds true for him who would receive grace outside the visible Church. But in the ultimate purpose and meaning of the Mystical Body, it is the prerogative of the Church, as the Body of Christ the head, to be the carrier and executor of His will and operation. In that light one may say that no grace, not even the most intimately personal one, is granted to the individual for himself alone; it must redound to the progress of the apostolate and to the general good of the Church.

Christian humanism

Since through the incarnation all things have become instruments of Christ's almighty power, we are in duty bound to press into service anything that is good or useful to make Christ known. Grace and human nature are two widely different realities: grace belongs properly to the divine order, human nature does not. The latter should not be neglected on that account. Culture, humanism, civilization, adequate welfare, corporal and psychic health, artistic refinement, alliances between nations, even science and technology—normally, all have their share in the call of contributing to the salvation of mankind.

All things are called to serve. First, they serve as a negative preparation for grace. The less a man is hampered in his worship of God, the better for him. Culture, science and refinement may differ in nature from grace; competently used, however, they clear away many obstacles that hinder the action of God's Spirit. Herein precisely lies their negative role. It stands to reason that people will not be ready to lend an attentive ear to the message of grace as long as they are weighed down by ceaseless worry over how they will secure their daily morsel of bread; in such conditions they cannot but grow stunted and brutalized. No doubt God sometimes works in surprising ways, but experience has taught the Church that such is not God's *usual* way. Cardinal Newman had this same thought in mind when he wrote that persecution, with its ensuing ghetto mentality, leaves such an impression of the Catholic masses that few among them escape from it immune. A certain degree of political and social freedom is necessary to create a climate favorable to grace. And that is why the Church has always actively promoted a civilizing uplift whenever her missionary work lay among primitive races. She was far from thinking that a new convert could not be a good Christian unless he was also a good Portuguese or a good Spaniard, as has been asserted by some writers; but she knows that poverty, slavery and barbarism are obstacles to the efflorescence of grace.

Though the purely human values are not—let us repeat—grace in essence, they possess a positive value all their own in God's salvific plan. Contrary to ignorance, barbarism and backwardness, they provide signs and symbols of God's eternal glory. History shows that the Church has always considered it a divine mandate to foster science and culture, even when she had to face the task alone; her architecture and her liturgy are there to prove it. The Church firmly believes that in the beauty of nature and art and in the truth of science lie hidden the marvels of God's own beauty and wisdom. Should we ask for an unquestionable charter for Christian humanism, we have only to turn to the Epistle to the Philippians. Paul spoke first of the grace, the joy and peace caused by Christ's living presence in our midst: " Rejoice in the Lord always; again I say, rejoice. Let your forbearance be known to all men. The Lord is nigh! ... and the peace

of the Lord, which surpasseth all understanding, keep your
hearts and mind in Christ Jesus. " The Apostle then continued,
" For all the rest, brethren, whatsoever things are true, whatsoever
venerable, whatsoever just, whatsoever pure, whatsoever lovely,
whatsoever commendable, if there be any virtue and if anything
is praiseworthy, think on these things " (Phil 4:4-8).

The world, a life's task

It is possible to proceed still farther in the consideration of the
world's positive value. The world is God's gift. Every divine
gift imposes an obligation because it is conferred on a free
person. The world, it is true, has been singularly damaged by
sin and robbed of its original purpose; but rampant evil cannot
alter the fact that the world remains a gift, a workshop to serve
as both room and instrument for culture and knowledge.

This last remark enables us to round off our argument. When
we grant that a life of grace is simply a life of obedience on the
very spot where God has placed us and where His grace and
calling reach us, it follows that our earthly task of civilizing and
mastering the universe falls within the wide scope of that very
same obedience. For those who are servants of God and brothers
of Christ in and through grace, the world with all it contains
recovers its primordial meaning. And so grace means really
everything to the baptized Christian. Whether good or evil, all
things turn through grace into a definite duty and task. Paul
said as much when he enlarged on the glories of the spirit and
of grace, adding, " We know that to them who love God, all
things work together unto good, to such as, according to his
purpose, are called to be saints " (Rom 8:28)—a text which might
be interpreted: we know for certain that God directs all things
to secure the good of those who love Him, those whom He has
called for the fulfillment of His designs.

Christian humanism, then, is not entrusted only with the
negative role of clearing external obstacles out of the way
of grace, or the task of merely serving the Church in her
apostolate. It should take pride in the profound *positive and
religious* vocation received in and through grace. God's word
makes the world transparent, turns it into a shrine and tabernacle
of the divine, living presence. More still, all goodness, truth,
virtue and beauty concealed in the world have been given to us
in commission. Our humble obedience to grace, which is the
secret of our salvation, demands that we take it all in hand, use
it, cause it to bloom. A Catholic doctor finds in his faith a
deeper, more convincing motive for a competent practice of his

profession; so also the poet, the engineer, the social worker, any laborer or farmer. To put it in other words, our earthly career does not lie *outside* our Christian calling but on the contrary, well *within* it. Or more correctly still, our fundamental self-surrender to God in faith and charity has to find expression in the concrete details of our earthly career and dedication. On this level, too, we are God's fellow workers. The world is to us a *divine milieu* in which our earthly life achieves its fullest meaning, thanks to God's love.

These thoughts offer us the welcome opportunity of quoting a text of Ruysbroeck, often alluded to on previous occasions. The quotation shows how all the views set forth so far are brought together into one sober, genuinely religious vision of the world: "You know well that a meeting is a gathering of two persons coming from different places which in themselves are opposite and apart. Now, Christ comes from above as a lord and generous donor who can do all things. We come from below [from earth] as poor folk, devoid of strength and in need of everything. Christ comes in us from within outwards, and we come to Him from outside inwards. And for this reason, a spiritual meeting must here take place."[8] The words "we come from outside inwards" are now very telling. Beyond but through our *exterior* deeds of obedience, occupation and dedication, we tend to Christ *interiorly*. Here as always, especially in the supernatural order, we humans are concerned with the interiorizing process. Our scattered, insignificant daily actions should lead us, deep down in our hearts, to the great surrender in faith and love from outside inwards.

Divine grace and matter

So far we have emphasized rather strongly how sharply grace is divided from the world. We accepted the term *world* in its twofold meaning: first, the meaning of space and "stage" for our human activity, and second, the meaning of kingdom of the evil one. This emphasis was necessary mainly in reaction against a lowering, ultimately pagan humanism which bypasses the exalted, unique nobility of a life of grace. But all reactions in the field of thought suffer fatally from onesidedness. Accents are shifted to the extent of falsifying the picture as a whole or of blotting out the correct accents. That was the way with heresy in the past.

[8] Jan van Ruysbroeck, *Die Gheestelike Brulocht,* tr. Eric Colledge as *The Spiritual Espousals* (London: Faber & Faber, 1952), p. 143; see also p. 92.

When dealing with what is peculiar to grace, one is apt to strain after orthodoxy to the point of not doing justice to the wealth of God's Revelation. In the mind of the Greek Fathers, there existed no doubt whatever that the sacraments acted also on man's body. With apparent unconcern, they looked upon grace in terms of our bodily substance: grace meant immortality and everlastingness. This is all the more remarkable because the Greek Fathers were the great exponents of the transcendence of grace; grace was for them a divinization *(theopoiesis),* just as for Irenaeus the Eucharist was the food and drink of immortality. It is probable that those Fathers were indebted for their manner of expression to some of their contemporaries, disciples of Plato and Plotinus, two philosophers who ruthlessly differentiated what (to their mind) is divine in the spirit from what is sinful in matter; but the essential of their faith they drew from other sources: they found it in Holy Scripture.

The modern mind has recaptured something of this sense of totality. We have already pointed out that we are not souls tied to foreign bodies. As man, each one of us is but one unit, always itself, though in two manners of being which conflict with each other. We are wholly spirit and person, but have spiritual, autonomous self-possession. We are wholly matter, but have a being that grows and expands in time and space. We have here not two substances, rather unhappily stuck together, but two poles, two sources of energy, one subordinate to the other. That is why it is more exact to speak of two elements of one complex spiritual being which is confined to time and space but of which the spiritual element, aided by grace, holds the primacy.

Earlier in this book we stressed the fact that grace affects only our innermost spiritual core, permeating it and raising it.

Along the same line of thought, we have shown that the significance of miracles consists in a manifestation of the divine presence in this world of ours, from which God might seem to some to be absent. These statements must stand. But in order that they not become onesided and false, the other aspect must be kept in mind as well: that man, even under the influence of grace, remains a single organic whole.

Maintaining all we have said before, we now assert that grace affects our being also in its material aspect, already here on earth. Both our body and the entire cosmos (which do not have to be thought of as divided from each other) receive a true germ of immortality, everlastingness and resurrection, in virtue first of Christ's redemption and second of our own personal grace of reconciliation. Our whole cosmic existence is necessarily involved in the reality of our rebirth in Christ. At the risk of dangerous misunderstandings and exaggerations on the part of literal-minded readers, we shall make bold to say that the sacraments, too, have their significance for cures of the body. The danger we allude to is not an imaginary one. We find evidence of it in some theologians who teach that the first and principal fruit of extreme unction is the physical healing of the sick. It is not hard to see what vain and false anticipation such unqualified statements are likely to raise in the mind of the average Catholic; but they nonetheless contain some elements of truth.

In the same order of thought, we could prove positively that miracles, seen in all their implications, convey to man a foretaste, a pledge and anticipation of the final cure and resurrection. They are more than mere symbols of Christ's victory over sickness, suffering and death; they are pregnant symbols, containing in germ what they witness to and signify. Neither our body nor the cosmos as a whole remains unaffected by the mighty upheaval God's love causes in the silent secrecy of the heart. And in this sense, we are justified in asserting that grace means everything in life. From now on, we have the pledge of our resurrection; or better, we are risen already, seminally. We possess within us the seed of everlasting life, the remedy for all sickness, pain and death. What are infirmities, grief and dying if not sin made visible and tangible in this world? Besides, it is fitting that from now on the triumphant Lord should conquer the countless manifestations of sin rampant in the world. But let us repeat once more: all this does not alter the fact that we are living in a world of sin and evil, of sickness and death, and that it is in this world that we have to find God in and through His first love.

Grace and psychology

Something more has to be said. A great deal of attention is focused today on man's psychology, his nature and way of life. The question arises: Does grace exercise any influence on man's psychology?

It has already been pointed out that in the present order grace leaves man's psychology fundamentally unaltered. But thus set down, our words run the risk of oversimplifying matters. It bears repeating that psychic health and balance are in themselves quite different from grace, though on this point we have made some important corrective qualifications. To some extent we can acquire or improve them or redress them after one or another disturbance; we can in part maintain them by human methods, sometimes by medicaments or even surgery. But grace is exclusively God's gratuitous gift in Christ. Further, the life of grace is made known to us only through faith. This is precisely why we drew attention a few pages back to the fact that grace is also granted to those who are burdened with a psychosis or are sorely tried in their psychic equilibrium. Should such men, always with the help of grace, surrender themselves to God in the depth of their souls, they could actually reach a high state of sanctity, though their lives would perhaps not be of the kind of perfection which the Church likes to guarantee by a solemn canonization.

The purpose of canonization is largely conditioned by the requirements of the Church's history on earth. Canonizations, to be sure, remind the faithful of heaven. But when the Church canonizes, she intends primarily to propose to the piety and imitation of the faithful those followers of Christ whom divine providence has raised up to be models of a virtuous Christian life. The providential design of raising canonized saints in the Church according to the needs of the times has been dwelt upon by many writers in recent years. Now, in the case of persons undeniably privileged by grace but psychologically disordered through no fault of their own, spiritual oddities or morbid character traits would prevent them from being held up as models for imitation in the Church. Nonetheless, psychological disturbances are not necessarily obstacles to grace. God's ways are wonderful: He may, when He wants, destine some distraught souls to the sublime but harrowing vocation of imitating Christ forsaken and desolate in the Garden of Gethsemani, and this in spite of, or rather by means of, their shattered psychic condition. The essential requirement for holiness is the same for all: a faithful " yes " to the call of God, manifest in the particular concrete situation of existence which His wisdom has chosen for each one. The case of the psychotic is no exception to the rule.

From the moment such a man has made his fundamental surrender to God, he will tend to express it and live up to it in his daily actions; like any other human being, he has no other option. In him, however, the expression, execution and consciousness of this surrender to grace will be heavily handicapped, muddled up and traversed by psychic anxieties and disturbances. He may be tried by endless scruples; he may live under the permanent sway of a dark interior depression; he may forever relapse into aggressive fits of temper. But though he may suffer from any form of psychic disease, he is in no way prevented from accepting himself from God's hand as he is, with the right dispositions of wholehearted humility and self-abasement. Though he may be hovering on the brink of insanity, in moments of lucidity he can still answer the merciful voice of God, throw himself in His arms and moan with the psalmist, " Out of the depth I have cried to thee, O Lord " (Ps 129:1). In his own depressed and anxious manner, he can exclaim with and in Christ, " Father, into Thy hands I commend My spirit " (Lk 24:26). Such cases do occur; they belong to history; but unfortunately they are not generally known.

However, such is not the normal way of grace. To quote Ruysbroeck for the last time, Christ comes in us " from within outwards. " God's grace transforms, heals and raises our fundamental option. The normal way with God's saving action is that an efficacious virtue flows from this interior rebirth of the heart, and little by little permeates, strengthens, unifies and enkindles human activity as a whole. In the ordinary designs of divine love, the process of interior unification in God brings about a behavior authentically human, a perfect psychic integration. The divine action of grace promotes an interior harmony of all our powers, aspirations and impulses, not only in order to purify them but also to give them deeper root and greater intensity. God works " from within outwards. " Grace radiates outward when it is given free scope in our life.

Grace brings with it peace and joy, even in the midst of pain, trials and desolation, because it attaches and directs the heart to God. That peace and that joy do not well up from a mundane source, but they prolong themselves and re-echo in the human psyche. Increasing attention is given today in psychology and psychiatry to the energy and balance generated by interior repose, by contentment with self and others, by joy and above all by esteem and love. Nothing enriches or fulfills human life so much as the genuine respect and affection of others; they act potently upon the human psyche, and contribute to our bodily functions and general health. The Christian is indebted to faith for a deeper insight into his sinfulness, but he also owes to it a blissful awareness of the Father's unique love in Christ for his lowliness and impotence. No one can fail to see that faith purifies, unifies and even strengthens on the merely human level—the *normal* outcome of a living, supernatural faith.

Few people seem to realize and acknowledge this after-effect, because too many deliberately refuse to cooperate with grace. Within that class must be reckoned a number of persons specially consecrated to God. Victims of neurasthenia and moral depression are met with in religious houses. The causes are not always the same. In the case of cloistered communities, the blame lies sometimes with the neglect of elementary laws of corporal and psychological hygiene on the part of the superiors; these are often appointed to leadership more on account of their overwrought piety than because of their knowledge of men. And that cannot be helped. However, the source of mental upsets, with far worse consequences, must be sought on a deeper level. They are to be traced back to infidelity to grace, shown perhaps in the spiritual mediocrity with which the divine call is lived up to.

Let a man give himself to God entirely and definitively, and without ceasing to be a limited onesided human being, and he will take up his stand on another level: the level of the saints. All the lives of the saints are enchanting, unique, arresting. Blinkered, moralizing hagiographers do their best to portray them all in the same drab colors, stripped of all originality. But a look at the actual facts of their histories is enough to convince us that originality and intensity of life are nowhere so finely displayed as in the world of the saints. Each one of them, borne along by grace, was surprisingly faithful to the bent of his own particular temperament and character, as given to him by providence. The wellspring of originality lies hidden in each one's fundamental liberty. And because grace heals and raises just that fundamental liberty, the world of the saints cannot but be fascinating.

Scripture teaches the same lesson. Whatever some moralizing preachers may say, Holy Scripture, especially the Epistles, insists on the fact that Christ's grace in us must shine as a *witness and revelation* of God's glory. "So let your light shine before men, that they may see your good works, and glorify your Father who is in heaven" (Mt 5:16). Nowhere do we find attention so frequently called to the high duty of *rejoicing* in the risen, redeeming Christ. Christian joy is our principal testimony. The Church has traversed periods of such ruthless persecution that joy remained the one way in which the Christian could bear witness to his faith, though harassed and sent to death. Georges Bernanos makes his Carmelite nuns sing throughout the night preceding their trial in prison, and after the trial, up to the very steps of the guillotine. In this, history bears him out. Grace is indeed all-important to us, even from the point of view of human psychology.

How could it be otherwise? To a lover everything shines with love. Shadows vanish and light illumines all things. Sickness, care and failure become trifling, easy to bear. If this is so with human love, what must it be in the case of a man filled with the love of God? Gone are the conventions of a routine Catholic life that has locked itself up and stiffened into lifeless, set formulas and practices. Can true religion be lived in a rut? The question answers itself.

Conclusion

Catholicism is without illusions; it is levelheaded and realistic —like God, Who sees all things and judges all things in the light of truth. The Catholic outlook on life, based on the theology of grace and redemption, is probably a great deal more pessimistic than that of some pagans of antiquity; it is also more somber than what modern pagans advertise today as enlightened wisdom. Basic in our faith is the knowledge that we dwell in a world of sin, that we are affected by it in the core of our being and that the absolute heinousness of sin is to be discovered only in the shadow of the cross. No one can show himself naively optimistic, though here and there we meet Christians who play up to the mood of their contemporaries by sweetening our pessimism with their own brand of humanism, which keeps too little of Christ's teaching.

In the course of this book, we have made good use of Chapter 8 of the Epistle to the Romans, in which Paul summed up in a masterly way what he held on the subject of divine grace. It is typical of the man to have concluded that chapter with the lines which we now quote.

" What else can we add to all this? If God is on our side, who can be against us? He did not even spare His own Son, but gave Him up for us all. How then would He not freely give us all things along with Him? Where is the man who can bring any charges against the elect whom God has justified [and thus freed and saved]? Where is the man who will pass sentence against us, when Jesus Christ, who died, nay, rose again, and sits at the right hand of God, is pleading for us? Who will separate us from the love of Christ? Will affliction, or hardship, or persecution, or hunger, or nakedness, or danger, or the sword? ... But in all these circumstances we are conquerors, through Him who granted us His love. Of this I am fully persuaded [and for us, too, this ought to become a certainty and a consolation]: neither death, nor life, nor angels and principalities, nor powers [in the heavens, according to Jewish notions in Paul's time], neither what is present, nor what is to come, nor any force whatever, neither the height above us, nor the depth beneath us [all of which are supposed sources of opposition which serve to enlarge in concrete terms on the word *nothing*], nor any other creature, will be able to separate us from the love of God which comes to us in Christ Jesus our Lord " [Rom 8:31-39].

Our life of grace is so deeply rooted in Christ that our triumph in and with Him is assured already here below. " Have confidence, I have overcome the world " (Jn 16:33): these words, taken from the farewell speech of Jesus to His disciples, are a lasting treasure for all of us to carry in our hearts. The conscious remembrance of them will cause happiness and joy to grow in a steady crescendo. We are saved. To the saved in grace and love, everything existing takes on a new look. In everything, everywhere and always, we recognize the features of Christ—" the bleeding head so wounded " no less than the glorified face on Tabor and on Easter morning. " This is the day which the Lord has made. Let us be glad and rejoice therein. "

APPENDIX

AIDS FOR INDIVIDUAL AND STUDY GROUP READING

It is not our purpose to offer a general index of names and themes.

This book has been written for laymen and priests who lack the leisure for prolonged theological study : the Greek work *scholè*, whence the English work " school "—means leisure! With such readers in mind, we have avoided all systematic divisions, technical definitions, and the formal methodical development customary in textbooks. We jave also limited footnotes and references to those which we judged essential.

Nevertheless, we trust that the present volume may prove helpful to individuals and groups. That is why we have drawn up study aids. But we do not offer a complete bibliography; rather we cite works which give an overall view of a problem or offer a valuable insight into a particular point. We do not refer to well-known theological or other encyclopedias, such as *The New Catholic Encyclopedia* (New York, 1966); *A Catholic Dictionary of Theology* (New York, London, 1962; still in process of publication); *Sacramentum Mundi, An Encyclopedia of Theology* (New York, 1968, still in process of publication); *Catholicisme* (Paris, 1949). Such publications seem obvious as a start in the study of any particular topic : they provide a basic survey of the problems and good bibliographies.

A. THEOLOGY AND RELIGIOUS INVESTIGATION:

PROBLEMS OF METHOD

1. Theology in relation to the positive sciences : pp. 179, 295.
2. Theology in relation to philosophical thought : pp. 24, 164 f.
3. Theology differs from the other sciences about man : pp. 147-150, 157-159, 278 ff., 327 f.
4. The nature of dogma : p. 19.
5. The need of determining the exact meaning of theological language : pp. 206, 246, 263, 319.
6. Myth and reality : pp. 157-159, 322.

For further reading:

P. Fransen, " Three Ways of Dogmatic Thought, " *The Heythrop Journal* 4 (1963) 3-24, or *Cross Currents* 13 (1963) 129-48. Dealing more particularly with the Councils: " On the Need for the Study of the Historical Sense of

Conciliar Texts, " *Problems of Authority*, ed. John M. Todd (Baltimore, London, 1962) 72-78. More historical and practical: " The Teaching of Theology on the Continent and its Implications, " *Theology and the University*, ed. John Coulson (Baltimore, London, 1964) 78-104. As applied to the subject of grace: " How Should We Teach the Treatise of Grace?," *Apostolic Renewal in the Seminary in the Light of the Vatican Council*, ed. Keller and Armstrong (New York, 1963) 139-63.

G. Philips, " De ratione instituendi tractatus de Gratia sanctificationis nostrae, " *Ephemerides Theologiae Lovanienses* 29 (1953) 355-373 (reprints available).

Herbert Vorgrimler, ed., *Dogmatic versus Biblical Theology* (Baltimore, 1964, London, 1965).

John L. McKenzie, *Myths and Realities* (Milwaukee, London, 1963).

B. THEOLOGY OF GRACE

I. BIBLICAL THEOLOGY

a.   *The original meanning of some words:*

spirit and flesh : pp. 33, 45, 52, 73, 152, 300, 316 f.
grace : pp. 14 f., 151, 156.
graciousness (love) and fidelity : pp. 15, 60, 217.
glory of magnificence : pp. 43, 50, 67, 155, 216.
heart : pp. 235, 255, 267, 298, 316.
Lord : pp. 68, 71.
to know, to see : p. 42 f.
justice : p. 46.
temple : pp. 69 f., 75 f., 182, 316.
truth : p. 115.
world : pp. 44, 308, 329 ff., 345 f.

For further reading:

J. Guillet, *Themes of the Bible* (Notre Dame, Ind., 1961); id., *Jesus Christ, Yesterday and Today* (Chicago, London, 1965). For an understanding of the words listed above, see John E. Steinmueller's *Catholic Biblical Encyclopedia* (New York, 1956); also *Encyclopedic Dictionary of the Bible* (New York, 1963).

Some useful works for biblical study: A. Robert and A. Tricot, *Guide to the Bible* (2nd ed., rev., New York, 1960-61); " Articles of Introduction, " *A Catholic Commentary on Holy Scripture* (London, New York, 1953); L. H. Grollenberg, *Atlas of the Bible* (London, New York, 1957); X. Léon-Dufour, *Dictionary of Biblical Theology* (New York, 1967); John L. McKenzie, *Dictionary of the Bible* (Milwaukee, London, 1965); Raymond E. Brown, *et al, The Jerome Biblical Commentary* (New York, 1968).

b. *Some Old Testament themes:*

Corporate personality : pp. 31, 35, 76.
Servant of Yahweh : pp. 29 ff., 49, 66, 68.
the Spirit, messianic gift : pp. 49 ff., 117 f., 157, 245, 298.
graciousness (love) and fidelity : pp. 10-12, 16 f., 153, 156 ff.
symbolism of marriage : pp. 10 f., 75 f.
symbolism of the temple : pp. 75 f., 182.
theology of the Covenant : pp. 16-18, 62 f., 117 f., 157, 168 f., 215-217.
people of God : pp. 65, 75, 160.
election and reprobation : pp. 157 f., 161 f.

For further study:

Y. M. Congar, *The Mystery of the Temple, or the Manner of God's Presence to His Creatures from Genesis to the Apocalypse* (Westminster, Md., London, 1962); J. Corbon, *L'expérience chrétienne dans la Bible* (Bruges, 1963); A. Gelin, *The Key Concepts of the Old Testament* (New York, London, 1955); id., *The Poor of Yahweh* (Collegeville, Minn. 1964).

For a more general orientation: H. H. Rowley, *The Re-Discovery of the Old Testament* (Philadelphia, 1946); *The Faith of Israel* (London, 1956; Philadelphia, 1957).

c. *The New Testament*

1. Some basic themes:

the cross, sign of grace : pp. 20 f., 31, 59, 155, 330.
obedience : p. 62.
love : pp. 60 f., 249.
redemption : pp. 65-70, 74, 160, 191 f.

For further reading:

M. Van Caster, *L'Homme en face de Dieu* (Bruges, 1958); id., *Redemption* (New York, 1966); C. Spicq, *Moral Theology of the New Testament* (London, 1968).

General orientation:

J. Bonsirven, *Theology of the New Testament* (London, Westminster, Md., 1963); J. Lebreton, *The Spiritual Teaching of the New Testament* (London, Westminster, Md., 1960); C. Charlier, *The Christian Approach to the Bible* (Westminster, Md., 1958; London, 1959); J. Castelot, *Meet the Bible:* Vol. II, *The New Testament* (Baltimore, 1961); Kathryn Sullivan, *God's Word and Works* (Collegeville, Minn., 1958); I. Hunt, *Understanding the Bible* (New York, 1962; Dublin, 1963); Robert-Tricot, *Guide to the Bible*, 2 Vols. (New York, 1960 ff.); W. Harrington, *Record of the Fulfillment: The New Testament* (Chicago, 1965; London, 1967).

2. The teaching of the Synoptics:

Christ, the Emmanuel, or God-with-us : pp. 24 f.
Christ, Son of Man : p. 29.
Christ, the Son : p. 31.
Christ, Servant of Yahweh : pp. 29 f.
assimilation to God : p. 34.
God's Kingdom : pp. 63 f., 68, 197.
merit : pp. 211 f.
God's People : p. 64.
freedom : p. 115.
sin and conversion : pp. 229 f., 247 f., 250, 254 f.
parables : pp. 12-14.

For further reading:

Basic orientation in modern exegesis: X. Léon-Dufour, *The Gospel and the Jesus of History* (New York, London, 1968); Jean Levie, *The Bible, Word of God in Words of Men* (New York, London, 1961); P. Fannon, *The Four Gospels* (London, 1964; Notre Dame, Ind., 1966); Robert and Feuillet, *Introduction to the New Testament* (New York, 1965); B. Vawter, *The Four Gospels* (New York, 1966; Dublin, 1967).

Other studies:

H. Van den Bussche, *Understanding the Lord's Prayer* (London, New York, 1964); L. Cerfaux, *Apostle and Apostolate according to the Gospel of Saint Matthew* (New York, 1960); id., *The Four Gospels* (Westminster, Md., 1958); J. Daniélou, *The Theology of the Jewish Christianity* (London, Chicago, 1964); J. Jeremias, *The Parables of Jesus* (Chicago, 1955; London, 1958); W. Harrington, *He Spoke in Parables* (Dublin, 1964) or *A Key to the Parables* (Glen Rock, N.J., 1964).

3. The Teaching of Saint John:

Christ, our image and model : pp. 28 f.
Christ, the Son in love : p. 31.
the " divine categories " :
   light and life : pp. 68, 76, 307 ff.
   love : pp. 14 f., 61 f., 66 f., 74, 183 f., 249 f., 275, 280 f., 303 ff.
fellowship with God : pp. 24 f., 42-46, 68 f., 74 ff., 223, 298 ff.
divine sonship : pp. 18, 31 ff., 48, 221, 300, 307.
freedom in the Son : pp. 114 f., 118.
completion, fulfillment : pp. 299 f.

For further reading:

R. Brown, *New Testament Essays* (Milwaukee, London, 1965); G. Vann, *The Eagle's Word. Apresentation of the Gospel according to St. John* (London, New York, 1961); W. Grossouw, *Revelation and Redemption* (Westminster, Md., 1955); H. Van den Bussche, *Last Discourses of Jesus* (Baltimore, 1966);

C. H. Dodd, *Historical Tradition in the Fourth Gospel* (New York, 1963). For exegesis see A. Feuillet, *Johannine Studies* (Staten Island, N.Y., 1964).

4. The Teaching of Saint Paul:

    Christ as image : pp. 28 f., 218 f., 221, 223 f.
    Christ as the Servant : pp. 30, 68, 330.
    Christ as the Son of love : pp. 31, 70.
    grace and the " works " : pp. 208 ff., 213.
    obedience of the faith : pp. 68, 116, 118.
    assimilation to God : p. 33.
    indwelling of the Trinity : pp. 45 f., 70 ff., 118, 316.
    divine sonship : pp. 32, 45 f., 73, 300.
    body of Christ : pp. 70 ff., 218.
    a new creation : pp. 70, 134, 231.
    fulfillment of all things and of all men in Christ : pp. 41, 162, 196.
    freedom from the law : pp. 115-122, 124 f.
    fruits of the Holy Ghost : pp. 285 ff., 300, 303.

For further reading :

F. Prat, *The Theology of Saint Paul* (Westminster, Md., 1946, London, 1934); L. Cerfaux, *The Church in the Theology of Saint Paul* (New York, 1959); A. Wikenhauser, *Pauline Mysticism: Christ in the Mystical Teaching of St. Paul* (Freiburg, New York, London, 1960); F. Amiot, *The Key Concepts of St. Paul* (New York, London, 1962); Cox and Knox, *It is Paul who Writes* (New York, 1959; London, 1960); J. Blenkinsopp, *Paul's Life in Christ* (London, 1965), in U.S.: *Jesus is Lord* (New York, 1967); J. Cantinat, *The Epistles of St. Paul Explained* (New York, 1966); R. Schnackenburg, *Baptism and the Thought of St. Paul* (New York, 1966); J. Murphy-O'Connor, *Paul and Qumran* (Chicago, London, 1968); F. X. Durrwell, *The Resurrection* (New York, London, 1960).

II.   POSITIVE THEOLOGY

a. *The doctrine of the liturgy :*

    nature of the liturgy : pp. 84-86, 113.
    grace-life in the liturgy : pp. 41, 68, 79, 83.

For further reading :

J. D. Crighton, *The Church's Worship* (New York, London, 1964); J. Miller, *Fundamentals of the Liturgy* (Notre Dame, Ind., 1960); I. H. Dalmais, *Introduction to the Liturgy* (London, Baltimore, 1961); G. M. Braso, *Liturgy and Spirituality* (Collegeville, Minn., 1960); L. Bouyer, *Life and Liturgy* (London, 1956), in U.S.: *Liturgical Piety* (Notre Dame, Ind., 1955); A. G. Martimort, *The Church at Prayer*, Vol. I (New York, Dublin, 1968, other volumes in process of publication); W. Barauna, ed., *The liturgy of Vatican II*, 2 Vols. (Chicago, 1966).

Basic books:

J. A. Jungmann, *Liturgical Worship* (New York, 1941); id., *The Mass of the Roman Rite: Its Origins and Development (Missarum Solemnia)* (New York, 1950); C. Vagaggini, *Theological Dimensions of the Liturgy* (Collegeville, Minn., 1959).

b. *Councils and heresies:*

    1. Council of Carthage in 418 : p. 111.
       Council of Orange in 529 : pp. 110, 112, 128 f.
       Council of Quierzy-sur-Oise in 853 : pp. 140, 232.
       Ecumenical Council of Vienne in 1312 : pp. 92, 319.
       Ecumenical Council of Trent : pp. 92 ff., 101, 104, 106 f., 112, 214 f.,
          219, 243.

    2. Heretical conceptions:
       Pelagianism : pp. 110 ff., 124.
       Semi-Pelagianism : pp. 105, 111 f., 207 f., 215, 219.
       Predestinationism in the eight century : p. 232.
       Reformation : pp. 89-95, 201, 206, 208, 210, 229, 256, 317.
       Jansenism : pp. 138 ff., 226, 256.

c. *Short themes taken from the theology in the course of centuries:*

    1. The Greek Fathers:
       divinization : pp. 18, 42, 78, 83, 345.
       theology of the image of God : pp. 29, 37.
       grace as " immortality " and " incorruptibility " : pp. 317, 322, 346.

    2. The Latin Fathers:
       Augustine : pp. 22 f., 100, 102, 104, 106, 111 f., 129 f., 132, 162,
          166, 169 ff., 175 f., 180.

    3. In the Middle Ages:
       Peter Lombard : pp. 88, 97, 102.
       Thomas Aquinas : pp. 88, 97, 112, 117, 162 ff., 206.
       Jan van Ruysbroeck : pp. 21 f., 28, 34 ff., 46 ff., 52 ff., 97, 131, 150,
          239, 241, 345.

For further reading:

Interesting and perceptive historical survey of the question of grace: H. Rondet, *The Grace of Christ* (Glen Rock, N.J., 1967).

For consultation or reading:

1. Church Fathers

R. Gleason, *The Indwelling Spirit* (Staten Island, N.Y., 1966); T. F. Torrance, *The Doctrine of Grace in the Apostolic Fathers* (Edinburgh, 1948, Grand Rapids, 1959); G. Chéné, *La théologie de Saint Augustin, Grace et Prédestination* (Le Puy, 1962).

On Saint Augustine: E. Portalie, *A Guide to the Life and Thought of Saint Augustine* (Chicago, 1960); V. J. Bourke, *Augustine's Quest of Wisdom* (Milwaukee, 1945).

2. The East

J. Gross, *La divinisation du chrétien d'après les Pères Grecs* (Paris, 1938); V. Lossky, *The Mystical Theology of the Eastern Church* (London, 1957); id., *The Vision of God* (London, 1963; Portland, Me., 1964).

3. The Middle Ages

— early Middle Ages: A. M. Landgraf, *Dogmengeschichte der Frühscholastik*, parts 1/1 and 1/2 (Ratisbonne, 1952-53); J. Schupp, *Die Gnadenlehre des Petrus Lombardus* (Freiburg, 1932).

— Great Scholastics: Saint Thomas Aquinas, *The Gospel of Grace*, in *Summa Theologiae*, Vol. 30 (in preparation, London, New York); H. Bouillard, *Conversion et grâce chez S. Thomas d'Aquin* (Paris, 1944); G. Ladrille, *Grâce et motion divine chez S, Thomas d'Aquin* (Turin, 1950); R. Garrigou-Lagrange, *Grâce* (St. Louis, 1952).

— On the Franciscan School (Duns Scotus, Bonaventure, etc): E. Bettoni, *Duns Scotus: the Basic Principles of his Philosophy* (Washington, D.C., 1961); E. Gilson, *The Philosophy of Bonaventure* (London, New York, 1940).

General studies on Medieval philosophy: D. Knowles, *The Evolution of Medieval Thought* (London, Baltimore, 1962); E. Gilson, *The Spirit of Medieval Philosophy* (London, New York, 1936).

— Nominalism: M. H. Carré, *Realists and Nominalists* (New York, 1946); F. Copleston, *A History of Philosophy*, Vol. 3 (London, 1950; Westminster, Md., 1953); H. A. Oberman, *The Harvest of Medieval Theology* (Cambridge, Mass., 1963).

— On Jan van Ruysbroeck: P. Henry, *La mystique trinitaire du Bienheureux Jean Ruusbroec* in: *Mélanges Jules Lebreton* (1951-52) 335-368, and its continuation in *Recherches de sciences religieuses* 41 (1953) 51-75.

— Some works on grace in general, more or less on traditional lines: J. Daujat, *The Theology of Grace* (London, New York, 1959); R. Gleason, *Grace* (New York, 1962); C. Journet, *The Meaning of Grace* (London, New York, 1963); T. J. Higgins, *Dogma for the Layman* (Milwaukee, 1961); M. J. Scheeben, *The Mysteries of Christianity* (St. Louis, 1940); P. de Letter, " Indwelling (divine), " *The New Catholic Encyclopedia* (7: 492-94).

4. The Council of Trent

R. Jedin, *A History of the Council of Trent*, 2 (London, New York, 1961).

5. The Reformation

A few works only are cited, of easy access to most readers.

a.   From the Catholic point of view:

P. Hughes, *The Reformation in England* (London, 1950-54, New York, 1963);
H. Kung, *Justification according to the New Testament*, a study to be compared
with the study by T. F. Torrance on *Justification: its Radical Nature and Place
in Reformed Doctrine and Life*, both studies found together in *Christianity
Divided, Protestant and Roman Catholic Theological Issues* (New York, 1961);
J. P. Dolan, *History of the Reformation* (New York, 1965).

b.   On Luther's and Calvin's ideas and development:

F. E. Cranz, *An Essay on the Development of Luther's Thought on Justice, Law
and Society* (Cambridge, Mass., 1959); E. W. Zeeden, *The Legacy of Luther*
(London, 1954); F. Wendel, *Calvin. The Origins and Development of His
Religious Thought* (London, New York, 1963); J. M. Todd, *Martin Luther*
(London, Westminster, Md., 1964).

c.   From the Anglican point of view:

E. G. Rupp, *The Making of the English Protestant Tradition* (New York,
Cambridge, Mass., 1947); J. P. Whitney, *The History of the Reformation*
(Naperville, Ill., 1940); F. J. Foakes—Jackson, *Anglican Church Principles*
(New York, 1924); W. H. Carnegie, *Anglicanism, The Thought and Practice
of the Church of England* (London, 1957); E. J. Bicknell, *The Thirty-Nine
Articles* (3rd ed., London, 1955; New York, 1966); C. E. Simcox, *The
Historical Road of Anglicanism* (Chicago, 1968).

d.   On ecumenical confrontation:

R. M. Brown and G. Weigel, *An American Dialogue* (New York, 1960); id.,
Christianity Divided (New York, 1961); L. Cristiani and J. Rilliet, *Catholics
and Protestants, Separated Brethren* (Westminster, Md., 1960); P. Fransen,
" Grace and Sacraments, " *The Eastern Churches Quarterly*, in reply to the
questions raised by Dr. T. F. Torrance, " The Roman Doctrine of Grace
from the Point of View of the Reformed Theology, " *The Eastern Churches
Quarterly* 16 (1964) 290-329; L. Bouyer, *The Spirit and Forms of Protestantism*
(Westminster, Md., 1956; London, 1963); W. H. Van de Pol, *The Christian
Dilemma* (London, 1952); id., *The End of Conventional Christianity* (Glen Rock,
N.J., 1968); C. Moeller and G. Philips, *The Theology of Grace and the
Ecumenical Movement* (London, 1961); J. Hardon, *The Spirit and Origin of
American Protestantism* (Dayton, 1968).

III.   THEOLOGICAL REFLECTION

1.   Basic synthetic views on the nature of grace : pp. 27, 38 f., 231-233, 307 f.

2.   Fundamental structures of grace-life:

a. Grace, a personal presence of God :
     the main theme of this book : the presence : pp. 5-9, 24-28, 55 f.,
     76 ff., 102, 106, 113, 121, 129, 141 f., 146, 148 ff., 154 f., 160,
     168 ff., 182, 190 f., 199 f., 207, 220, 227-230, 243, 299, 302,
     308, 340.

grace, a likeness to Christ : pp. 27-39, 134, 154 f., 305, 308 ff.
the manner of this likeness, i.e. servants in the Servant and sons
in the Son : pp. 38 f., 55 ff., 76 f., 102 f., 308, 330.
immediate union with the Father and the Spirit : pp. 40-46, 54-58,
76.
indwelling of the Father : pp. 46-48, 56.
of the Spirit : pp. 48-54, 56.
of the Trinity : pp. 54-57.

For further reading :

Critical and historical expositions of the more recent development in the
theology of grace, understood as a divine indwelling: P. de Letter,
" Sanctifying Grace and Our Union with the Holy Trinity, " *Theological
Studies* 13 (1952) 33-58; id., " Created Actuation by the Uncreated Act;
Difficulties and Answers, " *Theological Studies* 18 (1957); L. B. Cunningham,
The Indwelling of the Trinity (Dubuque, 1955).

Studies that have had a decisive influence on this development:
K. Rahner, " Some Implications of the Scholastic Concept of Uncreated
Grace, " *Theological Investigations* 1 (Baltimore, London, 1961), pp. 319-46;
M. de la Taille, " Actuation créée par Acte incréé, " *Recherches de Sciences
Religieuses* 19 (1928), trans. in *Hypostatic Union and Created Actuation by
Uncreated Act*, pp. 29-41, see also pp. 41-76 (West Baden Springs, Ind.,
1952).

Some recent studies in Christology: J. Daniélou, *Christ and Us* (London,
New York, 1961); F. Ferrier, *What is the Incarnation?* (London, New York,
1962); C. V. Héris, *The Mystery of Christ* (Cork, Westminster, Md., 1950);
K. Rahner, *Theological Investigations* 3 (London, Baltimore, 1967).

Works on the Holy Spirit :

A. M. Henry, *The Holy Spirit* (London, New York, 1960); A Gardeil, *The
Holy Spirit in Christian Life* (St. Louis, 1952).

b. Dialectic of the out-flowing and back-flowing grace, i.e. " from God
to God " : pp. 21 f., 50, 52 ff., 56, 79-86, 93-95, 141, 150, 171,
220 f., 232, 245.
c. Dialectic of person and community :
of the person : concrete situation and its acceptance : pp. 5-9, 22,
27, 38 f., 48, 58 f., 102, 103 ff., 129 f., 235 f.
of the community : pp. 58-87, 182-186.
person as " core of density " : pp. 233-237.
d. Dialectic of love :
of love that goes out to the neighbor : pp. 5-9, 15-23, 36 f., 128 ff.,
151, 157 f., 175, 220, 223-227, 244, 305-308.
e. Dialectic of the encounter : pp. 99 f., 103 ff., 131 f., 223.
f. Dialectic of the donor and the donee : pp. 133 f., 214, 226.
g. Dialectic : total gift and yet fully human, and this in spite of sin :
pp. 10 ff., 22 f., 25 f., 93-95, 105 ff., 133-137, 170, 206-215, 219 ff.,
284.

For further reading:

J. Buytendijk, *Phénoménologie de la rencontre* (Bruges, 1952); G. Madinier, *Conscience et amour*. Essai sur le nous (Paris, 1938); G. Marcel, *Présence et immortalité* (Paris, 1959); id., *Homo Viator*, (Chicago, London, 1951); M. Nédoncelle, *La réciprocité des consciences* (Paris, 1942); id., *Love and the Person* (New York, 1966); E. Mounier, *Existentialist Philosophies* (London, 1948; New York, 1949); id., *Personalism* (London, New York, 1952); id., *Personalist Manifesto* (New York, 1938).

3. The main definitions and descriptions of grace:

    a. as created and uncreated grace : pp. 22, 87-106, 231-236, 243 ff.
    b. as interior power and dynamism : pp. 233-236.
       formally as fundamental option : pp. 162 f., 226 f., 276 f.
    c. as healing and elevating grace : pp. 56, 99-103, 241, 312.
    d. as " offered " (situation-appointing) and accepted grace : pp. 153 f., 242 f.
    e. as new personal core and density-ground : pp. 27, 234 ff.
    f. as supernatural " existential " in each individual man : pp. 156, 168.
    g. classical definitions of grace :
       sanctifying grace as fundamental option : pp. 96, 226 f., 236-245, 267 f., 274, 315.
       actual grace or assisting grace : pp. 96, 241, 245, 327.
       sufficient and efficacious grace : pp. 138-141.
    h. The theological virtues :
       in general : pp. 245, 277.
       faith : pp. 292-298.
       hope : pp. 298-303.
       charity : pp. 126, 136, 275, 303-312.
    i. The " fruits of the Spirit " : p. 245.
       discernment of spirits : pp. 127, 287-292.

For further reading:

On the three theological virtues together: H. Bars, *Faith, Hope and Charity* (New York, London, 1961); A. M. Henry, *Theological Library*, Vol. 3, chaps. VIII-X (Cork, Notre Dame, Ind., 1952); F. Prat, *The Theology of Saint Paul*, Vol. 2, book VI, ch. III, 332-41 (London, 1945); L. Trese, *You are Called to Greatness* (London, Notre Dame, Ind., 1964).

On faith: St. Thomas Aquinas, *Summa Theologiae*, Vols. 31 and 32 (in preparation, London, New York); E. Joly, *What is Faith?* (London, New York, 1958); M. C. d'Arcy, *The Nature of Belief* (London, New York, 1951); id., *Belief and Reason* (Springfield, Ill., 1947); R. Guardini, *Faith and Modern Man* (New York, 1952); J. Coventry, *Faith Seeks Understanding* (New York, 1951); G. Marcel, *The Mystery of Being*, Vol. 2: *Faith and Reality* (Chicago, 1957); J. Daniélou, *The Christian Today* (New York, 1960); G. B. Montini (Paul VI), *Man's Religious Sense*, A Pastoral Letter to the

Ambrosian Diocese (London, Westminster, Md., 1961); P. Babin, *Crisis of Faith* (New York, 1963; Dublin, 1964); J. Miller, *Conscience Training* (Dublin, 1964); H. de Lubac, *The Drama of Atheistic Humanism* (New York, 1953); I. Hermann, *The Experience of Faith* (New York, 1966).

On hope: St. Thomas Aquinas, *Summa Theologiae*, Vol. 33 (in preparation, New York, London, 1968); P. Delhaye and J. Boulangé, *Rencontre de Dieu et de l'homme*, 3rd part, *Espérance et vie Chrétienne* (Tournai, 1958); G. Marcel, *Homo Viator* (Chicago, London, 1951); R. Olivier, *Christian Hope* (Westminster, Md., 1963); P. de Letter, " Hope and Charity in Saint Thomas, " *The Thomist* 13 (1950) 204-42, 325-52; W. M. Conlon, " The Certitude of Hope, " *The Thomist* 10 (1947) 75-119, 226-52; R. Troisfontaines, *De l'Existence à l'être* (Namur, 1953); W. Lynch, *Images of Hope* (Baltimore, 1965); G. Moltmann, *Theology of Hope* (New York, 1967).

On love: St. Thomas Aquinas, Summa Theologiae, Vols. 34 and 35 (in preparation, London, New York, 1968); G. Gilleman, *The Primacy o Charity in Moral Theology* (London, Westminster, Md., 1960); M. C. d'Arcy, *The Mind and Heart of Love* (New York, 1947, London, 1955); C. S. Lewis, *The Four Loves* (London, New York, 1960); A. Nygren, *Agape and Eros* (London, 1932-39; Philadelphia, 1953); P. Rousselot, *Pour l'histoire du problème de l'amour au moyen âge* (Paris, 1933); M. Scheler, *The Nature of Sympathy* (London, New Haven, 1954); C. Spicq, *Agape in the New Testament* (St. Louis, 1963); L. Trese, *Love in Action* (Paterson, N.J., 1956); A. Watkin, *The Enemies of Love* (London, New York, 1958); id., *The Heart of the World* (London, New York, 1954); P. Chauchard, *Our Need of Love* (New York, 1968); J. Cowburn, *Love and The Person* (London, 1966; Staten Island, N.Y. 1968).

4. Basic problems connected with grace and its distribution:

A. Grace and election:

election : pp. 107-144, 284.
God's primacy : pp. 108-110, 207, 211.
Christ's election : pp. 154-156.

For further reading:

P. Altmann, *Erwählungstheologie und Universalismus im Altem Testament* (Berlin, 1964); E. Portalié, *A Guide to the Life and Thought of Saint Agustine* (Chicago, 1960); see especially " Grace as Developed by Augustine " (including Augustine's teaching on original sin and predestination, pp. 190-229).—For other considerations on Augustine's notion of original sin, see H. Staffner, " Die Lehre des Hl. Augustinus Uber das Wesen der Erbsünde, " *Zeitschrift sur Katholische Theologie* 79 (1957) 387-416, summarized in *Theology Digest* 9 (1961) 115-120; E. Przywara, *An Augustine Synthesis* (New York, London, 1936), see especially Augustine's thought on man as coming from God and going to God through love, pp. 299-356;

E. Gilson, *The Christian Philosophy of Saint Augustine* (New York, 1960), see "Christian Liberty," pp. 143-64; A. M. Henry, *Theology Library* (Cork, 1952; Notre Dame, Ind., 1955) (in Vol. II, good reading on providence, sin, death: "Divine Government in the Tradition of the Church," and "A Sketch of a Theological Synthesis," pp. 375-496); H. H. Rowley, *The Biblical Doctrine of Election* (London, 1950; 2nd ed. Naperville, Ill., 1965); R. A. Dyson and A. Jones, *The Kingdom of Promise* (London, New York, 1961).

B. Grace and freedom:

   a. General considerations : pp. 35, 80, 99, 107-144, 122, 128, 139, 168.
   b. Theological freedom : the freedom of the children of God : pp. 114-144, 287, 289, 292.
   c. Philosophical freedom: fundamental option and freedom of choice : pp. 128, 236-241, 247, 273-277.
   d. Psychological freedom : pp. 273-277.
   e. Grace and Law : pp. 60 f., 109 f., 122-128.
   f. Grace and sin :
      Sin in general : pp. 238, 246-272, 312.
      original sin : as "sin of Adam" : pp. 154 ff.
                        as state of perdition : pp. 19 f., 155 f., 167, 274.
      mortal (final) sin : pp. 247-250.
      mortal and venial sin : pp. 250, 253 ff., 231-270, 274.
   g. Grace and merit : pp. 25, 77, 90, 92 f., 104 ff., 116 f., 125, 135, 137, 201-232.

For further reading :

On freedom: M. J. Adler, *The Idea of Freedom* (New York, Vol. I: 1958; Vol. II: 1961); H. Morris, éd., *Freedom and Responsibility: Reading in Philosophy and Law* (Stanford, 1961).—Freedom from the philosophical and psychological aspects: *Determinism and Freedom in the Age of Modern Science*, ed. S. Hook (New York, 1958).—Freedom seen from the traditional philosophical aspect: J. de Finance, *Existence et Liberté* (Paris, 1955); Saint Augustine, *The Problem of Free Choice*, in *Ancient Christian Writers* (London, Westminster, Md., 1955); R. Guardini, *Freedom, Grace and Destiny* (London, New York, 1961); Dom Mark Pontifex, *Providence and Freedom* (London, 1960; New York, 1961); M. Lawlor, *Personal Responsibility* (London, New York, 1963); D. J. B. Hawkins, *Christian Ethics* (London, New York, 1963); J. Courtney Murray, "The Problem of Religious Freedom," *Theological Studies* 25 (1964) 503-75; C. van Ouwerkerk, "Gospel Morality and Human Compromise," and J. H. Walgrave, "Is Morality Static or Dynamic?" in *Concilium* 5 (Glen Rock, N.J., London, 1965); J. C. Murray, ed., *Freedom and Man* (New York, 1965); B. Häring, *The Liberty of the Children of God* (Staten Island, N.Y., 1966).

For an historical conspectus: J. Farrelly, *Predestination, Grace and Free Wlli* (London, 1964).

On sin:

Historical survey of the question of original sin: J. Gross, *Entstehungs-geschichte des Erbsündendogma* (Munich, 1960).

Biblical and theological studies: H. Rondet, *The Theology of Sin* (Notre Dame, Ind., 1960); A.-M. Dubarle, *The Biblical Doctrine of Original Sin* (London, New York, 1964); S. Lyonnet, " Le péché originel et l'exégèse de Rom 5:12-14, " *Recherches de Sciences Religieuses* 44 (1956) 63-84, summarized in *Theology Digest* (1957) 54-57; B. Rigaux, " La Femme et son lignage dans Genèse 3:14-15, " *Revue Biblique* 61 (1954) 321-48, summarized in *Theology Digest* 6 (1958) 25-30; B. Häring, *The Law of Christ* (Westminster, Md., 1961); S. Kierkegaard, *Fear and Trembling* (London, New York, 1939); M. M. Labourdette, *Le péché originel et les origines de l'homme* (Paris, 1953); L. Ligier, *Péché d'Adam et péché du monde* (Paris, 1960-62); K. Rahner, " *The Theological Concept of Concupiscentia,* " Theological Investigations 1 (Baltimore, London, 1961), pp. 347-82; S. Trooster, *Evolutie in the Erfzondeleer* (Bruges, 1965); R. Schnackenburg, *The Moral Teaching of the New Testament* (New York, London, 1965); T. Worden, " Meaning of Sin, " *Theology Digest* 8 (1960) 42-44; H. Rondet, " Toward a Theology of Sin, " *Theology Digest* 4 (1958) 171-76; B. Vawter, " Scriptural Meaning of Sin, " *Theology Digest* 10 (1962) 223-26; G. Gille-man, " Sin as Revealed, Some Notes of Biblical Theology, " *Clergy Monthly* 29 (1965) 253-62; P. de Letter, " Meaning of Sin, " *Clergy Monthly* 23 (1959) 49-61; id., " Sense of Sin, " *Clergy Monthly* 26 (1962) 77-88; M. Huftier, " Nature of Actual Sin, " *Theology Digest* 9 (1961) 121-25; C. Journet, *The Meaning of Evil* (New York, 1963); P. de Rosa, *Christ and Original Sin* (Milwaukee, London, 1967).

On merit: G. Didier, *Désintéressement chrétien*, La retribution dans la morale de St. Paul (Paris, 1955); P. Y. Emery, *Le Christ, Notre Récompense* (Neuchâtel, 1962); W. Pesch, *Der Lohngedanke in der Lehre Jesu* (Munich, 1955); W. D. Lynn, *Christ's Redemptive Merit*. The Nature of its Causality according to St. Thomas (Rome, 1962); C. Baumgartner, *La Grâce du Christ* (Tournai, 1963), pp. 205-26; P. J. Mackey, *The Grace of God, the Response of Man* (Albany, N.Y., 1967).

On the Law and the Christian:

The problem of Law and Gospel as seen by the Reformed:

— The Lutheran conception: P. Althaus, *The Divine Command* (Philadel-phia, 1966); R. Bring, *Das Verhältnis von Glauben und Werken in der lutherischen Theologie* (Munich, 1955); W. Joest, *Gesetz und Freiheit*, Das problem des Tertius Usus Legis bei Luther und die neu-testamentliche Paränese (Göttingen, 1951); G. Heintze, *Luthers Predigt von Gesetz und Evangelium* (Munich, 1958); H. Thielicke, *Theological Ethics*, 3 Vols. (Philadelphia, 1966).

— Other Reformed conceptions: K. Barth, *God, Grace and the Gospel* (Edinburgh, 1959); id., *Fur die Freiheit des Evangeliums* (Munich, 1933).

— Studies by Catholics on the same subject: H. Bouillard, *The Logic of the Faith* (New York, 1967); W. A. Van Roo, " Law of the Spirit and Written Law in the Spirituality of St. Ignatius, " *Gregorianum* 37 (1956) 417-43, summarized in *Theology Digest* 5 (1957) 156-58.

Bergsonian thought on morality and free will: H. Bergson, *The Two Sources of Morality and Religion* (New York, 1935); H. Gouhier, *Bergson et le Christ des évangiles* (Paris, 1961).

    C. Grace and community:

        a. Grace and redemption : pp. 64-70, 76 f., 169 ff., 329 f.
        b. Grace and Church : pp. 162-174.
        c. Grace and sacraments : pp. 78 f., 80, 86, 95, 100, 105, 148, 177 f.,
            182, 190 ff., 198 f., 217, 278, 294 f., 307, 317, 322, 342, 346.
        d. Grace outside the Church : pp. 82, 160 ff.
        e. Grace and history : pp. 36 ff., 142 ff.
        f. Grace and final fulfillment (eschatology) : pp. 74 ff., 154, 196-
            199, 216, 220 f., 299, 321-324.

    For further reading :

On the Church as primordial sacrament: P. Fransen, " The Idea of the Church and the Holy Trinity, " *The Eastern Churches Quarterly* 14 (1962) A. de Bovis, *The Church: Christ's Mystery and Sacrament* (London, 1961); Yves M. J. Congar, *Mystery of the Church* (London, Baltimore, 1960); O. Semmelroth, *Church and Sacrament* (Notre Dame, Ind., 1965).

On the sacraments as signs of grace: P. Fransen, " De Gave van de Geest. " *Bijdragen* 21 (1960) 404-23; id., " Inwoning Gods en sacramentele genade, " *Bijdragen* 25 (1964); K. Rahner, *Church and Sacrament* (New York, 1963); E. Schillebeeckx, *Christ the Sacrament of Encounter with God* (London, New York, 1963); id., " The Sacraments: an Encounter with God, " *Christianity Divided* (New York, 1961), pp. 245-73; K. Rahner, " Personality and Sacramental Sanctity, " *Theology Digest* 3 (1955); F. Taymans d'Eypernon, " The Blessed Trinity and the Sacraments " (Dublin, London, 1961); C. O'Neill, *Meeting Christ in the Sacraments* (Staten Island, N.Y., 1964).

Salvation outside the Church: L. Caperan, *Le problème des infidèles*, Essai historique (good survey of former conceptions) (Toulouse, 1934); M. Eminyan, *The Theology of Salvation* (Boston, 1960); J. De Reeper, " The Problem of the Salvation of the Heathen, " *Worldmission* 6 (1955) 355-70; J. M. Hamell, " No Salvation outside the Church, " *Irish Ecclesiastical Record* 88 (1957) 145-61; F. X. Lawlor, " The Mediation of the Church in some Pontifical Documents, " *Theological Studies* 12 (1951) 481-504; S. J. Ott, *Opinions of Modern Theologians on Membership in the Communion of Saints* (Rome, 1954); Y. M. J. Congar, " Salvation and the Non-Catholic, " *Blackfriars* 38 (1957) 290-300, summarized in *Theology Digest* 9 (1961) 173-74; M. Seckler, " Salvation for the non-evangelized, " *Theology Digest* 9 (1961) 168-73; Y. M. J. Congar, *The Wide World my Parish* (London,

Baltimore, 1961); H. de Lubac, *The Splendour of the Church* (London, New York, 1956); E. Cornelis, *Valeurs chrétiennes des religions non-chrétiennes* (Paris, 1965); H. R. Schlette, *Towards a Theology of Religion* (London, New York, 1966).

Some works, philosophical or theological, on the sense of history in general and on the history of salvation: N. Berdyaev, *The Meaning of History* (London, New York, 1936); H. Butterfield, *Christianity and History* (London, 1949; New York, 1950); E. C. Rust, *The Christian Understanding of History* (London and Redhill, 1947), in U.S.: *Toward a Theological Understanding of History* (New York, 1963); C. Dawson, *The Dynamics of World History* (London, 1957; New York, 1962); M. C. d'Arcy, *The Sense of History* (London, 1959), in U.S.: *The Meaning and Matter of History* (New York, 1959); H. Urs von Balthasar, *A Theology of History* (London, New York, 1963); id., *Science, Religion, and Christianity* (London, Westminster, Md., 1958); O. Cullmann, *Christ and Time* (London, 1952; rev. ed., Philadelphia, 1964); T. G. Chifflot, *Approaches to a Theology of History* (New York, 1966); J. Daniélou, *Essai sur le mystère de l'histoire* (Paris, 1960); J. Mouroux, *The Mystery of Time* (New York, 1964); P. Ricœur, *History and Truth* (Evanston, Ill., 1965); K. Rahner, " Weltgeschichte und Heilsgeschichte, " *Schriften zur Theologie* (Einsiedeln, 1962) 115-35.

Some studies on the theological bearing of Teilhard de Chardin's work: E. R. Balthasar, *Teilhard and the Supernatural* (Baltimore, 1966); F. Bravo, *Christ in the Thought of Teilhard de Chardin* (Notre Dame, Ind., 1967); P. Chauchard, *Teilhard de Chardin on Love and Suffering* (Glen Rock, N.J., 1967); R. Faricy, *Teilhard de Chardin's Theology of the Christian in the World* (New York, 1967); H. de Lubac, *Teilhard de Chardin: The Man and His Meaning* (New York, 1965); id., *The Religion of Teilhard de Chardin* (New York, 1967); Sr. M. G. Martin, *The Spirituality of Teilhard de Chardin* (Glen Rock, N.J., 1967); C. F. Mooney, *Teilhard de Chardin and the Mystery of Christ* (New York, 1966); O. A. Rabut, *Teilhard de Chardin* (New York, 1961); P. Smulders, *The Design of Teilhard de Chardin* (Westminster, Md., 1967); C. Tresmontant, *Pierre Teilhard de Chardin* (Baltimore, 1959); R. J. Nogar, *The Lord of the Absurd* (New York, 1966).

Some further works on grace in history: J. van den Berg, *Drie typen in evoluerend Kristendom* (Bruges, 1965); K. Rahner, " Die Christologie innerhalb einer evolutiven Weltanschauung, " *Schriften zur Theologie* (Einsiedeln, 1962) 183-221; E. J. Fortman, ed., *Theology of Man and Grace* (Milwaukee, 1966); C. Davis, *God's Grace in History* (New York, London, 1966); G. Stevens, *Life of Grace* (Englewood Cliffs, N.J., 1963); F. Cuttaz, *Our Life of Grace* (Notre Dame, Ind., 1958).

On death as finalizing task of grace: L. Boros, *The Mystery of Death* (New York, 1965); P. Fransen, " Het vagevuur, " *Streven* 13 (1959-1960) 97-107; P. Glorieux, " In hora mortis, " *Mélanges de Science Religieuse* 6 (1949) 185-216; R. W. Gleason " Toward a Theology of Death, " *Thought* 92 (1957) 39-68; id., *The World to Come* (New York, 1958); Y. B. Tremont, " Man Between Death and Resurrection, " *Theology Digest* 5 (1957);

J. H. Nicolas, " A la jonction du temps et de l'éternité, " *La Vie Spirituelle* 108 (1963) 298-311 ; R. Troisfontaines, *I Do Not Die* (New York, 1963).

5. *A More technical theological problem: nature and supernature*
Natural and supernatural : pp. 130, 133-137, 149 f., 182, 283.

For further reading :

H. J. Brosch, *Das Ubernatürliche in der katholischen Tübinger Schule* (Essen, 1962); U. Kühn, *Natur und Gnade*, Untersuchungen zur deutschen katholischen Theologie der Gegenwart (Berlin, 1961); H. de Lubac, *The Supernatural* (revised ed., New York, London, 1967); K. Rahner, " Concerning the Relationship Between Nature and Grace ", *Theological Investigations* 1 (Baltimore, London, 1961) 297-318; id., " Natur und Gnade, " *Schriften zur Theologie* IV (Einsiedeln, 1959) 290-313.

6. Some present-day problems:

A. Grace and psychology:

In general : pp. 167 f., 273-316.
Awareness of grace : pp. 237, 282-285, 287-298, 302 f., 309-312 ff.
Integration : pp. 274, 284, 317 f., 347 ff.
Tensions : pp. 277-282, 284, 348 f.

For further reading :

Concerning spiritual and mystical experience in general: C. Albrecht, *Das mystiche Erkennen* (Bremen, 1958); J. Bernhart, *Das mystische* (Frankfurt, 1953); J. Maréchal, *Studies in the psychology of the mystics* (London, 1927; albany, N.Y., 1964); E. I. Watkin, *The Philosophy of Mysticism* (London, New York, 1920); M. C. d'Arcy, *The Meeting of Love and Knowledge* (New York, 1957; London, 1958); D. Knowles, *The English Mystical Tradition* (London, 1961), chapter 1 : " Christian Mysticism " is recommended, so also chapter II; E. W. Trueman Dicken, *The Crucible of Love.* A Study of the Mysticism of St. Teresa of Jesus and St. John of the Cross (London, New York, 1963); M. E. de l'Enfant-Jesus, *I Want to See God* (Notre Dame, Ind., 1953); J. Mouroux, *The Christian Experience* (New York, London, 1955); id., " sur la possibilité de l'expérience chrétienne, " *Festschrift für K. Adam* (Düsseldorf, 1952), pp. 43-60; K. Rahner, *Glaube inmitten der Welt* (Freiburg, 1961).

On " discernment of spirits ": L. Beirnaert, " Discernement et psychisme, " *Christus* 4 (1954) 50-61 ; Y. M. Congar, *Si vous êtes mes témoins* (Paris, 1959); J. de Guibert, *The Theology of the Spiritual Life* (New York, 1953); O. Karrer, *Geist der Wahrheit und der Liebe* (Munich, 1964); E. Leen, *The Holy Ghost and His Work in Souls* (London, New York, 1943); C. S. Lewis, *The Screwtape Letters* (London, New York, 1943); W. W. Meissner, " Psychological Notes on the Spiritual Exercises, III, " *Woodstock Letters* 93 (1964) 178-191; id., *Directory to the Spiritual Exercises of Our Holy Father Ignatius* (London, 1925).

On such spiritual experiences with reference to the human psyche:
L. Beirnaert, *Expérience chrétienne et psychologique* (collected articles) (Paris,
1964); J. Bernhart, *Das Mystische* (Frankfurt, 1953); W. W. Meissner,
"Psychological Notes on the Spiritual Exercises," see above; J. Gold-
brunner, *Cure of Mind and Cure of Soul* (London, New York, 1958); id.,
Holiness is Wholeness (London, New York, 1955).

On mature moral conduct and conscience: A. Godin, *Child and Adult
Before God* (Chicago, 1965); L. Monden, *Sin, Liberty and Law* (New York,
1965); M. Oraison, *Human Mystery of Sexuality* (New York, 1967);
P. Regnier, *What is Sin?* (Cork, Westminster, Md., 1961).

B. Grace and World : pp. 344-347.

C. Grace and "secularization" (J. A. T. Robinson) : pp. 183 f.,
332-340.

For further reading:

J. A. T. Robinson, *Honest to God* (London, Philadelphia, 1963); id.,
Christian Morals Today (London, Philadelphia, 1964); id., *The New Refor-
mation?* (London, Philadelphia, 1965); R. McBrien, *The Church in the
Thought of Bishop Robinson* (Philadelphia, 1966); J. A. T. Robinson and
D. L. Edwards, *The Honest to God Debate* (Philadelphia, 1963; London,
1964); E. L. Mascall, *Secularization of Christianity* (New York, 1965);
R. B. Smith, *Secular Christianity* (New York, 1961); R. L. Richard, *Seculari-
zation Theology* (New York, 1967).

Concerning the sources of J. A. T. Robinson :

— on R. Bultmann :

H. Fries, *Bultmann, Barth and Catholic Theology* (Pittsburg, 1967); L. Malevez,
The Christian Message and Myth (London, 1958); R. Marlé, *Bultmann and
Christian Faith* (Glen Rock, N.J., 1968).

— on P. Tillich :

C. W. Kegley and R. W. Bretall, *The Theology of Paul Tillich* (New York,
1952); R. A. Killen, *The Ontological Theology of Paul Tillich* (Kempen,
1956); C. Rhein, *Paul Tillich, Philosoph und Theologe* (Stuttgart, 1957);
T. A., O'Meara, ed., *Paul, Tillich, Catholic Thought* (Chicago, 1964).

Some works of D. Bonhoeffer: E. Bethge, ed., *Letters and Papers from
Prison* (rev. and enl., New York, London, 1967); *Life Together* (New York,
London, 1954); *Temptation* (New York, London, 1955); *Ethics* (New York,
1965); *Cost of discipleship* (New York, London, 1960); *Christ the Center*
(New York, London, 1966).

On D. Bonhoeffer: W. Kuhns, *In pursuit of Dietrich Donhoeffer* (Dayton,
1967); J. Moltmann and J. Weissbach, *Two studies in the Theology of
Bonhoeffer* (New York, 1967).